THE HILL TO DIE ON

THE HILL TO DIE ON

THE BATTLE FOR CONGRESS AND THE FUTURE OF TRUMP'S AMERICA

JAKE SHERMAN AND **ANNA PALMER**

B\D\W\Y
BROADWAY BOOKS
NEW YORK

2020 Broadway Books Trade Paperback Edition

Copyright © 2019 by Jake Sherman and Anna Palmer
"Just Not Worth It" copyright © 2020 by Jake Sherman and Anna Palmer
All rights reserved.

Published in the United States by Broadway Books, an imprint of Random
House, a division of Penguin Random House LLC, New York.

BROADWAY BOOKS and its colophon are trademarks of Penguin Random
House LLC.

Originally published in hardcover and in slightly different form
in the United States by Crown, an imprint of Random House,
a division of Penguin Random House LLC, in 2019.

ISBN 978-0-525-57475-0
Ebook ISBN 978-0-525-57476-7

Printed in the United States of America on acid-free paper

crownpublishing.com

9 8 7 6 5 4 3 2 1

CONTENTS

NOTE ON SOURCES   vii

PREFACE   **IN THE OVAL**   ix

Prologue   **The Hill**   1

1   **Not a Trump Guy**   11

2   **"Fire Pelosi!"**   32

3   **Trump's Washington**   44

4   **Follow the Money**   56

5   **The Limits of Mitch McConnell's Power**   69

6   **McCarthy and Scalise**   92

7   **"Three, Three, Three"**   110

8   **Zero Tolerance**   133

9   **The Tax Bill**   150

10   **The President's Watchmen**   173

11 **Purity**   185

12 **"I'll Take the Heat"**   194

13 **Family Discussions**   214

14 **Storms Brewing Offshore**   234

15 **The Discharge Petition**   254

16 **Left and Center**   270

17 **Going Negative**   283

18 **The Second Seat**   301

19 **October**   325

20 **Election Day**   345

21 **The Speakership**   354

22 **Shutdown**   372

23 **"Just Not Worth It"**   400

ACKNOWLEDGMENTS   413

INDEX   417

NOTE ON SOURCES

THIS BOOK IS THE PRODUCT of roughly twenty-six months of reporting on Congress in the era of Trump. Most books indicate how many hours of interviews the authors have conducted, but that measure is not operative for this book. We spend much of our time in the Capitol, where we sit in the press galleries, observe the floor, and talk with elected officials and their aides. Our job as reporters lets us exist alongside the legislative process.

Many of the interviews we conducted for this book were on the record, with the stipulation that the quotes would not appear until the book's publication. Other interviews were conducted on deep background, an agreement where the information may be used but the source may not be identified or quoted. We interviewed characters in this book and aides involved in the legislative process as often as several times each week stretching from Election Day 2016 through February 2019. Most of the interviews were recorded and the audio files have been preserved.

When we write about the thinking of a character or his or her emotions, it came from either the source himself or herself or from someone he or she spoke to. In addition to interviews, sources in both parties agreed to share meeting notes, transcripts of telephone conversations, recordings of telephone conversations, and recordings of meetings, e-mails, and memos. On several occasions, sources allowed us to listen in to telephone conversations or conference calls as they were happening. Almost every meeting we write about had multiple participants, which helped us in confirming what was said. At times, we put remarks from closed meetings in quotes. On other occasions we used italics for dialogue between two individuals. When we put material in quotes, we often had a recording of the meeting or spoke to one or more principals involved.

We also traveled to report for this book. Members of Congress gave us access to closed fund-raisers and meetings with donors, strategists, and aides.

Very few people declined our request for an interview.

Our reporting for this book was done contemporaneously with the daily news cycle, and as such some information in this book has appeared in news stories in *Politico*, the *Washington Post*, the *New York Times*, and elsewhere. But we took great care to rely on our reporting for this book. We kept a daily diary, chronicling what we learned, and ventured to confirm it with as many people as possible. At times, in double and triple checking, we referenced our colleagues' stories, or *Politico Playbook*, the twice-daily newsletter we write, for questions about the timeline of events. A note section was not possible for this book due to agreements with sources. We spent countless hours observing the proceedings of the House and Senate, but C-Span's archives were invaluable to help reconstruct speeches and other public appearances.

This is a book about Congress. As such, we spent most of our time embedded on Capitol Hill and with the party committees. We did speak very frequently with White House aides, almost all of whom were not permitted to talk to reporters but were involved in the administration's decision-making process. We interviewed President Donald Trump for the book, and his comments were embargoed until publication, except for a few questions we asked for immediate use for *Politico*. Trump's remarks are sprinkled throughout the book and were helpful in understanding how he viewed major characters and major incidents from 2016 to 2019.

IN THE OVAL

"HEY," **PRESIDENT DONALD TRUMP** said as we walked out of the Oval Office. "If you're a bestseller, you better give me some."

It seemed like a throwaway line, what the president saw as good-natured ribbing after an interview about his relationship with Congress. But after nearly two years of his presidency, it also seemed like the most satisfying and fitting encapsulation of Washington in the era of Donald John Trump: Everything was about him. A city filled with more than five hundred hard-charging, ambitious politicians swayed with his moods. His idiosyncrasies and policy preferences sent markets soaring to new heights, then yanked them back to earth. His election broke up friendships, frayed or ended marriages, and tested the resilience of American democracy.

Eventually, after 728 days, Trump's Republican Washington was shattered. The power structures that propped him up and the robust majority that helped him govern were broken beyond recognition.

When all was said and done, there was no ambiguity: Republicans' defeat in the 2018 midterm elections was absolutely astounding and bordered on historic. The party lost deep-red districts in places like Oklahoma, Texas, and Virginia; it was decimated in California and walloped in Michigan. The election ended careers of promising up-and-comers and reinstalled Nancy Pelosi atop the Democratic House of Representatives.

But if you listened to Trump, it was all according to plan.

"I [say] this, and everyone says, 'Oh, it's just talk, sour grapes,'" Trump said, wearing a blue suit, red tie, and crisp white shirt, with "45" stitched into the shirtsleeve, speaking from behind the Resolute Desk in the Oval Office. "Let's assume we held the House, and let's assume I held it by one or two or three. It doesn't matter—or five. I would have never been able to get, rarely at least, the Republicans to put anything forward because you would always have somebody" blocking what the Republican leadership wanted to do.

This was Donald Trump explaining why he was at least somewhat pleased that his party no longer held the majority of the House of Representatives, an institution Republicans spent nearly a half-billion dollars trying to save between 2016 and 2018.

Trump thought if Republicans had kept the majority, it "would've been impossible" to get anything done because every time he tried, people would look to exact changes and concessions. Some might have said that kind of horsetrading was part of the complex and messy legislative process that the founders designed. Trump saw it as superfluous and cumbersome.

In Trump's thinking, a Democratic House majority was welcome, even freeing. "Now, I just say 'Hey, folks, let's go. Give me legislation. Let me see. And if we like it, we'll work on it,'" he said.

One of the many paradoxes of Donald Trump was that he demanded backbreaking loyalty from his party but showed almost none in exchange. The president cut deals with Democrats in front of Republicans' faces. At times he or his staff ignored the will of his party's leaders. He sometimes even took pleasure in his party's defeats. George W. Bush had humbly called his electoral defeat in 2006 a "thumpin'." Barack Obama called his in 2010 a "shellacking." But when voters tossed Speaker Paul Ryan's Republican Party to the side, the president—speaking during a news conference at the White House—assailed those who lost. "Mia Love gave me no love, and she lost. Too bad. Sorry about that, Mia," said

Trump, clearly not sorry after Love spent $5 million trying to overcome her party's tarnished image in deep-red Utah.

"Carlos Curbelo. Mike Coffman—too bad, Mike," the president said, ticking off some of the party's most popular lawmakers who fell in Trump's Washington. "Peter Roskam didn't want the embrace. Erik Paulsen didn't want the embrace. . . . Those are some of the people that, you know, decided for their own reason not to embrace, whether it's me or what we stand for. But what we stand for meant a lot to most people."

Perhaps it did, but by the numbers those voters did not support Republicans in the fall of 2018. It will take time to truly understand how much blame Trump deserves for his party's historic defeat in the House of Representatives. But some things are clear: Voters were sick of the chaos Republicans had wrought. They appreciated the upswing in the economy but ultimately did not give Trump or Republicans credit. They thought the GOP was looking to strip away critical benefits like health insurance coverage. All while Democrats, fueled by piles of cash, were able to unwind a decade of Republican dominance without breaking a sweat.

Publicly and privately, Trump accepted almost no blame. He often pointed his ire toward Paul Ryan, a foe turned ally, who announced he would retire from the speakership in the middle of the election year. Reminded of Ryan's harsh words during the 2016 presidential campaign— the Speaker had considered dropping his support for Trump—the president said that was why he called him "Foxhole Paul," a reference to the Speaker abandoning Trump during tough times. "He did disappear a couple of times on me, didn't he?"

One of those times, in Trump's telling, was when Ryan, in April 2018, said he would leave the speakership at the end of that year.

"I like Paul, but I just couldn't believe when I saw that," Trump said of Ryan's retirement announcement. "Because he was a lame duck. He made himself a lame duck. And the great way would have been to either get out and have somebody else take your place soon." Who would take his place? Logic would dictate Trump would want Rep. Kevin McCarthy, the jocular California Republican who was Ryan's number two.

But Trump said he would've been happy if Rep. Jim Jordan—McCarthy's sworn enemy—succeeded Ryan. "I'm a huge Jim Jordan fan, too," he said.

The president didn't hesitate to shower praise on Pelosi and Senate minority leader Chuck Schumer, Washington's top-two Democrats. He called Pelosi "talented," and said this of the pair: "So here's the story, I like both of them."

At that moment, Pelosi was working to corral support for her return to the speakership. On the campaign trail, vulnerable Democrats had abandoned her in a bid to show independence. But Pelosi was in the process of leveraging her considerable power to bring members into line.

Trump had a plan to catch Pelosi if she fell short: He would ask the Freedom Caucus, the most conservative members of Congress and his staunchest allies, to do the unthinkable and vote for Pelosi. "I think you'd get the most violent Freedom Caucus people," Trump said. He told us he thought the most conservative members of Congress would do him a favor by voting for Pelosi.

There was something perversely satisfying about that. Donald J. Trump planned to use the right wing of his party, the keepers of his creed, to hand the speakership to Nancy Pelosi.

In the weeks after we spoke to Trump, Pelosi would win the speakership entirely without the president's help. The gears of the federal government would grind to a halt, and Trump, Pelosi, Schumer, and Mitch McConnell, the Senate's Republican leader, would wind up in a historic standoff. Members of Congress found themselves frustrated, disillusioned, and disenchanted with the legislative process.

The first two years of Donald Trump's presidency—during which his party controlled the House, Senate, and presidency—were coming to a close.

"Quite an era," Trump said.

Indeed.

THE HILL

THE U.S. CONGRESS IS UNLIKE any other institution on earth. It is the most remarkable example of representative democracy, a political arena in which public servants have righted historical wrongs, initiated drastic interventions on foreign soil, and uncovered malfeasance in leaders at home and abroad.

At the same time, it is one of the pettiest collections of adults the planet has ever seen. Power is measured—and people are judged—in police-chauffeured Chevy Suburbans, campaign cash, the location of cramped Capitol office space, and appearances on daytime television. If this sounds like teenage melodrama, it's not far off. Congress is filled with 535 personalities who closely resemble high school class presidents, and just as in high school, on Capitol Hill popularity is king. Leaders curry favor with campaign contributions to the rank and file and visits across the country to raise cash; it's not unusual for someone like California representative Kevin McCarthy, the House Republican leader, to spend congressional recesses touring small businesses in barely there towns across America. Leaders dole out seats on powerful committees to their political allies. The less fortunate rabble-rousers get stuck with garbage assignments—the Small Business Committee, for example—and leadership might limit their ability to take taxpayer-funded trips abroad. Top lawmakers like McCarthy and Rep. Steve Scalise of Louisiana, the House Republican whip, distribute gifts like Vineyard Vines sweatshirts and Apple Watches to keep their allies happy and loyal. Seventy-nine-year-old representative Nancy Pelosi—who, along with her husband, is worth at least $33 million—still spends as many as one hundred nights on the road every year, raising money, gladhanding donors, and making sure her Democratic colleagues are indebted to her. Democrats put up with her bottom-of-the-barrel poll numbers for years because she could raise tens of millions of dollars for the party.

In Washington, messages are delivered through cable television, and being spotted in *Politico Playbook* can begin, or end, a political alliance. Lawmakers often ask their aides to take on menial tasks like picking up their dry cleaning or picking up after their pets on daily walks. Marital infidelity is not uncommon. Drinking is prevalent—even encouraged—during the workday. In 2010, as Congress readied to pass the Dodd-Frank Wall Street reform act, lawmakers sat on the porch just feet from the House floor, drinking whiskey. In late July 2017, as the House debated amendments to the defense authorization bill, Speaker Paul Ryan hosted a reception for lawmakers on his balcony, which has stunningly sweeping views of the National Mall. "In the hope to make our Members a little more comfortable tonight with late votes, please share with your boss that Speaker Ryan would like to open up H-218 and the H-218 Balcony tonight from 8pm onward for refreshments and light snacks," the invitation from Ryan's office read, referring to a room in his plush suite of offices. "Note—this is for Members ONLY." Show up at an evening vote, and you might find elected officials a bit looser than normal.

It takes a certain level of confidence—some would say narcissism—to believe that you, above all others in your congressional district, are the best fit to represent your community. Unlike the White House, which has one principal, each member of Congress is his or her own boss—an independent contractor, operating with little guidance or oversight and within few bounds. At their disposal is millions of dollars in government and campaign cash that, broadly speaking, they can spend however they please. Take, for example, Rep. Gene Green, the seventy-one-year-old veteran Democrat from Houston. He named his wife—a teacher—as his campaign treasurer, then spent more than one hundred thousand dollars on flights for her during his twenty-six years in Congress, on some occasions more than once a month. Green had one competitive race in two decades in Congress. He used his campaign account to fly himself and his wife to Canada for the wedding of a top-flight lobbyist, who was a campaign donor and once his top aide. Green also spent campaign money on gifts for his staff, for his colleagues, and for his family.

The phenomenon is confined neither to one party nor to a specific chamber. John Cornyn, the senior senator from Texas who was the number two Republican leader in the Senate during Donald Trump's first two years in office, once spent $336 from his campaign account on "beverages for meal" at an organic wine estate in South Africa, which is far from his day job in Washington and his political home base in Austin. Rep. Anna Eshoo, a Bay Area Democrat, spent more than $2,000 in campaign cash to buy her friend Nancy Pelosi scarves. When it comes to spending campaign cash and running their offices, Congress essentially operates on the honor system. Sure, Congress has created committees and oversight panels to keep lawmakers on the straight and narrow, but it takes a lot to rouse them to action. All this is legal, if a bit unseemly.

In the Capitol, little is hidden. Votes are public. Conversations often happen in plain sight of dozens of reporters. Try walking into work every day and facing dozens of iPhone-wielding journalists who ask about Donald Trump's every utterance. When Rep. Justin Amash, a libertarian-leaning Michigan Republican, missed his first vote in seven years, he cried; *Politico* had a story up within hours. Roughly six thousand journalists are credentialed to cover the Capitol, and the rules of the institution allow them practically unfettered access to members of Congress. It creates a massive feeding frenzy that would be abhorred by any sane, rational political actor—of which there are few in Washington.

Serving in Congress is, broadly speaking, an attractive proposition. The pay—$174,000 a year—is well within the upper-middle-class range in the United States. Although congresspersons swear up and down that they are just like you, they definitely are not. The government foots most of the bill for their generous health care plan. The congressional pension program gives many lawmakers fat postemployment checks. While serving, they get a staff and an office, which they can sleep in. They get access to a private gym and complimentary overnight parking in a private lot at Reagan National Airport outside Washington. Airlines might hold flights for them if they are running late. They get license plates that allow them to park wherever they please—the disgraced former congressman Anthony Weiner periodically parked partially on a curb in a hip D.C. neighborhood where spots are at a premium.

Washington is not like New York or Los Angeles, the nation's other two primary power centers. Money, for the most part, is a secondary currency in D.C. Power—gaining it, maintaining it, and being in proximity to it—is what matters. Members of Congress are, essentially, permanent VIPs in a city where power is the primary form of status.

The power is so consuming that many of the nation's richest men and women leave lucrative careers to come to D.C. to serve there alongside former city councilors, statehouse lifers, and political operatives. For example, you might have seen Rep. Darrell Issa, a California Republican who is worth upward of a quarter-billion dollars from creating the Viper car alarm system, chatting with Rep. Jim Jordan, an Ohio Republican who has spent his career in government and has a maximum of $400,000 to his name. Sen. Jon Tester, the Montana Democrat and party leader who lost three fingers in a meat grinder accident as a child, has most of his assets tied up in T-Bone Farms. But he serves alongside colleagues like Sen. Richard Blumenthal, the Connecticut Democrat whose wife's family owned the Empire State Building for decades.

People joke that Washington is Hollywood for ugly people. It's more like Hollywood for people who can't afford nice clothes because they stay in low-paying jobs for too long in their never-ending quest for power. Political aides on Capitol Hill often spend upward of a decade in the "building," as it is called, making a quarter or less of what they could be making in the private sector on K Street, or "downtown," as Washington's political class says. For example, Hugh Halpern, a lawyer, helped run the House floor for Republicans for more than a dozen years—only part of his thirty-odd years on Capitol Hill. Republican leaders from John Boehner to Paul Ryan successfully convinced him to forgo a six-figure salary bump to remain in government. He did it out of a sense of duty: Congress needs people with institutional knowledge to make sure the institution stays on track. That said, the access is a hell of a perk. While much of the D.C. political class watches Congress on flat-screen televisions around town, Halpern was there, standing in the chamber during the debate. (Halpern finally left when Republicans lost control of Congress in 2018.)

The beauty for these folks is that they often get to eat their cake and have it, because the option to depart for a windfall is always there. To give a sense of the raise political operators get when they leave government, look no further than Mike Sommers, John Boehner's final chief of staff. Sommers worked in government from 1997 to 2016—mostly for Boehner, with one short stint at the White House. In those jobs, he never earned more than $200,000. When he finally left, he went to work for the American Investment Council, a group that represents private equity firms in Washington, where he earned more than $1.5 million. In 2018 he took a job running the American Petroleum Institute, where his predecessor earned $6.7 million.

For each staffer who ends up spending years on Capitol Hill, ten times as many aides cash in to work at lobbying firms or companies trying to influence the lawmakers they made a previous career of sucking up to. After working in government for elected officials, tending to their quirks, minding their schedules, and plotting their political rises, many aides then turn and market their knowledge—and sell their access—to their new bosses. They often parlay their expertise and close relationships on behalf of corporate America, while at the same time acting as experts to junior congressional aides who don't understand the intricate details of legislating. Who knows better than an experienced ex-staffer how to write a bill favorable to a special interest?

Former chiefs of staff and top committee aides can earn more than double their public sector pay when they go to the "dark side." No longer logging long hours in the Capitol, these lobbyists then cut campaign checks to get into the good graces with lawmakers' offices so they can quickly get meetings with key staffers and elected officials. On the flip side, if a lobbyist meets with a lawmaker or his staff, the lawmaker's political fund-raiser will often follow up within twenty-four hours to ask for a contribution to their campaign.

Staffers are not the only ones who leave the Hill for the financial windfall—lawmakers also cash out. Trent Lott, the Mississippi Republican who spent almost thirty-five years in the House and Senate, now brings in millions for Squire Patton Boggs, an international law firm. By dint of his membership in Chowder and Marching, the Republican secret society—which meets Wednesdays in the Capitol—he is able to rub shoulders with top Republicans like Kevin McCarthy without anyone seeing. Lott strolls freely through the Capitol because even eleven years after retiring from the Senate, he wears a pin that identifies him as part of the chamber's membership. Former Virginia representative Tom Davis represented a slew of corporate clients as a lobbyist for Deloitte. He was regularly seen roaming the Capitol chatting up members and senior staff. Others like Dave Lugar, son of former senator Dick Lugar of Indiana, prefer to grab a coffee at Cups, the coffee shop in the basement of the Russell Senate Office Building, where a who's who of Senate staffers stop for their caffeine fix.

In the mid-2000s Congress tried to overhaul lobbying rules to cut down on the pay-for-play economy that had long thrived in Washington. Back in the day, twentysomething-year-old staffers threw back Bud Lights and chowed down on ten-cent wings at the Pour House at lobbyist-sponsored events. They charged Domino's pizzas to corporate cards on file at the party headquarters or swilled wine from a lobbyist's locker at the Capital Grille down the street from the Capitol on

Pennsylvania Avenue. Those days are over. Any transaction between corporations and political aides now comes as a disclosed, tightly monitored political contribution.

Even still, money is the lubricant that keeps the town running. Personal contributions and corporate political action committees are still extremely relevant, as they funnel tens of millions of dollars into the political system. Politicians or committees take golf trips to Kiawah Island, South Carolina; spend resort weekends in Sea Island, Georgia; and stay at country getaways at the Greenbrier in West Virginia. The sole point: to sell access to politicians. Senators like Orrin Hatch of Utah perfected the weekend fund-raising opportunity. Hatch, who led the powerful Senate Finance Committee, organized a weekend fundraiser at the swanky Montage Deer Valley resort for both his leadership PAC and a nonprofit dedicated to his legacy.

Donald Trump, like many politicians before him, may have said he was coming to Washington to drain the swamp, but he has changed the town very little. Companies snapped up Trump insiders after he won the presidency, turning some of his anti-D.C. warriors into high-paid advisers. K Street power brokers capitalized on the uncertainty and charged a killing to steer corporate America through Trump's uncharted waters.

Even critics of Trump were able to make a buck. Former representative Charlie Dent is a great example of cashing out during the Trump era. Elected to the House of Representatives in 2004, at the height of the Bush era, Dent was a popular, backslapping congressman who was friendly with reporters because of his ability to turn a good quote. Frequently those quotes were critical of Donald Trump. In September 2017 he announced he would not run for reelection in 2018 and privately told party leaders it was because he was discouraged by politics in the Trump era. In April 2018 he announced that he would leave Congress "in the coming weeks" but assured people that it was his "intention to continue to aggressively advocate for responsible governance and pragmatic solutions in the coming years." His "advocacy" took the form of new roles as a paid CNN political contributor and a senior policy adviser at DLA Piper, the global law firm.

Trump crowbarred the partisan divide ever wider, but Democrats retained their inside tracks in the Capitol. Steve Elmendorf, who last worked in the Capitol in the early 2000s, is still able to stroll through the building unrestricted. He was once a shadow officer of the House of Representatives, which gives him lifetime privileges to walk through the Capitol and visit friends—and beneficiaries of his largesse—like Reps. Nancy Pelosi and Steny Hoyer without fear of being stopped by a Capitol Police officer. He is regularly spotted walking the halls of the Capitol.

Has the swamp been drained in Trump's White House? No, it has only become murkier, deeper, and richer. Hot spots inside the Beltway continually change based on who is in the White House. Georgetown's Smith Point was hot during the George W. Bush administration, as was Stetson's, a western-themed bar on U Street where Bush's daughters were spotted drinking underage. The Obama administration brought urban chic to Washington. In Trump's Washington, the Trump Hotel became the spot to be seen. Open and airy with posh silver and baby-blue velvet furniture and a long, dominant bar, the Pennsylvania Avenue hotel has become the "it spot" for Republicans looking to make headway in the new era of politicking. Former campaign manager Corey Lewandowski is regularly spotted there, pacing with his cell phone between meetings. Anthony Scaramucci, self-described as "The Mooch," holds court there, captivating a bevy of men and women sprawled across the couches. People wearing MAKE AMERICA GREAT AGAIN hats mix with a host of suited operatives.

As Washington insiders play their power games, pat each other on the back, and take advantage of the wide ethical berth afforded to them, the public views the greatest legislative body on earth with deep suspicion and disdain. Gallup, which has tracked the public approval of Congress since the mid-1970s, found that just two in ten people approved of Congress for much of the first two years of the Trump administration. As a comparison, in 2009, 37 percent of people approved of the institution. After the September 11 attacks, 84 percent approved. Even worse, just 29 percent of people polled in October 2018 thought most members of Congress should be returned to office. The institution that writes the nation's laws remains loathed by the voters who put its members in power.

Chalk it all up to a perception that Congress is simply not working for everyday people. It works for itself. And when it needs to work for people, it screws things up. It shuts down the government. It raises taxes. It spends money on endless wars. All while its members collect fat paychecks.

The irony about Congress in the era of Trump is that the institution briefly became more popular than usual. In February 2017 its approval briefly jumped 9 points to 28 percent—a sign, perhaps, that the public thought the institution would become more responsible or responsive under the New York City billionaire. But if anything changed about the power dynamics in Washington under Trump, it was that Congress gained power but at times shrank in its willingness to exercise it. For example, because of Trump's ideological flexibility, Washington shut up the chattering class and cleared a tax reform bill quicker than anyone thought possible. With a White House bereft of firmly held opinions, lawmakers and aides with decades-long relationships were able to cobble together a bill largely unencumbered. A cooperative administration allowed the Senate to confirm conservative judges at a breakneck pace. But at the same time, the institution receded in important ways, refusing to shore up the investigation into the president's campaign and declining lawmakers' request to curb his ability to spark trade wars with allies.

Donald Trump's 2016 candidacy systematically and inextricably altered a host of institutions in American life: media, the Republican Party, the political consulting class, and the traditional checks and balances on executive power. Trump turned American life upside down—and promised to do the same to Washington.

But how would Congress—the geographical and ideological center of the capital city—react to the shred-the-playbook ways of the brash New York real estate executive? Would it buckle to him or collapse under him? Would the newly elected president stand alongside the rigid elements of his party that elected him? Would his ideological flexibility unlock the gridlock that had plagued Washington for nearly a decade, or would it become mired in a series of inextricable crises?

Sure, Donald Trump wanted to change Washington. The question was, would he succeed? Or would he somehow make it even worse?

1

NOT A TRUMP GUY

"IT'S A FLOOD WARNING? I don't see a flood coming anywhere."

It was Election Day eve 2016, and Speaker Paul Ryan was standing in the local Republican Party headquarters at a squat strip mall in Racine County, Wisconsin. A few moments earlier the air had been pierced by an ominous-sounding cell phone alert, warning of nearby flooding. "Where is the flood coming?" Ryan asked aloud to no one in particular.

At that moment, the only flood Paul Ryan was expecting was a blue high tide of Democratic gains. How could it be otherwise? He was looking at the same polling everyone else was, and it showed Republicans would likely narrowly keep their House majority, Hillary Clinton would win the White House, and Democrats would steal the Senate majority, making Sen. Chuck Schumer of New York the majority leader.

Ryan loathed the thought of being Speaker in a divided government, with his House the only island of red in a sea of blue. He was worried about the damage Trump was doing to the Republican Party. And yet after months of hand wringing and hours of talks with his close cadre of advisers about quitting politics, Ryan had decided to stick it out and remain in Congress. He couldn't abandon House Republicans—he thought he had a duty there. He was going to rebuild. He was going to stop Republicans from imploding. Obligation. Duty. Paul Ryan didn't want to be seen as a quitter.

But at that moment on Washington Avenue in Racine he was utterly preoccupied with reelecting the vanilla, conservative former business-man Ron Johnson to the U.S. Senate. By October and November, Ryan's political operation was helping turn out voters for Johnson's campaign, which the Senate's Republican leadership had dismissed, thinking Johnson was toast.

The shrieking emergency tone of the cell phone alert had momen-tarily distracted Ryan, but he made a quick recovery. The fifty-fourth Speaker of the House, in tailored pants and a fitted button-down shirt, jet-black hair gelled in place, said he had no idea where the sound was coming from or what it meant. Someone suggested it was an Amber Alert. Someone surmised that it was a warning: Democrats were on the march.

"It's the Democrats—yeah, exactly," Ryan joked to the room, filled with party faithful and a small clutch of reporters. "It's voter suppres-sion. That's what it is. You can tell we're all pretty slaphappy these days."

Slaphappy was one way to put it. These were indeed strange days for the Speaker. He had been waiting for eight years to toss Barack Obama out of the White House and replace him with a thoughtful conservative Republican who could help him fulfill his policy dreams. But in 2016, with Trump atop the ballot, the candidate and Ryan seemed like they were on different planets. Ryan—the nation's top elected Republican—did not campaign once with Trump. They didn't appear together at the Republican convention that Ryan chaired in Cleveland. Ryan even went so far as to cancel a joint appearance in Elkhorn, Wisconsin, in early October, after Trump was caught on tape suggesting famous men could grab women by their vaginas with impunity. Trump's team later re-buffed Ryan's offer for a late-fall rally in Wisconsin. They said Trump needed to be in Michigan and sent longtime Ryan friend Mike Pence in his place.

Publicly, the candidate and the Speaker talked as if they liked each other; in reality, Ryan thought Trump disgusting, and Trump thought Ryan useless.

But during the late days of the 2016 campaign, Ryan—nicknamed "Bowhunter" by his Capitol Police detail—put on his game face and pushed toward victory for everyone except Trump. "We have to win an election so we can get this country back on track," Ryan said at the Racine campaign office, repeating the broad outlines of a refrain he had started in 2012 when he was the Republican vice-presidential candidate. "It's all about unity."

It was a statement that, given the Speaker's behavior all year, seemed somewhere between unbelievable and disingenuous. "It's all about coming together. It's all about bringing all kinds of Republicans from all parts of the party together to actually deliver. There is one person that we really, really have to deliver for. Because this man has been delivering for us. This man is a man of high integrity and character and value and gift."

Ryan hit his punch line: "The point is, Ron Johnson's been there for us."

Obligation. Duty. Paul Ryan was there for Ron Johnson. He wanted to be there for Republicans when Hillary Clinton became president. What he didn't fully understand was that a pocket within his own party wanted to pull the Speaker's chair out from under him.

A FEW DAYS EARLIER North Carolina representative Mark Meadows—a leader of the conservative House Freedom Caucus—was in his downtown Washington apartment, glasses on his nose, cell phone in hand, sitting with his closest political allies as he read aloud a text message from Ryan. "If you're going to kneecap me, will you at least let me know in advance?" Ryan wrote, followed by a series of shamrock emojis. Ryan had heard rumors about the Freedom Caucus's unhappiness with him, but he knew little of their plans. The rumors were believable, though: The Freedom Caucus was never happy.

The group laughed nervously as Meadows read the text. The truth was that these members of the House Freedom Caucus were indeed planning to kneecap Ryan. They were plotting to take down the Speaker of the House.

They had done it before. On a steamy day in late July 2015, just before the House was set to break for its August recess, Meadows had marched to the House floor and filed a motion to vacate the chair, setting up a near-immediate referendum on Speaker John Boehner of Ohio. Meadows said he had prayed, spoken to his family and friends, and come to the conclusion he wanted Boehner out. Conservatives and moderates alike voiced what they thought were legitimate gripes with Boehner: He was too willing to cut deals with Barack Obama, too willing to give up a fight, too lazy, too much a picture of yesteryear.

In typical times with typical politicians, those concerns would be handled behind closed doors. Meadows, though, took his complaints public, filing a resolution that would put every lawmaker on record about the Speaker. It was the first time anyone had attempted to oust a Speaker in more than a century. Months later Boehner resigned to save himself, and the House, the embarrassment.

Paul Davis Ryan Jr. of Janesville, Wisconsin, was no John Boehner. He was strong—politically and physically—vibrant, smart, hardworking, and popular. He had an impossibly high level of internal support on Capitol Hill. Yet he also struck some of his colleagues as arrogant. He was fond of saying he had taken the speakership reluctantly, out of a sense of responsibility, turning the third-ranking job in American democracy into martyrdom. A year into his tenure, Meadows and the Freedom Caucus thought something was missing. Ryan hadn't followed through on his promise to relinquish internal power—in other words, he was too strong a leader. At the same time, they thought he was too eager to compromise his conservative ideals.

But perhaps more than anything, some of the group's leaders were frustrated that Ryan hadn't marched in lockstep behind Donald Trump's candidacy for the White House. Republicans had spent years pillorying Hillary Clinton for what they saw as her role in the massacre in Benghazi and the use of a private e-mail server to conduct government business. The Freedom Caucus, almost uniformly, thought anyone would be better than Clinton in the White House. How, Meadows and Jim Jordan wondered, could Ryan continue to lead the party when he wouldn't do everything he could to prevent a Clinton presidency? They needed a fighter. Ryan, they thought, was not a fighter.

The Freedom Caucus usually met at Tortilla Coast, a Tex-Mex joint across the street from Republican National Committee (RNC) headquarters and around the corner from the Capitol. But a meeting to plot a coup against the Speaker required discretion, and they couldn't be seen at Tortilla Coast this time of year—their presence in Washington during campaign season would raise too many eyebrows.

But the plan to get rid of Ryan couldn't wait any longer. So Meadows called some of his closest friends and instructed them to gather in his D.C. apartment. There was Rep. Raúl Labrador, a former immigration attorney from Idaho. Rep. Justin Amash, a baby-faced libertarian lawyer, from Grand Rapids, Michigan. Rep. Mick Mulvaney, a staunch budget hawk, from South Carolina. And Rep. Scott Perry from southeastern Pennsylvania.

This was the gang that would dump the Speaker of the House for the second time in two years.

THE FREEDOM CAUCUS'S GRIPES with Ryan were not entirely illegitimate. Ryan had not shied from sharply excoriating Donald Trump—in fact, in 2015 and 2016, he had made a cottage industry of it.

"I'm just not a Donald Trump guy," Ryan privately told his friends throughout the year, employing a frequently used rhetorical construct that helped explain his love for policy ("I'm a policy guy"), a preference for the standard rhythms of the House ("I'm a regular order guy"), and his adoration for Wisconsin ("just a couple of Wisconsin guys," he said when surrounded by fellow cheeseheads).

And yet since Trump became a candidate in 2015, Ryan had found himself inextricably, at times inconveniently, tied to the New York City billionaire. Ryan hated it. It ate at him, deep at his core. Here he was, a man who had spent his life climbing the political ladder, from congressional staffer slinging nachos at a Capitol Hill restaurant to Speaker of the House, being forced to answer if he, too, thought it was okay for celebrities to grab women by their private parts.

Ryan's friends and staff never thought they would see a President Trump. The National Republican Congressional Committee (NRCC)'s polling had Trump losing, and the Republican majority dwindling in the House. So for a good portion of 2016, Ryan met with his advisers and secretly discussed retiring. Why would he want to stick around? After eighteen years of elected service, the idea of being Speaker during a Hillary Clinton presidency wasn't terribly appealing. All his political goals—tax and entitlement reform—would be out the window, and he'd be left with managing the House, an institution that was unruly at best and completely broken at worst. He saw the humdrum of running the place under Clinton as an unfulfilling job with little upside. Not to mention, if Clinton beat Trump, Ryan knew he'd be seen as a Judas: the high-profile Republican who continually jabbed his party's nominee, allowing the Democrats another four years in the White House.

Ryan's friends envisioned him following in the footsteps of his mentor, former representative Jack Kemp, by setting up shop in the nonprofit arena. They mused about him building out his policy portfolio, sitting on a few corporate boards and living an idyllic life in his stately brick home in Janesville with his beautiful blond wife and three children—a family out of central casting. Not to mention, that kind of perch could provide Ryan with the springboard he needed to rescue the Republican Party after what insiders then saw as Trump's nearly certain implosion. Ryan could finally become the party's standard-bearer.

But throughout the talks with his close-knit circle—communications adviser Brendan Buck, political director Kevin Seifert, and Andy Speth, his longtime chief of staff—there was always a sense that Ryan would eventually relent and return to the House. The chats, which stretched for months, butting up against election season, revealed a pointed political reality about Ryan: He was just popular enough to stick it out atop the party.

So Ryan was going nowhere. Sure, people were agitating to push him out, but no one, it seemed, wanted to take the plunge. Ryan was always looking to push the limits of what his party's fringes would allow. He privately chatted with Senate minority leader Chuck Schumer about topics like immigration and tax reform, believing that his personality and charm might bend political reality. In the meantime, he wanted to dismantle the procedural motion that forced an immediate referendum vote on the Speaker of the House—the motion that had toppled John Boehner and threatened to topple him as well, if he wasn't careful. For Ryan, removing this anvil from above his head was a point of pride: If he was going to give up nights and weekends with friends and family, he shouldn't be subject to a referendum based on a single lawmaker's whims.

Ryan slowly came to the reality that he would return to the House and push to change the chamber's rules to remove that threat. If that ended his political career, so be it. Eventually, though, he dropped the rules demand and decided simply to remain in public life.

As the election neared, Ryan's aides and allies in the Capitol began envisioning just how much cooperation would be possible during a Clinton presidency. Meanwhile, the Freedom Caucus was already scheming to make sure Ryan would never have that chance.

LUCKILY FOR RYAN, the men in the Freedom Caucus were not the second coming of Lyndon Baines Johnson. They were outcasts—a bit insular, offbeat, and strange. Most of them hung out only with each other. They sat together in the middle of the House chamber, and when the House wasn't in session, they grew close snacking on Chick-fil-A sandwiches or nachos, swapping tales about their disillusionment with the status quo. Their feelings about Ryan and Boehner mirrored their overall disappointment with the Republican Party: Republicans had won the majority in 2010 by promising to deeply slash spending, tear up regulations, repeal Obamacare, and rearrange the House to better represent the will of the voters. Put mildly, the Freedom Caucus believed Republicans had failed on each of these fronts. If these men had their way, the Republican Party would stand firm to their values and work with them—not with Democrats—to solve the nation's ills.

Mark Meadows was the most complicated of the bunch. A North Carolina Republican with a sweep of gray hair, a folksy southern drawl, and a preoccupation with being liked, he played the part of D.C. outsider well. But it was just that: a part. Meadows, at fifty-nine, spent many weekends in Washington with his wife, Debbie. He was frequently spotted at parties around town: a ceremony for Tom Hanks receiving the Records of Achievement Award; socialite Adrienne Arsht's Hair of the Dog New Year's Brunch; and the British embassy's party for the royal wedding. Later he bought a half-million-dollar condo in Old Town, a tony enclave in suburban Alexandria, Virginia. The man who in 2012 said that the government should "stop doing things the Washington way" had become a part-time Beltway resident.

Many inside players in the Capitol thought Meadows was a fraud. One former top Republican leadership aide said Meadows was the most dishonest person he had ever met in the Capitol, convicted criminals included. Meadows had once dropped to his knees in Boehner's office, begging for forgiveness after having crossed the Speaker. When Kevin McCarthy dropped his own bid for Speaker, it was due in part to an insurgent push in the Freedom Caucus to throw him overboard, but Meadows privately told McCarthy's staff that he wanted to give him another chance. McCarthy balked. He doubted Meadows's sincerity, and in any case, he knew that agreeing would make him an eternal prisoner of the party's far-right wing.

Meadows, for his part, said his integrity was beyond reproach. He privately chalked up the criticism to jealousy of his power.

Regardless of how the Freedom Caucus members were perceived by their colleagues, they now had a plan, one that would likely cause a political crisis in Washington. Jordan, Meadows, and their top aides had been discussing it for months. The scheme was still a Hail Mary at best, but they were finally ready to make a move.

The Speaker of the House is second in line to the presidency and a constitutional officer of the U.S. government. So after the party takes an internal vote, the House of Representatives conducts an official election in public on the House floor a few months after Election Day. The Speaker needs the support of 218 of his or her colleagues, Democrat or Republican. Jordan and Meadows felt they could prevent Ryan from reaching that threshold.

Here's what they envisioned: The morning after Election Day, Jordan would travel to New York to announce on Fox News that he was challenging Ryan for the speakership in the upcoming internal election. He would also oppose him in the public floor vote. *We need new leadership,* he would say. The move would send shock waves through Washington. The Freedom Caucus would mostly back Jordan, allowing Ryan to win the internal election but cutting away at his mandate. Their goal was to throw the House into chaos, force Ryan out, and insert someone like Rep. Mike Pompeo of Kansas into the speakership. If all went according to plan, Jordan would become majority leader. In Meadows's apartment, the plan was met with general agreement, dashed with concern and excitement.

Meanwhile reporters had caught wind of the meeting from chatty members of the Freedom Caucus. They gathered outside Meadows's apartment as the meeting was ending. Mulvaney and others walked out the front door, but Meadows and Jordan, the ringleaders of the plan, hid in the back of Jordan's legislative director's silver Jeep as he drove them out of the garage.

THE SIXTEEN-AND-A-HALF-MONTH campaign was a torturous slog for Ryan, but it wasn't nearly as bad for his Freedom Caucus colleagues and other members of the Republican leadership. Kevin McCarthy grew close to Trump, as did Rep. Steve Scalise. Scalise and McCarthy were far less bound to the notions and conventions of the traditional Republican Party than Ryan. They found Trump thrilling, his antics mostly laughable, and his can-do attitude refreshing.

On July 2, 2016—sixteen days before the Republican convention in Cleveland—Scalise was in the western North Carolina mountains with friends and family for a getaway at his friends' cabin, so remote that cell phones didn't get reception. On this trip, that fact proved troublesome: Scalise was in the middle of trying to broker peace between Ryan and Donald Trump ahead of the party's confab in Ohio. Scalise and Trump had spoken on July 1, a Friday, and Trump had said to call him back the next day.

So on Saturday Scalise clambered into his car and instructed his Capitol Police detail to drive down the mountain toward Cashiers, North Carolina, a small town of roughly 150. As he neared the town, Scalise saw his cell phone suddenly pick up a full signal. He asked the driver to pull over so he could dial Trump. A moment later the nominee's already infamous voice came back through the speaker, but he wasn't talking about Paul Ryan: "Hey, what do you think about Mike Pence?" This conversation was not going to be about brokering a peace deal with Ryan, so Scalise quickly shifted gears. Trump had not selected a vice-presidential nominee yet, and Pence was pretty far down the list of potentials, but Scalise liked the sound of it.

"He's a great guy," Scalise told Trump. "I was the chairman of the Republican Study Committee, and so was he. He was our conference chair—he was great while he was there. He went to Indiana, where he was a great governor. He has great legislative experience and great executive experience."

"That's good to know, because he's right here with me," Trump said. He was quizzing Scalise about his friend Pence as the two sat at his golf course in northern New Jersey. (Scalise later laughed. "I was an unwitting participant in the vetting of Mike Pence in front of Mike Pence!")

Ryan ignited a firestorm in May when he told Jake Tapper he just was "not ready" to endorse Trump. In response, Trump played footsie with endorsing Ryan's primary challenger, Paul Nehlen, an anti-Semite, whom the Speaker eventually trounced by sixty-eight points.

An initial détente of sorts came in May, when Trump and Ryan met at Republican Party headquarters on Capitol Hill. The two teams, brought together by Ryan's friend Reince Priebus, the RNC chairman, had decided in advance that only a small cadre of aides would be permitted to witness the meeting. When the time came, Trump ignored this and brought his whole team of roughly a half-dozen people. Ryan responded in kind and allowed his aides in the room. It was always tit for tat.

The two then had a private session, where Ryan explained his suspicions of Trump: that he was not a conservative or even a Republican for that matter.

"What kind of president are you going to be, and how are you going to govern?" Ryan asked Trump. Trump said he was a conservative. He asked Ryan if it would be wise to put out a list of judges he might nominate if he were elected. Ryan said he thought that would be a terrific idea. Trump then asked him if he had heard of the Federalist Society, and Ryan laughed—he had known the group's executive vice president, Leonard Leo, for a quarter century.

The Speaker explained to the president what he cared about—his legislative priorities of slashing taxes and overhauling entitlements, and his political prerogative of electing Republicans—and the two came out with a better understanding of each other.

Ryan had brought a slide deck with details about Medicare and the nation's ballooning debt, but it was abundantly clear that Trump was not interested. When Ryan brought up reworking Medicare, Trump demurred. "I know that's your thing, but I think that's stupid," he told Ryan.

During the campaign, Ryan maintained some semblance of sanity by refusing to consume news. He was often made aware of the controversy du jour by reporters or by his top adviser, Buck. But 2016 gave Ryan a lot of time alone. He spent months on end zipping around America in his armored black SUV, so he used a dummy Twitter account to scroll through headlines as his motorcade made its way from airport to fundraiser to rally. This is how Ryan followed the presidential contest, and he was always shocked by what he saw.

Weeks before Election Day, Ryan's party was slumping in internal polls. The House Republican leadership was certain they would lose the presidency, and gripped by the fear that their majority would shrink. Then came the *Access Hollywood* video, which deepened their distrust for Trump and prompted a slew of alarmed phone calls from GOP lawmakers to the personal cell phones of Ryan and his number two, Kevin McCarthy.

Ryan was in Cleveland when the video was posted, hosting a fundraiser for David Joyce, a moderate Republican from northeastern Ohio. Ryan's aides pulled him out of the event, and he asked his aides what Trump said. They said he needed to see for himself, so they handed him earbuds and showed him the video on a cell phone. Ryan cringed in disgust.

Before he left Cleveland, Ryan called Priebus and said he was pulling the plug on a planned appearance with Trump at the Republican Fall Fest in Elkhorn, Wisconsin, an event he and Priebus had first put on decades earlier. "I'm not doing this thing tomorrow with him," Ryan told the RNC chair. "No way."

"Well, he's coming," Priebus said.

"No, he's not," Ryan responded.

Priebus told the Speaker that he himself would have to disinvite Trump. Ryan said he'd be glad to, but told Priebus it would be easier for Trump to pull out of the event. Priebus said Trump would never go for that. Ryan didn't call Trump—Priebus asked him not to. The New Yorker never showed up in Elkhorn. (Ryan was taken aback when he, Ron Johnson, and Wisconsin governor Scott Walker were booed at the event. The Speaker hadn't realized that Trump supporters were so fervent.)

Very few knew that Ryan also placed a call to Mitch McConnell, his counterpart in the Senate. McConnell and Ryan were friendly enough, but they were of different generations, and it often showed. Ryan was driven both by conviction and by ambition. He never seemed to let go of the idea that he was too big for Congress and belonged somewhere bigger. Ryan, of course, had been the vice-presidential candidate in 2012, and his political views were enhanced by that experience. McConnell, in his mid-seventies, was a southerner whose ultimate goal, reached the previous year, had been to become Senate majority leader. He was perfectly content living on Capitol Hill and controlling Congress from his ornate office overlooking the National Mall, while pulling the strings in

Kentucky, a place where he exerted tremendous influence. McConnell was a staunch conservative, but unlike Ryan, he didn't wear it on his sleeve. McConnell never let himself get boxed into a corner.

Which was why he was so alarmed by what he heard from Paul Ryan that day. Ryan told his Senate counterpart that he was on the brink of pulling his endorsement of Trump.

"Don't do that," McConnell told Ryan. McConnell knew that if Ryan did, it would tear the party asunder, a trauma from which it might never recover. "Listen," McConnell told Ryan, "just keep talking to me. We'll work through this together." Ryan stood down.

On October 8, the day before Trump was to face off against Hillary Clinton in a debate at Washington University in St. Louis, Ryan and his leadership team held a conference call. Greg Walden, the mild-mannered Republican congressman from Oregon who was running the party's campaign committee, was ready to pull his endorsement from Trump. Rep. Ann Wagner, from the tony suburbs of St. Louis, reneged on her endorsement before the call. (She later jumped back onto the Trump train and in 2018 was more than happy to stand by his side, smile on her face, while Trump was signing a banking bill.)

Kevin McCarthy got on the call late, and upon hearing that everyone was ready to jump ship, he delivered a strong rebuke. *What the hell are you guys all doing?* McCarthy asked them. *How can you do this and hurt our nominee the day before he has his debate? Leave him alone, and if something happens, it will happen in this debate.* Ryan agreed to sit tight.

Trump held it together and was widely seen as staying toe to toe with Clinton at the event. Ryan wasn't moved. During the debate, he got a string of text messages from Sen. Mike Lee of Utah, who was also bothered by Trump's behavior.

Ryan still wanted distance from Trump. He scheduled a rare conference call with all House Republicans.

Ryan's message on the call was blunt: Republicans should feel free to abandon Trump. They should focus on their own races and not worry about their party's standard-bearer. Ryan himself took the unusual step of saying he would no longer defend the Republican Party's nominee.

"I am not going to defend Donald Trump," Ryan told House

Republicans on the October 10 call. "Not now, not in the future." It was short of yanking his endorsement, but still a hell of a statement.

"Look," Ryan said, sounding exasperated. "You guys know I had real concerns with our nominee. I hope you appreciate that I am doing what I think is best for you, as the members, not what's best for me." Ryan felt like he was doing Republicans a favor: He was allowing them to do what they needed to do to save themselves. He couldn't shake the fact that Trump was so vulgar. *People just don't talk like that where I'm from,* he thought.

Making this decision left Ryan's team feeling relieved. His staff would no longer be bombarded with inquiries about what he thought of the president's most recent dustup.

But Ryan's colleagues in the Republican leadership thought the Speaker's stance was dumb. "My feeling was, when you get to the final days of a major election, in a presidential election, the weird things always happen at the very end," said Steve Scalise. "You know the other choice. The other choice is Hillary. You've got to, at that point, rally behind the person that's going to give our country the best chance on getting back on track, and that's Donald Trump. You have no choice at that point. It's all or nothing, and you gotta go all in."

Over the next few weeks, Ryan slowly inched back closer to Trump. He hadn't warmed to the man—nor did he think he would win—but he thought it would help propel Ron Johnson to victory in the Wisconsin Senate race. Ryan's team made an offer to campaign with Trump in the Badger State, but he was rebuffed by Priebus, who thought Trump's time would be better spent elsewhere.

Finally, just hours before Election Day, it was time for Ryan to do what he had never thought possible. He was standing in a warehouse in Waukesha with Johnson, Gov. Scott Walker, and Republican Party officials in a last-minute effort to turn out the base. Trump seemed to be everywhere but Wisconsin, making stops in Florida, North Carolina, Pennsylvania, and New Hampshire that day.

Privately, Republicans had been urging Ryan just to get out of the way and tell people to vote for Donald Trump. Ryan relented. With a touch more than twelve hours until polls opened, Ryan encouraged Republicans to do what he had once thought was unthinkable.

"I voted Trump, Pence, Johnson, some guy named Ryan, and every other Republican on the ticket, and that's actually what each and every one of us need to do," he said.

At that point, Ryan thought it was binary: Either he urged voters to vote for Trump, or Hillary Clinton would be president.

"I was just worried we were going to get our butts kicked," he later recalled.

THE HOLIDAY INN EXPRESS in Janesville, Wisconsin, is a drab business-style hotel on the side of I-90. The lobby is sterile—one aide remarked that it was "clean, at least." It's completely unremarkable and therefore is representative of the hotels across America that political insiders become accustomed to as they hopscotch the country in their quest for power.

But on Election Day, November 8, that Holiday Inn Express morphed into one of the epicenters of the political universe. Ryan aides wandered around the main lobby, scrolling through iPads on the faux marble tables and eventually clutching bottles of beer and glasses of wine, getting a head start on the long night ahead. A handful of television trucks were parked just steps from an indoor pool, and Capitol Police and private security guards screened partygoers who were drinking from a cash bar.

It was here that Ryan would watch the results roll in, and here that his political world would change.

Ryan began this Election Day the same way he always did: He grabbed his dogs and his brother or father-in-law and went pheasant hunting. His kids were away at school, and it was a nice distraction during an otherwise uncertain day.

When Buck and Seifert, two of Ryan's most trusted aides, showed up at the Speaker's home around six P.M., they too believed it was the beginning of a new chapter for the Speaker: the counterbalance to

President Hillary Clinton. Shortly after she became president, Ryan planned to give a speech tossing the Republican Party of Trump in the dustbin. For the next two years, he would have to carefully weigh his never-ending quest for legislative dealmaking with the reality that he would be a top presidential hopeful in 2020. He couldn't be too ready to compromise, his inner circle thought, but he had trouble acting as the staunch and unflinching opposition.

Buck and Seifert came to Ryan's home to swap gossip—who was up, who was down—and to discuss the schedule for the election night event. It had been carefully crafted. The plan was to have Ryan speak early enough to avoid talking about the results of the presidential race. What was he going to say about a Clinton victory? He decided he would much rather wait the night out and discuss it in the morning, after a decent night's sleep.

At around seven-thirty P.M., Ryan got a call from Priebus, who told him the exit polls were terrible for the Republican Party. Trump was going to get trounced, Republicans were going to lose the Senate, and Ryan's House Republican majority would be sliced in half. Get your mind right with President Hillary Clinton and Senate majority leader Chuck Schumer, Priebus told Ryan.

"Well, I can't speak to the presidential or the Senate," Ryan told Priebus, "but I think we're going to lose six seats. But I'll defer to you on the presidential race."

Ryan had been dreading election night. *This is going to suck*, he thought. *I'm going to be the last Republican standing, and I need to figure out how to stiff-upper-lip this.*

The room where the throng of Ryan supporters gathered was drab and small. Reporters were penned in the back of the room along a bleacher. Ryan's aides were easily identifiable, sporting red and blue pins in the shape of an arrowhead—a nod to Ryan's hunting hobby.

Just before nine P.M., the Associated Press called the House race for Ryan, an all-but-certain result in the district he had first won in 1998. As he walked onstage with his family, elections across the country were trending in Republicans' direction—and toward a Trump victory. But Ryan didn't believe it quite yet.

"By some accounts, it could be a really good night for America," he said to an exuberant crowd. "There are races we want to watch. So like you, I'm eager to watch the rest of the evening, I'm eager to enjoy this evening with you, so thank you so much for coming out."

He waved as he exited stage left, surrounded by his daughter, two sons, wife, brother, and sister-in-law. Backstage he popped in and out of the war room, where senior staff like Seifert and Jake Kastan, the number two on Ryan's political team, were monitoring races across the country.

As the hour wore on, Ryan was shocked by what he was seeing. His own election results were stronger than usual in Kenosha County, a Democratic stronghold for the previous fifty years. Ron Johnson's numbers were also solid. If Johnson was winning in Kenosha County, Ryan thought he could win this thing. He then took a peek at Trump's numbers, and by God, he thought, Trump was running strong, too, right alongside Johnson. He then pulled up the numbers for Marathon County in central Wisconsin, and Trump was winning there, too. If Trump could win Wisconsin, Ryan thought, he would win Pennsylvania and Michigan. *Oh my God,* Ryan thought. *This guy might've done it.*

At around ten P.M., long before the race was called, Ryan called Trump on his cell phone. Their relationship was exceedingly frosty, but this call was unexpectedly warm.

"This is unbelievable," Ryan told Trump. "It looks like you're going to win."

Trump seemed happy but shell-shocked. "Hey, you and I had our differences," he told Ryan. "But I'm looking forward to working with you and governing with you. Let's go fix this country."

Trump was willing to let all of Ryan's disloyalty go. "Because it's life and we sort of need each other a little bit," Trump recalled in 2018. "I didn't like what he did, but I get along with him."

In Bakersfield, California, Kevin McCarthy had prepared a statement only for Clinton to win the presidency. His aides, draining beers at McCarthy's election night party at Temblor Brewing, quickly drafted copy reflecting the new political reality.

Steve Scalise was at his usual election night haunt, Drago's Seafood

Restaurant in Metairie, Louisiana, home of the original charbroiled oyster, it claims. His own reelection race was called fifteen minutes after the polls closed, so he was intently focused on the presidential contest. Ohio and Florida were called for Trump early, but none of the networks had called Pennsylvania.

Scalise had been to Pennsylvania, a state where Republicans had picked up a handful of seats in recent years. He knew that Republicans were ascendant there, so he had instructed his political team to use Republican Party data to investigate whether the outstanding precincts would give Trump the victory.

Even as the night turned toward Trump, turmoil was brewing for Ryan. When it was becoming clear Trump would win, Sean Hannity, the Fox News host who had a tight relationship with the president-elect and a prickly rapport with Ryan, was on air railing against the Speaker.

"Paul Ryan is not going to be the Speaker of the House in January," Hannity said during Fox's live coverage of election night, dialing in to the broadcast by phone after speaking to Trump three times that night. "I was going to save that for my program tomorrow. He's not going to be the Speaker. I mean, an amazing turn of events because the establishment on both sides lost touch with the real lives of real Americans, and Donald Trump opened the door, said we're going to fix it and turn the table over."

McCarthy immediately texted Hannity from California and explained to him that Ryan would be on Trump's side. McCarthy was sure of it, he told Hannity.

Buck, in Janesville, heard about the remark and called Newt Gingrich, the former House Speaker and frequent Fox News guest, and Marc Short, the former House GOP leadership aide who was now working for the Trump-Pence campaign. "Let us know if there's anything we can do," Buck said to Short. He also asked if anyone internally was aiming for Ryan's head. Short assured him that he had nothing to worry about.

By two-thirty A.M., Scalise was thinking it would be a bit presumptuous to have a victory party, but he was telling guests he thought

Trump was going to actually win. Scalise's wife, Jennifer, turned to him and said, "Should we send the kids home? They have school tomorrow."

"You know what," Scalise said. "This is history."

An hour later, he was popping champagne with his supporters, Jennifer, and their kids. *The country is saved,* Scalise thought to himself.

THE MORNING AFTER ELECTION DAY—seven days after the Freedom Caucus had discussed their plan to dispose of Ryan—Jim Jordan made his own decision and his own set of phone calls: he was not going to challenge Ryan. It was time to "come together," he told Meadows. The surprise election results had changed the calculus: There was real opportunity with Trump in the White House, and Jordan was heartened that the Speaker was on board. The wall with Mexico. Tax reform. Slashing regulations. Jordan and Meadows now had someone who could fulfill their policy dreams. Jordan called Alyssa Farah, the number two Freedom Caucus aide, who was set to take the Amtrak Acela to New York to help Jordan announce his candidacy for the speakership on Fox. *Cancel your train,* Jordan told her. *The plan is off.*

Around the same time that morning, Paul Ryan's new world was dawning on him—and quickly. He talked to Trump and Pence again and decided they needed to have their two staffs meet as soon as possible.

On the one hand, Ryan was exceedingly pleased that Hillary Clinton was not president. On the other hand, he felt an enormous amount of responsibility to keep government on the rails. He understood that some Americans—indeed, many Republicans who supported Paul Ryan—were scared by the prospect of a Trump presidency. On November 9 he held a press conference in Janesville for the explicit purpose of trying to convey that there were, in fact, normal people still in government.

"This is the most incredible political feat I have seen in my lifetime," Ryan said, standing in front of a blue curtain back at the Holiday Inn Express. "Donald Trump will lead a unified Republican government. And we will work hand in hand on a positive agenda to tackle this country's big challenges.

"I want to close with this," Ryan said. "There's no doubt our democracy can be very messy. And we do remain a sharply divided country. But now, as we do every four years, we have to work to heal the divisions of a long campaign. I think President-elect Donald Trump set the perfect tone last night for doing just this."

Ryan's reversal—and his ability to align himself with Trump at the drop of a hat—led many to think he had completely abandoned his principles in pursuit of power. It was a fair criticism: How did you go from thinking a man was vulgar and nearly pulling your support, to saying you looked forward to working with him to pursue a conservative agenda? Ryan felt obligated to stay in Congress and make sure the country went in the right direction. He wanted to get government set up, and he saw the opportunity to pass an agenda he had been working on for his entire life. And he saw Trump as a vessel to do that.

"If I just huffed and puffed and 'Never Trumped' and just took my toys and left, I just didn't think that was the responsible thing to do," Ryan later recalled.

Ryan spent all day on November 9 calling his colleagues, ensuring he had the support to remain Speaker of the House. Some Ryan aides had remained in Washington on election night to begin doing the same. They found that Ryan would be completely safe. Trump's victory, in a sense, had saved him. Now that conservatives had the White House, the angst about Ryan disappeared.

On November 10, Ryan and Trump met face-to-face. The Speaker hosted Trump; his wife, Melania; and Mike Pence on Capitol Hill for lunch at the Capitol Hill Club, and a subsequent tour of the Capitol and the Speaker's balcony, the space off of Ryan's office.

When Ryan walked into the Capitol Hill Club, Trump grabbed the Speaker's hand and brought him close in. "I think I got you figured out," Trump said to him. "That thing really rattled you." He was talking about the *Access Hollywood* tape.

"Yeah, it really did," Ryan replied.

"I get you," Trump said. "You're just a Boy Scout. You're also kind of religious, aren't you?"

"You're like Mike on that, aren't you?" Melania chimed into the conversation.

"I'm a devout Catholic," Ryan said, "and yes, I take that stuff very seriously."

"Oh, okay," Trump said. "You're just a Boy Scout. That's what it is."

2

"FIRE PELOSI!"

DAYS AFTER ELECTION DAY, Nancy Pelosi was calling Democratic candidates. Dialing from an iPhone, using a sheet compiled by her staff, she spoke with Democrats who had won and many who had lost. Across the country and in Washington, Trump's victory had sent liberals reeling, but Pelosi was making these calls, as she did most things, with purpose.

A week earlier she had expected to leave Congress. She was going to watch Hillary Clinton's inauguration, then quickly resign, triggering a special election in her San Francisco district, a seat that many believed Pelosi would try to bestow upon her daughter Christine. It wasn't the first time Pelosi had thought of leaving—she had come close in late 2012, when House Democrats were deep in the minority. But then she could point to the success of passing Obamacare in the president's first term. This time, though, with a new Democrat in the White House and her party probably in control of the Senate, she thought she could finally put down her sword.

But overnight the calculus had changed. Her legacy, everything she had worked to build from 2006 to 2010, was in jeopardy. Now, she realized, as she worked methodically through her list of Democrats' phone numbers, that her leadership was needed more than ever.

Not everyone saw it that way. In fact, frustration among House

Democrats with Pelosi and her leadership team, once simmering below the surface, was boiling over, especially after the disaster on election night. There was no ambiguity: A growing contingent of them were sick of being led by two white people in their upper seventies. They thought Pelosi and Steny Hoyer were unpracticed in the modern tactics of political warfare, unwise to the demographics of the contemporary Democratic Party, and out of touch with the issues that animated the party's base. Many felt that Pelosi and Hoyer had held Democrats back for nearly a decade. In many ways, they saw Pelosi as synonymous with Clinton: a coastal member of the liberal elite detached from the struggles of the Midwest. And as Clinton's poor turnout among white males in Michigan and Ohio became apparent in the days after the election, Pelosi's status as a coastal liberal elite became another talking point for lawmakers looking to back another horse.

There was some truth to the criticism. Pelosi and Hoyer of Maryland, the House minority whip, had been the leaders of a young and increasingly minority-dominated party since 2002. Pelosi was most closely associated with San Francisco, but she was a Baltimore native and still gave off the vibe of an old-school, big-city party boss—just like her father, who had been a member of the House and mayor of Baltimore. She excelled at the inside political game, but many believed she fell short at understanding and mobilizing the grassroots.

As soon as Trump won, Pelosi started quizzing her staff. "What should I do?" she asked. Her aides thought this was a mostly rhetorical exercise. She never seriously considered leaving with Trump at 1600 Pennsylvania Avenue. They knew she was going nowhere. Now after another bruising election, she had to consolidate power.

NANCY PELOSI'S TO-DO LIST is never-ending and revolving, and requires constant care. That's why, on the 2016 night that decided the presidency and control of Congress, she was in Washington, tending to the cogs in her vast and powerful political network. Handwritten thank-you notes. Calls to candidates and operatives in the fields. Personal touches with donors who had written checks for tens or perhaps hundreds of thousands of dollars. These were the people who gave Pelosi her power. These were the people who made her the rainmaker who lorded over the House Democratic Caucus for more than a decade.

Pelosi's congressional district is San Francisco, the liberal enclave where she has lived with her handsome husband—a financier and investor—since 1969. But her political base is D.C., the city where she went to college and where she's represented the Bay Area since 1987. Her life is the House of Representatives. She relishes the hum of the floor, the ability to deliver for colleagues she likes. She made her political bones in the chamber, working her way up from rank-and-file appropriator to whip to Speaker of the House, breaking up the staid old boys' club, clearing out the smoke-filled rooms, and shaping—some would say violently kneading—the modern congressional Democratic Party into her image. She filled the Democratic Congressional Campaign Committee (DCCC)'s coffers with cash and kept the details of its affairs tightly held. She established almost paralyzing control over the party's political apparatus. Hundreds of people—lobbyists, consultants, lawmakers, and operatives—have made careers from being "Pelosi people," trading on their proximity to her.

Pelosi had plans in town for election night—stops she had to make in the capital to ensure her people felt good. Why not? She felt good, too. She was unnervingly certain that Hillary Clinton would win the White House. On election night, she wore a pearl-white pantsuit and a purple shirt with a purple necklace—the colors of the suffragettes, she told friends.

Pelosi's plan was to attend a staff rally that afternoon at the DCCC's headquarters, which took up an entire floor in the DNC's Capitol Hill office building. Then she was expected at a fete for donors at the Capitol Hill townhouse owned by über-wealthy Rep. John Delaney of Maryland. But first she climbed into her black Suburban for an election night interview on *PBS NewsHour.*

"Tonight I believe that the Democrats will come out in a stronger position," Pelosi told host Judy Woodruff, sounding jubilant and projecting confidence. "We will, of course, retain the White House with the election of Hillary Clinton. I believe we will gain the United States

Senate, it will be close, but we will gain the United States Senate, and we will pick up many seats in the House of Representatives."

It was the kind of arrogance that many Democrats felt in 2016.

"We really have a massive mobilization," Pelosi said, when asked why she was so confident. "We own the ground. And we will pull out that vote." In closing the interview, Woodruff pointed out that Pelosi was the highest-ranking female politician in America, and Pelosi looked at her Apple Watch and said, "At the moment!"

At that moment, Pelosi's world looked rosy—just how she liked it. Instead of rushing back to Washington to catch up on the election results, she asked her ever-present police detail to point the Suburban deeper into the Virginia suburbs for a quick pit stop. Love or hate Pelosi, there was near universal admiration for her attention to detail. She never forgot a birthday, a birth, or a funeral. Case in point: The election night jaunt to the southern part of Alexandria had nothing to do with politics. She wanted to drop off flowers at her college roommate's house. Her roommate wasn't even home. As night fell, Pelosi's motorcade headed back into the city to Delaney's East Capitol Street townhouse, which, by then, was filled to the brim with donors, many of whom wanted to celebrate victory with elected Democrats like Pelosi.

Pelosi probably knew she wasn't headed back toward the speakership. In the days leading up to the election, she had felt exceedingly bullish about Clinton, but she had privately grown sour at the prospect of leading Democrats back into the majority in the House. It was a marked shift. In the months before Election Day, she had openly predicted her party would regain control of the lower chamber. In September, while sitting in her Capitol office, she said that if her party fell short, it would come "down to probably a single digit, one way or another." But as the election drew nearer, her outlook on regaining the majority grew darker. She was particularly miffed about FBI director James Comey's decision to reopen the investigation into Clinton. She told associates Comey was the best Republican operative in America.

Of course, for Pelosi, another failed attempt to regain the House majority would not be merely a blow to her ego. It would be, for Democrats writ large, the third consecutive election cycle during which they had failed to take control. As such, it represented an existential threat to the party and, more acutely, to Pelosi's leadership. The party's rank and file were growing weary of both her style and her substance and were beginning to line up against her. Junior Democrats—Reps. Ruben Gallego of Arizona, Seth Moulton of Massachusetts, and Kathleen Rice of New York—were publicly agitating against her, the loudest opposition to Pelosi in some time. They were publicly bellowing that the party should seek to elevate new leaders.

It was a steep fall from grace for the first female House Speaker in American history. In 2006, with the help of Rep. Rahm Emanuel, Pelosi and House Democrats rode an anti–Iraq War wave into the majority, dismantling the Republican strongholds in the South and the Midwest. It was historic. On January 23, 2007, for the first time in his presidency, George W. Bush came to the Capitol to give his State of the Union address to a Democratic House.

But Bush—with whom Pelosi had a pile of disagreements, not least the Iraq War, which she was agitating to end—recognized the historic moment. Speaking on the House floor, he said, "Tonight, I have a high privilege and distinct honor of my own, as the first president to begin the State of the Union message with these words: Madam Speaker." Pelosi looked around and beamed.

"In his day," Bush said, "the late Congressman Thomas D'Alesandro Jr., from Baltimore, Maryland, saw Presidents Roosevelt and Truman at this rostrum. But nothing could compare with the sight of his only daughter, Nancy, presiding tonight as Speaker of the House of Representatives. Congratulations, Madam Speaker." This kind of civility and kindness would come to seem quaint in the Trump era.

Pelosi widened the party's appeal, giving Barack Obama a healthy majority for the first two years of his presidency. Then came the stimulus bill, the auto bailout, Obamacare, and a failed attempt to pass cap and trade, a pollution-control law. Republicans, led by John Boehner and Eric Cantor, branded Democrats as profligate spenders and poor stewards of government, and perhaps most critically, they demonized Pelosi as the embodiment of a bureaucracy run amok. They hung a FIRE

PELOSI banner outside the window of RNC headquarters, and they drove around the country with the phrase emblazoned on a bus.

It worked. In 2010 Republicans won a stunning sixty-three seats, making Boehner Speaker of the House and relegating Pelosi to the minority. There she would stay, mostly watching Obama's presidency from the sidelines, hopeful she could win back the majority before too long.

Fast-forward to 2016. Democrats were still in the minority, and though operatives thought the outlook was good for the party, they were uncertain how good it could be. "We knew we would be up seats," said one senior Democratic aide. "The rest was up to Hillary Clinton's coattails." Either way, with Clinton headed to the White House, Pelosi figured it was time to move on.

The early returns, which Pelosi was briefed on by aides that evening, did not look good. Standing around top donors and Democratic operatives, Pelosi stayed busy making calls, trying to find out what was happening on the ground. She was particularly concerned about Virginia and Pennsylvania. She called Rep. Bob Brady, the Philadelphia party boss and a longtime ally. Brady, built like a refrigerator, was married to a former Philadelphia Eagles cheerleader, and was driven to Washington each morning and returned to Philadelphia each night. Nothing happened in Philadelphia politics without him knowing. Brady told Pelosi he had delivered strong numbers in the inner city, but areas around Pittsburgh went overwhelmingly for Trump.

The night ended in sharp disappointment. By the next morning, Pelosi, ever the operator, called Trump Tower to speak with the president-elect. Trump acted optimistic about working with Democrats and said Pelosi was the reason why.

"I think we'll get things done . . . 'cause I know what you do. . . . You're somebody that gets things done, better than anybody," Trump told Pelosi, showing his behind-the-scenes flexibility, praising the career politician who crafted Obamacare and helped write many of the regulations he wanted to unwind.

"Don't forget I was a supporter of yours, a good one," Trump told

Pelosi. "I think you're terrific. That was in my developer life, my business life."

TRUMP MAY HAVE SOUNDED keen to work with Pelosi, but there was no certainty he would get the chance. While Pelosi was busy making congratulatory or conciliatory postelection phone calls, some of her colleagues were surveying the landscape, trying to discern whether it was time to strike at her.

One of them was Rep. Joe Crowley of New York. The six-foot-four Irishman from Queens shared a similar background with Pelosi. Both were wise to the ways of machine politics: Pelosi had learned at the knee of her father, while Crowley had been the chosen successor to Thomas Manton, the New York Democrat who resigned his seat just in time to allow voters to tap Crowley for it in 1998. They both had a strong presence at home but spent lots of time in Washington: It was an open secret that Crowley lived with his family in suburban Virginia, not in Queens.

Crowley had long eyed a run for the top slot in the House Democratic Caucus, biding his time in lower-level leadership jobs. His politics weren't dissimilar to Pelosi's, but he brought different sensibilities. He was twenty-two years Pelosi's junior and represented working-class communities in Queens. There was no doubt he was well liked. He played guitar and was often seen at parties with a beer in hand. He had two major strikes against him in his leadership quest: He wasn't a natural Pelosi ally, and he wasn't a policy wonk. But now, finally, his distance from Pelosi seemed like it would play in his favor. Democrats from all corners of the party, from midwestern moderates to East Coast liberals to newly elected southwesterners, pulled him aside in the days following the election pleading with him to run. His team sprang into action, setting up a whiteboard in his office on which they mapped out his potential paths to victory.

Steny Hoyer, too, was always nipping at Pelosi's heels. In 2010, after Democrats lost the House, Hoyer had spoken with top advisers about trying to topple Pelosi. Democrats had just suffered the worst electoral defeat in six decades, and Pelosi had been the central figure in every race. Her face had been plastered on billboards, buses, and campaign signs everywhere from Florida to Iowa. Hoyer's team came to the conclusion that her support was too solid, and it would be better for him to remain her mostly loyal deputy.

During the following six years, Republicans had shut down the government, almost defaulted on the debt, and stumbled through legislating like a drunkard through a dive bar. Yet the Democrats had not been able to capitalize on this by taking back the majority.

Just days after the 2016 election, the mood was sour as Democrats met for their first postelection all-party caucus meeting in a nondescript room in the Capitol. Many Democrats were agitating to delay the imminent leadership election to give more time for "conversations." Quick elections, of course, favor the incumbent—especially Pelosi, arguably one of the best internal vote counters in modern congressional history. Her operation could snap into action at the drop of a hat. But this time even some of her traditional allies were agitating against her. Rep. John Larson, a Connecticut Democrat who left the leadership in 2011, asked for a delay, as did the Congressional Black Caucus, a group Pelosi worked assiduously to keep in her corner. The party, led by Pelosi, exempted the caucus's members from paying their full dues to the party committee and backed their push to lose term limits for committee chairs. Now they were abandoning her.

Despite the frustration, Pelosi kept her head down. "I've got 125 votes," she told her staff on numerous occasions—two-thirds of all Democrats—a signal they should not make phone calls to shore up support. Some of them made calls anyway.

In the tense caucus meeting, Pelosi was perturbed. Perturbed about the push to delay the internal election. Perturbed about House Democrats' perpetual station in the minority. And perturbed that she was being blamed for the party's electoral woes. The party sat there stewing over coffee and pastries, relitigating the prior twelve months.

"Don't lay this at my feet," Pelosi said defensively. The raw nerves among Democrats were also on display when Massachusetts representative Seth Moulton tried to compliment Pelosi by saying she was the hardest-working member of the Democratic Caucus.

"I like to think of myself as the smartest worker," she shot back.

Pelosi quickly moved to delay the internal election to November 30—a concession to ease the tension—and gave up some power to appease her disgruntled ranks, implementing many changes Hoyer and others had been pushing for behind the scenes for years. Pelosi allowed the Democratic Caucus to vote on the chairman of the DCCC, a post she traditionally appointed. She bought some space from the agitators but also exposed a bit of weakness: She had never given up power like that before.

At that point, Joe Crowley was feeling under a dizzying pressure to make a decision. He couldn't walk down a hallway without being stopped and quizzed about his interest in taking on Pelosi. Nine excruciating days after the election, he decided against a challenge. It wasn't the right time. He didn't think the support would materialize.

He picked up the phone and called Pelosi to inform her of his decision. "I wanted to let you know," Crowley said, "I'm not going to run."

There was a pause. It was almost as if Pelosi were taken aback—either at Crowley's decision not to run or at his call to tell her he was even considering it.

She responded, "Good decision."

Steny Hoyer never got that far. Pelosi knew that, at the end of the day, the Maryland Democrat wouldn't step up to challenge her. And, indeed, she was right.

Instead, it was a rabble-rouser, Ohio representative Tim Ryan, who challenged Pelosi for the job. This wasn't the first time Ryan, a partier turned meditation-and-clean-eating devotee, had bucked the establishment. He had first run for Congress by mounting a bid against his former boss, the embattled James Traficant. Nobody thought he had a shot in hell of winning against Pelosi, not even Ryan himself. But that wasn't the point. Ryan, like so many others, was tired of losing. He was fed up with being in the minority and tired with what he saw as an out-of-touch leadership team. The 2016 election had jolted him to life. Trump had won Trumbull County, Ryan's home base, the first

Republican presidential candidate to win there since Richard Nixon in 1972.

Ryan had bucked Pelosi before, in 2010. "We had some really good, substantive things to talk about that we didn't talk about, and there's plenty of blame to go around. She's obviously in charge, so she needs to take the brunt of the responsibility for it," he told *The Youngstown Business Journal* then. "I was brought up to be loyal to people who helped you, and I want to be—but at the expense of what? I think we have to sit down as a Democratic Caucus in D.C. and ask what direction are we going in."

After that comment ran, Ryan said, he got a couple of calls from her inner circle. *What are you doing?* Pelosi's allies asked him. *Aren't you on the team?* He quickly dropped his criticism.

But this time, after Trump's victory, when it became clear that Hoyer and Crowley were going to take a pass, Ryan decided to make a move. He knew that mounting a bid against Pelosi came with risks. The last challenge to her reign had come in 2010, when North Carolina representative Heath Shuler launched a long-shot bid. Pelosi drubbed Shuler 150 to 43. Shuler left Congress two years later, creating an opening for an upstart North Carolina conservative named Mark Meadows.

To complicate matters for Ryan, Pelosi had been one of his mentors, installing him on the coveted House Democratic Steering Committee when he first came to Congress. Ryan capitalized on that by getting himself on the powerful appropriations panel, which allowed him to bring big bucks back to his down-on-its-luck Ohio district.

Despite the uphill battle, Ryan began trying to cobble together a bid against Pelosi. He started during Thanksgiving break. In a sign of just how ill prepared he was, he had to scramble to get many of his colleagues' phone numbers. Yet as he called from his Ohio home, he found kindred spirits. Young lawmakers like Gallego of Arizona and Moulton of Massachusetts were more than happy to lend a hand to the long-shot bid to topple Pelosi. Quickly, Ryan had the public support from all factions of the caucus, including from prominent Congressional Black Caucus members like Reps. Alcee Hastings of Florida and Marcia Fudge of Ohio. Then more establishment Democrats, like Rep. Ed Perlmutter of Colorado, signed onto his bid.

Ryan's big mistake was waiting to get into the race just before the House left for its Thanksgiving recess. He had trouble reaching lawmakers by phone to shore up support. For example, Rep. Ron Kind, a veteran Democrat from Wisconsin who was skeptical of Pelosi and therefore an ideal Ryan supporter, was hunting with his kids and out of the reach of his cell phone.

So Ryan turned to television to supplement his phone outreach. A satellite van parked outside his home in Ohio for three days so he could appear on television to talk about his bid for Democratic leader.

"I knew [Democratic members of the House] were watching TV," he said. "People were cooking Thanksgiving dinner with CNN on. So we did every show and just made the case. They need to start seeing me as the leader. They need to see how I do on TV. Like how that would look for frontline members. How that would look for the party if Tim was in charge."

Ryan called Pelosi to tell her of his plans. He never heard back.

True to her word, Pelosi won another term atop the party on November 30, 2016. And just as she had predicted, she received support from two-thirds of her caucus. Still, it was a significant blow. She beat Ryan handily but lost more than sixty votes. Ryan ran "a very aggressive campaign," she told reporters afterward. "I feel very confident in the vote that I have received, and I quite frankly feel more liberated than I have after a vote, after such a hard-charging campaign."

But her victory didn't come without challenges. House Democrats had won only six seats, not the twenty-something she promised, putting Pelosi in the weakest state of her leadership tenure. She added new positions to her leadership team to ease tension. She created leadership roles for people who had been in Congress for less than a decade.

Tim Ryan, of course, was not among them. Before his challenge, Pelosi's team said they had been ready to name him to the leadership team and groom him to be a future Democratic leader. Instead, after his challenge, he was on the outside.

Ryan seemed skeptical of those claims. "Yeah, I don't remember any of those conversations," he said.

But Pelosi's victory and her power-sharing concessions did not stop the griping and grumbling about her leadership. Democrats were circulating a video clip from a CNN special of Pelosi struggling to remember Donald Trump's name, instead saying "whatever his name is"—trying to illustrate her age. Pelosi's advisers said it was a tactic so she didn't have to say the president's name. Crowley continued to plot ways to succeed her, envisioning leadership slates and building his support networks. Hoyer, meanwhile, hadn't given up the dream, continuing to work privately with lawmakers and lobbyists, telling them he should succeed Pelosi for a one-term reign.

Tim Ryan, meanwhile, became a darling of the left. He traveled to Alabama, Iowa, South Carolina, and Florida, trying to talk about the Democratic Party as he saw it. After he lost to Pelosi, he shook her hand, gave her a kiss, and said he was on her team.

Pelosi had consolidated her power—but now she had to figure out how to wield it. With Donald Trump in the White House, it was sure to be a tumultuous few years. But they would need Pelosi. Republicans would need her to keep the government open, and Democrats would need her to fund-raise and keep the party flush with cash. Nancy Pelosi was always needed.

3

TRUMP'S WASHINGTON

THERE ARE RHYTHMS TO THE way Washington works, decades-old conventions that help get things done in a town soaked in tradition and custom. The rules are mostly unwritten, passed down in wood-paneled Capitol Hill offices and carried out through the Speaker's office and the White House. They ensure continuity. They ensure the country does not slide off the rails.

Before Donald Trump, these rules allowed backroom deals to be cut before they leaked into the public. They allowed political foes—Barack Obama and John Boehner, for example—to seamlessly keep in touch with each other, swapping tips and gossip, keeping tabs, but more accurately, preventing legislative calamity. Boehner often slipped into the White House, out of the sight of cameras, to chat with Obama. Nancy Pelosi quietly cut deals with George W. Bush as she railed against his foreign interventions in the Middle East.

Tradition and convention, in other words, have kept America afloat.

But as the sun rose in 2017 on Trump's Washington, the city's accord—its intraparty traditions and its secret alliances—was quickly torn up, stomped on, set on fire, and tossed in the trash.

Trump's confidants were a Washington cast of misfits, many of whom had little qualification and no experience on Capitol Hill to prepare them for the jobs they were given. They had no care for the city's norms and, in fact, delighted in circumventing and ignoring them.

Stephen Bannon, long considered an outcast, sniping from the sidelines as the chairman of *Breitbart,* became Trump's chief strategist. Publicly, Bannon played nice with Paul Ryan, his nemesis, telling the Speaker in a December meeting at Trump Tower that he was in favor of a complex border tax. "That's good populist tax policy," he said. But privately, as Ryan worked to rally support behind the tax, Bannon worked with the conservative House Freedom Caucus to kill it.

Even the Washington operators Trump brought in were miscast and had no applicable experience for the job. Sean Spicer, the White House spokesman, was regularly criticized for his poor performance at the podium, but he also was ill-suited for backroom dealing between the White House and Capitol Hill. On the day of the Supreme Court nominee Neil Gorsuch's hearing, Spicer was in close contact with the Hill, asking how the White House could get a question to a senator during the hearing. Each senator's questions had been carefully choreographed, and they certainly weren't going to tear up the script for Spicer.

Trump did not understand, or care for, the official Washington that Paul Ryan and Mitch McConnell operated in. He was the embodiment of the electorate's frustration with Washington dysfunction, and his prescription for relief was all stick and no carrot. He mostly did not care about the pomp, tradition, or rules. His governing philosophy was simple: muscle and mouth. He tried to will his legislation through Congress. When that didn't work, he mouthed off using Twitter, his favored form of communication. First he tweeted about the Freedom Caucus— "The Republican House Freedom Caucus was able to snatch defeat from the jaws of victory." Then he tweeted to McConnell: "Mitch, get back to work and put Repeal & Replace, Tax Reform & Cuts and a great Infrastructure Bill on my desk for signing. You can do it!"

In Washington, this was mostly met with snickers by party leaders. Dealing with Trump meant listening to what he said, guessing what he meant, and proceeding with caution toward an uncertain end. When asked about Trump's utterances, Ryan was likely to say he hadn't seen the tweet. Privately, he shook his head or grimaced when told about Trump's most recent missive. This reality was one that not only top lawmakers and aides had to deal with but the president's own staff as well. For a company town accustomed to process, timelines, and general pragmatism, it was an unusual predicament. It bred uncertainty. And Washington loathes uncertainty. Lawmakers of all stripes quickly came to repeat the mantra over and over again when it came to Trump: "I was here before him. I'll be here after him."

Denizens of Capitol Hill treated the White House like dangerous agents who could not be trusted. Mitch McConnell asked the White House in April 2017 to brief the Senate about North Korea, looking to understand the nuclear threat before it spiraled out of control. When Trump heard about the request, he relayed to aides that, instead of dispatching an emissary or two to the Capitol, they should invite the entire U.S. Senate to the White House for the briefing. This invitation sent multiple senators—including Chuck Schumer, the minority leader—into a panic. They speculated Trump was trying to buoy flagging approval ratings before his hundredth day in office by staging a photo with the entire Senate in the West Wing. Even worse, many Democrats held a deep-seated conspiracy theory that the White House would force them to relinquish their cell phones to participate in the briefing, and the administration would hack into them to steal their private data.

On multiple occasions early on in the administration, Trump got crosswise with Republican leaders. Perhaps the best example was Trump's brief flirtation with naming Rep. Cathy McMorris Rodgers of Washington State to be his secretary of the interior. McMorris Rodgers, the number four House Republican leader from 2013 to 2018, had several meetings with incoming administration officials during the transition period. Then she got word that the president wanted to see her. This was it: the big interview. The appointment seemed a done deal; a "source close to the transition team" told media outlets from *The Hill* to

USA Today that McMorris Rodgers was the pick for Interior. But when she paid a visit to Donald Trump in his office at Trump Tower, suddenly things didn't seem so certain: The president-elect had a folder of media clippings at the ready, detailing various times McMorris Rodgers had spoken out against him. A few days later Trump offered the job to Rep. Ryan Zinke, a Republican from Montana.

Trump appeared to struggle reconciling smart congressional politics and his own whims. When Trump was assembling his cabinet, McConnell privately urged the White House to appoint a Senate Democrat, especially from a state with a Republican governor, so that Republicans could gain a seat. He even held discussions with West Virginia's governor about whom he would appoint if Trump tapped Joe Manchin to the cabinet. Manchin went to Trump Tower in 2016 to talk about the idea but backed away after it was made clear that he would not be able to bring his staff with him. Trump instead appointed former Texas governor Rick Perry to run the Energy Department, putting him in charge of an agency he once said he wanted to eliminate. Senate Republican leaders were left shaking their heads.

The discomfort—and distaste—with the president and his style was understandable. Republicans had spent the better part of the last decade trying to convince voters that they were the party that could soberly lead the country by restoring fiscal discipline at home and bolstering American leadership abroad. But Trump's presidency immediately undermined this well-laid case; he and his team stumbled through town like they'd never flipped on C-SPAN.

The basics of governing in this centuries-old system eluded them from the beginning. They'd tipped their hand well before the election during a meeting between top Paul Ryan and Trump aides, when Jared Kushner, the president's son-in-law, scoffed at Congress's snail-like pace. Kushner said congressional committees, which write and examine legislation, were "inefficient."

"We'll get to that later," Kushner told Ryan's aides, giving the impression he wanted to—and believed he could—single-handedly rewrite Congress's two-hundred-year-old rules.

When Sen. John McCain visited the White House early in the administration, he was in the midst of telling Trump about military procurement reform, a longtime passion, when Kushner interjected.

"Don't worry, Senator McCain. We're going to change the way the entire government works," Kushner said without a hint of irony.

"Good luck, son," McCain responded.

The norms of the Capitol were completely lost on Trump's operation. Gary Cohn, Trump's first national economic adviser, and Steven T. Mnuchin, the treasury secretary, scheduled a meeting with the House Freedom Caucus in the middle of a critical set of votes during which Republican leaders were trying to corral support for Trump's health care bill. Mnuchin and Cohn soon grew frustrated that the lawmakers weren't skipping the floor action to meet with them.

"You are wasting important people's time," one of their handlers said to a Freedom Caucus aide, as the entire group of lawmakers remained on the House floor, unmoved by their high-profile visitors.

Senior GOP staffers quickly grew frustrated with the White House. Like Trump, the president's top people early on treated Capitol Hill as an afterthought. Before the announcement of Trump's first Supreme Court pick, Neil Gorsuch, senior Senate Republicans, political operatives, and White House aides were scheduled to meet at the National Republican Senatorial Committee office to coordinate strategy. The White House staffers, including Boris Epshteyn, who later became a pro-Trump television host, were twenty-five minutes late, and when they finally arrived, they didn't apologize. They sat through the meeting without writing down a single note on how the different factions would work together to get Gorsuch confirmed.

Trump's phone calls to legislators—which he made at all hours of the day and night—were often unfocused and curt. During the early part of the health care debate, Trump called Mark Meadows to ask about the status of an ancillary negotiation he was involved in. Yet within minutes, Trump had veered off topic to talk about Susan Rice—Barack Obama's national security adviser—and whether she had improperly handled classified information.

"Can you believe her?" Trump asked Meadows.

The president periodically engaged in all-out arguments with Republican lawmakers, leaving them bitter and perturbed. He once implored the House Freedom Caucus not to worry about the "little shit" in the Republican health care bill; he asked them to simply vote for the legislation to give him a victory. In one meeting, Rep. Bill Posey, a veteran member from Florida, told the president to quit the "tweets and whining about crowd size."

"Who the fuck are you?" Trump shot back, before once again incorrectly positing that he had had the "biggest inauguration" ever.

Even more disconcerting, the president's governing strategies sometimes seemed to develop at the whim of cable television hosts. In May 2017, after Congress passed an omnibus spending bill to avert a government shutdown, Trump called Mitch McConnell and told him he was considering vetoing it. Why? He had seen a segment on *Fox & Friends* that focused on the fact that the Republicans' bill did not fund Trump's wall on the border with Mexico.

"I would strongly suggest you do not veto the bill, Mr. President," McConnell said. Only later, after a call with former House Speaker John Boehner, did Trump change his mind. Despite his apparent unease with establishment Washington, he listened to advice from Boehner, his old golfing buddy.

In a town that prizes hierarchy, Trump circumvented the leadership structure to cut deals with rank-and-file lawmakers. Reince Priebus and Steve Bannon, who were both ousted from the White House in the first year, frequently gathered low-level members of Congress for powwows in their West Wing offices—unthinkable in any other White House. They griped about the Capitol Hill leadership, all while members of Congress tried to tether Trump closer to reality.

Priebus, who had never worked a day in federal government before ascending to the top slot in the White House, often panicked when it came to dealing with Congress. His nerves and stress were the topic of constant gossip, as he frequented the Capital Grille, a Washington power spot, with close confidants to throw back a few glasses of wine.

In its early days, this White House was partly hobbled by the infighting and sniping between even top advisers as they all vied for Trump's favor. Priebus, in particular, was known for being sensitive, trying to promote his star to other aides and to Trump in the West Wing. He also employed his emissaries to push back on palace intrigue stories that for weeks predicted his impending departure. Priebus loyalists like Spicer regularly tried to kill stories about him.

Even when the White House was on the brink of success, it doubted its efficacy. In May, as members of the House gathered on the floor to vote for a health care bill, Priebus sat in the House cloakroom, a hangout for members of Congress just off the chamber floor. In normal times, the chief of staff would be nowhere near the House floor, but Priebus, Trump legislative affairs director Marc Short, and another top aide kept an open phone line to the president, just in case a lawmaker needed last-minute arm twisting.

AS CHIEF EXECUTIVE, Donald Trump could accomplish much unilaterally through executive order, but for the truly big-ticket items—killing Obamacare, tax reform, Supreme Court justices—he required the cooperation of the House and Senate. His cabinet secretaries would need approval, his bureaucracy would need funding, and his legislative agenda would need to be refined and okayed. The president was accustomed to running a family business in which he gave the final word. Now to achieve the success he so desperately wanted, he would have to contend with two chambers filled with politicians whom he could not fire, and who kept first in mind their own self-interest and self-preservation.

Perhaps no institution in the world was as essentially polar from Donald Trump as the U.S. Senate. The president often seemed to have no use for norms, but the Senate lived and died by them, and Senate traditions and customs dated back to the earliest days of its existence.

While America remains a global leader in innovation, its legislative body has not kept pace. Walking into the Senate chamber on the north side of the Capitol is like traveling back in time. Spittoons are scattered across the chamber's floor. Unlike the House, where lawmakers vote using an electronic system, Senators still vote by giving a thumbs-up or thumbs-down to the chamber's clerk, who sits at the front of the chamber and tallies the vote by hand. The Senate still employs pages, high-school-age boys and girls who serve the members of the body and who must know whether senators like their water with ice or at room temperature. They open the chamber's doors as senators approach and help them out when they leave.

The Senate's atmosphere is calm and genteel. The floor is often quiet for hours at a time, although the chamber's soaring orators of yore— Ted Kennedy and Paul Wellstone—took advantage of the silence to deliver passionate speeches about the issues of the day. Each senator has his or her own desk in the chamber, allowing for orderly proceedings. But senators aren't immune to enjoying the trappings of the job and the clubbiness of membership in an exclusive group of one hundred. They carve their names into their desks so insiders will know that Joe Biden had the same work space as John F. Kennedy, Cory Booker shared one with Joe Lieberman, and Bernie Sanders with Harry Truman. Each of the one hundred senators has a small hideaway in the Capitol where they can escape reporters, and they often spend their own money furnishing these spaces to their liking. If they want to go back to their main office in the Dirksen, Russell, or Hart Senate Office Building, two subway lines wait to ferry them there, as long as they are able to navigate hordes of reporters waiting to shout a question or two on the way.

Senators are an emboldened bunch because, unlike most House members, they represent an entire state, and in the Capitol they have the ability to hold up legislation single-handedly. For example, late in 2018, Rand Paul put a stop to a major U.S.-Israeli defense bill. The rules of the Senate allow a single senator to grind proceedings to a halt.

But the chamber is much more collegial than the House. The leadership—Chuck Schumer, the New York Democrat, and Mitch McConnell, the Kentucky Republican—typically glide through internal elections without any opposition. Since senators serve six-year terms, they are more likely to move to Washington, which gives them the opportunity to become friendly with their colleagues—even ones on the other side of the aisle—and get to know each other's spouses.

The Senate membership is also, historically, older than that of the House; octogenarians abound. During the first two years of the Trump administration, Thad Cochran of Mississippi, at eighty, often needed assistance getting around the Capitol. Chuck Grassley of Iowa, the chairman of the Judiciary Committee, was eighty-five. Agriculture chairman Pat Roberts of Kansas was eighty-two. Appropriations chairman Richard Shelby of Alabama, Armed Services chairman Jim Inhofe of Oklahoma, and Finance chairman Orrin Hatch of Utah were all eighty-four. Dianne Feinstein of California, the ranking member on the Intelligence Committee, was eighty-five. At an age when most Americans approached retirement or headed into nursing homes, many senators were just taking the helm of powerful committees.

As with much of Washington in the Trump era, fissures were bound to emerge in the Senate. Along with older power centers, people like McConnell, Grassley, and Schumer, both Republicans and Democrats, had a crop of younger lawmakers who had burst onto the scene and into the public consciousness. On the right were lawmakers like Tom Cotton of Arkansas, an Ivy League–educated Republican who counseled the president on foreign policy, and Ben Sasse of Nebraska and Jeff Flake of Arizona, who opposed Trump more than other Republicans. Tim Scott of South Carolina, James Lankford of Oklahoma, and Cory Gardner of Colorado walked a fine line, criticizing Trump when he deserved it, and supporting him when he was pushing traditional Republican policies.

Democrats like Cory Booker of New Jersey, Elizabeth Warren of Massachusetts, Chris Murphy of Connecticut, Amy Klobuchar of Minnesota, and Kamala Harris of California used Clinton's electoral whiff to establish a new face of the party: energetic, progressive, and unafraid to fight. Warren took Trump head-on on his favorite platform: Twitter.

The Senate was a breeding ground for future Democratic presidential candidates, with several members considering runs in 2020. Early in Trump's presidency, Warren and Bernie Sanders were considered national political celebrities and top contenders for the Democratic nomination in 2020. Harris, Klobuchar, Sherrod Brown of Ohio, and a whole pile of other Democrats were nipping at their heels. All this made the Senate a proving ground, and the chamber a bit more combustible than usual. At the same time, the emerging liberal stars on the campaign trail didn't get the same star treatment in the Capitol. Bernie

Sanders barely turned a head as he charged down the hall, his hair mussed, trailed by aides. Warren didn't answer reporters' questions in the hallways until late in 2018, when she was on the brink of her presidential run. She was far more popular in Concord than she was in the Capitol.

Where Democrats like Warren could feel free to position themselves opposite the president, Republican senators were forced to answer for every Trump utterance, which quickly grew tedious. They disagreed with most of his asides, had no use for his non sequiturs, and were a tad uncomfortable with where he was taking their party. Not to mention, on a practical level, they didn't have much of a margin in enacting their agenda: Trump and McConnell could only lose a couple of votes on any given bill that could be passed by majority, and in many cases Republicans needed sixty votes to advance legislation, which meant they needed to attract Democratic support. McConnell could've ended the sixty-vote rule but chose not to, recognizing it would be a useful tool if Republicans ever again found themselves in the minority. That constantly chafed on Trump, who believed the rule to be dumb and thought Chuck Schumer would blow up that custom if he were in the majority.

Paul Ryan had much more of a margin for error. There were 241 Republicans in the House, which meant twenty-three GOP lawmakers could take a pass and Republicans would still be in business. That meant Ryan could cater more to his conservative extremes. Ryan's Republican conference was deeply split. He had the conservative House Freedom Caucus, which saw itself as the keepers of Trump's creed and which represented a powerful bloc when Meadows and Jordan kept them together. But at the same time, he had a healthy core of moderates from suburban America—lawmakers who swelled the majority to historic highs.

The House was frenetic, and its floor was perhaps the last central meeting place in American politics. House lawmakers don't live in Washington, so they don't go to dinner together on the weekends. Their weeknights are taken up by votes. Where they meet and talk is in the chamber of the House of Representatives.

The chamber is probably best known as the venue for the president's State of the Union address. It's a rectangular room, and the horseshoe-shaped seating is oriented around the Speaker's chair. The floor has 446 chairs, more than enough to conduct its business. The Speaker of the House—or his or her designee—presides over the chamber whenever it is in session. The House is traditionally in session four days a week—either Monday night to Thursday afternoon, or Tuesday through Friday.

Anyone can watch the House proceedings all day on C-SPAN, but being inside the chamber gives a much better perspective of raw politics. From the Speaker's chair, Democrats are on the right, and Republicans are on the left. Mirroring the country at large far more than the Senate, the chamber fosters regional and tribal politics. Like-minded people from the same part of the country sit together, chat, and vote. For example, in the back left corner of the chamber, northeastern and moderate Republicans hang out. One might have seen Peter King of Long Island, New York, and Dan Donovan of Staten Island, chatting with Rodney Frelinghuysen of New Jersey, whose family is one of the most storied political dynasties in America. California Republicans sit in a row nearby.

Gulf State Republicans—Mississippians and some Louisianans—sit in the back of the chamber. Texans sit together in a row in the left-center section of the room, directly behind the leadership's table. One of two tables in the House is controlled by the Republican whip team and the majority leader. From there, the whip's office conducts vote counting with pink, blue, and yellow whip cards. They keep the desk stocked with gum, mints, and pens. (Jim Jordan, who frequently thwarts leadership's plans, has no problem snagging his daily piece of gum.) Aides keep a close eye on who is voting how. The Freedom Caucus sits together toward the center of the chamber—far enough from both Republicans and Democrats, but in a prime spot so nearly everyone who enters the chamber has to pass them by. Their seating was a perfect metaphor for their role in Trump's Washington—the Freedom Caucus would have to be reckoned with. With their members so close to the margin of the Republican majority, this bloc of conservatives were poised to have an impact on virtually every piece of legislation that Congress would take up, especially if Paul Ryan was hesitant to look to Democrats for help.

The House is up for election every two years, which makes its members much more responsive to the country's momentary political whims. That was why, perhaps, Trump found himself simpatico with House conservatives like Mark Meadows, Jim Jordan, Steve Scalise, and Kevin McCarthy. They ran alongside Trump and were more likely to follow his politics and defend his whims. Unlike members of the Senate, who considered themselves high-minded and oftentimes skirted the president, these conservatives were part of Trump's America. They would do what was needed to help Trump navigate the unfamiliar confines of Washington.

"It's a strong group of people," Trump said of Meadows, Jordan, and the Freedom Caucus. "They're great people. Those are the people that defend me. . . . They are unbelievable."

4

FOLLOW THE MONEY

THE DEMOCRATIC CONGRESSIONAL Campaign Committee has its offices at the Democratic National Committee's headquarters on Capitol Hill, and on Inauguration Day 2017, it told staff to take the day off. Democrats had nothing to celebrate, and the crowds in town were expected to be gigantic.

So on that day—January 20—Dan Sena, the DCCC's forty-one-year-old executive director, packed up his Toyota Highlander with his wife and child and headed roughly ninety miles northwest of Washington to a Cracker Barrel in Chambersburg, Pennsylvania.

Sena, strangely enough, was a Cracker Barrel devotee; he had the app on his cell phone and was eager to show he could beat the restaurant's popular peg game. But Sena wasn't headed to Cracker Barrel just to chow down on the green beans. He wanted to have a better sense of what he was up against, so he could figure out how to proceed. He recognized that Donald Trump's election was a major inflection point for the Democratic Party, one that had produced among the party faithful what many described as PTSD. But he also knew that millions of Americans were jubilant at the election results, and he thought he needed to see that firsthand. "I wanted to be able to understand the opposite and equal reaction Trump has," he said.

Sena had grown up on a dirt road in rural New Mexico, so he knew the Democrats had work to do to reconnect with just about everyone besides coastal elites. Still, he wasn't prepared for what he was about to find. On Inauguration Day at this Cracker Barrel, there was one star: Donald J. Trump.

Sena was stunned at the enthusiasm. Employees were wheeling in additional televisions. People high-fived. The crowd cheered. One woman sitting next to Sena reassured her daughter that they were recording the inauguration show at home.

"This is a different world," Sena thought to himself, as he dug into his food. "It was like I was watching the goddamned Super Bowl."

Five days later Sena and his team at the DCCC put staffers on the ground in twenty-one districts across America. They chose some of the most vulnerable Republican districts, in places like California and Florida, where the incumbent would be easy to pick off. It was Democrats' first move to try to take back the House.

Sena was an easygoing man with curly brown hair, a wide forehead, and eyes that tend to drift downward during conversation. His office was in the corner of the DCCC's war room on the third floor of the DNC, and like many political offices in Washington, it was covered with posters of the United States overlaid with the congressional map and the partisan leanings of every district. He also had a list of field offices opened by an outside Republican political organization to make sure he was staying on top of the enemy.

Sena had a picture-perfect résumé for the DCCC. He volunteered in field politics, knocking on doors and getting people to vote. He had worked on House and Senate races in New Mexico and California, managed a failed mayoral bid in Los Angeles, and even tried to help the co-founder of BlackBerry buy the Coyotes, Phoenix's professional hockey team. In 2010 Sena directed Hispanic media for a group that supported Harry Reid, the Senate majority leader, in his reelection. Sena even had a political pedigree: His great-uncle was Dennis Chávez, who decades earlier served as a member of both the House and the Senate from New Mexico.

At Sena's right hand was Meredith Kelly, a friendly twenty-nine-year-old and DCCC veteran, charged with crafting the party's message. Kelly was an alumna of Chuck Schumer's office, which counted for a lot. Washington insiders respected Schumer alumni like they did Mitch McConnell's progeny: They worked hard and understood the game because they had learned from the best. If you could survive Schumer, you could survive anything. And Kelly had. She and Sena had slogged through the last election cycle at the DCCC weathering loss after loss after loss.

Donald Trump's 2016 victory and the House Democrats' complete whiff had most Democrats completely shocked. They didn't know what to say, what to think, or what to believe. The DCCC's internal polling had shown the political winds blowing Nancy Pelosi toward the speakership, not relegating the party to two years in the minority with a Republican in the White House. In fact, the DCCC had been so confident in its electoral standing and in Hillary Clinton's pull at the top of the ticket that it had invested in only thirty House races nationwide. It created a terribly small needle to thread: To win the majority, Democrats would've had to win most of those contests. They were confident they would. Pelosi and New Mexico representative Ben Ray Luján—the chairman of the DCCC, and Sena's boss—thought Democrats would thrash through the congressional map. Instead, they were again relegated to the minority. No victory party. No control of the congressional agenda. Two more years in the wilderness.

After taking paternity leave right after Election Day, Sena returned to his office on South Capitol Street to find his party upside down. Pelosi's leadership was in mortal peril, with newly emboldened challengers nipping at her heels. Donors were up in arms, wondering why the tens of thousands of dollars they had forked over to the DCCC had resulted in eight consecutive years of losses.

The soul-searching was just beginning. Democrats were calling everything they knew about their party into question. Were they equipped for modern political warfare? Were their leaders too old, too stale for today's politics?

It wasn't going to get easier. Democrats were heading into a two-year battle with Republicans, unable to push a liberal agenda to attract new voters. The party's deep divisions were only beginning to come to the surface. Barack Obama was gone. The future was looking complicated, and Democrats' prospects were bleak. The DCCC—an organization under intense scrutiny and pressure from elected officials, and under the constant watch of Pelosi—would be the party's nerve center for the first two years, the operation that would seek a slice of control in Donald Trump's Washington.

THE DCCC AND ITS Republican counterpart, the NRCC, are multimillion-dollar nonprofit enterprises that exist for the sole purpose of electing members of the House of Representatives. They operate out of buildings a few blocks from each other on Capitol Hill, and they act as clearinghouses for massive amounts of cash brought in from donors and parceled out to various House races across the country. Crafting a message is an essential part of a campaign, but amplifying that message with money is just as important. While messages can travel infinitely, money is a finite resource, and it's the committees' job to raise money and then figure out how to deploy it across the country for two years.

The committees are funded by donations from lobbyists, corporate PACs, and individuals, but they also get millions of dollars from members of Congress. In theory, government business and outward politicking are supposed to be kept separate, but in reality they are inextricable and completely intertwined. The NRCC and the DCCC base their dues structure for members of Congress on what committees they sit on. If you're a rank-and-file Democrat, you owe $125,000. But do you have a seat on Ways and Means, the prized tax-writing committee, or on Financial Services, which puts you in touch with Wall Street honchos? That'll cost you between $200,000 and $500,000 from your campaign coffers if you're a Democrat, plus another $250,000 raised directly from donors.

If you have ambitions to serve in the leadership of the Democratic Party, as leader, whip, or Speaker, you're particularly unlucky. Between 2016 and 2018, the DCCC suggested that House Democratic leadership contribute anywhere from $350,000 to $800,000 and raise another huge lump from supporters. Nancy Pelosi had to contribute $800,000 and raise another $25 million during Trump's first two years.

(Exceptions were made. If you were a Democrat in a tough race, the party spared you. Many members of the Congressional Black Caucus did not contribute to the committee, because they argued that they could not raise the money in their rural or inner-city districts.)

In short, next time a politician says that money doesn't play a role in politics, you should be skeptical.

The DCCC and the NRCC make it very easy to raise cash. They even offer dialing booths into which lawmakers can slip away from the Capitol to make phone calls to bring in dough. Throughout the year, they hold massive fund-raisers at places like the plush Nemacolin Resort in Pennsylvania or at homes in Martha's Vineyard, New York, Chicago, and Los Angeles so lawmakers can be brought into the rarefied world of the über-wealthy.

But the real rainmakers are the party leaders. Any time Congress was not in session, Pelosi and Paul Ryan flew all around the country raising money. Ryan oftentimes found himself on private jets, which were paid for by the Congressional Leadership Fund and the American Action Network, a network of outside political organizations that helped fund the Republican Party. Pelosi, worth millions, flew commercial.

Because members of Congress pay dues to the party committee, they expect a certain kind of white-glove service. They want financial support from the party regardless of their political prospects. A frequent gripe is that lawmakers pay hundreds of thousands of dollars into their committee and receive no help when they are in a tough race. Democrats, unlike Republicans, often outwardly picked favorites in primary elections, a thorny exercise that caused heartburn at the time and then sometimes again later when the favorite got shellacked by the underdog.

SOON AFTER SENA RETURNED from paternity leave, he began sifting through his party's wreckage. There was plenty of it. When all was said and done, Democrats were staring slack-jawed at the results: They had gained just six seats, and they were twenty-four away from the majority.

"Of course, we're all very disappointed," Pelosi told reporters, as her caucus met behind closed doors wrestling with the results. "More than disappointed. Hard to accept the results. But accept we do. Peaceful transfer of power is what America and our democracy is about."

It was a nice sentiment, but it was up to Sena, Luján, and Kelly to figure out how to get things back on track. "Everything was magical in the Obama years," Sena said in an interview in the early days of the cycle. Now "we need to apply actual skills."

One of the first sets of phone calls Sena made illustrates just how far behind Republicans the Democrats were. When Sena rang Google and Facebook, it was something like a cold call: The House Democratic election arm had no meaningful previous relationship with the two largest technology companies on earth. Republicans, on the other hand, already had an extensive online presence, which they deployed with tremendous success in 2012 and 2014. Obama had ushered in a technological revolution during the 2008 election, but the Democrats had stopped innovating after that. They needed to start getting wise with today's technology: targeted advertising and searches, using the large platforms to their advantage. Sena was making tentative first steps into new tech ground, but the reality of how far behind the Democrats were was massive: Republicans said they had already moved on from things that Democrats were just discovering in 2017.

It was a sad truth: The party was a shell of what it should be. Democratic organizations like the DCCC didn't innovate as much as they should've during the Obama years, because the president's own organization brought people out to vote. So it was up to Sena to build the DCCC from the ground up.

The first order of business was to get Democrats comfortable with their party committee. Luján, the DCCC chair, was moderately well liked by his colleagues, but some Democrats viewed him warily because he had been installed as chair by Pelosi in 2014. He won election to the position in 2016, an initial sign of strength, but fairly or not, Luján was still seen by some as a Pelosi stooge. To overcome this skepticism, and to ensure he was responsive to the concerns of all House Democrats, Luján set up a member services operation early in 2017 that helped sitting congressmen build campaigns. All Democrats could take advantage of the committee's expertise in setting up their organization and get advice on things like best practices for social media.

What the DCCC had going for it thanks to Trump was massive energy among voters. The Women's March on the day after Inauguration Day drew millions of protesters to the capital and the DCCC knew it had a lot to work with. Though the organization had decided not to get involved in the march itself, it used its digital capabilities to grow its e-mail list by several million people in the following months. The DCCC also spent $9 million—much more than ever before—to acquire targeted voter data, including e-mail addresses and contact information, knowing that people would likely be participating in the political process in far higher numbers than usual.

The DCCC also set up focus groups in Orange County, California; suburban Detroit; and Philadelphia—white middle-class House districts—to get an early sense of what the electorate was hankering for. They heard the same thing over and over again: Voters wanted a check and balance on the White House. Private Republican polling showed the same, with nearly 60 percent of independents saying they would prefer electing someone who would put a check on Trump to someone who would help the president. But when the voters were asked if they wanted Nancy Pelosi back in the speakership, the margin tightened: 47 percent wanted to elect someone who would put Pelosi back in the speakership, and 41 percent wanted to elect someone who would help Trump. Pelosi was toxic in many of the districts that mattered for control of Congress.

Sena's game plan for the 2018 cycle coalesced over more than a year, and it was multifaceted. First, he and the DCCC knew they needed to set a massive electoral battlefield. The Democrats widened their target to any House district that Trump had won with 55 percent or less. That gave them ninety-five seats to try to capture—20 percent of the House of Representatives.

"Last cycle we had forty races and invested in thirty in a presidential year everyone thought we'd win the presidency," said Sena. "That's not a knock on anyone. We're going to be eighty to ninety-five races deep. I'm not going to invest in them all, but we are going to make those races real. That forces Republicans to spend there."

Sena distilled it this way: "We need as many viable races so Republicans are looking over their shoulder a little bit and not donating to their colleagues." Indeed, that was a key part of the Democrats' plan: to make the battlefield so large that Republicans had to spend money in races that they typically could ignore.

With all these races, Sena set up a new team inside the DCCC called the "expansion pod." The idea was to create a SWAT team of sorts that could be dispatched around the country to do immediate analyses of campaigns. "They have the ability to go in and review—look at your campaign operations, how you're raising money and what your digital and communications apparatus looks like," Sena said. If a race looked like it was becoming competitive, Sena could send this team out to confirm so the candidate and party could adjust.

Luján and Sena realized that if their battlefield was to be so massive, they would need candidates with interesting stories. Cookie-cutter Democrats weren't going to be enough. "Where you come from and your story is going to carry an enormous amount of weight in that small portion that gets to happen outside the federal frame," Sena said. But it would become clear that the DCCC would not be the final arbiter of whose story would have the most impact—voters would.

Democrats saw this with Jim Gray, the former mayor of Lexington, Kentucky, who a year later ran in a primary to face Rep. Andy Barr, a Republican incumbent the Democrats were looking to knock off in the northeastern corner of the state. In the Democrats' minds, Gray was an example of a local man with a great story and great credibility. He was a popular mayor who had lost a race against Rand Paul for the Senate in 2016. Except, after Gray launched his race for the House, he went absolutely nowhere. In the primary, his fellow Democrat Amy McGrath, a fighter pilot with a compelling family story, topped Gray by eight points. This happened to the DCCC in several places across the country: It boosted candidates in Democratic primaries who ultimately lost. Their view: The voters spoke, and in some cases they chose the stronger candidate.

Much is made every election cycle of the party's national message: What did Democrats stand for this year? Sena and the DCCC sought to find out by spending heavily on a "national research project" involving a battery of polls and focus groups to survey the mood of the electorate. Democrats discovered that voters, more than ever, didn't want traditional candidates—they wanted people outside the political class.

Why wasn't Trump part of the Democrats' focus? He was. But the DCCC saw 2018 as a three-party election: Republicans, Democrats, and Trump supporters. Democrats had to make the check-and-balance argument subtly to have a chance to pull from each segment of the voter population. The way Democrats saw it, why talk about Trump? He talked enough about himself, and that gave Democrats an opening to talk about their priorities.

As for Nancy Pelosi, eleven days after Election Day she made clear what she was aiming for. "In 2005 and 2006," she said, "I orchestrated the takeback of the House of Representatives. I'm very, very proud of that, and as I said, we see that as an opportunity now."

But within a few months, the DCCC was giving Democratic candidates across the country this shocking advice: Supporting Pelosi was up to each individual campaign. Pelosi's national approval ratings were hovering in the twenties, making her the least popular leader in Congress. In many districts, getting behind Pelosi could spell political suicide. The DCCC told their candidates to work through whether they could support her and to let the national party know.

"We're not telling them what to do in either direction," said one top House Democratic figure. "We're telling them to tell us where they land ahead of time. We outline to them what the options are. And we tell them what the benefits and ramifications are."

REPUBLICANS, MEANWHILE, KNEW THAT holding on to the majority in 2018 would be no small accomplishment. They had to contend with a challenging climate and a challenging president. The historical data was plainly obvious: The president's party loses an average of twenty-nine seats in his first midterm election. In 2018 Democrats needed to win twenty-three to take back the House. The winds were blowing stiffly in the GOP's face.

Republicans essentially had two party committees working to hold on to the House: the NRCC and a pair of outside groups called the American Action Network (AAN) and the Congressional Leadership Fund (CLF). The two men who ran these groups—and their visions for a path to electoral success—couldn't be more different.

The chair of the NRCC was Rep. Steve Stivers, fifty-two, of Ohio's fifteenth district, a former banking lobbyist who, after a failed run for Congress in 2008, finally made it to Washington in the gigantic Republican class of 2010. Stivers was a brigadier general in the Ohio National Guard and frequently escaped for service, where he was just another soldier, not a high-ranking member of Congress. But Stivers was hardly the picture of military seriousness: He had a wide boyish smile that made him seem mischievous, and he laughed often, his face turning deep red, as if he believed the pedestrian, ho-hum thing he was saying was the funniest thing in the world. Stivers had been close to John Boehner—a member of Boehner's informal "Ohio mafia," as it was called—and was long seen as a savvy operator in Washington. He had spent his career in D.C. in close proximity to power, and when he was elected chairman of the party committee in 2016, he finally had a fiefdom of his own.

Corry Bliss, at thirty-seven, ran both the AAN and CLF. The AAN was, ostensibly, a think tank organized as a nonprofit 501(c)(4). As such, it was able to take dark money, then turn around and run advertisements urging congressmen to support the Republican issue du jour—tax reform or spending restraint, for example. The Congressional Leadership Fund was a related super PAC that accepted unlimited but disclosed donations, but unlike its sister organization, it ran explicitly sharp political advertisements. Both organizations were blessed by Paul Ryan and the Republican leadership.

Stivers won election to the chairmanship of the NRCC, so he had to keep his constituents—his fellow Republican lawmakers—happy. But Bliss faced no such constraints around the need to get along. He was bombastic and energetic, a figure more out of Wall Street than Washington. Though he was legally prohibited from discussing the details of political spending with elected officials, he felt free to speak his mind to them and about them. He seemed to relish attention from the media. As an affectation, he kept a Louisville Slugger next to his desk, and sometimes, when he was greeting guests outside his private office, he held it in his right hand.

A Westchester native, Bliss had trod a well-worn path through Republican politics, making his bones on big-time statewide elections in Vermont, Georgia, and Connecticut. He led a campaign to help save veteran Kansas senator Pat Roberts in 2014, then steered Rob Portman to reelection in his 2016 Senate race. On the walls of his corner office, on Pennsylvania Avenue not far from the White House, Bliss had newspaper clippings from both victories, and a *New York Times* column by Frank Bruni, celebrating Bliss as "one of his party's most closely watched young strategists." Bliss was interested in running the NRCC, the equivalent of Sena's job in the DCCC, but Stivers chose instead John Rogers, a low-key, longtime party hand. Rogers was the polar opposite of Bliss—understated, calm, and private. But Bliss wouldn't have to sit on the sidelines: Portman, Jake Kastan, and Kevin Seifert—Paul Ryan's top three political hands—liked him and recommended he run the pair of outside organizations.

Bliss talked about House elections with uncanny confidence, which was slightly odd because before taking the helm of this multimillion-dollar House election apparatus, he had not been involved in a single House race, ever. He saw this as a positive attribute and boasted that he knew how to win elections. He claimed to despise super PACs despite the fact that he ran one. He loved to tell reporters and donors that super PACs practically existed to enrich an entrenched class of political consultants.

But Bliss was truly a neophyte in understanding the House of Representatives, its members, and their races. During a dinner in January 2017 in the basement of Trattoria Alberto's on Capitol Hill—John

Boehner's favorite restaurant, because they let him smoke inside—Bliss was giving Kastan and Seifert his rundown of the political consultant business. He had taken the reins of CLF and the AAN just weeks earlier.

Bliss was quizzing Kastan and Seifert about which members of Congress were their favorites. They both shrugged, but Bliss pushed for an answer: "Just give me one name, for shits and giggles. Give me one fucking name, someone you love."

Kastan and Seifert said Don Bacon, a retired air force brigadier general who represented the area around Omaha, Nebraska. Bacon had just beaten a Democrat in 2016, and he was a nice man who could use the help in 2018.

Bliss got in the car and called William Inman, his top deputy, and told him to Google Don Bacon. He then dispatched a young aide to Omaha, explaining to him, "It's in the middle—by Kansas." They opened their first field office there and began to boost Bacon.

No polling, no prep, just a name thrown out almost at random by two aides over dinner. This is how one of the nation's most important Republican groups started the 2018 cycle.

But for all Bliss's bombast, he had an important ally: Paul Ryan. The two had grown close since Trump won the White House, hopscotching around the country, raising big money for the pair of political groups. With no limit on CLF's intake, Bliss would be expected to go after big fish, a job that suited his ego brilliantly. In 2017 Bliss told Ryan he wanted to raise $100 million for the election cycle. Ryan's response: "Let's do it."

Bliss and Stivers saw the political universe very differently. Stivers knew he would spend most of the NRCC's money in the last few months of 2018, when the electorate was starting to tune in to politics. It was a well-worn and usually effective strategy. Voters tune in to the election around Labor Day, and that's when the NRCC would begin to blanket the airwaves. Stivers and the NRCC believed they could pour money into saving thirty Republican incumbents, preventing Democrats from expanding the political map.

Bliss, meanwhile, offered a different theory of the case. He planned to run a massive political advertising campaign. But in addition he started a program to open offices in districts around America, where he would hire people to knock on doors in support of Republican candidates. For a candidate like Bacon, that meant reminding voters that he supported Offutt Air Force Base, while Democrats wanted it shuttered. (Never mind that that wasn't exactly true.) Many people involved in elections questioned why it was useful to have people knocking on doors more than a year before Election Day, but Bliss thought it was novel, plus donors liked it. They thought their money was being well spent.

The aides at CLF thought the NRCC was practically useless. The two camps didn't get along but, theoretically, had the same mission: keeping Republicans in power, even as strong headwinds picked up against them. And they would need all the help they could get from congressional Republicans. If Congress couldn't pass legislation or confirm conservative judges to the nation's court, neither Stivers nor Bliss would have a thing to stand behind.

5

THE LIMITS OF MITCH MCCONNELL'S POWER

DURING DONALD TRUMP'S FIRST TWO years in office, Senate majority leader Mitch McConnell was the most powerful person in Washington, a man who inspired such loyalty in his colleagues that they never crossed him, and such hatred in his Democratic foes that they angrily dismissed him as a power-hungry, intellectually dishonest monster who would do anything to advance the cause of rabid conservatism.

McConnell was absolutely, perhaps maniacally, focused on power and how to exercise it with the maximum impact. Unlike other congressional leaders, who swayed back and forth with the political winds, McConnell was stubbornly stoic. He walked through the Capitol hallways slowly, ignoring questions he didn't like as if they hadn't been shouted at all. Asking him a question he did not want to address— about a Trump press conference gone awry, the importance of the president's former aide Steve Bannon, or special counsel Robert Mueller's investigation—would prompt some version of this answer: "I don't have any observations about that." There were no pretenses with McConnell.

He was first elected in 1984 and was involved in a host of critical issues during his time in Washington. He opposed landmark campaign finance reform legislation, and he offered stunningly prescient predictions about the massive mess that would become of the money in elections after that legislation took effect. He crafted bipartisan agreements to avoid government shutdowns and defaults on U.S. debt, and to avoid tax hikes.

But the Trump era gave Addison Mitchell McConnell Jr. an identity that will stick with him and will impact America for a generation: He moved the federal judiciary sharply to the right, ensuring conservative judges for decades to come. The numbers are staggering. Republicans confirmed scores of judges to lifetime appointments—thirty circuit court judges, fifty-three district court judges, and two Supreme Court justices. It was something McConnell had been eyeing since he was a young aide to Kentucky's Sen. Marlow Cook in the late 1960s. During his time working for Cook, a member of the Judiciary Committee, McConnell saw two of Richard Nixon's Supreme Court nominees defeated: Clement Haynsworth in 1969 and G. Harrold Carswell in 1970. From his early days, McConnell saw clearly the importance of the long-lasting contribution he could make by getting conservative justices confirmed to the Court.

Observers are fascinated about what drives McConnell. His opponents say he's like a black hole, which has produced endless speculation about his motives. Yet what drove him was actually quite simple: winning.

McConnell thought everybody in politics was ambitious, himself included. But he had come to think that perhaps he had a slightly higher tolerance for unpleasantness than most of his colleagues. That trait came in handy. Sure, perhaps past majority leaders had been less of a target, but those were different times. Being the majority leader now meant taking a lot of slings and arrows. It could tank your approval rating, as it had in both of his last two elections. In the end, he had won both races handily, but dealing with all the incoming had made it that much harder. Some members, he thought, probably just wouldn't want to deal with all that.

"But I . . . ," said McConnell, reflecting on it all in his Senate office, "in a weird sort of way, I love it."

. . . .

ON FEBRUARY 13, 2016—269 days before Election Day—McConnell had just touched down to start a vacation with his wife, Elaine Chao, when he received news that Antonin Scalia had died. The upper echelons of conservative political circles are small, and McConnell and Scalia were friendly. They also had a shared history, going back to their days as young conservatives in Gerald Ford's Justice Department. McConnell was a deputy assistant attorney general then, and he recalled being surrounded at staff meetings by brilliant people: Robert Bork was the solicitor general. Laurence Silberman was the deputy attorney general. Scalia was the head of the Office of Legal Counsel. McConnell found it all so intimidating that he never opened his mouth.

But forty-plus years later, when Scalia died, McConnell was quick to speak. He was the Senate majority leader, and he was not going to let Barack Obama confirm a third Supreme Court justice, moving the Court decidedly to the left for years.

So just hours after Scalia's death, McConnell personally wrote and released a statement that ended with a bombshell: "The American people should have a voice in the selection of their next Supreme Court Justice. Therefore, this vacancy should not be filled until we have a new president."

When he penned the statement, McConnell had a hunch that Democrats would have done the same thing if they were in his position. Later he found statistics to back up his "hunch" that he should not fill the seat: No opposition party had filled a Supreme Court seat during a presidential election year since the 1880s. And in 1992 Joe Biden, the chair of the Senate Judiciary Committee, had held McConnell's view: "It would be our pragmatic conclusion," Biden said, "that once the political season is underway, and it is, action on a Supreme Court nomination must be put off until after the election campaign is over."

Merrick Garland—Obama's nominee—was deprived of a hearing and a vote. McConnell knew it was a controversial move, but he didn't much care. He would ultimately consider ignoring the Garland nomination the single most consequential decision he made in more than three decades as a U.S. senator.

At the time, McConnell's bet was risky for many reasons. First, most Republicans thought Hillary Clinton would win and thereby get to fill the seat. Donald Trump was on the cusp of becoming the Republican presidential nominee, and McConnell hardly knew the guy. But in May 2016, Trump—with the help of Don McGahn, his campaign attorney and a longtime D.C. hand—put out a list of eleven judges he would consider for the Scalia seat. Neither Brett Kavanaugh nor Neil Gorsuch was on this original list.

Mike Davis, a conservative lawyer in Denver who had clerked for Gorsuch, was not pleased. Davis was a well-known entity within judicial circles, a man with a bit of a hot head and a foul mouth. Although he was living in Denver, the Iowa native had plenty of experience in conservative circles in D.C. He had been an intern on Capitol Hill for Chuck Grassley, Iowa's senior senator, and for Newt Gingrich, the former Speaker of the House. Later he worked in George W. Bush's White House. And he had loose associations with Trump, serving as a volunteer attorney for the campaign in Colorado.

Trump's list drove Davis crazy. He called everyone he knew on the campaign, lobbying for his man Gorsuch to get a spot. Finally in September, Gorsuch landed on a revised list of possible nominees. Davis assumed the campaign had done it to shut him up.

The whole idea of candidates detailing whom they might nominate to the Supreme Court was highly unusual, but the ploy worked. It galvanized Republicans to support Trump's campaign, and it reminded the nation that a seat on the highest court was at stake that year.

McConnell himself liked the tactic of releasing the list. After all, the party he led was "about to nominate somebody who was doing fund-raisers for Chuck Schumer three or four years ago," he recalled. "So there were a whole lot of Republicans saying, really? What's this guy going to be like?" McConnell found the list reassuring, and as the campaign progressed, he could see that it was similarly reassuring to regular voters on the fence about Trump. "The single biggest reason he ended up getting nine of ten Republicans," said McConnell, "just like Mitt Romney, was judges. Because Republicans care about judges."

Roughly one week after Trump was elected, the Federalist Society—the conservative group that helped Trump populate his Supreme Court list—held a gala at the Mayflower Hotel in downtown Washington. Mike Davis was there and spotted McGahn from across the room. Davis didn't know McGahn well, but he reminded him that he helped confirm him to the Federal Election Commission during George W. Bush's administration. That evening, however, Davis had another agenda: getting Gorsuch on the Supreme Court.

"You should consider Neil Gorsuch for the Supreme Court," Davis said to McGahn.

McGahn laughed. "If he wasn't on the first list, he's not going to get picked," he shot back.

"We'll see about that," Davis said.

That same week McConnell had his own conversation with McGahn.

"Don," McConnell said on the phone to the president's lawyer, "I think we have a chance to do something really important for the country."

McConnell suggested that McGahn take absolute control of all judicial nominations and elbow out the Justice Department and other factions that might want to have a say. "My advice to you, if you can pull it off, is to maintain firm control of the nominating process in the White House counsel's office," he said.

Snatching control of the process wasn't hard for McGahn, since Trump was mostly clueless about Washington. His knowledge of the legislative process was elementary, and his relationship with McConnell was nil.

McConnell had a willing partner in McGahn, but he knew he needed buy-in from the president. "This is a guy who is largely unfamiliar with a whole lot of stuff, as we know," McConnell later said of Trump. "I don't think he fully comprehended the significance of judicial appointments." So on January 9, 2017—less than two weeks before Trump's inauguration—an overcoat-clad McConnell went to Trump Tower by himself, with no staff, and just one topic in mind: how Trump and the

Republican Senate could reshape the federal judiciary. He explained to Trump the importance of the federal judiciary and how the "stars were aligned" in an all-GOP Washington for Republicans to overhaul the nation's courts.

On January 31—with McConnell's blessing—Trump nominated Neil Gorsuch for the Supreme Court. Gorsuch's nomination was a walk in the park. Three Democrats—Sen. Joe Donnelly of Indiana, Sen. Heidi Heitkamp of North Dakota, and Sen. Joe Manchin of West Virginia— voted for Gorsuch, which was quite the statement given Democrats' disdain for the president. He was sworn in on April 10.

MCCONNELL'S DECISION TO HOLD a Supreme Court seat vacant for fourteen months was one of the greatest political plays in modern memory. It demonstrated the remarkable extent of his power and his unshakable resolve: He had defied a sitting president and used his position to seat a justice who promised to bring decades of conservative returns. The spotlight it gave McConnell embodied a reality that was growing more apparent by the year, maybe even by the month: With congressional legislation increasingly gridlocked, the balance of power in American government had flowed toward the courts, which meant a corresponding rise in the power of the Senate and especially the majority leader, for the upper chamber alone controlled the fate of all nominees. To be sure, McConnell had had help from the previous majority leader, Democrat Harry Reid, who had knocked down the bar for clearing judges to a simple majority. But the Garland-Gorsuch imbroglio showed that the majority leader had the power to keep a vote from even coming to the floor, the power to utterly control the process. No doubt most Democrats thought McConnell's gambit undemocratic, unfair, and disgustingly partisan. But the very seating of Gorsuch showed that these concerns meant little in the face of legislative reality. McConnell had won, he had done so legally, and Democrats could only cry anguish.

As McConnell's power vis-à-vis the Court grew, though, it also became clear that there were limits to his power, especially when it came to actually passing legislation. Perhaps no moment underscored these limits better than in the wee hours of the morning of July 28, 2017, when McConnell stood in the middle of the Senate floor and watched his longtime colleague John McCain walk in through a door next to the presiding officer. It was a tick before 1:30 A.M., and McConnell was about to watch seven months of effort—and his party's best chance to make good on a promise it had been repeating for over six years—go down the drain.

For days now, McConnell and the other top public officials in America—Paul Ryan, Donald Trump, and Mike Pence—had been trying to persuade McCain, the eighty-year-old Arizona Republican who was stricken with brain cancer, that he should support a slapdash effort to repeal Obamacare. Republicans leaders were calling it the "skinny repeal," which was an apt title, because the legislation on the Senate floor that night was thin on details. Gone were the days of trying to jam a massive health care bill through the Senate. This bill would have to do. It repealed the mandate that individuals buy health insurance, a central element of the law that helped provide coverage to millions of Americans. It ended the mandate that employers provide health care to their workers. It did not end the government subsidies that helped people afford insurance. In short, it was a halfhearted attempt to repeal the law and did almost nothing to replace it. But McConnell, Ryan, and others tried to make the argument that passing something—anything, as a matter of fact—would allow the Senate and House to enter into formal negotiations to craft the large-scale replacement for Obamacare they had long promised.

McCain was unmoved. And given all the fits and starts over the previous seven months in getting this legislation to the floor, he was probably right to ignore his colleagues' argument. As he rode the subway over to the Capitol that night, McCain told Sen. Chris Murphy—a Connecticut Democrat with whom McCain had a good relationship—that he was about to do something that would make his party angry at him forever.

As he approached the Senate floor, reporters—including *Politico*'s Burgess Everett, the Senate beat reporter—asked him how he would vote.

"Watch the show," McCain said mysteriously.

McConnell stood with arms crossed as McCain entered the room, and as McCain stopped just a few feet from him in front of the clerk's desk, the majority leader hung his head and went stone still. McCain stuck his hand in the air, notifying the presiding officer that he wanted to vote. McCain's arm stretched only as high as parallel to the floor, a relic of his time being tortured while in captivity in Vietnam.

If one were able to press pause on that moment and hover over the Senate floor as McCain stood ready to vote, it would be a tableau worthy of a museum. McConnell was statuesque in the center of the room. Sen. Marco Rubio stood with his hands clasping his waist, as did Sen. Bill Cassidy, a physician from Louisiana who was in his first term. Sens. John Cornyn of Texas and John Thune of South Dakota, both members of the leadership, leaned against the desk at the front of the chamber. Minority leader Chuck Schumer was sitting at his desk, glasses on his nose, watching carefully. The chamber's floor was packed with aides, there to find out if the hitherto most lasting part of Barack Obama's legacy was about to be unwound.

"Mr. Peters," the clerk said, referring to Sen. Gary Peters, the Michigan Democrat, who was voting at the same time.

"No," Peters bellowed from the back of the chamber.

Then all eyes turned to McCain, who almost seemed frozen in time, arm stretched away from his body. In one motion, he lowered his arm, said "No," and plunged his fist, ending Republicans' efforts to repeal and replace the health care law.

After McCain voted no, he turned and for a moment looked directly at McConnell.

His vote shouldn't have come as a surprise. A few days earlier McCain had arrived on the Senate floor to a round of applause and voted—that time with two thumbs up—to proceed to debate the health care bill. Bearing a gruesome scar over his eye, and "a little worse for wear," in his telling, from his illness, McCain gave a spirited speech decrying the breakdown in Congress's processes. Bipartisanship was necessary to solve America's problems, he said, and the arcane procedures of the Senate helped achieve those ends. "Incremental progress,"

McCain said, "compromises that each side criticize but also accept. Just plain muddling through, to chip away at problems and keep our enemies from doing their worst, isn't glamorous or exciting. It doesn't feel like a political triumph. But it's usually the most we can accept from our system of government.

"Stop listening to the bombastic loudmouths on the radio, and television, and the Internet," McCain exhorted, his voice rising in fervor. "To hell with them. They don't want anything done for the public good. Our incapacity is their livelihood.

"We're getting nothing done, my friends," McCain said, his tone spirited. "We're getting nothing done. All we've really done this year is confirm Neil Gorsuch to the Supreme Court. Our health care insurance system is a mess. We all know it, [both] those who support Obamacare and those who oppose it. Something has to be done. We Republicans have looked for a way to end it and replace it with something else without paying a terrible political price. We haven't found it yet, and I'm not sure we will. All we've managed to do is make more popular a policy that wasn't very popular when we started trying to get rid of it."

McCain's stemwinder of a speech, more than fifteen minutes long, was as important as it was unrealistic. He wanted Congress to go back to the old days of bipartisan legislating, both parties working together to deal with the nation's big problems. He wanted a break from the Trump era. McCain made it plain: The GOP health care bill was not thought out and had been developed by just one party. That would not be acceptable to him, but it was the path down which McConnell and Ryan had headed.

THE REALITY WAS THAT Congress had veered wildly from those storied days McCain wanted to reclaim. The process by which the Republican Congress tried to repeal and replace the health care law was driven by partisan personalities, beset by fits and starts, and had all the markings of a newly empowered party learning to pull the levers. In his speech, McCain urged senators to treat the president as if he were the representative of an equal branch of government. But Donald Trump leaned on lawmakers to support the health care bill specifically to give him a victory. During a closed party meeting, Trump told Mark Meadows that he would campaign against him if he didn't vote for the bill, then conceded that he was joking and said he thought Meadows would get on board. McCain encouraged his colleagues to ignore the television pundits, but in April 2017, Paul Ryan and Mark Meadows were on a healthcare-strategy call with Trump, and Fox News's Sean Hannity was on the line. McCain extolled bipartisanship, yet Republicans dragged the bill to the right to appease the party's fringes. Democrats were barely an afterthought. The process got so dire that Ryan told Trump he would provide cover from critics: "Let me take the arrows. This is the last job in politics I'll have."

The promise to gut the health care law had been made by a party that was shifting to the right in the Obama era. But that promise eventually collided with an American electorate that had become accustomed to the Affordable Care Act's benefits and broadly comfortable with an expanded social safety net. Either the Republican House didn't realize that the law was gaining tremendously in popularity, or it didn't care. Mark Meadows and the rest of his conservative Freedom Caucus colleagues forced Republicans to embrace measures that could've been interpreted as ripping protections from patients with preexisting conditions. This gave Democrats the opening to paint the party as cruel and indifferent to the suffering of the poor, the sick, and the indigent. Republicans bet that failing to repeal Obamacare would hurt with the base, but their opposition to the program turned off the rest of the electorate. At the time, Republican leaders thought it necessary to spend seven months slamming a repeal and replace bill through the Congress. But in this circumstance, McConnell and Ryan's political gamble did not pay off.

REPEALING THE HEALTH CARE law had become perhaps the central promise of the Republican majorities. In 2010, when Republicans took the House, they did so in part because of broad distaste for the health care law and unease with how it was passed. *They rammed it down the* *throats of the American people,* Republicans said on the campaign trail. *It was written in secret in back rooms,* they cried. Not a single Republican had voted to put the Affordable Care Act into law in 2009 and 2010, and whether it was true or not, the bill became emblematic of Democratic governance gone amok. Republicans had a poll-tested line at the ready: Democrats had enacted a government takeover of health care. Everyone had complaints about health insurance, and Republicans made sure that Democrats owned it.

After the Republicans won sixty-three seats in Obama's first midterm election, they had to make good on their promise. During Obama's final six years in office, House Republican leadership forced more than sixty separate votes to repeal parts of the health care law. On a few occasions, Obama, John Boehner, Harry Reid, and Mitch McConnell were able to tweak the law on a bipartisan basis. The changes were mostly technical, though, and did not fundamentally change the Affordable Care Act.

But after Trump won the presidency, Paul Ryan knew he had an opportunity to repeal the law. So during a trip to Trump Tower in December 2016, the Speaker came armed with a plan that he had designed with McConnell. At this point, Ryan hardly knew Trump. He didn't know how to communicate with him, but he did know he was a builder. So Ryan designed a Gantt chart, a visual timeline popular in the building trade that indicates expected progress on a project. Ryan's chart laid out the timeline of Republicans' legislative priorities: Obamacare repeal in the first months of the administration, then tax reform, followed by a quick shift to a massive infrastructure project. Skeptics in the administration and on Capitol Hill thought Republicans should lead off with something positive, like tax reform, instead of delving into the messy politics of health care, but Ryan thought repealing the spending in Obamacare would give the Congress the budgetary space it needed to rewrite the tax code. Trump agreed.

The need to speed through repeal and do just about anything to get the votes defined how Republicans handled this process. On January 12, CNN's Jake Tapper asked Ryan if he would be able to repeal and replace Obamacare in the first hundred days of the Trump presidency, and Ryan left no doubt that that was his plan. It was an insanely ambitious deadline. As a comparison, it took six months for Democrats to pass Obamacare into law in 2009 and 2010, and that process was captained by veteran lawmakers, a well-prepared House and Senate majority, and a president who had served in the Senate and filled his White House with legislative tacticians.

From the earliest days of the Trump administration, it was clear that repeal and replace would be a heavy lift. First, the party had no unified plan. Republicans had ideas—allowing consumers to purchase health insurance across state lines, for example—but they needed to come up with something comprehensive, and quickly. On January 4, even before Donald Trump and Mike Pence were sworn in, the vice president–elect went to Capitol Hill for meetings with House and Senate Republicans and heard divergent opinions about how long the party should give to phase out the law. Sen. Rand Paul, the Republican from Kentucky, wanted the party to repeal and replace the law immediately. But some in the administration and on Capitol Hill thought a two-year off-ramp made sense.

It was clear that the president was torn as well. Republicans on Capitol Hill had privately been saying that the country would move from "universal coverage"—the goal under Obamacare—to "universal access." But on Saturday, January 14, Trump called the *Washington Post*'s Robert Costa at home and unveiled a new standard.

"We're going to have insurance for everybody," Trump told Costa, who had been covering the New York billionaire's campaign since its early days. "There was a philosophy in some circles that if you can't pay for it, you don't get it. That's not going to happen with us." It was as if the president-elect had internalized the complaints that the party would be ripping health care away from people and was seeking to quash them. Republicans had never planned to insure more people than Obamacare did, but Trump seemed to want them to, details be damned. "What I do want is to be able to take care of people," Trump told Costa.

But it was not Trump who needed to come up with the details, it was the Republican Congress, which was on a bit of a sugar high from winning the election and only beginning to focus on the herculean task ahead of them. Privately, some in the GOP were fretting. At their retreat in Philadelphia on January 26, they aired their very sharp grievances. Rep. Tom McClintock, a California conservative, warned his colleagues that whatever they came up with would "be called Trumpcare," adding that Republicans would own it "lock, stock, and barrel, and we'll be judged in the election less than two years away." Rep. John Faso, an upstate New York Republican, warned his colleagues that they shouldn't use the health care debate to take a whack at Planned Parenthood, which the party had targeted because of disagreements about its abortion services. Rep. Tom MacArthur, a New Jersey Republican from the suburbs of Philadelphia, said if Congress moved too quickly, "we are, in fact, going to pull the rug out" from under Americans who rely on the government-backed health care.*

As the House went back and forth on the proposal, Trump grew frustrated. On February 27 he told the National Governors Association that "nobody knew that health care could be so complicated"—a view that elicited its fair share of snickers from Washington stalwarts, who in fact were well aware of the complexities. He then suggested that Republicans simply sit on their hands for two years and let Obamacare collapse: "Let it implode, and then let it implode in '18 even worse. Don't do anything, and they will come begging for us to do something. But that's not the fair thing to do for the people. It's not the fair thing."

Of course, letting Obamacare sink wasn't a palatable option for any Republican. But they had a hell of a time getting their act together. On March 6 they finally laid bare what they had been working on for two months: the American Health Care Act. It did exactly what Republicans had promised. It repealed the individual mandate that Americans buy health insurance. It choked off the expansion of Medicaid, the mechanism by which many Americans were receiving affordable insurance for the first time. It instituted subsidies for low- and middle-income earners. Most important, it appeared to have the support of the only person who mattered: Donald J. Trump. The president told a meeting

---

*An anonymous e-mail sent a full audio recording of the January 26 retreat to multiple news outlets, including the *Washington Post* and *Politico*.

of House vote counters gathered at the White House that he was supportive of the bill.

But otherwise the rollout was a complete and utter train wreck. Conservatives came out of the woodwork opposing the bill because it didn't fully repeal Obamacare. They dubbed it Obamacare Lite and said it was an abandonment of everything the GOP had been fighting for for years. Conservative groups such as Heritage Action also came out in opposition.

Most important, the House Freedom Caucus was staunchly opposed, and they had enough votes to stop anything in its tracks. As Mark Meadows and Jim Jordan circled around the Capitol, they felt the president was being taken for a ride by the Republican leadership. This Republican bill was just Obamacare by another name, they said. Tax credits were being left in place, as were taxes that were part of Obamacare. This was not the best Republicans could do, they thought. We can give the president something better.

Meadows and Jordan met with various White House officials, including Pence and Health and Human Services secretary Tom Price, hoping to convince them to negotiate with the Freedom Caucus for a better bill. They threw anything at the wall, hoping something would stick. Could the Senate do away with the legislative filibuster and pass things with a fifty-vote threshold in exchange for moving the health care bill? That was a long shot. Meadows and Jordan were also a bit befuddled by the party's strategy. Why wouldn't Republicans simply gut the law, as they had done dozens of times when Barack Obama was president?

At the same time the Freedom Caucus was stewing, so was Mitch McConnell's Senate. Senators were expressing concern on things ranging from the treatment of Medicaid to the repeal of funding for Planned Parenthood. Sen. Tom Cotton, a Republican from Arkansas who had served in the House, said on MSNBC's *Morning Joe* on March 8 that his former colleagues were moving too quickly. That Sunday he followed it up with another broadside. Appearing on ABC's *This Week,* Cotton said that his "friends in the House of Representatives" should "not walk the plank and vote for a bill that cannot pass the Senate, and then have to face the consequences of that vote." That was a pretty dire warning from a hero of the conservative movement. He was asking the House to change their Obamacare strategy midstream.

As others equivocated, Mitch McConnell was blasting ahead. The way he saw it, it was time to act. Obamacare had been an issue in four straight elections, and the American public had just handed Republicans all levers of government in an unambiguous endorsement of their ideas, their policies, and their tactics. It was time to deliver—and quickly. The president supported the bill, and McConnell wanted to push it through. He was going to take advantage of the power.

McConnell vowed to have the bill through his chamber by Easter. "I encourage every member to review it," he said from the Senate floor around ten A.M. on March 7, "because I hope to call it up when we receive it from the House. It's clear to just about everyone that Obamacare is failing."

On that same day, Ryan guaranteed victory. When the bill got to the floor, Ryan said he would have the votes to pass it. "I can guarantee you that," he told reporters.

Scalise privately told Trump on the day of the rollout that Republicans would "be moving this quickly to get it to your desk." Trump nodded. At this point, understanding just how sticky health care was, the president was hoping to dispense with the repeal and replace process quickly and move on to tax reform, which he found much more appealing.

Then came a major thud. On March 13 the Congressional Budget Office (CBO), the nonpartisan budgetary scorekeeper for Congress, said the American Health Care Act would result in 24 million fewer Americans with health insurance. The report sent shivers through the Republican ranks. On Capitol Hill, many Republicans wondered privately if the party could overcome this. At the White House, the president's advisers, including HHS secretary Price, said the CBO's score was not to be believed. Indeed, both parties had complained that the CBO was constrained by rules that forced it to judge legislation through a narrow lens. That said, overcoming a budgetary score of this nature required a herculean political effort. Republican leadership told their troops in closed party meetings to focus on the upside of the report: that the bill would lower the budgetary deficit by $337 billion.

Amid flagging vote counts, the congressional leadership and the White House tried to employ the president, who called himself the ultimate dealmaker, to shore up support. And he had some luck. On March 17, Trump invited Scalise and a gaggle of House conservatives to the White House to try to flip votes. The concern at hand was the treatment of the elderly in the health bill. "These are my people, I will take care of them," Trump said. As he listened to concerns from roughly a dozen House Republicans, he made similar promises, then went around the room and asked each lawmaker if they were on board. Every single one of them said yes.

But Ryan and House Republicans were forced to make significant changes in the bill to satisfy holdouts. These changes were made on the fly in private agreements among members of just one party. Republicans instituted work requirements for Medicaid recipients. Additional tax credits for seniors. A Medicaid change that would specifically benefit New York. Changes were being doled out like Halloween candy.

Still, that wasn't enough for Meadows and Jordan. So with leadership short of the votes needed for passage, the Freedom Caucus duo took their concerns to Mick Mulvaney. Mulvaney was Trump's budget chief, but, more important, he had been a founding member of the Freedom Caucus during his days in Congress from South Carolina. Meadows and Jordan told Mulvaney the price for their votes: removing so-called essential health benefits. The Affordable Care Act forced insurers to provide a minimum standard of coverage, but conservatives thought everyone shouldn't have to cover things like maternity care if they didn't need it. So Jordan and Meadows got it yanked.

Even as the bill snowballed to the right, conservatives kept holding out, and on March 23 Ryan was forced to push back a vote because he still hadn't gathered commitments from a majority of the House. But on that same day, Mulvaney attended a closed House GOP meeting and said that the president was demanding a vote on the bill the next day, a Friday. Trump was through negotiating, he said. Ryan would have to take it to the floor not knowing if he had the votes.

Early in the afternoon on Friday, just before the bill was scheduled to come to the floor, the president spoke to Ryan by telephone and asked him to pull the bill. Trump had become aware it wouldn't pass and didn't want to suffer the embarrassment.

"We came really close today," Ryan told reporters in the Capitol around four-fifteen that afternoon. "But we came up short." He ruefully said, "Obamacare is the law of the land. It's going to remain the law of the land until it's replaced. We did not have quite the votes to replace this law. And so, yeah, we're going to be living with Obamacare for the foreseeable future."

Trump? He wasn't too concerned. "I never said, I guess I'm here, what, sixty-four days? I never said . . . repeal it and replace it within sixty-four days. I have a long time. But I want to have a great health care bill and plan and we will, it will happen."

The bill still had no pulse in early April, and that was when Meadows decided to insert himself into the debate once again. He started holding secret talks with the White House to revive the bill. The Freedom Caucus's new price: axing protections that prevented insurance companies from jacking up costs on high-risk medical patients, and allowing governors to opt out of some types of coverage. It wasn't exactly cutting coverage for preexisting conditions, but it was giving states the berth to skirt those bare-bones requirements. Some moderate Republicans grew concerned about the policy, and the potential for political fallout.

That was when Ryan, Trump, Meadows, and, much to everyone's surprise, Sean Hannity gathered on a conference call. Ryan's leadership team was incredibly wary of Meadows's push because they understood the political implications of kicking sick people off of their health care plans. So did Hannity, who, on that call with the Speaker, the president, and Meadows, expressed pause at the wisdom of dragging the bill in that direction.

Meanwhile the White House was upping its pressure on Ryan's House to vote on a health care bill before the end of April. The House was scheduled to leave town for a two-week April recess, and Trump's one hundredth day was April 29. He was hungry for the symbolism. White House aides hounded the GOP leadership, inquiring when the bill would finally come up for a vote. They also got into a bad, and dangerous, habit of whispering to reporters that the bill was coming to the floor imminently. This infuriated congressional aides, who angrily sniped behind the scenes that the White House had no idea when legislation was scheduled for a vote. They quickly grew tired of Trump meddling in their process and wished he would stay away.

At the same time, Meadows began quietly talking to Rep. Tom MacArthur. Meadows and MacArthur were an odd couple, a conservative North Carolinian and a moderate New Jerseyan, but they shared one trait: They both fashioned themselves better-than-average deal-makers. The deal they came up with, though, was considered toxic by many House Republicans. In essence, MacArthur and Meadows crafted an amendment to the health care bill that would allow governors to apply for "limited waivers" to the health care law, which was seen almost universally as gutting coverage for preexisting conditions. Even MacArthur's fellow moderates bailed on him, saying they didn't support the legislation. On April 22, recognizing the political and substantive reality, Ryan slowed the process down. On a twenty-five-minute conference call with House Republicans, the Speaker rebuffed the White House and said a vote was nowhere close. The GOP would take its time.

That it did. Even though the Freedom Caucus was mostly behind the newfangled bill by the end of April, the Republican leadership had scrapped plans for voting on health care. Meanwhile the Senate leadership had a message for the White House: No matter what, the Senate would not vote in May. The earliest Trump would get anything was June.

Trump was beginning to get accustomed to the snail's pace, but during a speech for the Air Force football team in the Rose Garden on

May 2, a few members of the House were in the audience, and Trump tried his best to prod them along. "How's health care coming, folks?" Trump said. "How's it doing? All right we're moving along? All right. I think it's time now, right? Right? They know it's time."

The next day, Trump himself had work to do with the House. He finally got a chance to strike a deal when Reps. Billy Long of Missouri and Fred Upton of Michigan indicated they might vote against the party's health care efforts. White House staff recognized Long would not commit to voting for the bill without speaking to the president in person. When Long and Upton arrived at the White House, they melted, all for an amendment worth $8 billion that would be aimed at helping cover people with preexisting conditions. Upton had rejected a previous version worth $5 billion but settled for the higher number.

The next day Republican leaders were finally ready to bring their bill to the House floor. In a closed party meeting, Paul Ryan got a standing ovation for navigating the choppy waters of repealing the law when, after four months of haggling, they squeezed it through the chamber on a party line vote. When it passed, Democrats started singing, "Na na, na na na na, hey hey hey, goodbye." They thought voting for the bill ensured that Republicans would lose the House.

The president, though, was jazzed. He invited the entire House Republican Conference to the Rose Garden for a celebration. It was akin to holding a victory parade at halftime. Several House Republicans skipped the ceremony altogether, thinking it was too strange, but the leadership had no choice but to attend.

"[W]e have an amazing group of people standing behind me," Trump said, with Vice President Mike Pence, Speaker Paul Ryan, and Rep. Mark Meadows at his back. "They worked so hard and they worked so long. . . . It's going to be an unbelievable victory, actually, when we get it through the Senate."

TRUMP MAY HAVE BADGERED Paul Ryan and House Republicans to no end, but in the Senate he took an entirely different tack: He was going to allow Mitch McConnell to handle health care the way he wanted. The White House viewed the Kentuckian as a savvy tactician, someone who knew how to navigate the currents stirred up by his membership, unlike Ryan, about whom the administration had constant doubts.

There were several early signs, however, that the Senate's waters would be choppy. First, McConnell could lose only two Republican senators and still pass repeal. But his moderates were concerned, as were some conservatives. McConnell's early moves confounded and frustrated some Republicans, starting with his appointment of thirteen white men to handle the party's legislation, which was clearly bad optics. And the party's top health care dealmakers, like Sen. Lamar Alexander of Tennessee, were already promising that the House's bill was dead as a doornail in the Senate.

McConnell, meanwhile, handled the early stages of the process in his trademark methodical yet secretive fashion. He called lawmakers to his Capitol Hill office suite to absorb their concerns. They didn't like the House bill, that much was clear. They thought the House had gone too far in gutting preexisting conditions. They thought the House was rolling back the state-based Medicare expansion far too quickly. But what Senate Republicans did want was by no means clear. By Memorial Day, nearly halfway through Trump's first year in office, the Senate had no real plan of its own. The June deadline turned to the end of July, and even that prediction seemed generous.

It wasn't only Senate Republicans who were cool to the House's bill. Unbelievably, just two months after celebrating with House Republicans in the Rose Garden, Trump started dumping on it. On June 13, Trump gathered a group of roughly a dozen GOP senators at the White House for a meeting about the health care agenda, and he called the House's legislation "mean." He implored the Senate to do better and to be more generous in taking care of people. It was a truly gobsmacking set of statements. The reaction from the House was apoplectic. House Republicans had shuffled down a plank for Trump, and this was what they got in return?

Finally, on June 22, Senate Republicans put themselves on the line and unveiled their 142-page Obamacare repeal and replace bill. It was certainly kinder, in the eyes of many Republicans, than the House bill. Most important, the legislation rejected Meadows and MacArthur's suggestion that Congress allow insurance companies to charge everyone the same rate.

Trump continued to be hands-off with McConnell in the Senate's process. He made a few phone calls to allies, including the skeptical Rand Paul, but he was generally happy to allow McConnell to do his handiwork. McConnell privately urged senators to keep their concerns to themselves and not announce opposition to the bill. His message: *We can work it out together.*

But they couldn't. Rand Paul and his fellow conservative senators— Ted Cruz of Texas, Ron Johnson of Wisconsin, and Mike Lee of Utah— expressed concern shortly after the bill's unveiling, as did moderates like Lisa Murkowski of Alaska. The situation did not improve from there. At the end of the month, McConnell sent the Senate home for a ten-day break. His chamber had made no headway.

Now Trump was getting frustrated with him. "If Republican Senators are unable to pass what they are working on now, they should immediately REPEAL, and then REPLACE at a later date!" he tweeted. McConnell's retort didn't come on Twitter, but came rather from Kentucky, where he was wheeling around the state doing events. He rejected Trump's tactical advice, putting it thusly: "It's not easy making America great again, is it?"

When the chamber returned on July 10, there was immediate trouble. Sens. Susan Collins of Maine and Rand Paul both announced they would oppose efforts to proceed to the bill. Then, on July 15, the clubby group of one hundred got bad news: John McCain would need surgery. A blood clot had formed above his eye, his office said, and he would be resting in Arizona for the week. Two days later, conservative senators Jerry Moran of Kansas and Mike Lee of Utah said they would oppose the Senate's bill. It was increasingly clear that, without a lot of persuading, McConnell would not have the votes to pass it.

So he announced he would put the House bill on the floor with a grab bag of amendments for senators who were thirsting for legislative action. But he couldn't even get that vote to the floor; a wide range of lawmakers thought the plan was half-baked and could throw the insurance markets into chaos.

For the first time in recent memory, McConnell looked weak, weary, and bruised. The White House was growing tired of him. But in reality, the Senate majority leader was trying to squeeze through a piece of legislation that did not have the support of the majority of his members. Repealing Obamacare, it turned out, had been little more than a tagline. The politics became inextricably tricky since every senator had constituents who were enjoying the law's benefits and would be detrimentally affected if it was repealed.

The next week the news got worse for John McCain. He was diagnosed with a glioblastoma, a deadly form of brain cancer. He remained in Arizona until July 25, when he traveled back to Washington to give his stemwinding Washington-is-broken speech.

But after he voted to proceed to the bill on July 25, McCain was edgy. The Republican leadership did not have a good read on where he stood. He indicated to his colleagues that he was queasy about the process the Senate was using—he didn't like that, despite his exhortations, one party alone was restructuring the nation's health care system.

On July 27, just a few hours before the bill would get a vote, he appeared at a news conference in the Capitol with Ron Johnson of Wisconsin and his dear friend Lindsey Graham of South Carolina. Graham explained the state of play. The Republican leadership was asking the Senate to vote on the "skinny repeal" just to get into a formal negotiation with the House. But senators were increasingly concerned that the House, in a rush to repeal Obamacare, would take the bill up and actually pass it and send it to the president. No Republicans thought the bill was ready for law, but they didn't trust the House not to do something rash.

"I need assurances from the Speaker of the House and his team that if I vote for the skinny bill, it will not become the final product," Graham said. "It will be the vehicle to have a conference between the House and Senate, where we can consider a true replacement. If I don't get those assurances, I'm a no because I'm not going to vote for a pig in a poke and I'm not going to tell people back in South Carolina that this product actually replaces Obamacare, because it does not. It is a fraud."

McCain said with a laugh that he had "nothing to add." But of course, he did. He said he was in touch with Doug Ducey, his state's governor, about how he should vote. But he needed assurances that there would be a "normal conference"—a negotiation with Democrats and Republicans.

"I believe that one of the major problems with Obamacare was that it was rammed through Congress by Democrats without a single Republican vote," McCain said. "I believe we shouldn't make that same mistake again."

McCain's legacy was not going to be a vote for another health care bill that would split the country. Obamacare, in his estimation, "split us for years." "It's time we sat down together and came up with a piece of legislation that addresses this issue," McCain said.

Before leaving, he said, "Right now, I am voting no."

A few hours later—after resisting entreaties from Pence, Ryan, and Trump—McCain voted no.

"This is, you know, clearly a disappointing moment," McConnell said, with the best chance to repeal the health care law receding in the rear view. "From skyrocketing costs to plummeting choices and collapsing markets, our constituents have suffered through an awful lot under Obamacare. We thought they deserved better. It's why I and many of my colleagues did as we promised and voted to repeal this failed law. We told our constituents we would vote that way, and when the moment came, when the moment came, most of us did."

6

MCCARTHY AND SCALISE

DON'T LET ME BLEED OUT on this field.

That was what Steve Scalise—the number three Republican in the House of Representatives—thought on June 14, 2017, as he lay bleeding and damn near death next to second base at Eugene Simpson Stadium Park in Alexandria, Virginia. Thoughts were racing through his head. Would he live to walk his daughter, Madison, down the aisle? God, he hoped so.

The bullet had torn through Scalise, shattering his femur and hip bones, and left his lower extremities a mess. He should've been dead. In fact, he *was* briefly dead, technically. And beyond the obvious gravity of the situation—a man's life hung in the balance, a leader cut down in his prime—the irony here was rich: This congressional baseball game was perhaps Scalise's favorite part of being in Washington.

The game hit all the notes for him. It was played under the white lights at Nationals Park. There was masculine camaraderie, mindless but intense competition, backslapping fun, and partisan pride. He got to compete against one of his old buddies, New Orleans Democrat and lights-out pitcher Rep. Cedric Richmond, a man who had once saved his career. Scalise always showed up wearing a jersey representing some slice of Louisiana: the University of Louisiana Ragin' Cajuns, the Tulane

Green Wave, the University of New Orleans Privateers, the Archbishop Rummel Raiders (his alma mater), the Southeastern Louisiana Lions, or his beloved LSU Tigers. His round stomach—the evidence, perhaps, of too many steak dinners and glasses of red wine—always protruded over his white baseball pants. He laughed. His staff partied.

But on this morning, James T. Hodgkinson, a deranged bespectacled man from Illinois, shattered that serene sense of innocence with a Russian rifle and a 9-millimeter pistol.

The next few moments were gory; few who were there that day care to relive them. Scalise dragged his near-lifeless body as best he could across the field. Rep. Brad Wenstrup, an Ohio Republican who served as a medic in Iraq, bandaged up his wound, trying desperately to stop the bleeding. Jeff Flake, a senator who had served with Scalise in the House, took the phone from his pants pocket and called Scalise's wife to alert her to the mayhem. Scalise was in trouble.

The Alexandria Police Department arrived by 7:12 A.M., three minutes after receiving the call. At least seventy shots had been fired in a ten-minute period that, to those involved, seemed like it stretched an hour. Scalise's Capitol Police detail and Alexandria police shot and killed Hodgkinson. In Scalise's telling, when he was on the ground, he almost immediately heard a different-sounding gun, which he believed was the Capitol Police going after Hodgkinson.

Scalise, draped in a white sheet, was somewhat alert as he was carried to the helicopter that would take him across the Potomac River and over Washington to the MedStar Washington Hospital Center. But after the quick ride across D.C., the doctor found no blood pressure and no pulse to speak of. Scalise was at death's door. His doctor later told *60 Minutes* that the number three House Republican was "hovering on the border between life and death."

Kevin McCarthy and Paul Ryan—Scalise's leadership colleagues—were frightened and horrified. McCarthy and Ryan were working out in the House gym when they heard the news about Scalise. Their Capitol Police details told them of the shooting, and they immediately went back to the Capitol into a leadership meeting.

McCarthy was absolutely shocked. By that afternoon, he and his wife, Judy, arrived at the hospital, where some of Scalise's closest friends were gathering. Kevin Brady, the Ways and Means chairman from Texas and Scalise's roommate, was there, as was Brett Horton, his chief of staff. Jennifer, Scalise's wife, had not yet arrived. But when she got there, she asked McCarthy and Brady if they would coordinate a statement with Scalise's surgeon.

For McCarthy especially, Scalise was not just any House colleague. For two decades their careers had been inextricably intertwined as they made their way from hungry young Republicans to the top of the party. Now, at the peak of their power, one was watching the other fight for his life.

Kevin Owen McCarthy and Stephen Joseph Scalise were the number two and three Republicans in the House, and the heirs apparent to a party in the midst of a massive transformation. Paul Ryan's party—of steady and levelheaded foreign policy, fiscal restraint, and aw-shucks demeanor—was nearly extinct. In fact, few thought Ryan would make it as Speaker through the two-year congressional session. McCarthy and Scalise, figures of the Fox News Republican Party, were next up to take the GOP through the Trump era, or rebuild it when it crumbled.

IN THE FALL OF 2007, Bobby Jindal was elected governor of Louisiana, and the following January, McCarthy—a brand-new congressman from the sweltering dust bowl of Bakersfield, California—thought it would be fun to fly to Baton Rouge to attend his inauguration. McCarthy had served in the House for a year with Jindal, and they were friends. Young. Conservative. Next generation. If McCarthy was known for anything, it was his ability to become fast friends with just about everyone.

McCarthy was also in the process of earning a reputation for doing things he thought were fun. Whether it was escaping with a colleague to fish in southern Florida or touring SpaceX with Elon Musk, McCarthy loved to leverage his minor celebrity for his personal enjoyment. This inauguration was the kind of thing he loved. He'd have the opportunity to travel. Pomp and circumstance. Later in his career, when he would ascend to the Republican leadership, he took photos with people like Beyoncé, Jay-Z, and Elena Kagan; stole placards from congressional dinners; and got to know athletes and country stars. Why not? He was pleasant, funny, and inquisitive, and people enjoyed his company.

On inauguration day—January 14, 2008—McCarthy saw his old pal Steve Scalise in Louisiana. Scalise was a mere state senator and only recently had confirmed his interest in running to replace Jindal in Congress. Just a year earlier Scalise was term-limited out of the Louisiana house; instead, he ran for and won a state senate seat, but now, just a few months later, he was ready to abandon that job when Jindal's House of Representatives seat came open. Scalise had long had his eye on Washington. He had considered and then passed on two previous races for Congress. This time he wasn't going to wait.

"His heart and soul are in Washington," his father, Al, told the *New Orleans Times-Picayune* in February 2008.

On that day, with Jindal taking the oath, Scalise took McCarthy on a tour of the Capitol in Baton Rouge, the building he served in for the previous decade. The two men had by then known each other for almost twenty years—and the pecking order between them had long been established: McCarthy, big dog; Scalise, underling. In the 1990s, in the heady days after the sunset of the Reagan Revolution, McCarthy was the national chairman of the Young Republicans. Scalise was a local Young Republican leader in Louisiana. It was McCarthy who spoke at the 2000 Republican National Convention in Philadelphia on the main stage, where he was hailed as a luminary of the "innovative, high-tech approach to politics" that was breaking through.

Eight years later Scalise was still a state legislator, but well on his way. He was a rambunctious and ambitious Louisiana State University graduate who had won a statehouse seat at just thirty-one years old. He was known as an able legislator, if a bit inflexible, a staunch conservative no matter the circumstance. In his campaigns, he vowed to fight gay marriage, protect the offshore oil industry (a business that nearly crippled the Louisiana economy a decade later), and work to shield gun manufacturers.

When Scalise made the plunge into the race to replace Jindal, he did it with the speed and precision of a savvy pol. He quickly locked up crucial endorsements from nearly all the Republicans in the Louisiana congressional delegation, and he put to work the six-figure campaign kitty he had stashed away from an earlier abandoned run for Congress. In March 2008 Scalise won a three-way primary by twenty points, then dispatched a well-financed Democratic challenger by fifty-three points. This district was red as hell, which meant Scalise couldn't be far enough to the right. In all likelihood, he would never have to worry about re-election again.

On May 7 Scalise took the oath of office on the House floor from Nancy Pelosi, with his daughter, Madison, in his arms. It was his wife Jennifer's birthday, and from the floor, Scalise said he promised he would not sing to her in public. When it was time for him to address the chamber, he handed Madison to David Vitter, the Louisiana senator.

"Do you solemnly swear or affirm that you will support and defend the Constitution of the United States against all enemies foreign and domestic, that you bear true faith and allegiance to same, that you take this obligation freely, without any mental reservation or purpose of evasion, and that you will well and faithfully discharge the duties of the office on which you are about to enter, so help you God?" Pelosi said from the Speaker's rostrum.

"I do," Scalise responded.

"Congratulations, you are now a member of the one hundred and tenth Congress," Pelosi said, as the Louisiana congressional delegation encircled him and cheered.

Congratulations were not really in order for Scalise, however. When the Louisiana Republican got to Washington, his party was in the dumps. Democrats were 235 votes strong in the House, compared to 199 Republicans. The 2008 presidential campaign was raging, Barack Obama was surging, and George W. Bush's days in D.C. were quickly coming to a close. Republicans got torched in the national elections later that year. They lost the White House and were plunged deeper into the House minority, as Democrats picked up another twenty-one seats. Rep. John Kline, a Republican from Minnesota, used to joke to Scalise that no one knew who he was because no one could believe that a Republican had actually won an election.

With their party on the skids, Scalise and McCarthy saw opportunity.

McCarthy banded with Paul Ryan and Eric Cantor to write a book—and create a brand—called *Young Guns: A New Generation of Conservative Leaders*. They were positioning themselves as fresh faces in a tired party. The whole thing was a bit kitschy: They shot a corny video—"America is at a crossroads, and Washington remains out of touch. . . . There is a better way, and a new team is ready to bring America back," a TV-like narrator said—went on a book tour, projecting themselves as the cavalry coming to save the Republican Party. The 2010 book was sharply critical of the party, saying it was irresponsible with power. In a triumph, or tragedy, of timing, the book was released nine days before the GOP put out its own election-season treatise, *Pledge to America*.

The whole thing chafed on much of the party's elder guard, which wondered why Ryan, McCarthy, and Cantor were broadcasting just months before Election Day that the party needed to evolve. No one viewed the effort with more skepticism than John Boehner and his inner circle, which saw this as part of Cantor's never-ending quest to claim power.

"The three of them know that my job is to make sure that they're well-qualified and ready to take my place," Boehner said at their book release party, held at a bar a stone's throw from the Capitol, "at the appropriate moment."

MCCARTHY AND SCALISE ROSE to prominence in unison. They were, in their own ways, beneficiaries of the 2010 Tea Party revolution that swept Republicans into power for the first time since 2006.

McCarthy, for his part, used the *Young Guns* platform to recruit many of the candidates, traveling to godforsaken towns like Frog Jump, Tennessee, to convince people to run for a job in Washington. He spared no details in shaping their campaigns, even telling two 2010 candidates—Scott DesJarlais in Tennessee and Jim Renacci in Ohio—to shave their goatees. Both did, and both won.

They weren't the only two whom McCarthy helped bring to D.C. in 2010. That year he, Cantor, and Boehner ushered sixty-three

Republicans to Washington, giving Republicans a historic majority, and McCarthy a power base.

Scalise, meanwhile, was making a name for himself as an unflinching conservative, the kind of guy ready to fight to the death for policies that caught fire on the right. His first big vote was a no on TARP, the bailout that prevented a collapse of the global financial system.

"I was getting calls from bankers back home saying, 'My whole bank could collapse if y'all don't pass this thing,'" Scalise recalled. "I heard members who had been here for twenty years saying that was the toughest vote they had in their career. I was thinking I have only been here a few months, but I have seen things similarly bad in Louisiana politics and my first rule of thumb is when somebody comes in a room and yells 'The sky is falling, and the room's on fire,' you shouldn't just run out of the room. You should take an assessment because many of the times what they're saying is not the full picture."

He was emboldened by the burn-the-house-down conservatives who swept the party into power in 2010. In 2012, just two years later, they supported Scalise in a tough, come-from-behind victory to win the chairmanship of the Republican Study Committee, a large conservative caucus that held sway in the GOP.

Scalise was playing the Washington game as well as anyone. In 2009 he opened up the Eye of the Tiger political action committee and immediately began stroking $500 checks. He also started bringing his colleagues to Louisiana to tour offshore oil rigs. It was a chance for him to bond with elected officials in his hometown of New Orleans. They ate food and raised a few bucks, and reporters got to witness Scalise expanding his power base in real time. These trips had reporters paired in the middle of the Gulf of Mexico with conservatives like firebrand Rep. Michele Bachmann and Rep. Mark Sanford, the former governor of South Carolina. One had no choice but to bond.

McCarthy, meanwhile, ran for Republican whip in 2011, using the newly elected class as the anchor of his power. He was elected with Scalise's wholehearted support. When McCarthy's mentor and chief booster, Eric Cantor, lost his primary in 2014, McCarthy moved up to majority leader.

Scalise wanted the whip job but found himself with a fight on his hands; McCarthy's chief deputy, Chicagoland representative Peter Roskam, was gunning for the job as well. McCarthy stayed completely silent, refusing to endorse either man, which was a massive blow to Roskam and a boost to Scalise.

Scalise was plain about why he, not Roskam, should be the next member of Republican leadership: He was conservative and from the South. Scalise said there were too many midwesterners, northerners, and others in the leadership, and no one representing the South, the region that made up the largest voting bloc of the House Republican Conference. The unspoken message: *The rest of these guys are pinky liberals. Let a real conservative in.*

In the opening days of the whip election, Scalise unleashed a decisive operation in the Capitol, locking up vote after vote. His aides wore "Geaux Scalise" shirts. He handed out Louisiana fare. And he handily defeated Roskam.

Conservatives were on the rise, and Scalise was up to the task.

As Republicans grew in prominence, and the House Republican majority grew to 247 in 2015 and 2016, some Republicans began looking for bigger things. Cory Gardner of Colorado, Tom Cotton of Arkansas, and James Lankford of Oklahoma became senators. McCarthy and Scalise might have been expected to seek the same, but they both suffered from the same political flaw: They had a deep love of the House of Representatives. They loved the churn and the fight of the House. They loved the camaraderie, the youth. The Senate was older. Being governor would be lonely. Being in the House fit both their personalities. Rep. Patrick McHenry from North Carolina, a close friend to Scalise and McCarthy, once said, "If Kevin McCarthy is alone, does he exist?"

Scalise was a font of talking points, affable to the point of annoyance (according to some of his colleagues), and singularly focused on the state of Louisiana; he gave out pralines as a lagniappe, a Cajun word for a little bit extra. He was light on policy and heavy on playing the game of internal politics. Meanwhile McCarthy could barely stick to talking points. His speech, at times, was halting. Still, he built deep relationships with lawmakers across the political spectrum, frequently getting to know their families and often staying in close touch by text and phone.

Both men were uniquely suited for the House, a political arena filled with quirks and offbeat politicians, where their strengths boosted their ascension to power.

But suddenly their rise came to a halt.

ON DECEMBER 28, 2014, WASHINGTON had already emptied for the Christmas holiday, and Scalise was in Louisiana when Lamar White Jr., a little-known Louisiana political blogger, published a post with this headline: HOUSE MAJORITY WHIP STEVE SCALISE WAS REPORTEDLY AN HONORED GUEST AT 2002 INTERNATIONAL WHITE SUPREMACIST CONVENTION.

The details were brutal. White wrote that Scalise "was allegedly an honored guest and speaker at an international conference of white supremacist leaders." The group, the European-American Unity and Rights Organization, was an unmistakable front for modern-day Nazism. David Duke, the former grand wizard of the Ku Klux Klan, was involved with the group. Three days after White's post, on New Year's Eve, Stephanie Grace, a local political columnist, led her column in the *Baton Rouge Advocate*: "This is what I remember about the first time I met Steve Scalise nearly 20 years ago: He told me he was like David Duke without the baggage."

Scalise was thrown back on his heels. At first, his staff declined to comment, saying that the blogger was making allegations about a speech a dozen years ago, a period of time when Scalise was operating with a single aide and for which he had no records. That line of thinking lasted about one day, as reporters and political operatives began to pick apart his legislative record, which included votes against establishing Martin Luther King Jr. Day. Scalise needed to do something to stem the bleeding, or his career was over.

So he moved to defuse the situation and released a statement saying he regretted the speech. "Twelve years ago, I spoke to many different Louisiana groups as a state representative, trying to build support for legislation that focused on cutting wasteful state spending, eliminating government corruption, and stopping tax hikes.

"One of the many groups that I spoke to regarding this critical legislation was a group whose views I wholeheartedly condemn. It was a mistake I regret, and I emphatically oppose the divisive racial and religious views groups like these hold. I am very disappointed that anyone would try to infer otherwise for political gain."

At the same time, Scalise began to work the phones. He called his colleagues, seeking to explain the incident and bolster his internal standing. Some Scalise allies whispered to reporters and other Republican elected officials that speaking to abhorrent Nazi-related groups was the cost of doing business in southern Louisiana.

If it weren't for Democratic representative Cedric Richmond, Scalise would've likely found himself out of Congress. Richmond, who is black, came to Scalise's immediate defense by saying that the Republican didn't have a racist bone in his body. The two had served together in the legislature in Baton Rouge, and that relationship—which continued to D.C.—gave Scalise the bipartisan cover he needed to keep his job.

Still, inside leadership, there were lingering concerns that Scalise, the number three Republican, would never recover. A man who palled around with Nazis couldn't raise the millions of dollars Republicans needed from tony enclaves like New York, Los Angeles, and San Francisco.

The allegations about McCarthy were far more sordid.

Rumors had circulated for years that McCarthy, who is married to his high school sweetheart, was carrying on an affair with Rep. Renee Ellmers, a married North Carolina Republican who was elected to the House in 2010. Ellmers and McCarthy were close, but McCarthy was close with everyone, so his buddy-buddy demeanor with her wasn't surprising. He told everyone who would listen that the rumors were not true.

Shortly after John Boehner announced he would retire from the speakership in 2015, McCarthy launched his bid for the party's top job. His aides, backed by a network of allies in the Capitol and on K Street, were so confident that he would prevail that they barely concealed their glee. McCarthy was hopeful he could split the votes of the conservative Freedom Caucus and waltz into the speakership.

He did not. McCarthy's fall wasn't only sordid, it was weird, painful, and hugely embarrassing.

It all started on September 29. McCarthy was intent on addressing some concerns on the right, enumerated by the Freedom Caucus, that he was a faux conservative who was too close to John Boehner and too willing to deal with Barack Obama. Sean Hannity of Fox News had been hammering him with text messages and e-mails to come on his show to speak to the GOP base. Frank Luntz, McCarthy's informal adviser who worked as a pricey pollster and message guru, was against McCarthy going on the program, but McCarthy did it anyway. He was confident, perhaps overly so. He thought he could win anyone over given the opportunity, and he had a few decades' worth of evidence that people were easily charmed by him. Surrounded by his security detail, McCarthy and Matt Sparks, the congressman's communications director, walked over to the cavernous Cannon House Office Building, where a camera waited that was dialed into Hannity's show in New York.

From beginning to end, the appearance was an abject disaster.

Hannity blamed McCarthy for funding Obamacare and "executive amnesty"—Obama's immigration policy. Then he scoffed when McCarthy said John Boehner deserved a B minus for his work as Speaker; Hannity thought he deserved a D minus.

"The question I think you really want to ask me is how am I going to be different," McCarthy said. "What are you going to see differently?"

"I love how you ask my questions," Hannity said with a smirk, seemingly annoyed, "but go ahead, that was one of my questions. Go right ahead."

"I knew you'd want to ask it," McCarthy said with a smile, clearly trying to charm Hannity's doubts away.

McCarthy continued, "What you're going to see is a conservative Speaker, that takes a conservative Congress, that puts a strategy to fight and win. And let me give you one example. Everybody thought Hillary Clinton was unbeatable, right? But we put together a Benghazi special committee—a select committee. What are her numbers today? Her numbers are dropping. Why? Because she's untrustable. But no one would've known any of that had happened had we not fought and made that happen."

"I agree, that's something good, I give you credit for that," Hannity said.

Very few other people gave McCarthy credit. Republicans had said for months that the 2016 presidential campaign had nothing to do with their party's investigation into Hillary Clinton. McCarthy had just explicitly tied them together. He knew immediately how badly he had screwed up. In fact, many believed that that was the beginning of the end for McCarthy's speakership hopes. The next morning Sparks, the McCarthy spokesman, was forced to issue a statement walking back the remark.

"The Select Committee on Benghazi has always been focused on getting the facts about the attacks on our diplomatic facilities in Libya that led to the death of four Americans. This was the right thing to do and the committee has worked judiciously and honestly," Sparks said. "These inquiries have nothing to do with politics and everything to do with the consequences of what the former Secretary has done and her confusing, conflicting, and demonstrably false responses."

McCarthy was losing support fast. Rep. Jason Chaffetz of Utah, who had just dropped out of the Speaker race, went on CNN and said the criticism of McCarthy was justified. On October 6 Hillary Clinton cut a campaign advertisement called "Admit," which put the McCarthy gaffe on screen once again and made him the centerpiece of what she saw as behavior from Republicans that was simply not on the level. It was a terrible look for McCarthy.

Republicans were turning against him, but there was no dissenter more hurtful to McCarthy than South Carolina representative Trey Gowdy. That same day Gowdy—McCarthy's close friend who was running the Benghazi probe—told the *Washington Post* that he had heard from McCarthy the next morning seeking to explain the remark, but Gowdy almost seemed too distressed to discuss the episode: "'Kevin is a friend, which makes the disappointment, frankly, even more bitter. If faith tells you to forgive somebody . . .' Gowdy trails off. 'It's tough,' he says after a moment."

All the while, McCarthy was fighting two other massive battles: one against the House Freedom Caucus, a skirmish he would come to know well, and another against the rumors he was having an affair with Renee Ellmers.

The Ellmers rumors quickly turned stranger than fiction. Two days before the internal election, Rep. Walter Jones, a genteel, elderly North Carolina Republican who inherited his House seat from his dad, sent a letter to the leadership asking that "any candidate for Speaker of the House, majority leader, and majority whip withdraw himself from the leadership election if there are any misdeeds he has committed since joining Congress that will embarrass himself, the Republican Conference, and the House of Representatives if they become public." Imagination wasn't needed to understand whom he was talking about.

The next day the House Freedom Caucus made its endorsement for Speaker: Rep. Daniel Webster, a Florida Republican who had served as Speaker of the House in Tallahassee. Webster didn't have a prayer to win, so it was a move designed especially to send a message to McCarthy. It wasn't deadly, since the caucus leaders made it clear that members could support McCarthy in the official floor vote, but it landed a blow.

Why was the Freedom Caucus—Jim Jordan, primarily—holding out its endorsement of McCarthy? A whole host of reasons. Its members thought the Fox News appearance was a disaster. Some of them believed the Ellmers rumors. Then there was a host of other issues: They wanted to get cash from the party's campaign committee without paying their own dues, they wanted prime committee slots, and they wanted McCarthy under their control. They wanted everything.

On October 8, when McCarthy walked into the cavernous Ways and Means Committee room, a large, high-ceilinged space adorned with columns and a massive chandelier, he knew he was doomed. The uncertainty, the lingering doubt about whether he could win, was consuming him. With the entire party sitting in the room, the Californian dropped his bid. McCarthy's chief Tim Berry, an imposing two-decade veteran of House Republican politics, told John Boehner that his boss was dropping out of the race.

Moments later McCarthy said the party needed a new look. "There's something to be said about a fresh face," he told *Politico* that day.

It was the most painful day in McCarthy's political life. He was forced to concede that the political career he had molded had been seriously interrupted. The charm could take him only so far. The smile, the backslapping, and the can-do demeanor were gone.

Moments after McCarthy dropped out, he walked through a sea of people, trailed by his wife, to a bank of microphones, where he tousled his trademark gray hair and started to explain.

CNN's Manu Raju asked if the Benghazi debacle had forced him aside. McCarthy responded with a smile, "Well, that wasn't helpful! . . . I could've said it much better." Mike DeBonis, a reporter with the *Washington Post,* asked about the alleged affair and the letter from Walter Jones. With his wife standing at his side, McCarthy shook his head, waved his hand, and said, "No," with an extended emphasis on the *o*.

"Can you just put a rest to this right now?" DeBonis asked.

"No, come on," McCarthy said.

If that wasn't enough, the next day Ellmers stood up in a closed party meeting and thanked her colleagues for their "prayers and support" as the rumors raged. It was such an obscenely stupid move that the entire room practically gasped. McCarthy's aides didn't even offer a comment on that one.

After McCarthy dropped out, his colleagues started calling, ensuring he'd stay on as majority leader. And Meadows came to his office and said he should reconsider running for Speaker. He politely declined. For House Republicans, it was a sign that McCarthy was not invincible.

ON SCALISE'S SECOND DAY in the hospital, he was barely alive. He was unresponsive. There was serious doubt that he would make it through another night. Jennifer, who had arrived in Washington by private jet, turned to Brett Horton and said, "Under no circumstances is anyone going to mention the word *retirement* to him.

"He likes this job," she said. "I'd be happy if he wanted to go home and be a UPS driver, but I know he's happiest doing this job. And I'm fine with him going back."

The next day was the baseball game the team had been practicing for when Scalise was shot. The team members arrived at Nationals Park—the stadium can be seen from the hallway off the House floor—to a heavy police presence, men with rifles or machine guns, and helicopters flying overhead. Amid the sadness, the pomp was overwhelming. David Bailey, one of the police officers on Scalise's detail who was injured in the shooting, threw out the opening pitch. Paul Ryan and Nancy Pelosi donned gear in honor of Scalise: Ryan a muscle-fit U.S. Capitol Police shirt and a Louisiana hat, and Pelosi a purple LSU T-shirt. CNN's Jake Tapper interviewed Ryan and Pelosi from Nationals Park.

"We're all close to Steve Scalise, he's a lovely person," Pelosi said, speaking of the man she'd sworn in nine years ago. She had had extraordinarily little interaction with Scalise since then, but this was Congress, where people tended to overstate their relationships. "Tonight we're all Team Scalise."

(Scalise didn't seem to think a ton of Pelosi's show of solidarity. During a closed New Orleans fund-raiser in August 2018—a few months before Election Day—he said, "It's not that we don't like Nancy Pelosi. She actually wore an LSU hat on that baseball game a year ago. I'm not sure what she felt about that or what LSU felt about it, but you know what? There is a difference. There's a difference between the approach we want to take to keep the American dream alive, and what they're approaching.")

An outpouring of support for Scalise came from around the world. Theresa May, the prime minister of the United Kingdom, Benjamin Netanyahu of Israel, and King Abdullah of Jordan all reached out. Barack Obama sent a handwritten note. George W. Bush called. Donald and Melania Trump visited with a bouquet of flowers on June 14.

Sean Hannity called several times. The first time, he reached Horton.

Hannity wanted to know how Scalise was. After a quick progress report, Hannity said, "Man, you'd be so proud of your president," before telling Horton that Trump had stayed on message and was discussing the importance of preserving the Second Amendment.

Just because Scalise was unresponsive did not mean that his life, professional or personal, was on hold. His phone was ringing off the hook. Jeff Flake showed up at the hospital with Scalise's phone and tried to hand it to Jennifer, who promptly gave it to Horton. Horton unlocked the phone at the end of each day and tasked a staff assistant with chronicling the incoming messages on a spreadsheet. Roughly nine thousand came in during the period in which Scalise was unable to tend to them. His staff alphabetized the incoming texts so he could review them when he was able.

Meanwhile Scalise became awake and alert but remained hanging between life and death. In his cognizant moments, he was wondering not whether he'd be able to return to Congress but whether he'd make it through the night. Still, in June, when Scalise's condition began improving, one of his first questions was about legislation on the House floor that would extend red snapper fishing season.

For a while, though, it was touch-and-go: Every time his condition took a proverbial step forward, he slid backward. There would be another infection, which would lead to another arduous, hours-long surgery. When Scalise would wake up after the procedure, he'd look around and think, "What just happened?" Once the cascade of surgeries stopped, he started to think about the long road ahead of him: learning to walk again and the next surgeries to stitch together his insides.

In the early stages of his recovery, the doctors worked judiciously to insulate Scalise from practically all outside stimuli. His mind and body were exhausted from the shooting and the hours upon hours he'd spent under the knife. They had orders: no cell phones, no iPads, and certainly no work. But Scalise didn't much care. He found himself stealing phones from visitors, his wife, his Capitol Police detail, and his friends.

But when Jennifer took their children back to New Orleans after a summer in Washington, Scalise placed a phone call to Horton from the hospital with pretty blunt instructions.

"I know you know where my phone is," he said. "I'm fifty-one years old. Bring me my phone."

Within an hour, Horton was at MedStar Washington Hospital Center with Scalise's iPhone. Scalise's first text was to Jennifer, and it said, "Surprise!" with a bunch of smiley face emojis. Jennifer was not amused.

All told, Scalise was in the hospital complex for three and a half months. He went absolutely stir crazy.

But on September 28, a skinnier and grayer Steve Scalise returned to the House floor—the place he had been dreaming about his whole adult life. He had a purple scooter decked out in LSU gear, and two canes to keep him stabilized when he walked. His shoes were adorned with rubber edging to make sure he didn't slip when he took steps.

Scalise entered the chamber from the Speaker's lobby, a long hallway behind the floor where he was known to dish to reporters. He had on a dark suit and a red tie, with a look of amazement on his face. Horton walked behind him, and the chamber's sergeant at arms in front of him. The room was deafeningly loud with cheers.

He slowly ascended to the whip's table—the podium from which he would speak—and standing there waiting for him were Kevin McCarthy and Cedric Richmond, the Republican and Democrat with whom he was inextricably linked. McCarthy put his hand on Scalise's shoulder, opened his notes, and pulled the microphone up to Scalise's mouth. In the gallery watching was Jennifer, standing not far from where she had been the day her husband was sworn in as a member of Congress just nine years before.

Paul Ryan banged the gavel, McCarthy motioned for everyone to sit down, and the room grew quiet.

"The chair wishes to mark the return to the chamber of our dear friend and colleague from Louisiana, Mr. Steve Scalise," Ryan said. The room erupted once again.

"Our prayers have been answered," Ryan said, choking back tears. "His bravery and his family's strength have been such an inspiration to this House and to the people it serves. America is grateful for this moment. The chair now proudly asks: For what purpose does the gentleman from Louisiana seek recognition?"

"To speak out of order, Mr. Speaker," Scalise said with a chuckle.

"The gentleman is recognized for as much time as he may consume," Ryan said.

"Wow, thank you Mr. Speaker," Scalise said. "You have no idea how great this feels to be back here at work in the people's House.

"As you can imagine, these last three and a half months have been pretty challenging times for me and my family," he went on. "But if you look at the outpouring of love, of warmth, of prayer, my gosh, Jennifer and I have been overwhelmed with all that outpouring. It's given us the strength to get through all this and to get to this point today."

Scalise had made it. He was back. He had no fear. And that newfound swagger and confidence augured a new phase in his relationship with McCarthy, planting the seeds of a battle that would roil the Republican leadership right up to the next election.

7

"THREE, THREE, THREE"

CONGRESS OFTEN TAKES ON the cadence, tone, and tenor of a soap opera. Steny Hoyer feuded with Nancy Pelosi for decades. Jim Jordan never liked Kevin McCarthy. Ben Sasse and Jeff Flake were at constant war with Donald Trump. Dozens of miniplots are playing out at any given time. But periodically the major players get engaged in a high-wire act that ends up setting in motion a series of events that define a party and the course of the country.

That's what happened over the summer and fall of 2017. Trump, Chuck Schumer, and Nancy Pelosi cut a deal in front of Paul Ryan and Mitch McConnell that, in the long run, sent the Republican and Democratic parties into a tailspin. It was a deal that Republicans uniformly despised. It was an accord essentially designed to screw the GOP, a legislative package that led to months of brawling over the nation's immigration laws. It was the beginning of Congress slowly kicking the can down the road when it came to the federal budget. It prevented Donald Trump from getting his wall along the southern border with Mexico. It led to a migrant crisis, with children being torn from their parents' arms, that made the United States resemble a third-world country. And it was the beginning of a long chain of events that led to the December 2018 brawl over Trump's border wall.

But at the time, Nancy Pelosi and Donald Trump were busy celebrating. After months of mostly negative dealings with Paul Ryan and Mitch McConnell—the two men who blew his best chance to repeal Obamacare—the president cut a quick and clean deal to lift the nation's debt cap and avoid a government shutdown, all while providing piles of cash for hurricane-stricken Texas. It was something Trump hadn't experienced in his eight months in office: success.

Republicans on Capitol Hill felt differently. "Trump. So bad at this," one senior Republican aide texted just moments after the deal was cut. "I can't even type it. . . . He just folded to the Dems. . . . [He] just gave us a bat to beat us over the head with. . . . I'm just here banging my head against my desk."

In September 2017 Trump was reminded, perhaps momentarily, of a dynamic that Republicans had long feared: He had no problem cutting deals with Democrats, namely Nancy Pelosi and Chuck Schumer. Chuck and Nancy, as he called them. Like them, Trump was born on the East Coast, and for years the trio had moved comfortably together in wealthy enclaves like New York, Palm Beach, Washington, and Los Angeles. They rubbed shoulders with the same people, sharing similar experiences in the rarefied upper echelons of America's political-finance-media axis.

Back in Washington, though, Trump was using Schumer and Pelosi to write his own Hollywood-like script with himself as the star: the Republican president who ditched his own party and, theoretically, for the good of the country cut a massive deal with Democrats. Suddenly some Democrats were saying that maybe Donald Trump wasn't as bad as they thought he would be. After the deal, Schumer and Pelosi released a statement saying they "look[ed] forward to working together on the many issues before us." How about that!

The incentives were clear. Trump was looking for a quick and easy end to a government funding fight, and a bit of flair that would come with cutting a deal with Democrats. Some in Trump's orbit figured Republicans would come to the president's side quicker if they knew he would ditch them for the minority. Democrats figured they could force Donald Trump into a large-scale immigration deal.

All sides were sorely mistaken.

. . .

THROUGHOUT RECENT AMERICAN HISTORY, Congress has thought it wise to knowingly set itself up for a crisis. Think of it like this: Imagine if, for some reason, you purposely set up a date on which all your household appliances would break down and need to be fixed, on the assumption that fixing them all at once would somehow be easier. Congress does this all the time.

A great example was on display between 2010 and 2012, in the rolling train wreck of a crisis known as the fiscal cliff. The insanity started at the end of 2010, when income tax rates were about to go up on every single American on New Year's Day. Congress decided to extend the tax breaks until the end of 2012. Yet on the same date that the tax cuts were now set to expire—December 31, 2012—automatic steep spending cuts were also slated to slash government spending by billions of dollars. Unemployment benefits were set to run out. Congress had piled a bunch of deadlines together, hoping that some sort of large-scale deal would be cut to avert disaster. That's almost never how it went.

"America wonders why it is that in this town, for some reason, why you can't get stuff done in an organized timetable. Why everything always has to wait until the last minute. We're now at the last minute," Barack Obama said at the White House on December 28, which, as he observed correctly, was indeed the last minute. "The American people are not going to have any patience for a politically self-inflicted wound to our economy. Not right now."

Congress stopped just short of going fully over the fiscal cliff when it cleared a bill on New Year's Day. What followed was five years of lunging from one legislative crisis to the next, plunging congressional approval ratings to new lows and making the legislative branch of the U.S. government look like a banana republic.

The latest crisis greeted Chuck Schumer, Nancy Pelosi, Paul Ryan, and Mitch McConnell when they returned in the fall of 2017 from a month-long summer break. A two-headed legislative Medusa was rearing its head: The nation's debt limit needed to be lifted, and the government needed to be funded by the end of September. Kept separately, each item would prove a heavy lift for the Republican Congress, which would have to weather defections from conservatives on raising the debt limit and fend off others who would hold up the funding bill in an attempt to use it as a cash grab bag for a variety of political issues: defunding Obamacare, raising military spending, and cutting funding for Planned Parenthood. Put together, the two problems could be deadly. A government shutdown combined with a crisis over the nation's borrowing limit would send shock waves through the global economy. Added to that, Houston, the nation's fifth-largest metropolis, was practically underwater, reeling from a historic storm days earlier that analysts said could set the city back a decade. The cleanup would require Congress to authorize a big pile of cash.

For years, funding the government had been a partisan battle. In the mid-1990s, Newt Gingrich's Republican House had shut down the government after a series of policy and personality differences with Bill Clinton. In 2013 John Boehner's House shut it down after Barack Obama refused to strip funding from Obamacare, the president's top legislative achievement. Broadly speaking, government shutdowns could be damaging in the short term. Agencies would shut down. Federal workers might get furloughed. The stock market often dipped. But in the long run, the party in power was typically spared the blowback. In 2014, a year after the shutdown, Republicans gained thirteen seats in the House and won the majority in the Senate.

Toying with the debt limit, though, was far more potent. The mechanism was created in 1939 as a safety valve, a way to keep members of Congress honest about accruing more federal debt. For years, Congress had routinely raised the limit, and the president signed it. Lawmakers of all stripes saw it as a vote necessary to allow the largest and most robust economy on earth to pay its bills. In the last decade, though, the vote had become toxic. Both parties branded it as a reckless stamp of approval on a profligate legislature that spent with no regard for the nation's ballooning debts and deficits.

During the 2000s, politicians proved to be somewhat flexible on the topic, but the Tea Party class of 2010 was far more rigid. Its candidates ran campaigns almost entirely focused on the ballooning national debt, and they vowed endlessly on the campaign trail to come to Washington to clean up a budget awash in red ink. In 2011, recognizing the political winds that had blown him into the speakership, John Boehner said he would demand that Obama cut a dollar for every dollar that the debt limit was lifted. But taking a strong stance had real risks: If Congress couldn't lift the debt limit, the country couldn't pay its existing obligations, and credit agencies might downgrade the nation's creditworthiness.

Since 2011 the GOP majority had slowly retreated from its hard-line position, which brought Congress to the political pickle in which it found itself in 2017. For the entirety of the Obama administration, congressional Republicans had leveraged these issues to extract policy concessions from the Democrat in the White House. Now that the Republicans controlled both the executive and the legislative branches, this should've mooted the issue; the problem was that Republicans, especially in the House, wouldn't be able to lift the debt limit or fund the government without Democratic votes. Pelosi and Schumer would be called on to save Republicans from themselves, and what would they get in return? Nada.

The one unknowable? The president. No one knew how Trump would act in a situation like this.

THE WHITE HOUSE UNDERSTOOD the situation was dire and that it would need help from Democrats come September. Marc Short, the president's legislative affairs director, invited the top four Democratic aides in Washington to the White House during Memorial Day week for a chat. Nadeam Elshami from Pelosi's office got the invitation, as did Alexis Covey-Brandt, Steny Hoyer's top aide; Mike Lynch from Chuck Schumer's office; and Illinois senator Dick Durbin's top aide, Pat Souders. For these Democrats—deep in the minority, still recoiling from Trump's election—going to the White House was not a fun prospect, especially during the Memorial Day recess, when the great weather sent most of D.C. outside to hit the links or congregate at patio bars. But

Short, the president's top Capitol Hill liaison, wanted to chat, and when the White House calls, you answer, even if you're in the minority.

The gathering turned out to be completely unremarkable. The White House wanted cooperation from both parties when it came to important items like raising the debt ceiling and funding the government, Short said. Keep the lines of communication open, he implored. It was the kind of reach-across-the-aisle crap that sounded good on *The West Wing* but never worked in reality.

When the chiefs of staff got into an Uber to head back to the Capitol, Lynch—Schumer's chief of staff—urged everyone to keep their powder dry when talking about the debt limit. Lynch was trying to get his colleagues to understand that, just as Republicans had for years, they might get some concession for their votes. In response, Covey-Brandt gently reminded the group that more than a hundred Democrats had asked for a clean debt limit—one without policy provisions attached.

But Lynch was right: Republicans' weakness had opened a window for Democrats. And during a series of conversations in late July and early August, Pelosi and Schumer began considering the kind of hostage taking they had claimed to abhor during the Obama administration: extracting concessions in exchange for their votes on the debt limit. They figured they would have the most leverage if they forced Republicans to pass a short-term debt ceiling bill until the end of the year, when members of Congress are desperate to flee the capital for the holidays and are thus more willing to compromise.

Republicans, meanwhile, were planning a government-funding bill that would keep the government open until December, and legislation to raise the debt cap until after the 2018 election. Schumer and Pelosi calculated that if they could get both deadlines—for the debt limit and government funding—set to the end of the year, it would create such a legislative inflection point that the White House would have no choice but to give in to a large-scale immigration deal—something Pelosi's troops were eager for.

Getting all the Democrats on board would not be a cinch. Steny Hoyer, Pelosi's number two and her frequent adversary, was staunchly opposed to asking for concessions when it came to passing the debt ceiling. He abhorred gamesmanship with something so important. Still, Schumer stayed in constant contact with him, urging him to refrain from public proclamations that Democrats would help Republicans lift the debt limit. Hoyer didn't necessarily agree with the strategy, but he made it clear that he wouldn't stand in the way.

In the middle of August, Elshami, Pelosi's short and sharp chief of staff, sent the House Democratic leader a memo detailing a series of conversations Pelosi had had with Schumer about government funding and the debt limit. "'MEMORANDUM TO THE LEADER.' Thursday, August 17, 2017 (3:30 P.M. Eastern time)" read the headline of the memo. In an era of capitalized, breathless tweets, acidic back-and-forths on cable news, and seemingly endless high-wire drama, the memo's title was understated. Yet it laid out Pelosi's options for battle against the new Republican president.

The first option was an eighteen-month debt limit increase with no other policies attached. It was a method favored by House and Senate Republicans, who did not want to vote on the borrowing limit more than once before the 2018 midterm elections. But it would mean Democrats were bailing out Republicans without getting anything in return.

Option two: Twin a debt-limit increase with a short-term government funding bill, and set both deadlines to December—creating a year-end leverage point. It was well known that the president wanted to end Deferred Action for Childhood Arrivals (DACA), an Obama-era program that prevented the government from extraditing people who had been brought to the United States illegally as children. Even more immediate were a set of upcoming court cases that would decide whether the government could continue deferring extradition. Pelosi and Schumer were under intense pressure from their colleagues to strike some sort of accord with the president on immigration before the cases were decided. If they set up another legislative deadline in December, they thought they could use it to get an immigration deal.

There were two more convoluted options, neither of which got much attention. Option three was that Democrats would lift the debt cap in exchange for Republicans dropping a plan to pass tax reform with only GOP votes.

"Schumer stated his 'moderates' are apt to support option 2 (two)," Elshami wrote to Pelosi. "But there is some support for option 3 (three)."

Those pesky moderates. Option number two it was. The Democrats would go into the White House armed with a unified strategy.

On September 3, the Sunday of Labor Day weekend, Pelosi and Schumer issued a rare joint statement that set the stage for their standoff without giving away their hand: "Providing aid in the wake of Harvey and raising the debt ceiling are both important issues, and Democrats want to work to do both. Given the interplay between all the issues Congress must tackle in September, Democrats and Republicans must discuss all the issues together and come up with a bipartisan consensus."

Both leaders were attuned to the political realities in Washington: Democrats had mostly been observers during the eight months of Donald Trump's presidency. But that wasn't necessarily a bad thing. Schumer was still getting accustomed to leading Senate Democrats, learning how to thread the needle between his fiery left and the vocal center. Pelosi, meanwhile, needed time to regain favor with her restless troops. The rank and file was frustrated from being in the political wilderness, and Pelosi was still being squeezed by young House Democrats looking for a change in the ranks.

But Republicans weren't exactly in fighting shape, either. They were slipping in polls. They could use a win as proof of governance. The NRCC and the AAN, the cash-rich campaign machines that made the party hum, warned Republican leaders that if they didn't pass tax reform later that fall, they would eventually lose their majority in a spectacular fashion.

Lending a hand and providing some votes could put Schumer and Pelosi back in the game.

ON SEPTEMBER 5 CONGRESS RETURNED from the month-long August recess. Racial tensions were at a high after a summer that saw the deadly

Unite the Right rally in Charlottesville, Virginia. The president's staff was split, with Jewish advisers like Gary Cohn deeply uncomfortable with the president's response to the violence. The president was warring with Mitch McConnell about the Kentuckian's inability to replace Obamacare. Houston was practically underwater, and the state of Texas needed billions of dollars in aid. No one had a damn clue how Washington would avert a government shutdown and raise the debt ceiling. Trump called congressional leaders to the White House the following day to kick off his negotiations with them.

As he did at the beginning of every week, Elshami took a right on his way out of his office in the Capitol and headed to the House Speaker's suite to meet with Jonathan Burks, Paul Ryan's chief of staff. Elshami was familiar with the space: Ryan's office was in the same spot Pelosi's was when she was Speaker, just off the Capitol rotunda, in the geographical center of Washington.

Burks told Elshami that House Republicans would pass a bill with a bunch of money to help fix Houston. The Senate would then load it up with the unpopular lifting of the debt limit and a short-term government funding bill. Then they'd send it back to the House and dare them to vote against the package. A chamber with twenty-five Republicans from Texas was unlikely to turn its back on the Lone Star State, even if it meant lifting the debt ceiling. Finally the bill would be on its way to Trump's desk. The assumption in all this was that the Democrats would play ball and not put up much of a fuss. Republicans were counting on the idea that the Democrats would follow the traditional Washington playbook, and they believed the Hurricane Harvey aid package—desperately needed by FEMA, which was on the brink of being unable to pay out claims—would seal the deal.

"Okay," Elshami said, knowing he had another plan in mind.

Even as GOP leaders thought they had the Democrats in line, not everything was going according to plan in their own party. House conservatives were furious that the party had embraced a plan to lift the debt limit without corresponding budget cuts. The GOP leadership was hoping the president would embrace their plan and help them get the right wing on board so they could get it through Congress and claim a legislative victory. Until that happened, though, it remained unlikely that the Republicans would have enough votes on their own to pass anything.

As if the negotiations weren't fraught enough, by four P.M. that day, Trump had announced that he would repeal DACA, effective March 2018. The president wanted to give Congress a six-month window to pass legislation that would replace the program, which allowed people who came to the United States illegally, mostly as children, to avoid deportation. Ending it was like the president driving a stake through the hearts of Democrats while pleasing his voting base, which largely supported restrictive immigration policies.

The repeal lit a fire under Democrats, especially with a fast-approaching government funding fight. That same day, September 5, top Democrats gathered in Schumer's office suite, just around the corner from the Senate floor. In the huddle were the most powerful elected Democrats in the country: Reps. Pelosi and Hoyer, Jim Clyburn of South Carolina, and Joe Crowley of New York; and Sens. Schumer and Durbin. Crowley and Clyburn represented different poles of the caucus: Clyburn, the black caucus, which was a powerful bloc, and Crowley the new guard, which had started looking to him as the next leader. Sen. Chris Van Hollen from Maryland, a former deputy to Pelosi in the House, was also in attendance. He now chaired the Democratic Senatorial Campaign Committee (DSCC), the party's reelection arm for the Senate.

Schumer had worked quietly over the August recess to get everyone on board with the hostage taking, dialing colleagues from Washington, New York, and even Italy, where he vacationed with his family. Now in his office, he opened things up by telling the group that the White House had floated a deal that would lift the debt limit until the end of Trump's presidency, which was a nonstarter for Democrats. Congressional Republicans were pushing for eighteen months, putting the next vote after the midterm elections. As Republicans struggled to coalesce around any plan, it was clear that the two sides would not have the time to cobble together a yearlong spending deal and debt limit accord. So Pelosi and Schumer used the meeting with their team to float only an immediate three-month debt-limit extension, leaving the government-funding fight to the end of the month. Despite Trump's decision to end DACA that afternoon, they would not push for an immigration accord as part of this deadline. Better, Pelosi and Schumer thought, to take the next three months to pull together a plan so they could maximize the gains from their leverage.

Some in the leadership were a bit skeptical, including Crowley, the newest member of the inner circle. Hoyer wanted to push Trump for an immigration deal now, as did Durbin, who was one of the Senate's champions of DACA. Van Hollen, however, backed Schumer and Pelosi.

Schumer and Pelosi issued a statement just before they went to the White House to meet with the president: "Democrats are prepared to offer our votes for the Harvey aid package, and a short term debt limit increase of three months. Given Republican difficulty in finding the votes for their plan, we believe this proposal offers a bipartisan path forward to ensure prompt delivery of Harvey aid as well as avoiding a default, while both sides work together to address government funding, DREAMers, and health care."

DURING TIMES OF LEGISLATIVE upheaval, it's common for the president to call the congressional leadership to the White House. Often these meetings are staid affairs, big-time photo opportunities before the two sides go into their corners.

That's what Republicans expected on September 6, when they were scheduled to head to the White House with Democratic leaders. Republican leaders spoke to White House aides before the meeting and were assured the president would agree to their plan. The Republicans expected that Trump's support of the package would help them get the votes they needed from conservatives. This short-term fix would give them time to cobble together a large spending package that, among other things, would lift spending caps and allow for Trump's wall.

This meeting, they thought, was a mere formality. Steven Mnuchin, the treasury secretary; Marc Short, the legislative affairs director; and Mick Mulvaney, the president's budget director, huddled with Trump in the Oval Office before the meeting. White House aides assured Ryan's and McCarthy's staffs that the president would be supportive.

McCarthy was the first lawmaker to enter into the Oval Office for the meeting that day. "Hey, Kevin, what's up?" the president said. The Californian had a special status with the president, who often called the majority leader "my Kevin."

After Pelosi walked in the door, Trump said, "I've gotta get Ivanka." When Ivanka eventually entered the room in the middle of the discussion, Trump said, "You know my daughter Ivanka. She's like a Democrat."

When everyone was gathered, Ryan, McConnell, and Mnuchin put forth their plan: debt ceiling extended past the 2018 election, government funding until December. Everyone agreed on the contours of the hurricane relief legislation, the first of many aid packages Congress would have to pass in Trump's first two years.

But Schumer, holding a folder, his glasses perched on his nose, said no: The most Democrats would go for was a three-month debt-limit increase, something Republicans were staunchly opposed to.

Mnuchin—whom the leaders saw as a bit of a lightweight when it came to politics—interjected, saying that the markets expected a debt limit into 2019.

"The markets expect a debt limit that happens to extend just past the midterm elections?" Schumer asked rhetorically. "I doubt it."

Pelosi and Schumer kept telling Ryan, McConnell, and Trump that they were welcome to pass whatever they wanted, as long as they could do it without Democrats.

Ryan and the other Republicans kept pushing for a longer debt-limit lift. Pelosi kept interjecting, "Do you have the votes, do you have the votes to pass it? If you don't need us, just do it." The longer this went on, the more an uncomfortable reality filled the air. Democrats were right: with conservatives still on the fence, Republicans needed Democrats to keep the government functioning.

Suddenly Trump had heard enough. He liked the Pelosi and Schumer offer—and agreed to it quickly.

"Let's just do that," he said. "Three, three, three." Never mind that there were only two threes: a three-month extension of the debt limit and a corresponding three months of government funding.

The Republicans couldn't believe what was happening. They had walked into the meeting with assurances that the president would side with them, and instead he sided with Pelosi and Schumer in front of their faces, allowing the Democrats to lump the debt-limit and government-funding deadlines together in December. It was an instant disaster, one that would give the minority party huge leverage in Washington and show that the president wasn't fully on the same page as his congressional cohorts.

The Republicans scrambled. Ryan tried to convince the president that the deal he had accepted was no good. But Trump would not listen. Mnuchin piped up again, trying to sway Trump to push for a longer debt-limit increase. Trump told him to quiet down, saying he was risking tanking the deal with the Democrats.

As Trump was scooting away from his treasury secretary, his closeness with Schumer was clearly evident in their conversation. Schumer tried to remind Trump that working people were part of his family's DNA.

"My wife's parents lived in Trump Village," Schumer mused, referring to the Coney Island housing development built by Trump's father, Fred, in the mid-1960s. "You guys built it for the middle class—cab drivers, seamstresses. When Fred would come down in his black Cadillac, 'FT' on his license plate, they'd say 'There goes Fred Trump.'"

The back-and-forth was unmistakably comfortable. Trump asked Schumer if he remembered when he hosted a Democratic fund-raiser for him at Mar-a-Lago, which the president said raised $1 million for the party. Schumer reminded him it only raised him $270,000. Trump said that he was Schumer's first donor. Schumer said that wasn't true. But it was all playful.

Republicans sat there, slack-jawed.

At the end of the meeting, Trump told Schumer he wanted to work with him on legislation relating to China's alleged currency manipulation, a longtime Schumer hobbyhorse.

"We'll do something on China," Trump said in Schumer's direction.

"Not without me," Pelosi chimed in. "I know more about China than everyone in this room."

Marine One had already landed on the South Lawn, waiting to carry Trump to Andrews Air Force Base and on to North Dakota, where he was scheduled to host a rally focused on tax reform alongside Democratic senator Heidi Heitkamp. Trump pulled Schumer near the door, seemingly aware that photographers were outside waiting for the president to emerge from the Oval Office. He wanted the photo, Schumer and Trump, New Yorkers, ignoring party labels to get things done for the country.

Ryan and McConnell were confused and frustrated, but once the initial shock wore off, they knew they shouldn't be surprised. It wasn't the first time the president had ignored their counsel. They did wonder, however, how the president's aides so badly misjudged his thinking. Ryan told Trump he took Schumer's bait by accepting the deal.

As Schumer returned triumphant to the Capitol, he quickly prepared for a press conference to announce the Democrats' victory. McConnell, meanwhile, was whisked up the elevator in the Capitol surrounded by Capitol Police. When told by staff of Schumer's plan to hold a press conference, he responded, "He should. He got everything he wanted."

Pelosi returned to her office on the second floor of the Capitol and was shell-shocked. "They capitulated," she said to a group of aides, including Elshami. "They took everything we asked for."

EARLY ON IN DONALD Trump's presidency, his White House had some difficulties reaching Nancy Pelosi. Trump officials like OMB director Mick Mulvaney would buzz her iPhone, but no one picked up. It was a bad strategy. The phone was usually buried deep inside her purse.

The best plan, they soon learned, was to call the office. And on that Friday morning, the day after the White House sit-down, that's exactly what the president of the United States did. He was jubilant about the deal he had just cut and seemingly pleased he had ditched his own party.

"Hey, Nance," Trump said to Pelosi on a private phone call. "It was great to be with you yesterday. You and Chuck are getting rave reviews. Me? I'm okay. Your two friends?" he said, referring to Paul Ryan and Mitch McConnell. "Not so good. The country needed a dose of this."

Trump was, for the moment, being heralded as bipartisan and unafraid to split with his party. His deal with Democrats was good for the country, he told reporters. Why? It was not clear. It merely set up another deadline a few months away. In fact, there was no argument to be made that the deal was good at all, beyond the surprise of its bipartisanship. But when Trump called Pelosi on her office phone, it seemed as if he had found a new partner.

Pelosi told the president the meeting was "useful" and said she appreciated his praise. Their conversation was more than cordial, it was collegial, almost as if Trump were willing to govern exclusively with Democrats.

Pelosi sensed the conversation was going well, that she had a moment with the president in which she might make some headway. She told Trump there was some concern about whether he would begin deporting DACA recipients immediately, bypassing the six-month window he gave Congress to get a deal.

"If you could put something out, when I say six months, I meant six months," Pelosi said to the president, trying to urge the Republican president to use the levers of power he had at his disposal to clear up a misunderstanding.

"I'll take care of it," Trump said.

Pelosi said she wanted the president to make clear that he wasn't aiming to split up families—a big fear of Democrats. "Don't do that," Pelosi said. "We don't want to scare people."

"I agree with that," Trump said.

Pelosi then raised the specter of passing the DREAM Act, legislation that would give legal status to young immigrants who came to the United States illegally through no fault of their own. She was testing the waters, using the moment to try to see what she might be able to get out of this president. Trump seemed game. "I'd love to do it," he said, seemingly unaware of his party's resistance to the legislation. "I'd love to do it quickly. Why should we wait six months? I'm okay—let's make a fast deal. Border security. The drugs are a big issue."

"I agree," Pelosi said, also noting that the Coast Guard has a role in keeping drugs from being transported into the United States. "We all want to protect the border." But Pelosi said Democrats would not accept an increase in interior enforcement or a wall.

"There are some conservative Republicans that will vote for this," Trump said of the DREAM Act. "But let's do it soon because people will forget what DACA is six months from now.

"We'll see you soon," Trump concluded, before adding a quick line to address Democrats' concerns about young immigrants being deported: "We'll get something done on social media."

PAUL RYAN, MCCONNELL, SCHUMER, and Pelosi may have all seen the deal as a win for the Democrats, but within the Democratic Party that was not the universal view. It was a particularly perilous time for Pelosi and Schumer to cut any deal with Trump. Internal Democratic polling showed that the party's base opposed almost all cooperation with the Republican president, and Pelosi's internal capital among House Democrats was already low. Many continued to question whether she could ever lead them out of the minority.

That was clear in a closed Democratic Party whip meeting the day after the deal was cut, just a short while after Pelosi's call with Trump. It was Steny Hoyer's meeting, but Pelosi called him that morning and asked him if she could bring Schumer and Dick Durbin to speak at the gathering. Pelosi wanted Schumer's help in sealing the debt-limit deal with House Democrats, and she knew Durbin's presence would help calm lawmakers like Reps. Luis Gutiérrez of Illinois and Raúl Grijalva of Arizona, who were fuming over the leaders' decision to move forward without forcing an immediate vote on the repeal of DACA.

Aside from Hoyer, Gutiérrez was Pelosi's biggest problem. The

Congressional Hispanic Caucus—which was anchored around the ideology of the fiery Chicago-area congressman—thought, with good reason, that Pelosi had just given up the store. A day earlier at a larger gathering of Democrats, Gutiérrez had gotten a standing ovation after giving an impassioned speech arguing that now was the time for Democrats to force the issue on DACA, that the party should draw a line in the sand. Hoyer had backed Gutiérrez in that meeting, suggesting that Democrats should withhold their votes on the short-term funding bill if there wasn't a clear path forward on DACA.

But there was no relief for DREAMers in this Pelosi-Schumer-Trump deal, and nothing real in sight but the possibility of a leverage point in December. Gutiérrez told friends and colleagues that he wished Pelosi would give him a heads-up before she sailed them down the river.

"You have to tie the DREAMers to one, the debt ceiling and/or the budget," Gutiérrez later reflected. "This is an opportune moment for us to ask for something since the Republican majority does not behave as a majority when it comes to the debt ceiling."

So the tension in the room at this whip meeting was palpable. But among the leaders, it was all laughs and smiles. They thought they had outfoxed Trump.

"Nancy, when you wear that green dress you always get us good luck," Schumer bellowed, in his good-natured, old-man humor, speaking of the outfit Pelosi wore to the White House meeting. "Don't throw away that dress."

Pelosi, meanwhile, said the entire leadership team was on the same page. But the friction between her and Hoyer briefly bubbled up to the surface.

"We were all in agreement. Well, most of us," Pelosi said pointedly, looking at Hoyer out of the corner of her eye.

THE HOUSE REPUBLICAN leadership was confused and a bit dejected, but they felt confident they would be able to pass the deal that Trump cut with Democrats. They had little choice: The leader of their party cut this deal, and Paul Ryan had to bring it to the floor. Though they expected some Republican defectors, they thought some Democrats would join them to squeeze it through. But they didn't own the deal—the Trump administration and Democrats did. McConnell even called the agreement the president's deal. So with the House conservatives restless and their votes not totally assured, Steven Mnuchin and Mick Mulvaney were forced to come up to Capitol Hill to defend it.

The White House aides arrived by motorcade and headed down the center steps of the Capitol. They walked down the carpeted hallway, still adorned with some of the bunting from Inauguration Day, and hooked a right into HC-5, the plain, soundproofed conference room where House Republicans hold their twice-weekly strategy meetings.

The mood was tense from the beginning. Mnuchin made a personal plea: Pass the bill "for me." The room grunted. Why would they do anything for Mnuchin, a former Hillary Clinton–donating Democrat whom they hardly knew?

Soon the lawmakers started to lace into the treasury secretary. Rep. Tim Walberg, a mild-mannered Michigander who typically had little to say, said the president needed to work with Republicans, not Democrats.

"Is it true you have forty-two open deputy director positions over there at OMB?" Darrell Issa of California asked Mulvaney.

"No, actually, I just have one opening," Mulvaney replied.

"That's too bad, because if we could send forty-two of our conference over they could become just like you," Issa replied. It was a withering shot at Mulvaney's swift ideological shift since joining the administration. Attendees noticed that Mulvaney turned bright red.

Rep. Joe Barton, a conservative, potbellied Texas Republican who was first elected in 1984, asked Mulvaney if the administration would commit to a deficit-reduction package when government funding expired in December.

"I don't know the answer to that," Mulvaney said. The room booed loudly.

Trying to get them back, Mnuchin told the lawmakers that the best way to address the deficit was to grow the economy. But this tack was a mistake: Spouting talking points to a roomful of politicians was the mark of a true political amateur. With the hostility unabated, Mnuchin ducked out with roughly a dozen lawmakers waiting to speak, telling the packed crowd he had other commitments.

After Mnuchin was gone, Rep. Lee Zeldin, a New York Republican who represented the red reaches of Long Island all the way to the Hamptons, was still angry.

"When the president undermines our unanimously elected Speaker, it pisses everyone in this room off," Zeldin said to very loud cheers.

THE VOTE IN THE House was September 8, a mere two days after the Oval Office deal, and perhaps surprisingly, given the rancor, there was a certain lightness on the floor. Kevin McCarthy, with a bit of a pep in his step, popped a breath strip into his mouth while walking down the center aisle. Rep. Rodney Frelinghuysen, the House Appropriations chairman, whose father and great-great-grandfather had been in Congress, was casually chatting in the front of the chamber with Rep. Hal Rogers, the gray-haired Kentucky Republican who held the spending gavel before him. Rep. Dave Brat, the Virginia Republican who toppled Eric Cantor in 2014, ran down the center of the House floor to cast his no vote on the package by hand.

Three hundred and sixteen members of the House voted for the deal, and ninety voted against it. Not a single Democrat voted no.

Pelosi was radiant. It was her and Schumer's moment. They were back. She laughed with Rep. Zoe Lofgren, her California Democratic colleague and ally. She chatted with Reps. Hakeem Jeffries, Gregory Meeks, and Joe Crowley, all New York Democrats. Crowley told her his prediction that, within days, Trump would try to cut a deal on the so-called DREAMers, the young immigrants who were brought into the country illegally by their parents.

Pelosi wheeled around the floor with a white slip of paper in her hand: the list of how each lawmaker had voted. She told everyone she encountered that Republicans needed Democrats to get anything done on the House floor.

Eventually she turned around and found Steny Hoyer, who had been skeptical of her dealing all along. "Steny, this is just brilliant," she said, detailing how this deal would help her notch another accord with Trump to save children who were in the country illegally. Hoyer listened. He was still very skeptical.

JOE CROWLEY'S PREDICTION WAS right, and Donald Trump was true to his word: the president was going to move quickly to try to strike an immigration accord with Democrats. On September 13—the week after the president cut a deal with Democrats to keep the government open and lift the debt limit—Trump hosted Schumer and Pelosi at the White House for Chinese food and a discussion about the country's immigrant policies. The food was a nod to one of the areas of agreement between the Republican president and top Democrats: that the U.S. needed to rein in China. The White House chef prepared crispy honey-sesame-glazed beef with sticky rice, and a chocolate cream pie for dessert.

They sat at a rectangular table in the Blue Room; the president at the head, flanked by Pelosi on the right and Schumer on the left. The meeting participants were all men except Pelosi. Trump brought John Kelly, Gary Cohn, Mulvaney, Mnuchin, and Marc Short. Pelosi brought Dick Meltzer, her policy director, and Schumer brought Mike Lynch, his chief of staff.

After half an hour's discussion on China, the conversation turned to immigration. Schumer laid out what he saw as the Democratic position: eight hundred thousand DREAMers needed to be given legal status, and then Democrats would accede to a border security package that could include technological upgrades, rebuilding roads, and more money for security. Under no circumstance would Democrats agree to fund a new physical wall on the southern border. Schumer and Pelosi made that point clear: The president's wall was a nonstarter.

"What's in it for me?" the president asked the group. It was as if the president fully understood that he was risking selling out his base by making a deal but wanted to know exactly what he was getting in exchange. Schumer quickly explained to Trump that he had disappointed Democrats on many fronts. He was threatening to pull out of the Iran accord, he had pulled out of the Paris climate agreement, and he had taken a hard line on just about every issue under the sun. Schumer thought it was time for the president to prove his mettle with the Democratic Party. If he wanted to get big things done in his presidency, Trump needed buy-in from Republicans and Democrats.

Later in the dinner, Commerce Secretary Wilbur Ross, an eighty-one-year-old dealmaker who earned hundreds of millions of dollars in private equity, reiterated the question: What does the president get out of the deal Schumer was proposing? Pelosi explained that wooing Democrats was important, especially if Trump was to be the dealmaker he set himself out to be. At that point, the room burst into cross talk.

"Do women get to talk around here?" Pelosi shot back.

At the end of the dinner, there appeared to be the makings of an agreement: the president would push his House and Senate Republican allies to give legal status to DACA recipients in exchange for border security—but no wall. A simple one-for-one trade. Trump made clear throughout the meeting he was not going to give up on getting his wall built but seemed to agree to put off the discussion for another time.

At around 9:30 that evening, the White House released a statement calling the dinner "constructive." But Pelosi and Schumer took it a step further. At around 9:45 P.M., they released a statement of their own. "We agreed to enshrine the protections of DACA into law quickly, and to work out a package of border security, excluding the wall, that's acceptable to both sides," their statement read. The Associated Press sent a bulletin alert at 9:52 P.M., saying a deal had been cut.

Immediately, alarm bells went off with the president's legislative staff and Capitol Hill Republicans—no one seemed to have a damned clue what the parties had just agreed to. The White House legislative affairs team was sending text messages and e-mails to Capitol

Hill aides, pushing back on the narrative that a deal was done. The president had simply said he would work to fix DACA soon, and he didn't agree to anything more, they told anxious Republican aides and lawmakers.

It wasn't enough. Conservatives lashed out, and the ratings for Trump's performance were brutal. AMNESTY DON screamed the conservative *Drudge Report.* Rep. Steve King, a conservative congressman from Iowa, tweeted, "If AP is correct, Trump base is blown up, destroyed, irreparable, and disillusioned beyond repair." The next morning, Chuck Grassley, the chairman of the Senate Judiciary Committee and also an Iowan, tweeted: "@realDonaldTrump Morn news says u made deal w Schumer on DACA/hv ur staff brief me/ I know u undercut JuidiCimm effort 4 biparty agreement."

In other words, the president was feeling the heat. At 6:11 on the morning after the dinner, the president was in the residence and promptly moved to crush the idea that he had sold out his party to Democrats. "No deal was made last night on DACA. Massive border security would have to be agreed to in exchange for consent. Would be subject to vote," the president tweeted. "The WALL, which is already under construction in the form of new renovation of old and existing fences and walls, will continue to be built."

But nothing was that cut-and-dried with the president. A few minutes later, he seemed to be making a case for DREAMers, tweeting, "Does anybody really want to throw out good, educated and accomplished young people who have jobs, some serving in the military? Really! . . . They have been in our country for many years through no fault of their own—brought in by parents at young age. Plus BIG border security." It was as if he was handcuffed. It seemed clear that Trump agreed with the framework Pelosi and Schumer said they agreed to. But once he started taking flak, the president backed off.

A few hours later, Schumer was on the Senate floor, and a hot mic caught him musing about his meeting with the president. "He likes us," Schumer said gleefully. "He likes me anyway. . . . Here's what I told him, I said, 'Mr. President, you're much better off if you can sometimes step right, and sometimes step left. If you have to step just in one direction, you're boxed.' He gets that. . . . Oh, it's going to work out, and it will make us more productive too."

It didn't exactly work out that way, though. For the moment, Trump had yanked the emergency brake. The immigration deal that Pelosi, Schumer, and Trump thought was in the offing was back on ice.

"Well, what happens is, he likes to sit there and agree with you," Schumer reflected in 2018. "But the next minute, when someone gives him blowback, he goes back."

Mark Meadows watched the dinner from afar with a bit of alarm, and his view of it was simple: "One dinner with two Democrats can't dictate your immigration policy."

8

ZERO TOLERANCE

LAWMAKERS GETTING OVEREAGER with their hands is not a new phenomenon. Congress is filled with middle-aged men who spend at least three nights a week away from their wives and hang around women looking to impress them. Men behaving badly at fund-raisers after a few too many cocktails was hardly a novelty, and many Washington women considered it the cost of doing business.

Back in 2010, in the wake of ethics scandals that had helped cost Republicans the majority in the previous election, Republican leader John Boehner pulled aside several House members who had a reputation for late-night boozing and carousing with young women and told them to "knock it off." But his best attempts to quash inappropriate behavior didn't change the culture. In February 2011, Boehner pushed Rep. Chris Lee, a good-looking and buff New York Republican, to resign after he was outed publicly for soliciting a female companion on Craigslist while holed up at a Marriott in Baltimore during a Republican Party retreat. In a strange twist, Lee told the woman he was soliciting online that he was a "fit" and "fun" thirty-nine-year-old divorced lobbyist.

Three months later another scandal upped the wattage. Rep. Anthony Weiner, a New York Democrat married to Hillary Clinton loyalist

Huma Abedin, was a rising star in the party when it became public that in May 2011 he had sent a waist-down photo on Twitter to a Seattle college student. Weiner initially claimed his Facebook and Twitter accounts had been hacked, but in early June he copped to having had inappropriate online conversations with six women before and after he was married. His situation grew even worse after police interviewed a seventeen-year-old girl in Delaware about online conversations she had had with the congressman. Weiner resigned from Congress but two years later tried to resurrect his political career. He made a bid for New York City mayor, but it quickly imploded as more inappropriate interactions with women and photos surfaced. He later went to jail after sexting with a minor.

Weiner's two-month congressional flameout served as a precursor to the wave of sexual misconduct allegations and resignations that would follow over the next few years. Rep. Tim Murphy, a Pennsylvania Republican who was first elected in 2002, was such a popular figure in the state that he ran unopposed in 2014 and 2016. But that all crashed to a halt in October 2017 after the *Pittsburgh Post-Gazette* published a story about how the antiabortion lawmaker not only was having an extramarital affair but had allegedly pushed his lover to have an abortion after she became pregnant. Amazingly, this alone didn't kill his House career. Only when congressional investigators started taking a closer look at how Murphy ran his congressional office—and at his potential mistreatment of staff—did several senior Republicans urge him to leave. Murphy's banishment from Washington wasn't long-term: He went on to join the Pittsburgh-based lobbying firm Cranmer Consultants.

Most current and former senior women staffers, when speaking candidly, would acknowledge a run-in, or two, with a male lawmaker or senior staffer that made them uncomfortable. Before the #MeToo movement, this kind of encounter was often dismissed in a town where forming a close relationship with the boss—a high form of currency in Washington—often meant working late nights in close quarters with little privacy and plenty of drinking at watering holes like the Capitol Hill Club and the National Democratic Club. Getting the boss's blessing could mean the difference between getting hired by a top law firm or lobbying shop and being relegated to a no-name association or company slot.

But in the wake of Trump's *Access Hollywood* tape and the allegations of monstrous behavior by producer Harvey Weinstein, a reckoning was rippling across the country, and Capitol Hill was not immune. As titans of Hollywood and sports fell, political icons also found themselves in the crosshairs. Trump's Washington may have been a boon to white male Republicans—they dominated his cabinet and top positions of leadership across the administration—but with the election of a president who had bragged about grabbing women "by the pussy," women in Washington were coming forward, telling their stories like never before, forcing a close look at the underbelly of the country's most storied institutions.

The Senate, so often billed as genteel in nature, turned out to be not so genteel after all. While sexual harassment allegations were far more prevalent on the House side, the Senate's clubby environs made the scandals even more complicated and personal. No matter if you were a Republican or a Democrat, you were one of just a hundred, and that meant your colleagues were there to take care of you—until suddenly they weren't.

AL FRANKEN HAD WORKED hard to make himself a model senator. The Minnesota Democrat was well liked by Republicans and Democrats alike, and since getting sworn into office in July 2009, the former comedian had become a close confidant to many of his colleagues, currying favor by helping them raise money. Franken's stature grew further as he became one of the most vocal and convincing Democrats to speak out against Trump. He so effectively railed against the country's chief executive that there was open speculation about whether he would be the party's standard bearer in 2020.

Franken was also a close friend of Chuck Schumer—he was one of the senators whom Schumer had helped elect when he was heading up the Senate's party committee. The two got to know each other well during that campaign, with Schumer regularly dispensing advice to the political novice and even dispatching a few top Democratic political aides to help Franken when his bid looked like it was faltering. Once in Washington, Franken was a staunch Schumer supporter, giving the New York Democrat some political cover with liberals who worried that he was too close to Wall Street. Franken later told the *Washington Post* that he had a nickname for Schumer: "The Jewish LBJ," a nod to Lyndon Baines Johnson, whom Democrats and Republicans alike revere as the most powerful majority leader in history.

But the arc of Franken's political career was about to change. On the morning of November 16, the website of Los Angeles radio station KABC published a photo of Franken seemingly fondling a sleeping woman who was wearing military fatigues. The woman was Leeann Tweeden, a model and sports commentator, and the photo was accompanied by an essay explaining that it was taken in 2006, when Franken was still a comedian and he and Tweeden were both part of a USO tour of the Middle East. In the photo Franken appeared to be playing for a laugh, but when Tweeden posted it online that morning, humor was the furthest response from most people's minds. Tweeden had since become a radio news anchor in Los Angeles, and she followed up her post with a radio interview and appearances on cable news shows in which she claimed that Franken had forcibly kissed her while rehearsing a skit. Her appearances gave life to the photo and made a compelling case that it was more than just a joke gone wrong.

The photo caught Franken and his staff completely off guard. Since Tweeden had posted a first-person essay rather than speaking to a reporter, they were never contacted about the allegation or photo before it was published online. Franken's chief of staff, Jeff Lomonaco, and communications director, Ed Shelleby, first heard about it when a publicist from the radio station e-mailed Shelleby for comment. Franken's staff quickly sprang into action, pulling the senator out of a committee hearing and getting him back to his office. He got there just in the nick of time. Less than twenty minutes later, more than three dozen reporters and TV cameras were camped out in the hallway in front of his Capitol Hill office, and his staffers' phones were ringing off the hook as hundreds of media requests piled in. It was a complete shitshow.

As Franken huddled with his top aides in D.C., and others in Minnesota dialed in on a conference call to figure out how to respond, Schumer canceled his regular press conference on Capitol Hill. Democrats were headed into crisis mode. Franken's team quickly decided that the senator needed to face the allegations directly by putting out a statement with an apology. It was released just hours later, with Franken saying that he remembered the incident differently and that he felt "disgusted with myself" over the photo. He said he would cooperate with a Senate Ethics Committee investigation. He told Minnesota Public Radio that he had apologized to Tweeden and that she had "graciously accepted my apology."

While many of Franken's Democratic colleagues in the Senate condemned the incident, there was no widespread cry for him to resign. Instead, they parroted Franken's call for an ethics investigation, including Schumer, who said that "sexual harassment is never acceptable and must not be tolerated." He added: "I hope and expect that the Ethics Committee will fully investigate this troubling incident . . . as they should with any credible allegation of sexual harassment." But if Franken hoped his old friend Schumer might give him some breathing room, he was disappointed. Schumer continued to hew to the party line.

Even beyond the broader context of #MeToo, Tweeden's accusation didn't surface in a vacuum. Capitol Hill was already on high alert after a deluge of news stories about Roy Moore, the Alabama Republican looking to win a special election in the Senate. The week before Tweeden went public, Moore faced the first of what would become a number of accusations that he had harassed or sexually assaulted numerous teenage girls and young women. That same week Rep. Brenda Lawrence, a Michigan Democrat who had been an outspoken critic of sexual harassment issues, saw her top aide resign amid allegations of harassment.

Meanwhile Franken practically went into hiding. He missed votes and canceled a sold-out appearance for his book *Al Franken, Giant of the Senate*. In his absence, his network of allies quickly went to work to save his reputation. Current and former staffers were in disbelief. There had never been a whiff of Franken making inappropriate sexual advances in the Senate, and many of them wanted to defend the senator. A group of former female staffers came forward to serve as surrogates on cable TV. Three dozen women Franken worked with at *Saturday Night Live* pulled together to defend Franken, writing that "not one of us ever experienced any inappropriate behavior." His former chief of staff Casey Aden-Wansbury also put out a statement that Franken "has always worked hard to create a respectful environment for his staff."

But in the new world of misconduct allegations, one often did not have to wait long for the other shoe to drop. For Franken, it came four days later, on November 20, when former Minnesota resident Lindsay Menz told CNN that Franken "put his hand full-fledged on my rear. . . . It was wrapped tightly around my butt cheek" during a photo op at the Minnesota State Fair in 2010. By that date Franken had been elected to the Senate, which made hash of excuses that tried to justify the Tweeden photo as a bad joke from his comedy days.

MEANWHILE, HOUSE DEMOCRATS HAD a crisis of their own.

On the same day Franken's second accuser came forward, Rep. John Conyers, the eighty-eight-year-old longest-serving member of Congress, was outed as a serial sexual harasser in a shocking story by *BuzzFeed*, made all the more controversial by the news site's decision to use Mike Cernovich, the conspiracy-theory-pushing right-wing operative, as a source for the article. The story detailed how Conyers's office had settled a claim with a former staffer in 2015 who said she had been fired after she rebuffed the Michigan Democrat's sexual advances, and four other aides had come forward signing affidavits in that case alleging that they also faced sexual harassment by the congressman. It opened the floodgates. Former staffers were coming out of the woodwork, cataloguing allegations of chronic sexual harassment and fostering an unprofessional workplace going back decades. And Melanie Sloan, a high-profile former Conyers staffer, came forward and said he had verbally abused and harassed her.

Despite the tidal wave of alarming evidence, Nancy Pelosi wasn't so quick to throw Conyers overboard. As ever, Pelosi wanted Democrats to follow protocol, calling on the House Ethics Committee to launch an investigation. The political implications of forcing out a black member of her caucus weren't lost on her. Holding their support was one of the keys to her power, so pissing them off wasn't something she contemplated lightly. And Conyers had his supporters: Rep. Jim Clyburn, Pelosi's link to the Congressional Black Caucus (CBC), complained that Democrats shouldn't jump to conclusions.

Timing in politics is, of course, everything. The unfolding Conyers scandal coincided with the long Thanksgiving weekend. The day before the holiday, Pelosi caught a break in the news cycle when Republicans got snared in their own scandal: Rep. Joe Barton from Texas admitted that explicit photos circulating on the Internet were indeed of him. He had sent lewd texts and pictures of his penis to a woman who said she didn't want them. The veteran House member, who had served in the chamber since 1985 and had been chair of the powerful Energy and Commerce Committee, announced his retirement eight days after the allegations surfaced.

Meanwhile Pelosi, her lieutenants, and top members of the CBC, including Rep. Cedric Richmond, were privately urging Conyers to step down. Their problem was that others in the party were telling him to hang on. Rep. Sheila Jackson Lee of Texas had the family's ear and urged Conyers to ride the scandal out. With his political future in question, Conyers and his family began pondering what life would be like after Congress. Conyers had been in office since 1965, and for decades everything had been taken care of. Questions abounded: Who would pay his bills? When would he get his pension? Could he shoehorn his son into his seat on the way out?

Pelosi was scheduled to appear on *Meet the Press* that Sunday. She wanted to blast the Republicans' tax reform plan, but she also knew she would be quizzed about the Conyers situation. At the same time, Pelosi and her allies were pressuring Conyers to step down from his position as ranking member on the Judiciary Committee and support an Ethics Committee inquiry. The hope was that Conyers would release a statement before Pelosi's appearance.

But the statement never came. So as Pelosi headed to NBC's studio, nestled in upper northwest Washington, near American University, to submit herself to a Chuck Todd grilling, she didn't have good answers to his Conyers questions.

"Define zero tolerance," Todd said to Pelosi. "You said there's now a zero tolerance."

"Yes," Pelosi responded.

"John Conyers—what does that mean for him, right now. In or out?" Todd asked matter-of-factly.

Pelosi equivocated. "We are strengthened by due process. Just because someone is accused—and was it one accusation? Is it two? I think there has to be—John Conyers is an icon in our country," she said. Her choice of words rang out like a bad note through the studio; she was calling a man accused of sexual assault an "icon."

"He has done a great deal to protect women—Violence Against Women Act, which the left—right wing—is now quoting me as praising him for his work on that, and he did great work on that," Pelosi continued, on the defensive. "But the fact is, as John reviews his case, which he knows, which I don't, I believe he will do the right thing."

"Why don't you?" Todd shot back.

"Excuse me. May I finish my sentence?" Pelosi said, trying to get control of the interview.

"And is the right thing what?" Todd asked. "Resign?"

"He will do the right thing in terms of what he knows about his situation. That he's entitled to due process," Pelosi responded. "But women are entitled to due process as well."

"Do you believe the accusers?" Todd asked, a seemingly easy softball served up for Pelosi to clobber.

"Excuse me?" she asked.

"Do you believe John Conyers's accusers?" Todd said.

"I don't know who they are. Do you?" Pelosi said, in an uh-oh moment that would stick out in lawmakers' minds. "They have not really come forward. And that gets to—"

"So you don't know if you believe the accusations?" Todd asked.

"Well, that's for the Ethics Committee to review. But I believe he understands what is at stake here, and he will do the right thing," she said, noting that she wanted the nondisclosure agreements to go away.

"I guess it goes back to what is this line? What is a fireable offense? You say it's zero tolerance," Todd reminded her.

"Yes," Pelosi said, at the same time as she was protecting Conyers on national television.

Pelosi's team was furious. She hadn't been asked a single question on tax reform. They privately vowed to avoid *Meet the Press* in the future. Still, her inner circle knew almost immediately how big of a belly flop she landed that day in NBC's Nebraska Avenue studios. Angry tweets and online takes followed almost immediately, and a statement with a partial walkback came later that day. Her fellow colleagues described her performance as "one of [her] worst" and that using words like "icon" to describe Conyers didn't help the Democrats' case. Pelosi haters like Rep. Kathleen Rice used her poor performance to trash her to reporters. "I think that her comments set women back and, quite frankly, our party back for decades," Rice said.

BY LATE NOVEMBER 2017, as the Franken and Conyers scandals were unfolding, panic had set in among Washington men. Sexual harassment claims were ricocheting through the Capitol, and lawmakers were having a tough time keeping up. There were simultaneous rumors that the *Washington Post,* CNN, and *Politico* were all preparing to unveil the names of thirty or more lawmakers who had been serially sexually harassing staffers and people around town. Top party officials were e-mailing and calling reporters, asking who was working on taking which member down.

It was an around-the-clock inquisition. Both Republicans and Democrats were squirming. Lobbyists and staffers were gossiping in the hallways and at happy hours telling war stories about members' bad behavior they had witnessed or heard about. Lawmakers themselves would bring it up in casual conversation during votes in the Speaker's Lobby, asking reporters, "Have you heard anything about me?" Or they might awkwardly ask, "I never made you feel uncomfortable, right?"

But the institution itself, which has a horrible record of self-policing, was completely and utterly clueless. In one closed party meeting on November 29, 2017, Rep. Markwayne Mullin, a chisel-jawed Oklahoma Republican who was once a professional mixed-martial-arts practitioner, told his colleagues they needed to learn how to hug: *Don't go under the armpit,* he said. Others were in denial. Rep. Louie Gohmert, an eccentric Texas Republican, said he didn't think lawmakers had to be trained not to harass and assault women.

THE WEEK AFTER THANKSGIVING, House Democrats huddled at their weekly caucus meeting trying to figure out what to do about Conyers. Pelosi's defense of the Michigan Democrat had bought her goodwill with the CBC, and now she was looking to Clyburn and Cedric Richmond to take the temperature of the caucus and figure out what was next.

Having Conyers stay became an untenable position, but he didn't make things easy on Pelosi. After ceding to pressure and relinquishing his position on the judiciary panel shortly after Pelosi's *Meet the Press* appearance, he still refused to resign. The following Thursday, November 30, Conyers was hospitalized, apparently as a result of the stress from the allegations and investigation. That day Pelosi and Rep. Joe Crowley publicly said Conyers should resign, a sentiment that was echoed by Clyburn. But Conyers's lawyer said the lawmaker would not step down.

Behind the scenes, Pelosi was grappling with how a man she had served with for decades and about whom she had never heard any mention of impropriety was now being accused of being a serial harasser. A day after her disastrous *Meet the Press* appearance, she spoke with Melanie Sloan, one of the women who had come forward about the abusive work environment in Conyers's congressional office.

Pelosi knew she was getting killed over the *Meet the Press* appearance, but she felt defensive about it. "I did my job. That's all I can do, is say who can serve in a capacity on a committee as a ranking member," Pelosi told *The New Yorker*'s Susan Glasser in an interview just days after the gaffe. In part, her hands were tied. She wanted to give Conyers the space to get his ducks in a row before stepping down. "Is it all right to give him time to tell his family? Is it all right to do that? Probably not, but we did. It was scheduled to happen, it was scheduled to happen. It was his announcement. I said, 'Why isn't it out there?' They said, 'Well, they want to change a word for the family's sake,' or this or that, whatever, and so it went out a little bit later."

Every day more problems landed on Pelosi's plate. House Democratic leadership was in a complete mess. Her deputies found themselves forced to respond in real time to the allegations against Franken and Conyers, and the responses were hardly coordinated. Crowley may have been speaking in unison with Pelosi when he called for Conyers's resignation, but he looked like he was freelancing when, that same day, he issued a call on his own for Franken's resignation after the emergence of new accusations against the senator. Then the next day, DCCC chair Ben Ray Luján was the first to call for the resignation of Rep. Rubén Kihuen, a Nevada Democrat who was facing allegations that he harassed a staffer. In other words, the number six House Democrat was getting ahead of the top Democrat.

Privately, Crowley called for the leaders to get together to create a system so they could all be on the same page. But the distrust among Pelosi and her deputies was almost palpable. She wanted House Democrats to try to avoid commenting on the Franken allegations and stick to their own domain. To compound the issue, Pelosi and Hoyer and their staffs were almost constantly trying to undercut each other. People close to both Pelosi and Hoyer were also beginning to see Crowley as more of a political threat, which didn't help encourage coordination between the leaders.

The problem posed by misconduct allegations was not limited to those currently in office, nor was that November the point of greatest danger. As fall was turning into winter in late 2017, polling data for the next year's midterms was beginning to look extremely positive for Democrats. Down the street at the DCCC, Dan Sena had increasingly rosy numbers that showed, for the first time, Democrats gaining on Republicans. But Sena couldn't afford surprises; he needed Democrats to be unimpeachable when it came to the #MeToo movement. In order for their strategy to stick, Democrats had to be sure there were no bad eggs in their own ranks.

Thus Sena and other DCCC senior aides began the awkward task of calling the party committee's candidates—many of whom they'd had to cajole into running in the first place—to ask them if there was anything in their past, or in their professional life, that could endanger their chances of winning. If they had anything they were hiding, Sena told them they should consider stepping down. None did.

AS PELOSI WAS WORKING to get Conyers out the door, Al Franken's situation was going from bad to worse. On the day before Thanksgiving, *Huffington Post* ran a story in which two unnamed women accused him of separate groping incidents in 2007 and 2008. Franken remained quiet through the holiday, but on Sunday, November 26, he finally made a statement. "I'm not going to make any excuses. I am embarrassed and ashamed of some of what has come out," he said in an interview with a local Minnesota CBS affiliate. Still, he vowed to return to work, saying, "I've let a lot of people down, and I am hoping I can make it up to them and gradually regain their trust."

Franken came back to his office the following Monday. It was time to face the music. He addressed reporters outside his office. "It's been clear that there are some women—and one is too many—who feel that I have done something disrespectful and it's hurt them, and for that I am tremendously sorry," he said. "I know that I am going to have to be much more conscious when in these circumstances, much more careful, much more sensitive, and that this will not happen again going forward." The next day he made his case to his Democratic colleagues in a closed-door meeting. He and his team continued to push the line that the appropriate venue for adjudicating the allegations was an ethics investigation.

On Thursday, Army veteran Stephanie Kemplin alleged that Franken had touched her breast when taking a photo when he was on a USO tour in December 2003. That same day the Senate Ethics Committee—which is charged with policing senators' behavior—put out a rare statement about Franken. "While the committee does not generally comment on pending matters or matters that may come before it, in this instance, the Committee is publicly confirming that it has opened a preliminary inquiry into Senator Franken's alleged misconduct." The statement, which was released by Sens. Johnny Isakson, Chris Coons, Pat Roberts, Jim Risch, Brian Schatz, and Jeanne Shaheen, seemed like an effort to show that the Senate was policing itself and not totally tone deaf to the cultural turmoil on sexual harassment that was roiling the nation.

But Franken's Democratic colleagues, particularly women, were peeved. They couldn't go on television without getting questions about Franken's behavior, and with Franken eschewing an all-out lobbying blitz in favor of waiting for the results of the ethics investigation, he wasn't doing much to make it easier for them to defend him.

Sen. Kirsten Gillibrand found herself in a particularly awkward position. The petite blond New Yorker had quickly risen in the political ranks from rank-and-file congresswoman to being the state's junior senator. She had also become an outspoken advocate against sexual assault. In 2013 she was a leading figure pushing the Senate to enact legislation to stem the tide of sexual assaults in the military and on college campuses. Her success on the issue was hardly assured, but she doggedly pursued her fellow colleagues, constantly working them over and getting both Republicans and Democrats to sign on to the bill.

As she got more involved in these issues, she had also worked with Franken on legislation that would ban forced arbitration in the workplace. But though they had grown close over their time in the Senate, Gillibrand was shocked by the allegations. She had found out about Franken's imbroglio like most lawmakers on Capitol Hill—a staffer alerted her to the photo—and couldn't believe what she was seeing.

Gillibrand wrestled with how to respond. She didn't want to call out a colleague, but at the same time, this was an issue she felt passionate about. As more women came forward, Gillibrand and her fellow Democratic women senators were texting and having side conversations during votes about what they should do. For many of them, Franken wasn't doing the things necessary to try to stem the bleeding. He wasn't engaging in the typical crisis-mode blocking and tackling. He didn't blanket his colleagues with phone calls, or buttonhole them in the Capitol, explaining the allegations. Instead, he left it up to his staff to respond with statement after statement saying Franken never "intentionally engaged in this kind of conduct" and that he "remains fully committed to cooperating with the ethics investigation." He didn't ask Senate investigators to speed up his probe, or talk to his accusers, both of which would have gone a long way toward helping his colleagues maintain their support.

The big question Gillibrand was wrestling with was how could she continue to lead on the issue of sexual assault if she was not willing to call it out when the alleged perpetrator was a person she loved. As she discussed the issue with staff, she kept going back to what she would tell her nine- and fourteen-year-old sons if she was not able to call out Franken's alleged behavior.

In early December, Gillibrand appeared onstage for an interview with reporter Annie Karni during a *Politico* women's empowerment summit. In front of the crowd of several hundred professional women, she struggled to address whether Franken should resign. She became visibly emotional but declined to respond directly. "I'm telling you, I'm so angry and frustrated and I'm not going to say that today," she said. "But it is something I am very troubled about."

Meanwhile John Conyers had become an island unto himself. With several members of the CBC urging him to step down or risk his legacy being sullied, the dean of the House made his decision public on December 5, announcing on a Detroit radio station his intent to retire. But his resignation almost immediately prompted fresh controversy in the Capitol. Black lawmakers publicly questioned why Conyers had to resign and Franken could remain in his job. *Was it because Conyers was black?* they asked. Franken had returned to work, attending committee hearings and votes, and tensions were rising.

The next day a seventh woman came forward to accuse Franken, this time one of the Senate's own: A former Democratic congressional aide told *Politico* that Franken had tried to kiss her in 2006, after a taping of his Air America radio show. The aide said Franken had told her, "It's my right as an entertainer." Franken denied the allegation. Later an eighth woman came forward, recalling that Franken had groped her when she posed with him at a party to celebrate President Barack Obama's first inauguration.

By this point, the Franken situation was becoming untenable for many senators in the Democratic caucus. His time was up. After the congressional staffer story broke, Schumer called Franken and told him his support in the caucus was crumbling. Meanwhile Gillibrand worked with her staff—including Glen Caplin, a former senior communications aide to Hillary Clinton—to craft her statement, which would be released on Facebook. She moved quickly on the morning of December 6 to call for his resignation. Scheduled to appear at a Capitol Hill press conference on the workplace bill—the same one Franken had helped shepherd before the sexual assault allegations erupted—at 11:30 A.M., with cameras from every network pointed in her direction, Gillibrand would be the first Democratic senator to publicly call for his resignation.

First, however, her statement went up on Facebook at 11:26 A.M. "While Senator Franken is entitled to have the Ethics Committee conclude its review," Gillibrand wrote, "I believe it would be better for our country if he sent a clear message that any kind of mistreatment of women in our society isn't acceptable by stepping aside to let someone else serve." Although her staff reached out to Franken's staff shortly before she publicly called for his head, the two senators never spoke.

In the next ninety minutes, sixteen Democratic senators, including ten women, and Republican Susan Collins publicly called on Franken to step down. Some of Franken's good friends like Sherrod Brown and Sheldon Whitehouse numbered among those calling for his resignation.

For Franken, being a pariah in his Democratic Caucus was tough.

At 3:50 P.M., Minnesota Public Radio published a story citing a Democratic official who had talked to the senator and staff saying that he would resign. Franken's office responded at 5:15 P.M. via the senator's Twitter account: "No final decision has been made and the Senator is still talking with his family." It was true. His two children had come to Washington and were huddled in the senator's Washington home, along with some of his most senior aides. Franken and his wife, meanwhile, went to Schumer's D.C. apartment. It was clear to Franken that Schumer wanted him gone. Exhausted and beaten down, the senator prepared to make the announcement the next day.

THERE WERE TWO CONGRESSIONAL resignation announcements on December 7. The second one got fewer headlines, even if the allegations were far more salacious. That evening Rep. Trent Franks, an Arizona Republican, resigned abruptly after Paul Ryan confronted him over allegations that he had solicited two staffers to serve as a surrogate mother for him and his wife. At one point, a former staffer told the Associated Press that Franks pressured her constantly to carry his baby and offered her $5 million.

Earlier that day Franken's resignation had landed with a thud. Addressing the Senate a day after Democratic senators had piled on calling for his resignation, Franken followed Conyers's lead and said he would leave office.

Accompanied by his wife, Franni, and Democratic consultant Mandy Grunwald, Franken took to the Senate floor. "I, of all people, am aware that there is some irony in the fact that I am leaving while a man who has bragged on tape about his history of sexual assault sits in the Oval Office and a man who has repeatedly preyed on young girls campaigns for the Senate with the full support of his party," Franken said, referring to Trump and the multiple allegations against Moore in Alabama. "But this decision is not about me. It's about the people of Minnesota. It's become clear that I can't pursue the Ethics Committee process and at the same time remain an effective senator for them."

And just like that, Franken's career in the Senate was over.

Franken would leave office on the second day of the New Year, but 2017 did not end without one last scandal, arguably the most distressing of all. The creep factor of Rep. Blake Farenthold, a Texas Republican, was already widely known—a picture from before he became a lawmaker, which regularly circulated on the Internet, showed Farenthold wearing duck pajamas next to a cocktail waitress wearing lingerie. But few imagined the extent of his lascivious behavior before early December, when it was reported that he had settled a 2014 lawsuit brought by former aide Lauren Greene. Greene alleged the congressman sexually harassed her and created a hostile work environment, and that Farenthold had told another member of his staff that he had "sexual fantasies" and "wet dreams" about her. She also said Farenthold had told her he was "estranged from his wife and had not had sex with her in years." Farenthold had used $84,000 in taxpayer money to settle the sexual harassment claim.

As outrage mounted, Farenthold said he would not run for reelection, and in April 2018 he announced he would resign immediately after the House Ethics Committee opened an investigation into allegations of sexual harassment and other charges from former staffers. His withdrawal from politics was only temporary. A month later Farenthold had found himself a job doing—what else?—lobbying for a port in Texas.

9

THE TAX BILL

IF THERE WAS ONE legislative salve that would calm Republican nerves in Washington, it was tax reform. Cutting taxes was safe ground for the GOP. It was something the party had campaigned on for decades, which is why they went to extraordinary lengths to ensure its success.

Republicans kept Donald Trump away from their work to rewrite the code for as long as they could. The president made regular phone calls to members of Congress about it—they usually started with him saying, "Hi, it's your favorite president." He received regular briefings from his economic team. But the House GOP leadership wanted him nowhere near large groups of lawmakers, especially when they were in the middle of trying to cobble together support for the party's current top legislative priority: a wholesale rewrite of the U.S. tax code. In the spring, Trump had gotten involved in trying to repeal Obamacare, and the result was a complete and utter failure. Something was sure to go wrong if the president got too close to this effort, Republicans thought.

But on November 16, 2017, a few days before the Thanksgiving break, they finally relented. Trump was going to come to the Capitol, and there was no convincing him otherwise. Fortunately for House Republicans, the votes for the massive tax package were locked up. Unlike health care, which was always going to be a heavy lift, tax reform was mostly a cinch. Just hours before Trump arrived at the Capitol, Rep. Patrick McHenry of North Carolina—the party's number two vote counter—was sitting in front of the fireplace in his chief of staff's office. "We have this vote in two hours," he said to his staff. "I guess I can text these last three people, but I think they're all going to vote for it." In other words, the mood was exceedingly light, and Trump's trip down Pennsylvania Avenue to nudge was completely superfluous.

But the president had just returned from a lengthy trip to Asia, and he wanted in on the action. He'd been getting itchy while overseas, frequently ringing Rep. Kevin Brady—the chair of the Ways and Means Committee—to make sure things were on track. The GOP leadership invited Trump to address the party at eleven-thirty A.M., with the vote scheduled for two hours later.

Reporters are usually allowed only a few feet from HC-5, the room where Republicans meet. On this Thursday, as the GOP gathered in the Capitol basement, everyone was kept roughly a football field away. Security was so tight that Dave Stewart, the Ways and Means staff director who was key in writing the tax bill, and Emily Schillinger, the committee's press secretary, were stuck outside.

Inside the room, the president quickly got on a roll, but his speech had little to do with the tax legislation scheduled for a vote on the House floor. Like many Trump speeches, this one was something between a ramble and a roast. "I call Kevin [Brady] and give him ideas," Trump said to laughter. "He usually rejects them, but at least I say them and feel better about myself." He then moved on to Steve Scalise, who, at that point, was still in rehabilitation from the gunshot wound that had nearly killed him in June. "Scalise is one tough guy," Trump said. "Isn't he one tough guy? I visited him that night and it was bad, but his color looked good though."

After telling the packed room that the United States now had better relations with Asian nations than ever before, Trump decided to let the room in on a secret. "Keep this confidential. We can keep it confidential, right?" he asked. Having satisfied himself, the president then told the crowd about how he had convinced Chinese president Xi Jinping to release a few UCLA basketball players who were being held by authorities for shoplifting from three separate stores.

After checking in with Brady again—"Kevin, have you ever stole sunglasses?"—he described his conversation with Xi. "You have three young guys who made a mistake," Trump explained. "I don't know how stealing $4,000 sunglasses is a mistake, but anyway. [President Xi] asked if it was important. I said it was really important. We gotta do it. And he did."

Only then did Trump turn to the issue at hand. "We have to have it," Trump said about tax reform. "It's not like 'oh gee.'" His eyes darted to a wall, where Louie Gohmert, a Texas Republican, was standing. "Boy, Louie, were you good on television yesterday," Trump digressed. "You were on fire. That man loves Trump."

Back on track: "You're gonna go up and vote and go home," Trump said. "Please go back home and say this is going to be the biggest tax cut in the history of our country. And if it's not the biggest, blame Kevin Brady. . . . It's a great cut."

Even in cheerleading mode, Trump's way with the backhanded compliment was undiminished. "We're gonna go from a party that's been scoffed at and laughed at to a party . . . if we get this, and straighten out health care and do welfare reform and fix our roads . . . we'll go from being scoffed at to the greatest Congress in history. . . . We can be the greatest Congress in the history of our country. That's a big step from where we've been.

"Whatever I can do, let me know," Trump said in closing. "I love you. Go vote."

Though Republicans were in a celebratory mood at getting the bill across the line, the sound of their heavy exhales of relief could be heard throughout Washington. Later, as the bill was about to become law, public perception was that tax reform had sailed through Congress without any of the fits and starts that plagued health care, government funding, or immigration reform. But that was only because Republican travails were kept behind the scenes. There were intraparty explosions. The president made and broke promises to Democrats, whom he vowed to include in the process. On multiple occasions, the process was on life support due to a clash of egos, diverging ideologies, and a White House that was not ready for the big time. Almost everyone involved in crafting the tax reform bill had the same takeaway: It was a success because of relatively limited involvement by Donald Trump and the White House.

THE PROSPECT OF TEARING up and rewriting the tax code was something approaching a fever dream for Republicans. The last time it had been overhauled was more than three decades earlier, in 1986. Rep. Tip O'Neill, the towering Democrat from Boston, had been House Speaker, and Ronald Reagan the Republican president. The process took two years, but at the end of the day, the conservative Reagan signed the bill flanked by righties like Rep. Jack Kemp and liberals like Rep. Charlie Rangel. It was a moment of bipartisanship that truly hadn't been replicated in Washington in the three decades that followed.

In fact, D.C. did a hell of a good job littering up the code. Three decades' worth of tinkering gave Americans tax breaks for private planes, the hedge fund profits that pay for the jet fuel, the luxury boxes where rich folks lounge, the country clubs where they play golf, and the second homes in which they relax. In short, all of Washington knew the IRS tax code seemed primed for a massive rewrite.

But Washington did what it was good at—it punted, over and over again. George W. Bush slashed taxes in 2001 and 2003, providing an immediate boost to the economy but saddling the United States with interminable deficits. Barack Obama locked arms with Republicans in 2010 to keep most of those tax cuts in place, much to the chagrin of Democrats, who privately called him a sellout.

Once Republicans had control of Capitol Hill, they again talked a big game about a tax overhaul but never got too far. In 2014 Republicans finally got around to putting out a plan to rewrite the code, but that framework hit a wall of resistance, a wall better known as Wall Street. Banking lobbyists pounced, threatening to stop bankrolling GOP campaigns because of a small tax on financial institutions. Threats were levied. Fund-raisers were canceled. Rep. Eric Cantor, then the House majority leader, told lobbyists behind closed doors that the Republican proposal was just that: a plan, with no backing from the leadership. The bill never came up for a vote. It disappeared into thin air, never to be seen again.

Through all the tumult, there was one man who kept a singular—some would say maniacal—focus on rewriting the tax code: Paul Ryan.

"I do think we should not walk away from the chance to reform our tax system so we have one that gives people a better chance of producing in their lives, keeping more money for their family in their paychecks—those are issues that are very important as we go into the next century," a twenty-eight-year-old Ryan said on November 17, 1998, two weeks to the day after being elected to Congress for the first time. "Our tax system is punishing all those qualities that make America great."

Throughout 2017, tax reform became somewhat of a meditative mantra for Ryan. Whenever he was made aware of an inopportune comment by the president, or a scandal within his ranks, he took a breath and reminded his inner circle that they shouldn't take their eye off the prize. Tax reform: they just needed to get it done.

By late 2017, getting tax reform passed was no longer just a matter of principle—it was an absolute political imperative for Republicans, especially after the collapse of the attempted Obamacare repeal. The Congressional Leadership Fund spent somewhere near $50 million on advertisements and other advocacy to promote tax reform, and Corry Bliss told anyone who listened that an overhaul was key to keeping power in Donald Trump's Washington. Bliss's theory was that people didn't vote for Trump because he was going to move the American embassy to Jerusalem or alter foreign policy. They wanted him to keep the economy ticking. "This will kind of, at some level, sell itself," he said early in December 2017. "If your taxes go up next year, you're going to be pissed. If your taxes go down, you'll be happy."

TAX REFORM GOT OFF to a confused start.

On January 26, 2017, Donald Trump headed to Andrews Air Force Base in suburban Maryland for his first flight on *Air Force One*. Just one week into his presidency, he was heading to Philadelphia to address the Republicans' legislative retreat. Typically, the annual retreat was a pretty boring and staid affair. Some years, some lawmakers even skipped it. But this year, it was nearly a full house because Trump was coming to town.

At 11:26 A.M. Trump arrived at Andrews by helicopter for his flight to Philadelphia. At 11:59 A.M. he touched down at Philadelphia International Airport, and his motorcade left for the hotel at 12:12 P.M. Clockwork timing.

But inside the ballroom where he would speak, there was a delay in starting the program: Trump was nowhere to be found. Everyone was confused. The Republican leadership was called onto the stage, and Kevin McCarthy, the House majority leader; John Cornyn, the Senate whip; and other low-level officials emerged and took their seats. But as time went by, it was clear that the president was not following. He was in the building—he arrived at the Loews Hotel at 12:33 P.M. But McCarthy, Cornyn, and Scalise were onstage alone for more than twenty minutes waiting for the president to come out.

Where was he? He was backstage with Paul Ryan. Just a month earlier Ryan had been up in New York with his Gantt chart, selling the president on his agenda. But now he was asking Trump to line up behind one of his most controversial proposals: the border-adjustment tax, or BAT. In essence, it was a proposal that allowed the government to tax imports to the United States instead of exports from the United States. The tax code needed something like BAT, Ryan argued, because the government needed to generate fresh revenue to offset all the money it would lose by slashing corporate and personal tax rates. In truth, no one gave a good God damn what it did, because Paul Ryan was about the only person who liked it. Most others thought it was confusing.

But Ryan, standing backstage that day in Philadelphia, was trying to get the president to rewrite his speech on the spot to embrace his proposal. A presidential endorsement, Ryan told Trump, would go a long way. And the border-adjustment tax would help the president cut rates as low as he hoped.

When the Speaker finally walked onstage, he was still not sure what the president would say, and even after Trump was introduced and began his talk, Ryan was on tenterhooks. Finally, fourteen minutes into

Trump's speech, after recounting the glory of his election, the president turned to tax reform.

"Well, we're working on a tax reform bill that will reduce our trade deficits, increase American exports, and will generate revenue from Mexico that will pay for the wall, if we decide to go that route," Trump said. "It is time that the American people had a president that was fighting as hard for its citizens as other countries do for theirs. And that's exactly what I'm going to do for you. Believe me. Thank you." Ryan's aides were pleased. In his comments on trade deficits and exports, the president, with whom they still had a tricky relationship, had just wrapped his arms around the Speaker's tax plan—at least he'd *seemed* to.

But only hours later, the kumbaya ended. Sean Spicer, the White House press secretary, began to walk it back, telling reporters on *Air Force One* that the president had not made a policy pronouncement. It already felt like the White House was making up the plan as it went along.

EVEN THOUGH TRUMP BEGAN talking about tax reform that day in Philadelphia, it took time for the real discussions to begin. In the summer of 2017, Kevin Brady, the Ways and Means chair, and Dave Stewart, his top aide, approached Steve Scalise's office with a request: help assemble small private dinners so Brady could start talking to Republicans about tax reform. They curated the groups based on region and legislative interests. Between June 7 and the fall of that year, Brady hosted eleven dinners around town to talk about tax reform. The GOP considered these so important that leadership reached into their political coffers to foot the checks.

Stewart, a veteran of Capitol Hill and a former aide to John Boehner, was just one of the top advisers to key members of Congress who played an outsize role in shepherding and drafting what would become a landmark piece of legislation. Brady was also backed by Barbara Angus, the committee's tax counsel. There was no one as steeped in tax policy as Angus—she wrote her third-year law school paper at Harvard on Congress's failure to fix the state and local tax deduction in 1986. Ryan's top tax aide was George Callas, who had worked in tax policy on Capitol Hill for nearly a decade. In the Senate, there was Jay Khosla, the top adviser to Orrin Hatch, the Utah Republican who chaired the Senate Finance Committee, and Brendan Dunn, the top adviser to Majority Leader McConnell. Both Dunn and Khosla were whip smart, politically, and they knew the policy inside and out.

On August 3, with the House already in its opening phases of writing its tax reform bill, McConnell started getting focused. He asked all members of the Senate Budget Committee to come to his office for a chat. Tax reform would need to clear two hurdles to succeed. First, Congress needed to pass a budget resolution. This would lay out what tax reform would look like and give Congress the ability to pass it with a simple majority. Without the budget resolution, Senate Democrats could throw up procedural hurdles that would force Republicans to muster sixty votes to get the plan through, which would almost certainly never happen. In the meeting, McConnell told the committee—including Sen. Mike Enzi of Wyoming, the chair of the panel—that they needed to pass a budget. It would be a heavy lift, but it would allow them to pass a tax overhaul with just fifty-one votes, obviating participation by Democrats.

SEPTEMBER 25 WAS A HOT Monday, the kind of swampy Washington fall day that would soak the suit-wearing town.

It was also the beginning of perhaps the biggest week yet in Trump's Washington. Republicans were finally rolling out their plan to rewrite the tax code. In theory, the party would rally around it, and then a few days later, Trump would head to Indiana—the home of Vice President Pence and endangered Democratic incumbent Joe Donnelly—to begin to sell it to the American people and pressure vulnerable Democrats to jump aboard.

But a strange and all-consuming fear was gripping Capitol Hill and the White House. Even as plans were being made to send Trump to the Hoosier State, top aides on Capitol Hill and in the White House feared that the president, ever unpredictable, might not be on board with the plan his party was readying to unveil.

The legwork had been done throughout the summer. For months Paul Ryan, Kevin Brady, Mitch McConnell, and Orrin Hatch had been huddling with treasury secretary Steven Mnuchin and Trump economic adviser Gary Cohn to hash out the details. Because it's Washington, the group got a name: the Big Six.

In spirit, it could've been called the Big Five, because most everyone discounted Mnuchin. He wasn't dumb—he was a Yale undergrad, with a net worth of $300 million—but he didn't garner the respect that Cohn, a self-made millionaire, did with the negotiators. Much like Trump, Mnuchin seemed to latch on to the last concept he heard. For example, the treasury secretary wanted to craft rules that would, in effect, allow earnings up to $1 million to be taxed at 20 percent. This could allow a lobbyist making $900,000 to pay a lower effective tax rate than a teacher. Some involved in the negotiation preferred that Mnuchin stay far away. One day in November, Mnuchin was at an event in Los Angeles, and a White House aide joked that he was going to find more events thousands of miles away from Washington for Mnuchin to attend.

The Big Six did one thing that helped move the tax reform process along: It did away with Paul Ryan's border-adjustment tax, the proposal Ryan had tried to get the president to embrace. The White House never fully embraced it, and it divided Republicans. Ryan was furious. When Senate negotiators met with him after the statement was released to talk about other ways to raise new government revenue, Brendan Dunn suggested he was going to release a proposal with some ideas.

"You can put out your proposal, and it's going to look like dog shit," Ryan fumed.

As the Big Six plotted behind closed doors, Mark Meadows was plotting outside them. Meadows didn't like being on the outside, and when bored, he had a dangerous tendency to stir the pot. He loved inserting himself in the middle of an issue, first causing problems and then later trying to patch them up. He frequently did this with the president's implicit consent. This kind of mischief kept him occupied and made him a force to be reckoned with on Capitol Hill.

This time, though, Meadows had a compelling argument with which to stir the pot: It was September, Republicans hadn't delivered Trump a single victory, and nary a detail was public on tax reform. The president had said he wanted tax reform signed into law by the end of 2017. They didn't have much time.

By dint of being chair of the Freedom Caucus, Meadows controlled somewhere between two and three dozen GOP votes, so he had the power to take down tax reform, first by sinking the Republican budget—the prerequisite for an overhaul—and later by throwing roadblocks in front of other procedural votes. His price? He wanted to be in the room. He wanted to be listened to. He wanted guarantees on what the tax plan would look like. At the front end, he wanted to know what the rates were going to be, and what loopholes were getting cut.

Meadows had tried to lay out his views to Paul Ryan, but he felt the Speaker was dismissive. He had also tried to make his ideas known to the president. Back in June, Meadows and Jim Jordan had gone to the White House for a lunch meeting with Trump. Meadows and Jordan were trying to talk about tax reform and fiscal policy, but the president kept interrupting. He asked Jordan, a champion high school and college wrestler, if he was "really the best wrestler in the country." Jordan, trying to be humble, said he was "one of the best." A few minutes later the congressmen tried to bring the conversation back to taxes, but Trump turned to Jordan and said: "Admit it. You're a winner. You were the best." They left without having broken through to the president.

In September, Meadows again tried to focus Trump. "We have to send a letter to the president outlining where we are," he told Jordan. Jordan agreed, and Alyssa Farah—Meadows's and Jordan's adviser, who later went to work for Vice President Pence—penned the letter. Its contents were the perfect mix of suck-up ("No one has been more focused on delivering pro-growth tax reform than you") and substance ("The Freedom Caucus stands ready to support the current budget as long as we are assured the following will be included in a final bill: A corporate tax rate reduction to be as aggressive as possible but in no event higher than 20 percent") and it was sure to get Trump's attention. "We have yet to see any commitment from our leadership on Capitol Hill that these basics outlined above will be included in a final plan," the letter concluded. "[W]e hope you will consider this proposal to bring about our full support."

Meadows and Jordan didn't hear anything from the White House. They suspected the letter was caught in a black hole somewhere in the West Wing. But on September 25, with Republicans readying to release the tax framework, Meadows was milling about 1600 Pennsylvania Avenue waiting for an immigration meeting to start when he ran into White House chief of staff John Kelly. The two men had a rocky rapport, mostly because the retired Marine general had worked to restrict the North Carolina Republican's freewheeling access to the president. But now Kelly was opening the door: "Can you come to a meeting with me in the Oval Office?" he asked Meadows. *Win*. Meadows had gotten the president's attention.

Meadows was a bit taken aback when he crossed the threshold into the president's private office. Inside was a who's who of the men running the country: Mike Pence, Steven Mnuchin, Gary Cohn, legislative director Marc Short, and other senior staffers. It was obvious they were gathered there with purpose.

"That was fast," Trump said to Meadows, surprised at his near-instant arrival.

"When you ring, I show up," Meadows told him, conveniently omitting that he had already been in the building.

"Where's Jordan?" Trump said, wondering why the Ohioan, whom he had also summoned, was skipping the meeting.

"He's on a plane," Meadows said, looking around the crowded and well-lit room. As if Meadows needed more evidence, this was proof positive that he was in the inner sanctum, the president's true tight-knit circle of advisers. Barack Obama had dealt with Nancy Pelosi and Harry Reid, the two Democratic leaders, and rarely dipped below the leadership level. But Trump had summoned Meadows—a mere five-year veteran of Congress—to the Oval Office as members of his cabinet discussed tax reform.

"Take my seat," Pence said as he turned to Meadows.

"Mr. Vice President, I'm not taking your seat," Meadows said. He eventually relented on Pence's insistence.

"We were discussing this letter," Trump told Meadows, handing him a copy of the letter the congressman had just sent.

Bingo, Meadows thought. He knew he had the president's ear, which came along with having his cell phone number, but he hadn't known that the letter he sent to 1600 Pennsylvania Avenue would be directly influencing policy decisions just hours before the Republican tax plan was set to roll out.

Trump looked at Meadows, and around the room, and said, "Well, Mark, you want a corporate rate as low as possible?"

"Mr. President, rate is king," Meadows said. "If you're willing to go fifteen percent, we'll support you."

"We can't," Cohn shot back. "There's not room in the budget. We need to be aggressive, but we can't."

Trump wasn't pleased. "Okay," he said, specifying an 18 percent corporate rate and a 23 percent pass-through. "The letter says be as aggressive as possible, if you are going to be as aggressive as possible, be as aggressive as possible," he said to the room. He was still using Meadows's letter as a baseline. "It says no more than twenty. Can't we do that?"

Cohn and Mnuchin said they could make that work.

"Check," the president said, looking at Meadows.

But Trump was still unhappy. He didn't like that his party was embracing a 20 percent corporate rate, and a 25 percent rate for pass-through companies as a starting point. He feared he would get hosed when Congress hashed it all out, and the rates would tick up to 25 and 30 percent.

Pence—himself once a House conservative—tried to reassure him: "No, if this gets to twenty-five and thirty, the Freedom Caucus will vote it down."

Meadows chimed in, "If that happens, we're glad to vote it down, if we have your support. If you want to be at twenty and twenty-five, we'll help you get there."

The meeting lasted thirty-five minutes, and Meadows felt he left with the president understanding where the Freedom Caucus stood. A rank-and-file member of Congress, he had successfully elbowed his way into swaying the president on his top legislative priority.

But Trump was still perturbed. The details were not set in stone, and the president seemed to want an 18 percent corporate rate. White House legislative affairs staff called top aides to Mitch McConnell and Paul Ryan, saying the president was on the brink of pulling his support for the tax framework. Someone needed to call Trump to assuage his concerns.

McConnell's aides told the White House that the Senate majority leader would not be helpful. The next day, Luther Strange was going to lose the Republican primary in Alabama's special election. Strange had been appointed to the Senate to replace Jeff Sessions, Trump's attorney general, but he was locked in a tight race against Roy Moore, an ultraconservative Republican who was accused of sexual misconduct with young women. Moore was about to win the race, which would be a black eye for McConnell, since he had talked Trump into supporting Strange.

Ryan called Trump and made him a promise: He would aim for an 18 percent corporate rate but would not go any higher than 20 percent. Privately, Ryan knew that the 18 percent rate Trump was seeking was fiscally impossible, but his promise seemed to mollify the president.

On September 27 Meadows and Jim Jordan sat through a GOP tax reform retreat in the auditorium at National Defense University, a government-funded national security college in Washington. Ways and Means chair Kevin Brady described the contours of the tax bill, ticking through the corporate and personal rates. Meadows winked and Jordan smiled back: They heard the numbers they wanted.

Trump was hardly as savvy with Democrats. On September 26, he had Republicans and Democrats at the White House to talk tax, and Rep. Richard Neal, the Massachusetts Democrat who was his party's top tax writer, took the face time to make a request: Could the president appoint a special envoy to Northern Ireland? Yes, the president said, that would be a great idea, perhaps thinking it might help persuade

Neal to vote yes on tax reform. Trump never appointed an envoy, and after that day the White House summarily ignored entreaties about the position. In fact, there was no real effort to include Democrats in the tax process—something Republicans would subsequently lie about on the campaign trail.

For all that the much-ballyhooed tax outline appeased Meadows and Jordan, upon release it was met with resistance from many Republicans. The GOP framework was seeking to ax the popular state and local tax deduction, a critical loophole for blue states like California, New York, Illinois, and New Jersey. Rep. Peter King, a longtime New York Republican, told his colleagues at the tax retreat that he was going to be excoriated in his Long Island district if he cut the deduction. Reps. Tom MacArthur and Leonard Lance, both New Jersey Republicans, also complained privately to their colleagues and to senior administration officials like Steven Mnuchin about changing the deduction. But top Republicans blew past that stop sign.

On October 5, House Republicans passed their budget, clearing the hurdle that unlocked the fifty-one-vote threshold for the Senate. But there were complications. On October 19, the Senate passed its own budget with a significant difference from what the House passed—the Senate had allowed for $1.5 trillion to be added to the deficit over the next ten years, hundreds of billions more than the House. Stewart, the House tax-writing aide, told Khosla, the Senate aide, that Congress needed "to be more serious about our fiscal health." But Senate Republicans largely blew past those concerns, too. The way the Senate aides viewed it, they needed all the budgetary room they could get to slash taxes.

Despite concerns from the House rank and file, Ryan and Brady privately decided that the House would adopt the Senate bill, which gave Congress the entrée to proceed with a process that would add piles of debt to the nation's ledgers. They called in President Trump to appear on a conference call with all House Republicans to help seal the deal with their reluctant membership, which wasn't happy with the extra padding the Senate had given the deficit.

It was October 22, the middle of a congressional recess. That meant that all across America lawmakers were at home, glad-handing constituents, holding fund-raisers, and catching up with their families. Trump would need to get on a giant conference call on a Sunday night. He considered this kind of thing his sweet spot: wooing members of Congress with his freewheeling verbal flourishes. But convincing House Republicans that they needed to take up the Senate's budget bill to speed up the tax reform debate would not be easy. Asking the House to accede to the Senate was no small request; both chambers are stubbornly prideful of their work.

So that night, there Paul Ryan was, on a private line with Kevin McCarthy, Cathy McMorris Rodgers, and Rep. Diane Black, the budget chair, waiting for the president to call in.

Black decided to use the wait to complain to the Republican leadership about Trump's decision to stay away from her race for governor of Tennessee. She wanted the president involved, she told them. In the Volunteer State, Trump could easily pave the way to victory. But Trump, she said, was not endorsing her.

Never one for political drama, Ryan interrupted Black, saying, "Cathy, do you know what time the president is getting on the call?"

Before McMorris Rodgers could answer, the president said, "This is Donald." He had heard the entirety of Black's screed.

After an introduction, Trump launched into sales mode with the whole House GOP.

"I use the word 'tax cuts,'" he told the captive audience. "The voters know the word 'cuts' and they like the word 'cuts.' . . . A lot of these tax cuts and reforms have failed because they use the word 'reform.' I've studied it very closely, believe me. The voters like to hear the word 'cuts.'" Trump wanted to call the bill the "Cut, Cut, Cut" bill.

There was no evidence, of course, that Trump had done any message testing. Worse, his suggested verbiage was in direct conflict with Ryan's, which encouraged Republicans to say they were reforming the tax code, not simply cutting taxes. The word *cuts,* Republican leaders said at the time, was heard by most people as a slash in rates for the wealthiest Americans.

"We just can't take any chances as a party," Trump continued. "We got hurt with health care. We're gonna get the health care passed, as soon as this is completed we'll go back to health care. Health care hurt us. We can't afford to make fifty different changes [to the tax bill], many of which won't really mean anything."

Those words—"health care hurt us"—represented a stark private admission that the party was truly backed into a corner as it worked on rewriting the tax code. It explained Republicans' itchiness, their stated desire to finish the massive overhaul by the end of 2017.

"I also think we'll get some Democrats voting for this," Trump said. "Mike and I won the states that we're talking about by twenty, thirty, and in some cases even more than that, forty-two points. It could be as many as four" Democrats who would support the eventual package, Trump said. Put bluntly, this was fantasy, and most people involved in the process knew that. Indeed, Republicans had designed the process to require *only* GOP votes.

"I am in the White House waiting if anybody needs anybody, if anybody wants to see me, you guys just let me know," he continued. "I'm a Republican inside out and backwards. Twenty-eighteen could be a phenomenal success instead of a phenomenal failure if we get some things passed."

The next day, though, Trump went back to being unhelpful. On October 23, as Republicans were working to put together the tax reform bill itself, he tweeted, "There will be NO change to your 401(k). This has always been a great and popular middle class tax break that works, and it stays!" In fact, Republicans *were* working to change the tax treatment of the popular retirement accounts; one item under consideration was lowering the amount someone could contribute before being taxed. Such a move would no doubt be unpopular, but they had to pay for the rest of these cuts somehow.

When Ryan, Scalise, McMorris Rodgers, and Brady came to the Oval Office, the president said, "That was a good tweet, right? That's what you wanted?"

The GOP leadership had no idea what the president was talking about. It was not what they wanted. No one, so far as they knew, had suggested he comment on the prospect of changing the tax treatment of retirement plans, and his doing so was entirely unhelpful. White House aides suggested to Republican tax writers that they keep them closer in the loop, so the president didn't torpedo any of their other plans.

On October 26, the House passed the Senate's budget bill. Twenty Republicans ultimately jumped ship: "No" votes came from across the spectrum, from fiscal conservatives like Rep. Justin Amash of Michigan as well as northeasterners worried about the elimination of the state and local tax deduction. But the budget reconciliation was accomplished. Now they just had to pass the bill itself.

THE HOUSE WAYS AND MEANS Committee revealed its full tax bill on November 2, and the political perils were immediately clear. Tom MacArthur was one rabble-rouser not afraid to express his concerns with the legislation and the political peril that came along with tax reform. When the bill came out with changes to the tax treatment of mortgage interest and state and local deductions, MacArthur told the Speaker, "You dropped a bomb on me." He didn't appreciate that the mortgage interest deduction was being decreased from $1 million down to $500,000 and was eliminated completely for second homes. Many of MacArthur's constituents had vacation properties on the New Jersey shore, and this could prove politically problematic to his reelection.

The GOP leadership heard the concerns on the two issues and conducted shuttle diplomacy, conceding that the mortgage and state and local tax issues were a problem and working through it with individual lawmakers. To help alleviate some issues, the party added a $10,000 deduction for property taxes, designed to ease the pain for blue-state Republicans.

On November 9, Chad Pergram of Fox News, a long-tenured producer who had attended Miami University of Ohio at the same time as Paul Ryan, reminded the Speaker at his press conference that the House majority usually crumbles in the president's first term. He asked why this bill would be the salve to help Republicans keep power.

"The crime bill in 1993, Obamacare—those were unpopular bills,"

Ryan said, highlighting two pieces of legislation that predated electoral defeat. "This is not unpopular."

THE HOUSE PASSED ITS bill after Trump's grand descent to the Capitol basement on November 16, and then the action turned to the Senate. Mitch McConnell took a diametrically different approach from the detail-obsessed Paul Ryan. When McConnell was asked what he supported in the tax bill, he said, "I support fifty votes." He wanted a victory. He was open to what that looked like.

"No red lines, no red lines," McConnell told his Senate Republican colleagues when they expressed pause about particular proposals under consideration. He wanted them to avoid firmly ruling out anything; no one should let a small or personal concern stand in the way of the bill's passage. "If you do that, you're going to make everybody's life harder," he said.

The Senate had watched warily as the House put together its bill. Senate Republican leadership aides had urged the House to steer clear of provisions that would allow the government to tax graduate tuition waivers, and another that would increase the tax burden on the blind. The House didn't listen, and the Senate dropped those provisions on its own. The Senate had also learned from its own mistakes. At times during the health care debate, lawmakers had felt scorned by the slapdash process. This time the leadership kept John McCain's aides apprised of everything they were doing; still bruised from his no vote on the health care bill, there was no way they were risking another. "No process fouls," they kept reminding each other.

In early November—one week before the Senate was set to hold hearings on its tax bill—Jay Khosla, Hatch's aide, and Brendan Dunn, McConnell's top staffer, were in a second-floor Capitol meeting room for an emergency session with members of the Senate Finance Committee, which had primary jurisdiction over tax matters. Even though Paul Ryan and House Republicans had resisted it, the Senate Republicans on the Finance Committee had decided to go for broke and repeal the individual mandate in the Affordable Care Act as part of the tax bill. Whacking Obamacare as part of tax reform would just be an added benefit, plus there was a budgetary upside as well. But Khosla warned the senators that every single one of them had to be on board in order for the bill to clear the committee. Everyone locked arms and agreed: They would repeal Obamacare's central component as part of the tax bill.

On Monday, November 13, the Senate began its markup with an opening statement from Hatch. But on November 14 at seven A.M., the process hit a fatal hitch. Tom Barthold, the chief of staff of the Joint Committee on Taxation (JCT), e-mailed Khosla with this message: "CALL ME." Khosla thought, *This is great.*

"After you guys repealed the individual mandate, you're seeing significant tax increases in the $10,000 to $40,000 [income] range," Barthold said when they got on the phone. The crux of the issue was this: Before they decided to repeal the individual mandate, the JCT's budgetary score indicated that every income category was getting a tax break. But when Republicans decided to ax the individual mandate, which the IRS was barely enforcing, they were essentially shrinking a tax credit that low-income earners were receiving. It set their bill on fire.

"You might as well just tell me that the bill is dead and I can stay home the rest of the day," Khosla said. "How much money do we need to fill the hole?"

Barthold said they'd need to find $84 billion to turn those tax hikes into tax cuts.

Khosla and Dunn immediately called all the Republicans on the Finance Committee into the committee's small side meeting room. Khosla said to no one in particular, "Close the door." He kicked out all the staff except Dunn. They pushed the markup to eleven A.M.

The two aides explained that the JCT was judging the Obamacare repeal as a tax increase, and somehow the GOP would need to find money to make up the difference.

All the senators, led by Pat Toomey of Pennsylvania, rejected the idea that they were hiking taxes. It was a failure to take a tax credit, they said. Instead, they plowed the unused tax credit money into doubling the child tax credit, which would make up the difference. This was, perhaps, the most understated rolling-back of the landmark health care law imaginable.

When they finally resumed consideration of the bill in committee, Senate Republicans were able to defeat every Democratic amendment to change the bill. McConnell still had to do a good deal of wheeling and dealing in his own party to get the bill through. Ron Johnson of Wisconsin had concerns with the bill's treatment of pass-through companies. Susan Collins of Maine had qualms about the state and local tax deduction, which the leadership agreed to fix for her; plus, to be sure she would be happy, they added a provision to allow the deduction of medical expenses. McConnell ended up promising Jeff Flake of Arizona that he would be involved in an immigration working group. In the wee hours of the morning of December 2, the Senate cleared its tax bill 51–49.

Now it was time to meld the House and Senate bills. The final package was to be put together in a formal negotiation called a conference committee. Both chambers would have to vote to begin negotiations.

Mark Meadows, though, was annoyed once again. He had shoehorned the tax reform bill into a place of his liking, but now he felt the bill was eating up all the attention and that Congress was not adequately focused on a looming government shutdown. He was also suspicious with the House and Senate entering formal negotiations, and he wanted assurances of what that process might produce. He didn't like having no control over such a big issue.

So on the evening of December 4, Meadows did what he did best: He stirred the pot. He temporarily blocked the vote to enter negotiations. Ryan, who was fund-raising in New York, called Meadows and asked him to drop his protest, annoyed by the drama. At Ryan's request, the president called Meadows and said, "Mark, I will commit, before we pass something, you'll be happy with it." Meadows acquiesced; he just wanted everyone to know, once again, that he had the power to take down the bill if it wasn't to his liking.

Not everyone was so humbled by Meadows's power. Kevin McCarthy sidled up next to him on the House floor and said, "Vote against it, I don't care. If the market drops five thousand points, it will be on you."

After voting to enter negotiations, one dynamic was plainly obvious: The Senate absolutely hated the House's bill and felt it was a mess. The horse trading was conducted almost entirely by aides. On December 8, Dunn and Khosla in the Senate thought they had submitted their final offer to Stewart in the House. It was late in the night on December 9, a Saturday, and Stewart sent back his rebuttal. But by the time it arrived, most of the aides working on the bill were blowing off steam at Dunn's Christmas party. Hungover the next morning, the Senate aides got together to work on their counterproposal for the largest rewrite of the tax code in decades.

Addition was hard that day, one aide said.

They tied up some loose ends and sent the bill over to Stewart. At 9:52 on Monday evening, Stewart sent back an offer, reiterating an odd request from the House that the Senate Republican negotiators had been ignoring. The subject was, to say the least, esoteric: The House was pushing hard to limit business interest expensing to 30 percent of earnings before interest, taxes, depreciation, and amortization, or EBITDA. The bill, as it stood, allowed expensing of earnings before interest and taxes but left out depreciation and amortization. The onion was being sliced very thin.

Dunn and Khosla were exasperated. There's no way House Republicans cared about this, they said to each other. But Stewart made clear that the request came from the absolute top of the party: Paul Ryan. At the eleventh hour, the Speaker of the House was holding up the tax reform bill for something absolutely arcane. The negotiators were eventually able to solve it, but the request left some shaking their heads.

Around six or seven o'clock that night, Khosla and Stewart sat down to cut the final deal. There were no lawmakers in the room, although the two were keeping their bosses apprised. To pay for last-minute fixes to the bill, they increased the tax rate by which companies could bring back profits to the United States. After a late-night phone call between Sen. Rob Portman of Ohio and Brady and the staff, they had a deal.

That was until Wednesday morning. Top Senate and House aides were gathered in a second-floor room on the Senate side of the Capitol, marking up the deal with a red marker, when Tom Barthold called once again. This time he told them they needed to add another $14.5 billion in revenue to ensure compliance with Senate rules. So once again they increased the rate by which companies could bring back profits from overseas, bringing it all the way up to 15.5 percent. Negotiators were quietly ticking up a tax rate that would impact massive corporations, and in turn the global economy, as they tried to close the deal.

Khosla got to his D.C. home at four A.M. on December 14. He had been working around the clock, and had a meeting scheduled with Dunn in three and a half hours. At 6:30 A.M. Khosla's alarm went off, and he headed to the shower. Almost simultaneously, his phone started ringing. *Who could this be?* It was a senior Treasury official.

"We heard you have reached a final deal," the official said.

"Yes," Khosla replied.

"Can you tell me what's in it?" the Treasury official asked. The final elements of the negotiation were done almost completely between senior aides on Capitol Hill, and the administration was starving for information.

Even then the drama was not over. For all McConnell's assurances, Flake and Collins remained undecided on the day of the Senate vote. Collins wanted the Senate leadership to commit to reinstating federal subsidies to help insurance companies cover low-income patients. The president had canceled such payments. McConnell agreed to hold that vote in the future, and the administration told Collins they would try to reinstate the payments, but they had failed to get Paul Ryan on board. After Ryan publicly said he would not put that bill on the floor, Collins called Marc Short, the White House's legislative liaison, a liar.

Meanwhile, Mike Pence called Flake, whom he knew from the House, and told him that "God brought us to D.C. for such a time as this. . . . You have a moment to make history," he said. "Trust my friendship."

Karen Pence, the vice president's wife, called Flake's wife, Cheryl.

Mike Pence stayed in the Capitol to preside over the vote, and Steven Mnuchin, Cohn, Short, Pence's chief of staff Nick Ayers, and

Alyssa Farah—who was, by then, Pence's press secretary—watched from Pence's office near the Senate floor. Cohn and Mnuchin expressed frustration at how long the Senate was taking to pass the bill. The Senate eventually cleared it by a 51–48 vote. All Republicans voted yes, and all Democrats voted no. The House passed the bill with 224 Republicans voting yes, 12 Republicans voting no, and all Democrats standing firm in opposition.

Trump was in the mood to celebrate. Now that the bill was law, he was going to have members of Congress to the South Lawn to celebrate. His staff had prepared notes for him detailing who he should thank at the December 20 ceremony, but he declined to look at them.

"So who should I thank?" Trump asked, sitting in the Oval Office before the ceremony. "Mark Meadows or Jim Jordan?"

What a visual it was for Trump. In an overcoat, accompanied by Pence, Ryan, and McConnell, he strode to a podium on the South Lawn. Dozens of lawmakers were standing behind him.

"Hasn't been done in thirty-four years, but actually, really hasn't been done, because we broke every record," Trump said. "It's the largest—I always say, the most massive—but it's the largest tax cut in the history of our country—and reform—but tax cut. Really something special."

Trump thanked McConnell, Ryan, Alaska lawmakers Don Young, Dan Sullivan, and Lisa Murkowski, John Cornyn, Orrin Hatch, Tim Scott, John Thune, Pat Toomey, Kristi Noem, Diane Black, Kevin McCarthy, Steve Scalise, and Kevin Brady. He forgot to mention Mike Enzi, the budget chair whose persistence in passing a budget had made tax reform possible. Enzi remained angry at the president for months.

Trump sent Meadows and Jordan's letter back to Meadows with an inscription: "Mark—Jim—Big Commitment—Pushing Hard . . . Going To China Etc. Will See You Both Soon." More than a year later, after the bill had turned out to be anything but Republicans' ticket to holding the House, the letter remained framed and hanging in Meadows's and Jordan's offices.

10

THE PRESIDENT'S WATCHMEN

IT WAS THE MIDWAY POINT—exactly one year since Donald J. Trump's stunning election, one year since the political order had been shaken and the power structure rearranged. And it was one year before Election Day 2018, when voters would render an interim judgment on Donald Trump's America. The president was in Asia, on a seven-day tour of China, Japan, South Korea, Vietnam, and the Philippines. His White House was busy negotiating the details of the tax reform bill on Capitol Hill.

Ivanka Trump was in Kevin McCarthy's Capitol office, part of her effort to edge herself further into the tax reform debate. She was pushing, with some success, to make the code more favorable for working parents and families. Lawmakers of both parties—even some who hated the president—took meetings with Ivanka, dined with her at her home, and took photos with her across the country. Republicans knew how important Ivanka was to the president, and they wanted to curry favor with her to get in better with him.

Tax reform was the stated purpose of Ivanka's visit with McCarthy, but the majority leader was consumed with more troubling thoughts. It was November 8, and McCarthy wasn't feeling particularly sentimental about Trump's anniversary. He had a dire message he thought Ivanka—and her father—needed to hear: Republicans were in mortal political danger.

"This election doesn't look good," McCarthy told Ivanka in his office, looking ahead to 2018. "And if things don't change, the House is in jeopardy, and this presidency will not be successful."

Ivanka and McCarthy had a good enough relationship, and McCarthy felt as if he could be honest with her. They had spent some time together privately. Ivanka and her husband, Jared Kushner, had invited McCarthy to dinner at their seven-thousand-square-foot Kalorama mansion, which is around the corner from Barack Obama's house. The two texted frequently about politics and policy, and they were often in agreement.

McCarthy also knew that Ivanka had her father's ear, and he figured this was a message only she could deliver to the president. Trump didn't want to hear anything negative about his political standing. The polls, he thought, were always wrong. The typical Washington hands that had crafted political agendas before his arrival were dopes compared to him. The president frequently glommed on to one piece of positive information in an otherwise gloomy presentation. He had no use for members of Congress who were looking to drag him down. He surrounded himself with people who would build him up. McCarthy thought he could get through to him, but the amplification from Ivanka would be useful.

McCarthy's concerns were real and acute. He was worried that Trump was completely unaware of the political peril Republicans were in. The way McCarthy saw it, history was clear: The GOP was poised to lose more than two dozen seats in the 2018 midterm election, which would hand the chamber to Nancy Pelosi and march Trump toward impeachment. The president needed to wrap his head around that reality. On the legislative front, McCarthy was hoping Trump would forget big-ticket legislating, incessantly sell tax reform, and turn his attention toward issues like the opioid crisis. Taking credit for a booming economy and focusing on the drug epidemic were political wins, congressional Republicans thought.

McCarthy wanted Ivanka's help in focusing her father. Back in May, during a spring barbecue at Ivanka and Jared's mansion, McCarthy had floated the idea of a getaway with the president and Republican leadership. Now in his closed quarters, McCarthy pressed it with Ivanka again, with new urgency.

"We need to get away, either at Mar-a-Lago or Camp David," McCarthy told the president's daughter. He thought the trip would give him the chance to focus the president on the midterms. He wanted the president to recognize that he was not invincible, and that Republicans would need his energy positively channeled in the coming months should he want to keep control of the House.

A few days later McCarthy got a call from Ivanka.

"Everyone loves the idea. Kelly loves the idea," Ivanka said, referring to the president's chief of staff, who responded to the first daughter even as he ducked calls from members of Congress. "We're going to do it."

THE WHITE HOUSE CHOSE Camp David, the presidential retreat in the mountains of Thurmont, Maryland, northwest of Washington. Camp David, of course, has played a big part in the recent history of America. Israel and Egypt cut a peace deal there in 1978. Barack Obama hosted the G8 summit there in 2012. Trump used the resort with some frequency as well. He went there a number of times in 2017—with his family, to hold a meeting about the war in Afghanistan, with Ivanka and Jared's family, and with his cabinet. This retreat would give Trump unfettered time with Republican leadership without the constant din of Washington grousing. The White House invited Paul Ryan, Kevin McCarthy, Steve Scalise, Mitch McConnell, and John Cornyn, five of the most powerful men in America.

January 5 was an auspicious day for Trump to head away with these congressional leaders. The stock market was roaring, with all major indices reaching new highs. The tax reform bill Congress had passed seemed to be working as they planned. Now it was time to use the momentum from the tax reform win to right the political ship.

But at the same time, the mood at the White House, and within Trump's circle, was tense. Michael Wolff, a New York–based journalist, had just released *Fire and Fury: Inside the Trump White House,* a book filled with salacious anecdotes about the president's administration. Wolff knew the president—he had interviewed Trump in Los Angeles for the *Hollywood Reporter* in 2016—and had pitched him on writing a book about his time in the White House. The book featured lots of source material from Steve Bannon, who by that time was out of the White House. Bannon used the book to call Ivanka "dumb as a brick" and generally presented the president as unfit for office. When the book was published, Wolff said he had been a constant fixture in the West Wing, but Trump said he did not give Wolff any access. The president took to Twitter on January 5 to respond: "Michael Wolff is a total loser who made up stories in order to sell this really boring and untruthful book. He used Sloppy Steve Bannon, who cried when he got fired and begged for his job. Now Sloppy Steve has been dumped like a dog by almost everyone. Too bad!"

Drama notwithstanding, Trump emerged from the White House that afternoon seeming particularly upbeat on his way to *Marine One.* "Hi, everybody. I'm going over with the senators," Trump said, forgetting or ignoring the fact that three members of the House leadership would also be in attendance.

The president boarded *Marine One* and headed north to the Maryland mountains. The members of the Republican leadership got a much cooler ride: Osprey helicopters. The twin-propeller choppers used by the U.S. Armed Forces lifted off from Fort McNair, a U.S. Army base on the southwestern tip of Washington. They flew along the Potomac River over Georgetown, past the CIA headquarters in McLean, Virginia, before heading north to Maryland. Trump arrived at Camp David just before three P.M.

Each member of the leadership got his own cabin, and most of them dressed casually, in open-collared shirts, khakis, or suits with no tie. The president wore a suit and tie. McCarthy and Scalise shared a two-bedroom cabin, and the staff, including multimillionaire Gary Cohn, took a van to a nearby Hampton Inn. The group held their meetings around a big wooden table in Laurel Lodge, the camp's largest cabin.

Most every player at the retreat seemed to have had a goal of his own. Ryan wanted to talk policy. He discussed a broad overhaul of the nation's entitlement programs, but McConnell shut him down, gently reminding him he would need to find sixty votes in the Senate—an impossibility at this juncture. McConnell briefed the group on the electoral climate in the Senate: *Good, but take nothing for granted,* he said. (McConnell frequently told Republicans that they shouldn't "fall in love" with the 2018 Senate map, which was favorable to his party. In other words, individual races had to be won.)

But McCarthy saw this getaway as his show, his chance to make the president understand the political pickle that House Republicans were in. Keenly aware that Trump was a visual learner, McCarthy came armed with a twenty-six-slide presentation depicting the "challenges and opportunities in 2018." The slides were eye-catching and sleek. They had a dark blue backdrop, white lettering, and lots of red and blue.

The message of the presentation was at once harrowing and dimly hopeful. McCarthy wanted to get Trump to understand that, at that moment, the House was lost—but he could turn things around.

He started off with the basics. The first slide was a representation of the breakdown of the current House of Representatives: 237 Republicans, 193 Democrats. Each member of Congress was represented by a blue or red dot. The dots were plotted along an axis that ranged from D+40 (meaning districts that Democrats normally win by an average of 40 points) to R+40.

Then came the warning. The slide was titled NET CHANGE IN HOUSE SEATS FOR PRESIDENT'S PARTY. It was a bar graph awash in red, and it showed that in past midterm elections the president's party lost anywhere from 55 seats in 1946 to 4 seats in 1962. The two outliers were 2002, when Republicans gained seats after September 11, and 1998.

A blunt message flashed on the screen: AVERAGE # OF SEATS LOST IN PRESIDENT'S FIRST MIDTERM: 29 . . . 2018 HOUSE MARGIN: 23.

There it was in plain English. McCarthy was telling Trump in no uncertain terms that, if history held, he was going to lose the House. He even transposed 2018 onto the bar graph and charted a twenty-something-seat loss.

But the next slide was meant to explain to Trump what could

happen if he were to heed the Capitol Republicans' advice. McCarthy highlighted 1994 and 2010.

"The reason they lost was they passed Obamacare but never sold it," McCarthy said of the Democrats in 2010. "It was unpopular. They tried to do Clintoncare," in 1993, "and it was unpopular."

Now McCarthy homed in on 1998. "Economy was good. Six quarters of economic growth," he said of Clinton's second midterm election, when Democrats had bucked the trend and picked up five seats. "Republicans lost the shutdown. He made small things look big. And he triangulated." McCarthy was thinking about Bill Clinton's ability to make something like the hiring of police officers seem like a major accomplishment.

He wanted Trump to see that if he played the next year right, he could be just like Bill Clinton in 1998: a scandal-plagued president presiding over a good economy, who bumbled a bit in legislating but worked with Republicans for self-preservation. A president whose party gained House seats in the midterms or, in this circumstance, held the House against all odds.

But it wouldn't be easy. McCarthy then illustrated just how stiffly the headwinds were blowing. The generic ballot—the measurement of a race between a nameless Democrat and nameless Republican—needed to have Republicans within six points if they were going to keep the House. At that moment, they were down twelve points.

McCarthy was trying to have Trump understand that the deck was stacked heavily in Democrats' favor. One slide showed that since Trump won the White House, 71 percent of Clinton voters had shown up for special elections. The president's voters? Just 55 percent had voted in 2017.

The presentation ended with a quote from Nate Silver, the election analyst: "The signal is the truth. The noise is what distracts us from the truth."

"We've gotta get the generic ballot down, and watch women and college graduates," McCarthy said. "I've got to sell the [tax-reform bill] so people see the effects and give us credit for it."

Trump nodded along for the entire presentation. When it was over, he offhandedly said to an aide, "I don't believe in these polls."

· · ·

LATER THAT NIGHT, THOUGH, Trump told Pence that he enjoyed the presentation. Pence told McCarthy on their way to dinner that it was important that Trump saw the numbers.

The weather was frigid at the retreat, and the group spent much of the time indoors.

Scalise was waiting outside his cabin for a ride to dinner, and Brett Horton, his chief of staff, said, "Steve, where's your jacket?"

"Oh, it's in my cabin," Scalise responded.

"Aren't you shivering?" Horton said.

"Yeah, but I had a rough summer, so I can deal with this," Scalise said with a laugh.

That night the group watched *The Greatest Showman,* the 2017 Hugh Jackman movie, which is loosely inspired by the life of P. T. Barnum. McCarthy and Trump sat next to each other and talked periodically throughout the 105-minute running time. It was clear they had the best relationship of anyone on the trip.

Aside from the dose of political reality that McCarthy had delivered, the second-most-important presentation came from Gary Cohn, the president's chief economic adviser. That weekend Cohn was on the brink of leaving the administration. His employment was always the subject of gossip—and in early January the chatter hit a high. During a news conference in a cold warehouse at the retreat, Trump was asked about Cohn's plans. Trump said he hoped he stayed, but "if he leaves, I'm going to say, I'm very happy that he left."

Still, Cohn had one of the marquee roles at the Camp David retreat: delivering a briefing on infrastructure. The next morning, Saturday, he laid out a plan to spend $200 billion in federal funds on roads, bridges, tunnels, and airports, which he hoped would unleash $1 trillion in private sector and local government spending. Trump told the Republican leaders he wasn't sure that plan would work, and the administration should consider other approaches.

But lawmakers and aides found Cohn's presentation particularly engaging. Infrastructure was a winner with voters if you could get it through—it produced actual, tangible results, and it meant more of that one word every politician loves to hear: *jobs*. Around the Laurel Lodge table, Steve Scalise, Paul Ryan, and Kevin McCarthy were all debating the merits of public-private partnerships and their prospects in Congress.

As the debate bubbled on, Trump was nodding his head, taking what appeared to be furious notes on a notecard in front of him. Was he moved by Cohn's public-private partnership talk? Was he eager for Ryan and McCarthy to bring the idea to the House floor? People in the room were impressed that Trump—who cared little about policy particulars—seemed to be so engaged in Cohn's proposal, especially after seeming so skeptical right after the presentation.

The notes had nothing to do with infrastructure.

"SLOPPY STEVE," Trump had scrawled on the top of the card in black marker. Copious notes then followed. As Cohn had detailed his plans to rebuild America's roads, the president was writing down how he wanted to trash Steve Bannon the next time someone asked him about it.

It may have been Trump's own key takeaway from Cohn's presentation. A few minutes later, with the Republican leadership standing by his side, the president leaned in to his new favorite nickname.

"Just so you know, I never interviewed with him in the White House at all," Trump said of Wolff. "I guess Sloppy Steve brought him into the White House quite a bit, and it was one of those things. That's why Sloppy Steve is now looking for a job."

The Republican leadership left the retreat Sunday morning feeling good. Ryan felt McCarthy was blunt about the party's political prospects. McCarthy believed they had given Trump something to think about. Sell tax reform as a positive, try to appeal to women and college graduates, and recognize that despite the stiff political winds, there was a way for the GOP to keep power—if only the president would listen.

MCCARTHY FANCIED HIMSELF a defender of the president, which dovetailed with his instinct to protect the party, but he was far from the only Republican working overtime to insulate the president from criticism and failure that winter. A cottage industry had sprung up among some Washington Republicans around protecting the president, and if that industry could be said to have a leader, it was Rep. Devin Nunes of California's twenty-second district, the chair of the House Intelligence Committee.

Virtually no one reading the tea leaves would have guessed this role for Nunes. In the early days of this Republican majority, Nunes had been a foot soldier in John Boehner's war against the right wing of his party. In 2013 he called those who wanted to shut down the government to repeal Obamacare "lemmings with suicide vests," and the next year he gave money to a primary challenger to Rep. Justin Amash, the future Freedom Caucus Republican from Grand Rapids, Michigan. He called Amash "al-Qaeda's best friend in the Congress" after Amash opposed the renewal of some of the National Security Agency's policies. Nunes was an easygoing guy who was eager to banter with reporters and seemed content with his role as the backup to and close ally of John Boehner and Paul Ryan.

Then Donald Trump got elected.

Nunes wasn't a Trumpster. He didn't endorse his candidacy or make many appearances on his behalf during the 2016 campaign. But after the election, Nunes, by then the chair of the secretive and powerful Intelligence Committee, was sucked into the Trump vortex. First, he accepted a role on the administration's transition team, where he helped tap his friend Mike Pompeo to lead the CIA and Gen. James Mattis to serve as defense secretary. He had close ties with some in Trump's orbit, including Mike Pence, whom he knew from Pence's days in the House, and he had a decade-old relationship with Michael Flynn, a Trump campaign mainstay and the president's first national security adviser. Nunes called Flynn "unbelievable." "He's a hero," Nunes said in December 2018. (Flynn later pleaded guilty to lying to investigators and began cooperating with the probe into Trump's activities with Russia.)

Nunes, who was first elected to Congress in 2002, became the embodiment of what most Democrats and even some Republicans saw as the permissive, hands-off attitude that GOP lawmakers took when it came to keeping Donald Trump in check. His detractors said he shielded Trump from congressional oversight.

First, in March 2017, just months after Trump first took office, Nunes shared with reporters that members of the president's campaign were being surveilled by the U.S. government. Nunes went to the White House to view the intelligence, which the *New York Times* reported was given to him by Trump officials Ezra Cohen-Watnick and Michael Ellis. The next month Nunes stepped away from the Russia investigation after congressional ethics authorities began probing whether he improperly disclosed classified intelligence to the public. The ethics investigation was dismissed.

Just weeks after the Camp David summit, Nunes and his staff released what became known as the Nunes Memo, which documented that the FBI might have surveilled members of the Trump campaign as part of a politically motivated investigation. The FBI urged Nunes not to release the memo out of "grave concerns" about the veracity of the document's claims. It was produced by Nunes's staff with no input from Democrats but under the watchful eye of Rep. Trey Gowdy, the Republican of South Carolina who led the investigation into the Obama-era attack on a diplomatic facility in Benghazi. Nunes was looking to detail what he thought was malfeasance in government. Ryan allowed the release of the document but urged caution in discussing its contents.

There was serious fallout from all the discontent. The Intelligence Committee, one of the few bastions of bipartisanship in Washington, was irreparably damaged. The two sides hardly had a relationship and sparred at every turn. Nunes's relationship with Rep. Adam Schiff, the California Democrat who was the committee's ranking member, became nonexistent. And in 2018, Nunes got a real challenger in his district for the first time in recent memory, prompting a race that would cost him mountains of cash and a fair amount of the padding he'd come to expect in his victory margin. Nunes told his staff that there was both good news and bad news in his newfound prominence: The good news was that everyone in America knew him now, and the bad news was that everyone in America knew him now.

. . .

NUNES WAS NOT JUST any member of Congress. As chair of the House Intelligence Committee, he was part of the elite Gang of Eight, which included the top Republican and Democrat on both the House and Senate intelligence panels, the Speaker of the House, the House minority leader, the Senate majority leader, and the Senate minority leader. These eight lawmakers have access to the most sensitive information on earth. They are briefed about American intelligence missions and war strategies and hear frequently from top military brass. They conduct these meetings in secret, in a room called a SCIF (Sensitive Compartmented Information Facility), where cell phones are confiscated and attendance is severely limited. Officials shuffle in and out of the room carrying black briefcases with the nation's biggest secrets.

Until the Trump administration, Nunes was happy to talk to reporters about almost anything besides what he learned in those closed, classified sessions. Taxes. Political strategy. Trade. But something happened to the once-friendly Nunes. Over the course of Trump's first two years in office, his mood grew darker. He practically cut off all media besides Fox News, feeling that he was getting an unfair shake from what he called the "mainstreamers," meaning the mainstream media.

It's not that he believed there had been no Russian interference in the 2016 election. He conceded Russia was a bad actor and had been involved in election meddling for "years and years," he said, "and they are always up to no good here. So are others." But he remained certain that Trump did not collude with the Russians to sway the elections and that Vladimir Putin's nation did not have a dispositive impact in 2016. He called Russia's activities on behalf of Trump a simple "trial balloon. . . . It was almost to create press stories." (Asked if the United States was involved in similar election meddling worldwide, Nunes said, "Well, I can't comment on that.")

Nunes even said he was initially in favor of Robert Mueller's appointment as special counsel, figuring that the former FBI director would come to the same conclusion that he came to. But eventually, he said, he viewed Mueller's probe as a "hit job." "They should've went in and figured out if there was any collusion between him and Russia," he said, sitting at a table just a few feet from the House floor. "But what it's turned into is bust as many people as you can around Trump for whatever you can get them on, and then make it sound like it's a lot of bad Russia stuff. But the truth is that there is no connection to Russia."

Mueller's employment is subject to the president's whim, and in the first two years of his presidency, Trump did not fire the special prosecutor. But Nunes thought Congress should have curbed Mueller. "When Mueller was clearly going off the rails, we should have done even more than we did," he said. "I think the criticism that would fall onto us as a whole is that we did not understand that Mueller wasn't there to do a credible job to get to the bottom of Russian collusion. He was there to put scalps up on the wall, and take down the party and the president." Of course, there was no evidence that this was true.

Nunes didn't get along well with Adam Schiff. But in the Senate, Mark Warner, Democrat of Virginia, and Richard Burr, Republican of North Carolina, conducted a bipartisan investigation during which the two sides worked judiciously together and were sharply critical of the Russian effort to sway the election. Nunes was dismissive of their work: "I don't know what Mueller or the Senate have that was not in our report."

Nunes saw the entire investigation into Trump as a political exercise aimed at removing Trump from the presidency. In his view, Democrats were working with "corrupt people at the FBI" to bring Trump down.

"People have been poisoned," he said. "There's a big percentage. . . . I bet if you did a poll right now of Democrats nationwide, you'd probably get, I'd guess, a sizable percentage—more than the teens, right?— that believe me and our investigative team and all our members—Trey Gowdy, et cetera—have run this massive cover-up operation. If it wasn't for us, Trump would've been gone by now because he clearly colluded with the Russians, and we're the ones that hid it from the American people. They really believe that."

11

PURITY

JIM JORDAN'S ENTIRE POLITICAL IDEOLOGY is wrapped up in an imaginary couple he likes to call the "second-grade teacher, second-shift worker." These people live just up the road from Jordan's Urbana, Ohio, home in a small town called St. Paris, and they are Jordan's constituents in Ohio's fourth district. The worker walks out of his house around two o'clock in the afternoon, and on his drive to work, he looks out his truck window to see a guy drinking beer and reading the newspaper—a bum who could be working but isn't. This infuriates Jordan's imagined man because, unlike the beer drinker, Jordan's guy is missing his kid's game that night to work at the Honda factory. The teacher sees the same man after her day working at the school. After the worker's shift, during his nighttime drive home, he flips on the radio and hears about something else Washington is doing that seems dumb and superfluous—hiking spending, putting government in control of health care, something like that. In Jordan's view, the worker and the teacher then turned around and voted for Donald Trump.

"Those kinds of guys," Jordan said, "I don't know why we aren't fighting for those people. They put us in power."

Jordan, fifty-three, is a founder of the Freedom Caucus and the keeper of the conservative creed. He was digging into a plate of eggs at

Studebaker's Country Restaurant near his home in January 2018, and he had a feeling he just couldn't shake. Donald Trump was in the White House, and his party was *still* acting like a bunch of losers.

They were weak.

They were feckless.

Jordan is a short but fierce man with cauliflower ears, a strong jawbone, and a big smile. In the Capitol, where men are forced to wear sports coats, he's rarely seen with his on; usually it's flung over his shoulder, as if he's readying to brawl. At Graham High School in St. Paris, Ohio, he was a four-time state champion wrestler, compiling a record of 150–1. He didn't take kindly to losing then, and he still doesn't.

More than perhaps anyone else in Congress, Jordan craves confrontation. It was he who urged the tear-it-down strategies that led to government shutdowns and other legislative crises. It was he who pulled the strings. The three dozen members of the Freedom Caucus followed him because he was a fighter. He was the man on Fox News telling it like it should be.

Even when it came to the bulk of his Republican House colleagues, Jordan was unafraid to be blunt: He thought they sucked. "We always say 'win to fight another day,'" Jordan said wistfully. "If we've heard that once, we've heard it a million times."

His view throughout the Trump presidency was quite simple and ideologically uncomplicated: He didn't think Republicans should be a bunch of wimps. Trump was president, for God's sake. Republicans held the House, the Senate, and the presidency for the first time in a dozen years. Why the hell were Republican leaders so willing to get in bed and cut deals with Democrats?

Two issues consumed outsize space in Jordan's mind: Republicans' weak-kneed stance on profligate government spending, and immigration. In Trump's Washington, government spending was in vogue, so on that issue Jordan found himself fighting an uphill and often hard-to-win battle. But immigration was a defining issue for him.

"Voters in Pennsylvania, Ohio, Michigan, Wisconsin," Jordan said on that cold January day in Ohio. "I think voters across the country, particularly in those four states, do not trust anyone in Washington when it comes to immigration. They just don't trust the town. The one person they trust is the president. But they're also smart about it. And if they see some kind of deal that Chuck Schumer likes and Nancy Pelosi likes, by definition, that's probably not an agreement that our core voters who put Republicans in power and made Donald Trump president are going to like."

Jordan thought Donald Trump had won the election on a few key issues: building a big, hulking wall on the southern border with Mexico and changing migrant laws to make it much tougher to come to America. And what should happen to the DREAMers? "It can't be citizenship," he said. "It can't be amnesty." You had to do security and immigration law first.

Jordan didn't have time for bipartisan immigration deals with Schumer and Pelosi, and he didn't think the president should, either. His entire thinking could be boiled down into one sound bite: "Any deal Chuck Schumer and Nancy Pelosi support, our voters who showed up are going to be against."

Immigration was conservative Republicans' hill to die on.

OUTSIDE WASHINGTON, JORDAN HARDLY cut the image of a man looking to slash and burn. At home in western Ohio, he ambled around his house in furry slippers; when he drove to D.C., he threw show tunes on in the car. Jordan calls himself a bit of a country bumpkin, because much of his family lives within a stone's throw of him in Urbana. In 1997, when he was in the Ohio House of Representatives, he and his wife, Polly, bought a stone cabin there that her family previously owned. The cabin, which was built in 1837, bears no visible trace of Jordan's life as one of the country's most prominent conservative politicians. During the summer, it's quite a pleasant scene. A creek runs through the front yard, although the bridge they installed for their daughter's wedding blew away in a storm. But in the winter, the cold can get nasty, so Jordan and Polly use space heaters, which affords them the opportunity to watch Fox News in warmth and peace.

On January 4, a frigid, snow-covered day in Urbana, they were packing up for a seven-and-a-half-hour drive to Washington, where they keep an apartment on Capitol Hill. Jordan's Washington apartment was newly purchased—he lived in his office for much of his tenure—but he was hardly a D.C. neophyte. He was elected in 2006, the waning years of the Bush administration and the year Nancy Pelosi's Democrats took the House majority. He came to Washington in a minuscule Republican class that included Kevin McCarthy, who later turned out to be his nemesis. Jordan's first time speaking on the House floor was to oppose Democrats' efforts to pay for new government spending. The floor was yielded to Jordan by Paul Ryan. Mike Pence sat directly behind him.

By 2010 Republicans were back in the majority, and Jordan was having a moment. He won the chairmanship of the conservative Republican Study Committee and began his ascent to prominence. He became a top tormenter of John Boehner, his fellow Ohioan, and sharply criticized the Speaker's inability, or unwillingness, to stand up to Barack Obama. Still, Jordan displayed a photo of Boehner in his office. No ill will, he told visitors, he just disagreed with him. That was an understatement; Jordan made a habit of dumping all over Boehner. But the photo was nice.

Jordan's seat atop the Republican Study Committee gave him a great perch on a sinking power base. Since 1973 the committee had been the caucus for conservatives in the House, but over the decades, it had grown large, losing both its luster and its power in the process. As its membership swelled to more than one hundred lawmakers, a significant fraction of House Republicans, it became impossible to hold every member to the same position on a given issue.

So in 2015 Jordan and Mark Meadows had banded together with other conservatives like Mick Mulvaney of South Carolina, Justin Amash of Michigan, and Ron DeSantis of Florida to create the House Freedom Caucus (HFC). Admission to the HFC required just one thing: The lawmaker had to be willing to vote against the Speaker of the House if the group took a position. Jordan was the group's first chair, but he and Meadows were always the combined center of gravity; Jordan was the ideological core, and Meadows the strategist. Jordan liked the fights and was convinced that if conservative Republicans took a stand on an issue, their idea would carry the day. He could drag the entire party to the right by taking a position, and he saw no real need to compromise, feeling that he had the responsibility to hold firm to his views. Meadows was more pragmatic; he understood there were always deals to be had. He wasn't looking to sacrifice his ideology, but he thought he understood how to put his opponents in a tough spot, where they couldn't refuse what he was offering. Meadows's power came from his flexibility. But on big issues Meadows was often the less powerful one simply because he was unwilling to be to the left of Jordan. His internal politics dictated that they could not split; if they did, the entire Freedom Caucus would lose its compass.

The Freedom Caucus counted only a couple dozen members, but a united front could stop pretty much any bill. And because of Meadows's and Jordan's power over the group, in many instances it took only their opposition to grind the chamber to a complete standstill. Many lawmakers bemoaned this circumstance, but Jordan and Meadows saw it as a savvy use of power.

"It's simple legislative fact," Jordan said. "If you're one senator, you have an influence based on their crazy rules. If you're three or more senators who could stick together—influence. If you're one member of Congress, you can lead. But to really get something done, you need a group. It's funny," he mused. "I say this to our guys—we're pro free-market conservative guys. But we're a union. And we have to function like a union if we're going to get something done."

In unity, strength. Enforcing that unity was something for which Jordan was particularly suited. In this key respect, he was different from almost every member of Congress: He wanted and expected purity. Most members of Congress just did what it took to win or to survive in the moment. They broke promises. For example, Markwayne Mullin of Oklahoma announced in 2012 that he would serve only three terms in Congress. In 2017 he should've been readying to return to his plumbing business in Broken Arrow, Oklahoma. But instead he announced he was running for a fourth term. "The last thing we want is to make people think we're going back on our word. That made this difficult," Mullin said in July 2017, according to the *Tulsa World*. "At the time, we were sincere. But where we're at today is a different situation." (Members of Congress often absurdly refer to themselves as "we.")

Jordan expected members of Congress to do what they promised on the campaign trail. Novel, right? And he expected Republican leaders to keep their promises.

DONALD TRUMP WAS NOT exempt from Jordan's expectations, and the singular spotlight of the presidency made deviations impossible to hide. The pressure to bend came from nearly every direction, as the political landscape during Trump's first two years was complicated at best and treacherous at worst.

Trump spent nearly all of the 2016 presidential campaign laying out an extraordinarily hard-line immigration position, including strict limits on legal immigration, and vowing that, if he were to win the presidency, not only would he build a wall, but Mexico would foot the bill for its construction. Jordan and his Freedom Caucus cohorts didn't all necessarily believe that Mexico would actually pay for it, but they did take seriously the idea that the United States was going to build a new physical barrier on the border with Mexico, and they expected Trump to keep his word.

Republican leadership was tasked with carrying out the broad outlines of Trump's vision, but it was an awkward fit, since their views on immigration were barely reconcilable with the president's. Paul Ryan had the most interesting history when it came to immigration reform: He was unabashedly for it and had worked with Congress's most liberal members to try to push it through. In 2013, while visiting Chicago with Rep. Luis Gutiérrez, an Illinois Democrat, he walked into a church with mariachi music playing and promoted a five-point immigration plan. It included a "pathway to earned legalization" that encouraged undocumented immigrants to "come out of the shadows." Ryan was also wholeheartedly for a special pathway for undocumented children born in the United States. All those policies became anathema to the GOP in Trump's Washington.

The following year Ryan was secretly working with people like Gutiérrez—and Mark Meadows, as a matter of fact—to squeeze what would now be dubbed amnesty through the House. At that time, some people considered Meadows a dove when it came to migrants; he had a district that benefited from immigrant agriculture workers. The House effort collapsed when Eric Cantor lost his race after being accused of a permissive attitude toward illegal immigration.

Like many of Kevin McCarthy's views, his take on immigration didn't fit neatly into what became Trump's Republican Party. When McCarthy was the Republican leader in the California Assembly—he didn't like the title "minority leader," and forced anyone who said it to put a charity contribution in a jar—he gave his clearest view on just how wobbly he would seem in today's Republican Party. In 2005, during an appearance at Marina High School in Huntington Beach, California, McCarthy was asked by a student if he thought immigrants should be permitted to run for president.

McCarthy, then a top ally of Arnold Schwarzenegger, didn't skip a beat. "I personally support it," he said, noting that the fear that underlay prohibiting immigrants from running had been driven by the idea that another country could take over America. "That was two hundred years ago. I think if people have lived here twenty-five years, they made a decision they want to be an American. They made a decision they loved this country. They understand this country well. And they should have the opportunity. I mean, a lot of our great changes in this country have been from immigrants. We have to recognize that. We're a country of immigrants."

Trump's policies did not require Jim Jordan to equivocate or evolve. When it came to holding the president to account on these promises, Jordan had two things that gave him power: some control over the votes of the three dozen members of the House Freedom Caucus, all of whom viewed him as an ideological barometer, and the attention of the president himself.

Trump "normally calls when you're on TV fighting with someone, or on CNN," Jordan said in Ohio. "I wish every American could meet him. . . . He's a fighter. He hates losing. That is America."

One of Jordan's first interactions with Trump was at the White House on February 16, 2017. Jordan, who has virtually no coal-related jobs in his district, was invited to the signing of a bill that repealed coal regulations. He was surprised to be asked but attended anyway. Trump spotted him before the signing and immediately approached him. "I saw you on TV," the president said as he shook Jordan's hand. "You kicked Cuomo's butt." Trump was referring to Chris Cuomo, a CNN host with whom the president and his aides had sparred. "I like your tie and shirt," Trump added.

Jordan immediately went back to his office and instructed his staff to put him on television more often. "Because you're talking to the president" when you're on TV, he explained later.

It was easy to see why Trump liked Jordan. He was, personally, a pretty pleasant guy. He liked to talk shop with the media, chatting with reporters and giving out his cell phone number. Trump also seemed taken by Jordan's wrestling prowess. He liked that Jordan was a fighter. "He was like the best wrestler in college," Trump said in an interview, talking about Jordan. "Jim was incredible. And part of that competitiveness that you see is why he was such a great wrestler."

Outside the president, though, Jordan was perhaps one of the least popular men on Capitol Hill. In his pursuit of purity, he tormented his leadership and tried to sink their legislative game plan at every turn. Ryan, McCarthy, and Scalise kept an eye on him but spent little time trying to extract a yes vote from him, because they felt he was predisposed to oppose whatever they were trying to achieve.

Despite closures at Washington's Dulles Airport, and snow bearing down on the national capital region, Jordan made it to Washington for the second year of Trump's presidency. He didn't know when it would happen, but he truly wanted his party to take a stand. He wasn't keen that Congress was getting ready to boost spending by $1 trillion, something Ryan, McConnell, and Trump were all aiming for. "You're now talking about the second-largest spending increase in a decade," he said. "Second only to the [Obama-era] stimulus package. That's the worst place you can go."

On spending and on immigration, Jordan didn't think he was asking for much. He merely wanted the president, and the Republican Party, to fight.

"It's going to require a showdown at some point," Jordan said of beating the Democrats and getting some wins in Trump's Washington. "You're going to have to have a debate. You'll have to work closely with the White House. The guy with the biggest bully pulpit in the world is on our side helping us win that debate."

12

"I'LL TAKE THE HEAT"

FRESH OFF THE CAMP DAVID retreat, during which he heard about the benefits of bipartisanship from people like Kevin McCarthy, the president invited Republicans and Democrats to the White House for an immigration roundtable. This was exactly the kind of gathering that drove Jim Jordan and the Freedom Caucus nuts. *Why is he sitting down with Democrats before he has an agreement with Republicans?* conservatives quietly griped.

Immigration was the issue that best showcased the paradox of Donald Trump. He had been elected by promising hard-line immigration measures that were anathema to Democrats, and yet he remained willing to keep bringing them to the table in hopes of striking a deal. This persistence reflected both his love of deals and the ego-driven faith that he alone could break the gridlock that typically strangled Washington. Get Republicans and Democrats in a room, he thought, and things could happen. They could talk it out. Trump had haggled with his fair share of contractors, and for him this was virtually the same thing: Stomach one bad policy in exchange for a good one. But this was politics, not skyscrapers, and that kind of bargain was difficult; on immigration, it approached impossible.

In December, Pelosi and Schumer's big plan to bundle deadlines at the end of the year in order to get an immigration deal had fizzled. They were locked in battle with Republicans on multiple fronts, from the tax reform bill to pushing for parity between domestic and military spending in 2018. Government funding was slated to expire December 7, and using it to fight for DREAMers seemed an afterthought. Speaking to reporters in the Capitol, Pelosi said she would not take the government to the brink of a shutdown to insist on language to protect DREAMers. "That is part of our priorities," Pelosi said, pointing to a poster of her top issues at a news conference. "We have student loans, you know, there are other subjects, too, that need attention." She and Schumer ended up agreeing to push funding to mid-January. Steven Mnuchin used what's referred to as "extraordinary measures" to delay the debt limit deadline into 2018 as well. Just like that, the Democrats' legislative leverage point disappeared, and the battle raged into the New Year.

Going into Trump's January meeting, the battle lines seemed clear: Democrats, of course, wanted to grant some form of legal citizenship to the DREAMers, who had come to America illegally, many as small children. Democrats weren't open to ending chain migration, which allowed people to bring family members to the United States, or the diversity visa, which allowed residents of small countries to gain legal entrance.

Still, Trump invited more than two dozen people to the Cabinet Room to, in theory, hash these differences out.

This meeting, on January 9, was designed to be closed, as most serious D.C. gatherings are. But Trump stunned the crowd when he invited cameras in and allowed them to stay for the duration of the session.

Trump was sandwiched by Democrats: To his right was Dick Durbin, the Senate's Democratic whip from Illinois. To his left was Steny Hoyer, the number two House Democrat from Maryland. Trump invited Kevin McCarthy and Martha McSally, an Arizona Republican who was running for the Senate. Attendees spanned the ideological spectrum: everyone from Dianne Feinstein, Democrat of California, to the conservative Idaho Republican congressman Raúl Labrador.

"I'm appealing to everyone in the room to put the country before party, and to sit down and negotiate and to compromise, and let's see if we can get something done," Trump said. "I really think that we have a chance to do it. I think it's very important. You're talking about eight hundred thousand people—and we're talking about lots of other people are also affected, including people that live in our country. That's from the security standpoint.

"So maybe the press can stay for a little while and a couple of folks can make statements and I don't mind the statements," the president continued. "We want to have this as a very open forum. I will say, though, that I really do believe Democratic and Republican—the people sitting around this table—want to get something done in good faith. And I think we're on our way to do it."

Durbin spoke first and was cautiously optimistic. Then Hoyer got into specifics, encouraging Trump to handle DACA first and quickly. "It seems to me, Mr. President, if we're going to move ahead in a constructive way, that we take that on which we agree [and] pass it," he said. "The American public will be pleased with all of us if we do that. Just as, in September, you recall, we did the extension of [government funding]. No drama. We were all for it. You and the four leaders met, we came to an agreement, and we passed that CR."

Trump listened to Hoyer, then promptly blamed Barack Obama for the nation's immigration woes. It was a typical Trump non sequitur, but his spirits seemed high, and he sounded like he thought he could defy political gravity and pitch a permanent solution for illegal immigrants in America, not just DACA but a big-picture deal.

"I also think that, after we do DACA . . . I really think we should look in terms of your permanent solution and to the whole situation with immigration," Trump said to Hoyer. "I think a lot of people in this room would agree to that also, but we'll do it in steps. And most people agree with that, I think, that we'll do the steps. Even you say, 'Let's do this, and then we go phase two.'"

Trump wasn't being entirely clear, but he seemed to be agreeing with the Democrats' two-step solution: DACA first, border security later.

"Kevin, what would you like to say?" the president asked McCarthy.

When it came to Trump, McCarthy felt his role was, at times, to put the cat back in the proverbial bag. Already he felt like Trump had gone too far in this meeting—pitching a wholesale rewrite of immigration laws to Steny Hoyer—and it fell to McCarthy to translate Trump not only to the rest of the room, but to Trump himself.

McCarthy, of course, preferred a different solution: He was willing to look at a big comprehensive immigration deal down the road, but he didn't want to cut a deal protecting DREAMers in the short term without also getting border security. For most conservatives, including Meadows and Jordan, these two issues were inseparable; many insisted on securing the border as a condition of giving status to anyone in the country illegally.

McCarthy thanked the president for bringing everybody together, then turned to Hoyer. "Yes, we've got to do DACA, and I agree with you one hundred percent," he said. "But if we do not do something with the security, if we do not do something with the chain migration, we are fooling each other that we solved the problem. You know how difficult this issue is. . . . I'll be the first one to tell you, we're all going to have to give a little, and I'll be the first one willing to. But let's solve the problem—but let's not tell the American public at the end that it's solved when it's not."

Trump didn't get that McCarthy was pulling him back from the brink. In fact, he seemed to want to shoot right over it. "If you want to take it that further step," he said, indicating a comprehensive deal, which would create a new pathway to citizenship for illegal immigrants, "I'll take the heat, I don't care. I'll take all the heat you want to give me, and I'll take the heat off both the Democrats and the Republicans. My whole life has been heat. I like heat, in a certain way. But I will."

Four months earlier McConnell and Ryan had sat in the Oval Office and watched Trump cut a deal with Democrats on the debt limit, and even then, on something as minor as a three-month extension, Republicans had threatened to bolt the deal. For what Trump was proposing to do with Democrats now, there would be mass defections from the right. The president was seemingly abandoning Republican orthodoxy and the promises on which he had campaigned.

Chuck Grassley quickly tried to bring the discussion back to earth. "I'd like to talk about the reality of the whole situation," he said. "We've always talked in the United States Senate about the necessity of getting sixty votes. And that's pretty darn tough.

"But if we would write a bill that you don't like and you veto it, we're talking about a sixty-seven-vote threshold—two-thirds in the United States Senate. So that's the reality of negotiating in good faith and getting something you can sign.

"You know, I would vote for a path to citizenship, which isn't very easy for me, but I would do it just as an effort," Grassley said, stunning some in the room. "But there are certain things that we got to guarantee that we're going to do."

Grassley was trying to make Trump understand that he couldn't just kick border security down the road; without it, there was no deal. But Trump was in full deal mode. "Chuck, I will say," Trump said. "When this group comes back—hopefully with an agreement . . . I'm signing it. I mean, I will be signing it. I'm not going to say, 'Oh, gee, I want this or I want that.' I'll be signing it, because I have a lot of confidence in the people in this room that they're going to come up with something really good."

Come up with something, and I'll sign it. It was a sentiment that revealed the president's ideological black hole. He wanted to do a deal. He wasn't going to make demands. On the other side, there was no guarantee that he wouldn't change his mind entirely once someone else had his ear, even as soon as thirty seconds from now. The conversation had become a form of political whiplash, with no one sure where the president would turn next.

Trump then did something that likely made every Republican in the room clench his or her teeth: He asked Dianne Feinstein what she was thinking. "Senator, would you like to say something?"

No one in the room was farther to the left than Feinstein, the eighty-four-year-old California Democrat, and her thoughts were very much in character. "I don't know how you would feel about this," she said, "but I'd like to ask the question. What about a clean DACA bill now, with a commitment that we go into a comprehensive immigration reform procedure?"

It was a strong, concrete ask of what Hoyer had been requesting:

legalize the 700,000 DREAMers without a corresponding border security package. This was the definition of amnesty, the policy track Trump had railed against during his entire campaign. Republicans would revolt over it.

Trump did not revolt. "I have no problem," he said. "We're going to come up with DACA. We're going to do DACA, and then we can start immediately on the phase two, which would be comprehensive."

"Would you be agreeable to that?" Feinstein said.

"Yeah, I would like—I would like to do that," Trump replied.

McCarthy was alarmed. There was no way he could let Trump agree to a clean DACA bill. Grassley had tried to walk him back and failed. Now McCarthy had to take charge. "Mr. President, you need to be clear though," he said, trying to act as the party's savior. He turned to Feinstein: "Are you talking about security as well?"

"Well, I think if we have some meaningful comprehensive immigration reform, that's really where the security goes," Feinstein said, trying to kick it down the road. "And if we can get the DACA bill, because March is coming and people are losing their status every day—"

"But let's be honest," McCarthy interjected, "security was voted on just a few years ago, and, no disrespect, there's people in the room on the other side of the aisle who voted for it. If I recall, Senator Clinton voted for it. So I don't think that's comprehensive; I think that's dealing with DACA at the same time. I think that's really what the president is making. It's kind of like three pillars: DACA, because we're all in the room want to do it; border security, so we're not back out here; and chain migration. It's just three items, and then everything else that's comprehensive is kind of—"

"And the lottery," Trump said.

"And the lottery," McCarthy echoed. Now he had Trump back.

"And I think you should add merit," said Trump, tilting further back to the right. *Merit* was shorthand for restricting immigration based on education level—anathema to Democrats. "I mean, if you can, add merit-based. I don't think—I don't know who is going to argue with merit-based?"

"I wanted to ask Mr. McCarthy a question," said Feinstein. "Do you really think there can be agreement on those three difficult subjects you raised in time to get DACA passed and effective?"

"Yes, because you have heard from Leader McConnell and Speaker Ryan, who said they will put the bill onto the floor if the president agrees to it," McCarthy said. "And us getting to the room, I haven't seen us be this close and having this discussion in quite a few years—or the whole last four years. So I think, yes, we can make this happen."

"I think what we're all saying is we'll do DACA and we can certainly start comprehensive immigration reform the following afternoon," Trump said. "Okay? We'll take an hour off, and then we'll start."

Suddenly, Trump seemed to have gone back to his previous position on a clean DACA. "Okay," Feinstein said, seeming befuddled. One could hardly blame her. It seemed like both Democrats and Republicans were trying to pin down a president who wasn't entirely sure where he himself stood.

After a few more comments from lawmakers, a reporter piped up with the obvious reaction: "I'm not the most politically astute person in the world, but it seems to me not much has actually changed here in terms of your position at this particular meeting."

"No, I think it's changed," Trump said. "I think my positions are going to be what the people in this room come up with. I am very much reliant on the people in this room. I know most of the people on both sides. I have a lot of respect for the people on both sides. And my—what I approve is going to be very much reliant on what the people in this room come to me with. I have great confidence in the people. If they come to me with things that I'm not in love with, I'm going to do it because I respect them."

It was as if the president of the United States had no guiding philosophy on immigration policy and was happy to defer as long as it meant he could notch a victory.

After the press left the room, McCarthy made clear to the group exactly what he wanted: The House should quickly pass a bill that satisfied Trump's previously stated four pillars of immigration reform: end chain migration, end the diversity visa lottery, give legal status to DACA recipients, and beef up border security.

But Democrats could never go for that. Hoyer would not agree to those conditions; any consideration of chain migration and the visa lottery had to come later, in a more comprehensive proposal, after DREAMers were legalized.

The meeting didn't functionally change any immigration policy, but it taught the two parties the same lesson: At that moment, the president had no true North Star when it came to this crucial issue.

THAT WEEK CONSERVATIVE REPUBLICANS went into a closed party meeting in the Capitol and urged leaders to adopt a hard-line proposal penned by Rep. Bob Goodlatte, chair of the House Judiciary Committee. The Goodlatte bill was tough stuff. It eliminated the diversity visa program, which allowed migration from underrepresented countries. It shrank the number of overall immigrants let into America, including on visas issued to family members. It created an system to electronically verify immigration status for employment purposes. It boosted border security, per Trump's request. And it sought to crack down on so-called sanctuary cities, areas that ignored federal immigration law. Even Republican leaders thought the Goodlatte bill was a poison pill, a piece of legislation so politically toxic that it would get something south of one hundred votes and could never pass the Senate.

As the immigration talks proceeded haltingly, the president, surprising no one in Congress, stuck his foot in his mouth.

On January 12, the *Washington Post*'s Josh Dawsey broke the news that Trump had told a few lawmakers he didn't exactly appreciate some of America's immigrants. "Why are we having all these people from shithole countries come here?" Trump was quoted as saying in Dawsey's piece, referring to migrants from "Haiti, El Salvador and African countries."

That all but ended any immediate prospect for an immigration deal. Democrats couldn't even negotiate with someone who spoke like that.

.   .   .

ON JANUARY 16, MARK MEADOWS was in his office, which had bloodred walls, a deer head tacked to the wall, and a photo of Donald and Melania Trump with Meadows and his wife, Debbie. It was midafternoon, and Meadows was sinking into his black leather chair seemingly weighed down by power. He just blurted this out: "It's all coming down to: Will the Freedom Caucus shut down the government?"

It was true. It was up to Mark Meadows, the Freedom Caucus's tactician, to decide whether a government funding bill passed or failed.

Republicans had been inching closer to the January 19 government funding deadline they had set in December, and yet with three days to go, they had no clear sense of how they would keep the government open. Roadblocks stood in every direction. Democrats were desperate to use the funding battle to get something on immigration even without the two-issue leverage they'd had in September and again in December. Ryan, McConnell, and the Republican leadership, on the other hand, worked mightily to keep the issues on separate tracks.

But immigration wasn't the only hurdle to passing a budget. Both parties were working to boost government spending limits. The leadership was looking to boost defense spending by $80 billion, and nondefense spending by $63 billion later that year—an increase almost unheard of for the party, and one that was producing blowback from fiscal conservatives.

So Ryan was in a box. Military hawks needed the spending increase, but conservatives weren't willing to put their stamp of approval on a massive boost in government spending. Democrats wanted a DACA solution, but conservatives weren't at all willing to okay it. And even if Ryan blocked Democrats and gave the hawks what they wanted, he could not pass a budget without support from the members of the Freedom Caucus, Meadows's gang of mostly ardent Trump supporters.

In Meadows's office that day, a cold one with temperatures in the midthirties, it was as if he were becoming ruefully aware of his power. He could plunge the government and country into chaos—or not. He could look to score political points—or not. He could screw over his president—who told him on a phone call he did not want a shutdown—or not. He and Jordan had absolute sway over twenty votes, and

Republicans could lose just eighteen. In other words, Meadows was king.

"There's all kinds of hyperbole on our influence and what we are and what we're not. This time, you know, for the last seventy-two hours, I've been sweating because now, I have to make a decision," he said.

He was sweating because this decision wasn't so easy. His colleagues in the hard-line Freedom Caucus didn't like the big spending on the horizon. Nor did they want to okay a bill that would again fund the government on a short-term basis. And they damn sure did not want a weak immigration deal. The problem, which Meadows knew, was that there was nothing they wanted that Ryan could offer to buy their votes.

"This is the first time since I've been in Congress that I've looked and tried to say, 'Okay, what strategy could I deploy?' And I can't come up with one," Meadows said. "I just don't see the leverage points. I don't see where it ends up."

Meadows was pretty sure that Republicans would suffer politically for a government shutdown. It would be in Democrats' interest to make it last for weeks, heaping political pain on the party one year after Trump took power. In two weeks, on January 30, President Trump was to deliver his State of the Union address. What if the government were shut down?

"I'm just sitting here, and I'm just sweating," Meadows said.

THAT NIGHT HOUSE REPUBLICANS were getting their bearings, readying for a long week of brawling over government funding and immigration. They announced a seven P.M. meeting in the basement of the Capitol, and for fuel, they ordered Italian food from Carmine's, an outpost of the New York City eatery that was a few blocks from the Capitol in Chinatown.

Ryan was ready for the fight. He arrived carrying a red folder, which contained his plan to avert an immigration-fueled government shutdown. The House was going to vote that week on a proposal to kick the can down the road and fund government for just one month while congressional negotiators tried to work out an immigration deal. To try to attract votes for the one-month funding bill from Democrats, Ryan attached language that would extend a children's health insurance program; to sweeten the deal for Republicans, he would kill off a tax on high-end insurance plans that was enacted as part of Obamacare.

But there was nothing to address the immigration crisis. Nothing that would assuage Meadows or his conservative cohorts. The DACA debate would be extended one month—to line up with the next government funding bill.

Inside the Republican meeting, as they munched on the Italian food, most Republicans were pretty pleased with Ryan's plan. They got to extend government funding while taking another whack at Obamacare, and to the delight of many, they were further delaying the immigration vote.

As usual, House members were frustrated with McConnell's Senate, which would have a tough time passing any immigration bill. It was an age-old Washington game: When the Republican House was in a jam and trying to work its way out, it blamed the Republican Senate, which, in the House's telling, could never stand up for conservatism. Senators usually snickered; they considered House members lesser beings who liked to complain.

The blame-the-Senate dynamic was particularly sharp that January evening as House Republican leaders told the rank and file that McConnell's chamber would never accede to their immigration demands.

"I can't wait until we get Martha McSally over there so there's finally some testosterone," said Rep. Tom Cole, an Oklahoma Republican, speaking about the Arizona congresswoman running for the Senate.

"Well," said Rep. Austin Scott of Georgia, as he approached the microphone, "I can guarantee Martha McSally has more testosterone than Mitch McConnell, because he has none."

"It's not about having testosterone," replied McSally. "It's about growing a pair of ovaries," she said to hoots and hollers.

Rep. Glenn Grothman, a Wisconsin Republican, announced that Trump's "shithole country" comment "should be celebrated" because a constituent told him she didn't mind the tough talk. In fact, she could envision herself speaking like that.

But Rep. Mia Love, a Utah Republican, was having none of it. Love was black, the only Haitian American in Congress, and the only black Republican woman.

"I joined the Republican Party because our party offers the best chance to lift people up from all corners of the earth," she said. "I hope that my colleagues view me the same way as everyone else."

The room gave her a standing ovation.

THE NEXT MORNING Nancy Pelosi gave her private assessment to Democrats gathered in the Capitol Visitor Center for their caucus meeting.

"We can't vote for what they're putting forth," Pelosi said bluntly of Republicans' proposed bills. "Not for what's in it, but [for] what's not in it. This is an important moment for our caucus, standing up for what we know is right. . . . We will not give up our leverage, for our priorities and for our DREAMers."

Democrats were not keen on helping keep government open this time. The short-term bill had nothing to solve the immigration woes, and only cursory spending increases for programs they cared about. Pelosi, speaking in a private party meeting, put it this way: "This is like giving you a bowl of doggy doo, put a cherry on top, and call it chocolate ice cream."

Given the good feelings in their conference, Republicans took to the House floor the next day—Wednesday, January 17, at 1:20 P.M.—to canvass the party for support. Whipping, the intricate process of judging and drumming up support—is an art and a science. There are about sixty appointed whips, and they are responsible for asking their friends whether they support the bill under consideration. For example, when leadership was circling the floor trying to judge whether they could keep the government open, Rep. Elise Stefanik, an upstate New York Republican whip, was chatting with a fellow upstater, Rep. John Katko, about how he would vote. The whip cards, which alternate between blue, pink, and yellow, have five boxes to indicate where an individual member stands on a piece of legislation: *no, yes, lean yes, lean no,* and *undecided.*

Republicans quickly found out they were short. The source was unsurprising: Mark Meadows was holding out the Freedom Caucus's support, and Democrats would not make up the difference.

The next day Ryan delivered the news to the president. Ryan told Trump that he thought Republicans would be able to avoid a shutdown, but it was tricky because the Freedom Caucus was holding out, as were Democrats. The president had not helped matters; he had just tweeted that "CHIP should be part of a long term solution, not a 30 Day, or short term, extension!"

"I feel we're making really good progress with our members," Ryan told reporters. "We're having great conversations, and I feel our members are understanding the gravity of the situation, and I think our members do not want to reward using the military as a hostage in this moment."

But in fact, those conversations were not going well. That day Ryan had a small private lunch with some Republican lawmakers, and he urged them to try to be louder about the damage that would be done to the military if government were to shut down.

Meanwhile the Freedom Caucus was agitating. Meadows, inspired by the president and backed by Jim Jordan, had finally proffered some demands he wanted met in order to keep the government open. But just as he'd suspected, there was no room for Ryan to give. The Freedom Caucus wanted to boost money for military equipment—the leadership said no. It wanted to give the military a pay raise—the leadership lightly informed Meadows and Jordan that Congress was already giving soldiers a pay raise. They said they would vote for the funding bill if Ryan would agree to declassify a House Intelligence Committee report on Trump and Russia. Republican leaders dismissed this out of hand.

Then Meadows had another idea. He approached his fellow North Carolinian Patrick McHenry and tried to make a deal. McHenry was the party's chief deputy whip, the most important unelected position in Republican leadership. He was no stranger to agitation; in his early days as a young congressman, he had been a thorn in the side of John Boehner, routinely voting against the leadership while reveling in the attention and the courtship that came along with being a pain in the ass. Eventually, he came to see the other side of the coin. McHenry was close with Eric Cantor, and when Republicans took back the majority in 2010 and Cantor became the number two House Republican, he quickly saw how difficult it was to run the Republican Party. Boehner liked to call McHenry "shithead," as in "Now you see how hard this is, shithead."

Meadows and McHenry had a complicated relationship. They had to get along because of their shared home state of North Carolina, but they weren't particularly friendly. Meadows gave McHenry's leadership a hard time, and McHenry felt like Meadows was never honest with him.

But even though Meadows didn't like the spending bill, he didn't want to shoulder a government shutdown, so he and Jordan decided to take a meeting with McHenry in the Speaker's office to try to negotiate an off-ramp. McHenry, at the moment, was the acting Republican whip, since Steve Scalise was in the hospital, recovering from a second surgery related to his gunshot wounds the previous summer.

Earlier that day Meadows and Jordan had privately met with John Kelly and Marc Short from the White House. They told the aides exactly what they told the president: that they were concerned about the upcoming boost in government spending, but even more concerned about once again putting off the immigration debate. This was what Meadows would use to try to leverage his vote.

"We want a pledge that you're going to have a vote on Goodlatte," Meadows said to McHenry, referring to the hard-line immigration bill. Most Republicans thought the bill wouldn't pass, and many in the leadership thought a vote on it was political suicide for President Trump and the Republican Party.

But that wasn't the discussion McHenry wanted to have now. "Look," McHenry said. "The first step here is we need to put a team together, and we're going to work it." Translation: He was going to ask around and see how many people would support Goodlatte. His guess: The support was in the gutter, a message he'd be happy to deliver to Meadows himself.

That wasn't enough for Meadows. "Well, you need to pledge you're going to whip it," he shot back. Meadows didn't want McHenry to just canvass for support; he wanted the Republican leadership to twist arms to get the bill across the finish line.

"Can't do that. The whip's not here," McHenry said, thinking it would be out of place to bind Scalise to such a politically tricky vote.

McHenry and Meadows both left the meeting having heard what they wanted. Unfortunately, they didn't hear the same thing. McHenry thought he'd been clear that he was only going to take lawmakers' temperatures on the Goodlatte bill. But Meadows and Jordan walked out of the meeting, marched straight to the House floor, and began telling people that the leadership—specifically McHenry—had promised a vote on the Goodlatte bill.

People were fuming.

"I heard you pledged to put Goodlatte on the floor," Rep. Charlie Dent, a moderate Pennsylvania Republican, said to McHenry's chief of staff, Parker Poling, in a sharp tone. "Why are you always doing what they want to do?"

That night McHenry and Meadows were on the phone until midnight, trying to negotiate a way to keep the government open. Meadows asked for a token increase in troop pay, and McHenry and McCarthy both separately said they would call Meadows in the morning.

But that night McHenry started calling Meadows's Freedom Caucus colleagues to try to peel them away. They may have been Meadows's bloc, but they were all Republicans, and as McHenry saw it, they were his voters, too.

The move infuriated Meadows. He thought the leadership had been negotiating with him in good faith. Instead, they were trying to peel away his supporters—and his power.

With the Freedom Caucus now in open war with leadership, the mood was exceedingly tense on the Republican side of the aisle. That night the Freedom Caucus met to try to figure out what else they might ask for. The door to their typical meeting place was broken, so they repaired to Jim Jordan's office in the Cannon House Office Building. They threw a bunch of things at the wall, including a full year of defense

funding instead of a short-term deal. Jordan told reporters he was negotiating for "all good stuff," reminding them that this was what the
American people voted for in 2016.

Ryan didn't cave to the pressure. He offered the Freedom Caucus a
vote on a yearlong stand-alone defense bill and said that he would "work
harder" to pass the Goodlatte bill. And in the end, Meadows and Jordan
agreed to commit their bloc of votes to keeping the government open.
What they got wasn't much, but it was better than owning a shutdown.
For Ryan, it was a sweeter victory. He had also made these promises to
members of the Armed Services Committee, so in his telling, he gave
absolutely nothing away to get the Freedom Caucus's votes.

The bill passed at 7:36 P.M. on January 18 with 230 votes, 224 of
which were Republican. Meadows and Jordan both voted yes. True to
Pelosi's word, Democrats voted nearly uniformly against the bill. Another government funding debate had passed in the House without a
solution for the DREAMers.

THE BILL WAS SENT immediately to the Senate, where it would need to
be passed before midnight on the nineteenth to avoid a shutdown. At
11:02 that morning, Ryan, McCarthy, and McHenry huddled around
the whip desk to discuss whether to send House Republicans home for
the weekend while the Senate picked up the work. "Keep them here,"
Ryan said, uncertain what the Senate would do.

That night, just hours before the government was slated to shut
down, the president called Chuck Schumer and invited him to the
White House to try to untangle the messy knot of issues. Schumer—in
a moment that surprised Republicans, dismayed some Democrats, and
would perhaps come to be seen as a remarkable, fleeting moment of
concession—offered Trump money for his border wall, if Trump would
agree to allow DACA recipients to stay in the United States. Schumer
pleaded with Trump to support a short two- or three-day government
funding agreement so that the two sides might hammer out an agreement around those terms.

In retrospect, Trump might have wished he'd jumped at the chance; before long, wall money would become a red line that no Democrat would dare cross. But in the moment, Trump was skeptical; he wanted changes to visa policy, not only construction of his wall. And so shortly after Schumer left the White House, Trump's chief of staff, John Kelly, called John Cornyn, the number two Senate Republican, and informed him that the president would not cut a deal with Schumer. It was up to Schumer to work something out with Ryan and McConnell.

HOUSE REPUBLICANS FOUND THEMSELVES waiting with nothing to do. Steve Scalise's office opened up for Five Guys burgers and beer around six-thirty P.M. Other lawmakers headed to the Senate floor to see the action up close. Rep. Robert Pittenger, a North Carolina Republican, and Jim Himes, a Connecticut Democrat, separately took front-row seats in the Senate gallery to see whether the chamber would be able to avoid the first shutdown since 2013.

The mood was tense with uncertainty. Senate Democrats, seemingly ignoring the four-week funding bill that the House had just passed, were pushing to solve the status of DACA recipients as part of keeping the government open.

An initial vote was scheduled for ten P.M., and about fifteen minutes past the hour, McConnell approached the microphone and immediately moved toward a vote.

One by one, senators cast their votes by voice or by hand. By 10:35 P.M., the vote stood at 50–48, well short of the sixty-vote threshold needed to move toward a final vote.

With failure clear, the Senate broke into a number of side conversations. In one of them were Republican senators Roger Wicker of Mississippi, Lamar Alexander of Tennessee, Susan Collins of Maine, and Lindsey Graham of South Carolina, along with Democratic senators Michael Bennet of Colorado, Tim Kaine of Virginia, Joe Donnelly of Indiana, Jeanne Shaheen of New Hampshire, Chris Coons of Delaware, and Debbie Stabenow of Michigan, and independent senator Angus King of Maine. The discussion centered on one thing: Could they somehow cobble together an immigration deal as part of this debate? The clock was ticking; the government would shut down in less than two hours. There were lots of ideas thrown out. Everything fell flat.

At 12:16 A.M., more than two hours after the vote started and sixteen minutes into a government shutdown, Ron Johnson, the Republican senator from Wisconsin, announced that the vote had officially failed. McConnell stood up to concede that the Senate failed to keep the government open—and began blaming Democrats.

"What we have just witnessed on the floor was a cynical decision by Senate Democrats to shove aside millions of Americans for the sake of irresponsible political games," McConnell said. "The government shutdown was one hundred percent avoidable, completely avoidable. Now it is imminent. All because Senate Democrats chose to filibuster a noncontroversial funding bill that contains nothing—not a thing—they do not support. . . . Perhaps across the aisle, some of our Democratic colleagues are feeling proud of themselves, but what has their filibuster accomplished? . . . The answer is simple: their very own government shutdown."

McConnell said—and rightly so—that Democrats were holding the government hostage over illegal immigration. Everyone wanted to help the DACA kids, McConnell said, but this was not the time. The deadline for that issue was in March. Government funding was running dry now.

At 12:23 A.M., it was Schumer's turn. He said he had thought he was on the brink of an agreement with Trump after offering him his border wall and seemed perplexed by what happened.

"Many Democrats don't want to go that far on the border," he said from the Senate floor. "Many Republicans don't either. But we were willing to compromise with the president to get an agreement. In the room it sounded like the president was open to accept it. This afternoon, in my heart, I thought, *We might have a deal tonight*. That was how far we'd come. That's how positive our discussion felt. We had a good meeting. But what has transpired since that meeting in the Oval Office is indicative of the entire tumultuous and chaotic process Republicans have engaged in in the negotiations thus far."

Then Schumer stuck the knife in: "What happened to the President Trump who asked us to come up with a deal and promised he'd take heat for it? What happened to that president? He backed off at the first sign of pressure." Schumer later said he'd thought he had a deal with Trump. "I went over, bent over backward because I care so much about the DACA kids, to give him a deal," Schumer said. "We didn't exactly shake hands, but we shook hands."

The brief shutdown was entirely useless. It did not bring Congress any closer to solving the immigration mess. Its only accomplishment was earning Paul Ryan plaudits from conservatives who were happy he'd had a stiff spine when he refused to talk about immigration with the government shut down. Even if the Senate got something done with immigration in its bill, Ryan said, he couldn't guarantee a vote in the House. *Take up the bill we passed,* Ryan told senators.

On Monday, January 22, Schumer went to the floor and said he would vote to reopen the government. No real progress had been made toward a DACA deal. But over a series of conversations, McConnell told Schumer that he would allow a free-wheeling immigration vote by February 8.

House Democrats who had taken the stand to oppose Ryan's bill felt like they had been hosed—and they had been. Schumer didn't have much room to maneuver, as the base wanted to solve the immigration issue and he had little leverage to deliver anything resembling a victory.

During a closed party meeting that Monday, Democratic Rep. Gwen Moore, who represented Milwaukee, said, "How do we know the Senate isn't screwing us?" Steny Hoyer said only this: "They are."

It was true. McConnell's promise to bring immigration bills to the floor in February had to be declared a win, but Ryan had not made a corresponding promise. House Republicans saw the March 5 deadline—when Trump said DACA would expire—as their action-forcing date.

"March is really the timeline," Steve Scalise said in an interview with *Politico.* "The House wasn't part of that deal."

Jim Jordan watched the whole episode and blamed Republicans. Instead of extracting some concession from Schumer to end a shutdown that he had caused, Republicans had folded.

"We were so poised to win, and we blew it, so poised to win," Jordan said. Jordan's view was that they had Democrats up against the ropes—they were withholding their votes to fund government—and they relented for no reason. In Jordan's telling, they could've used this opportunity to force a discussion about visa policy or even Trump's border wall.

But instead, the government was open. Jordan and Trump did not get their border wall. And Democrats had made no progress on DACA.

13

FAMILY DISCUSSIONS

IT WAS ALL SCRIPTED, hour by hour, minute by minute, down to the two-and-half-page call sheet detailing whom Paul Ryan would phone to warn that he was ending his career.

He left nothing to chance. On April 11, Ryan woke up in the Rayburn House Office Building—yes, the Speaker of the House slept in his office—and worked out as usual in the private, members-of-Congress-only Capitol gym. He arrived at his office that morning at 7:50 A.M., nearly thirty minutes earlier than usual. Brendan Buck, his counselor and close adviser, had arrived more than half an hour earlier to review the game plan. Now it was time to execute.

The day before, a Tuesday, Jonathan Burks, Ryan's chief of staff, had sent a calendar invitation to the senior members of the office, alerting them to a meeting in the Speaker's office that evening, and an all-hands meeting the next morning. *Normal enough,* aides thought. Congress was getting back into session. Maybe Ryan wanted to touch gloves. Buzz that Ryan was planning something had begun to reach the legions of Republican operatives around town, but no one was alarmed— Patrick McHenry of North Carolina, Steve Scalise's deputy, heard about the full-office gathering but shrugged his shoulders. *Weird,* he thought.

In that small Tuesday-night meeting of a dozen or so aides, Ryan broke the news: The next morning he would walk into HC-5, the dingy basement meeting room where the party had fought its most fervent and defining internal battles, and tell the 237-member House Republican Conference that he was through. His twenty-year career was over. The bulwark to, and later the partner of, Donald John Trump was going back to Janesville. He told the small group that he would loop in his entire staff first thing the next morning, make a round of quick phone calls to his leadership colleagues and friends, then inform the whole GOP at nine A.M.

In announcing the end of his political career—one marked by a rocket-like ascendance—Ryan didn't utter a negative word about Trump, not publicly, not privately. Those days were gone; Ryan had learned his lesson. Hours after he told his colleagues he would not run again, sitting in shirtsleeves in his office, he put it this way: "He appreciates that when we have disputes or differences of opinions that we air them out privately, and what I've learned is he learns and he responds and he respects." In other words, Ryan had learned to shut up.

This decision wasn't born of some deep-seated angst over Trump's conduct, Ryan and his aides said. Sure, the Speaker had misgivings about the president, and they were well known: the crudeness, the steady stream of affairs, the undermining of U.S. traditions, the tweets. Ryan frequently shook his head privately when told of the scandal du jour. But the trade-off, he said, was worth it. "The issue of the moment—the tweet of the moment—pales in comparison to the big policy changes I believe are going to make a difference in people's lives, and are going to move us in the right direction," he told a small group of reporters in his Capitol office the day he quit. "We've done so much stuff that I really think is going to have a lasting impact. And those things completely overshadow the frustration of the day or the moment."

Indeed, the publicly and privately available evidence was that Ryan was getting along fine with the president. By the time he announced his retirement, the two men were often talking several times a day. During the Obama years, it was a news story when the president called Nancy Pelosi or John Boehner. In the Trump years, the president was dialing Ryan all the time—often finding him in the gym. The president would call to check in on legislative strategy, and Ryan would listen, trade tips, and sometimes try to redirect his thinking on sensitive issues like trade policy. He had made the pointed—and controversial—decision that Trump wasn't worth trying to change.

You couldn't help but get the sense, however, that Ryan was just tired of Donald Trump. Couldn't-take-it-anymore tired. It had been a long year and a half since the president was inaugurated, and the endless back-and-forth was wearing. There was no better example than the recent mid-March fight over the omnibus, a massive, trillion-dollar spending bill that would keep government funded until the end of September. Though there was much in the bill for both parties, and $1.3 billion for Trump's border wall, Mark Meadows and Jim Jordan had been whispering to the president that he was getting a raw deal. Ryan went to the White House to explain to Trump just how big a win the bill represented for Republicans. The president blew up at Ryan, angry he had not gotten enough money for his border wall. He asked the Speaker if he could move money from military spending on things like fighter jets to be spent on a wall. "You can't do that," Ryan told him. Both chambers of Congress cleared the bill before going out of session on March 23.

Ryan was already back in Wisconsin when Trump, egged on by negative coverage on Fox News, tweeted that he was considering vetoing the bill, which would shut down the government. Ryan had to call the president and plead for him to sign it. He told Trump that if he vetoed the bill, Congress would simply pass it again—a rare dare from the Speaker to the president, which showed how invested he was in the giant spending bill. Ryan also secretly called Defense Secretary Jim Mattis and urged him to get to the White House to forcefully ask the president to sign the bill. Ryan wanted Mattis to remind Trump how good the bill was for the military. Mattis did meet with the president, and eventually Trump signed the omnibus, though not without calling it "crazy" and saying he'd never sign a bill like that again. The whole process was exhausting.

If Ryan wouldn't admit that he was tired of Trump, he was definitely tired of being away from his wife, Janna, and the kids. His three children were growing up, and Janna had essentially been a single mom for almost two decades. Ryan thought often about time, and how much of it he would have. It had been three generations since a male in his family had lived to sixty. Ryan was forty-eight. His team considered that narrative in their planning and leaned into it: Who could blame him for wanting to spend more time with his family?

But this decision would also have outsize impact on his other family: the Republican members in the House of Representatives. His staff privately warned him what most people were expecting him to do: run for reelection and quit after he won his seat for the eleventh time. This would avoid the chatter that the leader of the party was resigning in the middle of a tough campaign season during which the GOP was sure to lose seats—or control of the House. Ryan couldn't do it. His poker face was too bad, and the guilt would be layered on too thick. He wouldn't be able to sleep at night if he ran for office knowing he wouldn't serve. Sure, he was sending his troops into battle just as he retreated, but they'd be fine, he thought. Things would settle back into normalcy soon enough, Ryan said shortly after he announced his decision.

Not everyone felt sympathy for Ryan's need to honor what his heart was telling him to do. At times, it seemed as if external forces were dictating Ryan's decision making, leaving him a hapless bystander in his own life. He *just had* to get on board with Donald Trump after his election, despite spending months sharply criticizing the man. Running for Speaker *was not* his choice—he was called to duty. He *just had* to fire the House chaplain in the middle of the term, despite the outcry he knew would ensue. He *couldn't* run around Wisconsin, campaigning for another run, while knowing in his heart that he would step down after he won—never mind that his decision to announce his retirement during campaign season would impact more than two hundred members of his party, all of whom were running for reelection. This dynamic frustrated some of Ryan's Republican colleagues.

But this decision was made, and the fruits of a long five months of planning were about to go into effect. As he stood before staff in his office on that Wednesday morning amid Green Bay Packers memorabilia and the official handwritten vote tally of his Speaker race, Ryan laid out why he was jumping ship. The Speaker's keywords, as he spoke to his staff and later his colleagues: "weekend dad," which was something he didn't want to be anymore, and "run through the tape," which he promised to do in the remaining nine months of his speakership. He wanted people to understand he wasn't about to give up. He did not want to be seen as a quitter.

GUILT. IT WAS JUST one of the many feelings, ideas, and emotions raised and debated during seven intense "family meetings" that Ryan had held over five months before making the decision to end his two-decade career in D.C. In political circles and especially on Capitol Hill, the "family" concept is a bit overused. John Boehner, during his speakership, presided over intense intraparty squabbles over whether to shut the government down or default on the U.S. debt —he called those debates "family discussions." They were more like *Jerry Springer Show* episodes. But Ryan's inner circle was one of the few that truly exhibited familial loyalty.

The people in the room for these sessions represented the inner sanctum of Ryan's world. There was Brendan Buck, Ryan's counselor, who had first worked for the Wisconsinite during his 2012 vice-presidential run and was lured back to the Capitol to help guide Ryan's career when he became the chairman of the tax-writing Ways and Means Committee in 2015. Kevin Seifert was the brains behind Ryan's political operation, responsible for the sprawling network of donors that helped fund the Republican Party. Jake Kastan, a fresh-faced Ohioan who traveled with Ryan during the dark days after his vice-presidential run and was now his number two political operative, came to the meetings, too, as did chief of staff Jonathan Burks and Tim Kronquist, the Speaker's attorney. Andy Speth, a longtime Ryan hand who had first met Ryan in middle school, was also in the room. Speth traveled each week from Wisconsin to serve Ryan.

The first time they gathered was roughly one year before Election Day 2018. They met in the office of Team Ryan, the Speaker's political operation, which was located on the ground floor of the Republican National Committee headquarters on Capitol Hill—the same building where Ryan met with Trump when he first became the nominee. The expressly stated mission was to decide whether Ryan should serve another term.

Ryan's kitchen cabinet made every effort to keep their plotting secret. In the first meeting that November, the group made a pact: None of the staff would be permitted to discuss the private deliberations with anyone. But the aides also made it clear to Ryan that he should not discuss his potential retirement with his friends.

"Because if you do," they warned him, "it's going to get out there."

Ryan's political future was, of course, the stuff of rampant gossip around town. Even by that point—the winter of 2017—nearly no one in D.C. thought he could, or wanted to, continue in the speakership. *Politico*'s Rachael Bade and Tim Alberta published a story in December saying Ryan was going to leave the job at the end of his congressional term. Ryan's team shoulder-shrugged that one away, saying he had made no decision to announce, and he had to discuss it with his wife. But by then the internal discussion was seriously under way.

Over six meetings between November 2017 and March 2018, Ryan and his inner circle chewed over every possible consequence of Ryan leaving Congress. Would fund-raising suffer if Ryan cut bait midway through an election year? It was an important question, given how much money Republicans would need to be competitive, yet the answer was unknowable, the group decided. Because the discussions were so secret and private, Ryan's team didn't consult donors, Steve Stivers at the party committee, or Corry Bliss at CLF. Would Ryan's decision cause a rash of retirements across the Capitol? Unlikely. His team discovered that Wisconsin had one of the latest filing deadlines in America, which meant most incumbents would have already decided to stick it out. In other words, most House Republicans would be stuck running alongside a Speaker who refused to run with them.

How would the president react? they pondered. Would he lash out at Ryan and say he could no longer trust the Speaker? Or would he be gracious? Again, guesswork with this president. How would Kevin McCarthy, Ryan's number two, react? Would he push for an early election for the next Speaker? The general consensus was no, he wouldn't; he could use the time to build a winning coalition. Would the Freedom Caucus, wary of any Speaker, push for Ryan to resign immediately and force a vote to boot him to the curb? Ryan was confident he could weather that attack. "If it comes to that, and if people want me to go, that's fine," he said. "I think it's best for me to stay throughout the term, and do everything I can."

Ryan didn't come to the decision quickly. He vacillated a lot, and everyone in the room knew he was waffling. There was no real pressure for him to come to a decision until the spring, giving potential candidates for his Wisconsin seat enough time before Election Day to file their paperwork and get in the race. He set his own deadline as June 1—the Wisconsin filing deadline. So in the New Year he let the decision linger.

As late as February 2018, though, Ryan was still uncertain what he would do. He thought about the additional time commitment of staying on—two and a half years more, realistically, with Donald Trump in the White House—and balked at what it would entail. In a brief conversation that month with Buck, he brought this up but added he was "still thinking about it." One reason Ryan was considering sticking around was so he could take another whack at repealing and replacing Obamacare in 2019, when he thought Republicans would have a stronger majority in the Senate.

A few things soon tipped him to leave. One came on March 2, when Ryan was in Springfield, Missouri, raising money for Reps. Billy Long and Jason Smith, two backbench Republican lawmakers from the Show Me State. An older man approached him with advice. "I know you're a family man," he said to Ryan. "Let me give you a piece of advice I wish I listened to. They used to say it's not the quantity of time you spend with your kids, it's the quality of time. That's bull. It's both—and don't forget that."

Ryan said the advice hit him like a "two by four, more or less."

At the end of March, Ryan was about to decamp for Prague, where he was set to mark the one-hundredth anniversary of the U.S. relationship with the Czech Republic. He would meet with the prime minister and address the Chamber of Deputies, the lower house of parliament. Before departing, Ryan told his kitchen cabinet, "I'm going to go on spring break. I'm going to spend time with my family and have some final conversations."

That phrase, "final conversations," was all the small cadre of aides needed to hear. They knew Ryan was done, and they began to think about what his future would look like. Now the operation turned to planning his exit. They decided that if Ryan got approached with job offers after he announced, Kronquist, the attorney, would field those inquiries. Seifert, the political director, pushed for an aggressive party fund-raising schedule to ensure that Ryan reached an important mark, $40 million, before he announced he was going to retire. The media rollout plan for the step-down was quite simple: Ryan would tell the meeting of two hundred–plus Republicans and allow the news to leak from the room—which was certain to happen immediately.

In late March, Ryan and his family flew to Europe, where they spent six uninterrupted days together, touring and meeting with U.S. officials. During dinners, and as they wheeled around Europe, the family talked about Ryan retiring. Ryan's daughter, Liza, was beginning to look at colleges. Leaving felt right.

When Ryan and his family got back to the States, they had one last family dinner to discuss it. Around that table, in the house Ryan had spent so much time away from in the last twenty years, they finalized the decision.

As soon as Ryan walked into the office on April 11, the well-laid plan was already in motion. He had a two-and-a-half-page list of people to call to alert them of the decision. In quick succession, he called Kevin McCarthy, Steve Scalise, Cathy McMorris Rodgers, and Patrick McHenry, the members of his leadership team. He then held a conference call for Republicans in the Wisconsin congressional delegation.

Next came calls to donors, government officials, and friends. Mitt Romney, Ronna Romney McDaniel, Tommy Thompson, John Boehner, and Eric Cantor were among the other political figures Ryan dialed. And of course Donald Trump and Mike Pence got early phone calls. Trump was not pleased Ryan had announced his departure so far before the end of his term.

"Why don't you just wait until you're done to do it?" Trump asked Ryan.

"You've just got to know me. I can't live in dishonesty," Ryan said. "I just can't say one thing and do another. I can't do it."

Trump said he wished Ryan would stay. "You know how to get things done," Trump said. "People follow you. You're very effective at it. We could do a lot of good stuff together."

AS RYAN BEGAN MAKING phone calls that morning, it was completely unclear if his one big gambit would work. Would he be able to keep his speakership as a lame duck? In normal times, a party leader would have to step down immediately after making such an announcement. Ryan's old friend Eric Cantor tried to remain majority leader after he lost his primary challenge to an economics professor but ended up stepping down. Lame ducks are exactly that—lame. No one listens to them. Ryan was determined to be different.

The one thing that was completely out of his control was how his leadership team would react. Ultimately, it sparked a massive mess among Ryan's colleagues and turned grumbling and unrest that had been festering in the Capitol for months into an intraparty war.

The crux of the drama was this: It was clear to nearly everyone that McCarthy and Scalise, the number two and number three, were on a collision path. McCarthy, in many ways, was still licking his wounds from his last run at Speaker in 2015, which had been cut short when he realized he couldn't win. Scalise's allies seemed to realize that, and—whether they meant it or not—started sowing doubt about McCarthy's viability. This type of behavior threatened to split the party.

Scalise wasn't being coy. In March 2018 he invited *Politico*'s Rachael Bade to join him aboard an oil rig, the tactic he had used with reporters for years, and said he "wouldn't rule it out" when asked about a bid for Speaker. "Obviously, I've shown interest in the past at moving up," he told Bade. "I've enjoyed being in leadership. I feel like I've had a strong influence on some of the things that we've done, and I've helped put together coalitions to pass a full repeal of Obamacare."

Behind the scenes, Scalise's aides and allies had been saying the same thing for months: If McCarthy couldn't become Speaker, if the same problems dogged him this time that dogged him the last time, Scalise would step up and run. He had a hell of a story, right? Conservative. Nearly died in a politically motivated shooting. Who could vote against that?

Ryan was planning to stay until January 2019, when the new Congress was slated to begin. If Republicans lost the majority in November, McCarthy—"Dodger," to his Capitol Police detail, a nod to his favorite baseball team—would run for minority leader. If they kept power, he'd run for Speaker.

Before the Ryan retirement, Scalise and McCarthy thought they had cleared the air. The two men met frequently, usually right after the full Republican meeting on the first day of every week. In March, McCarthy asked Scalise if he would run for Speaker, and Scalise said no, he wanted to run for Republican leader—the number two slot. It seemed like everything was clear.

Until April 11.

YOU JUST COST US the House.

This was what Kevin McCarthy was thinking as he spoke to Paul Ryan. Ryan had just informed him of his plans to leave, and McCarthy wasn't happy. Sure, he'd heard the same rumors everyone else had in the last year about Ryan leaving, but he'd never thought it would happen midstride. McCarthy was worried—about morale, fund-raising, and the optics of the Speaker announcing his retirement in the middle of a congressional session.

Still, while Ryan's call may have perturbed McCarthy concerning the Republicans' future, personally the news wasn't all bad. Ryan had created a power vacuum, and no one was better poised to fill it. McCarthy was on the brink, and he could feel it, taste it. It was close.

The days of weakness were gone. Now when the Freedom Caucus tried to get in Kevin McCarthy's way, he stood up to them. When a problem needed solving, it was Kevin McCarthy who stepped up to solve it.

California needed more disaster-relief money after a spate of wildfires? Kevin's got it. He slipped it right into a must-pass spending bill, forcing Democrats to vote with Republicans to keep government open if they wanted their disaster aid. Texas wasn't happy with the billions they got after Hurricane Harvey? Kevin had a solution: He called the governor of Texas on speakerphone in front of the entire delegation—a powerful one at that—and made sure they knew that their state's chief executive was comfortable with the decision McCarthy had made. Everything is bigger in Texas, but no one had more juice than Kevin McCarthy.

The president of the United States was calling him frequently, often after hours when he was already asleep. Ivanka Trump was seeking him out for advice.

"A wonderful man who I've gotten to know very well—what a personality—Kevin McCarthy," the president of the United States had said about the gentleman from Bakersfield on March 20, 2018, at a massive, posh campaign dinner at the National Building Museum in Washington.

"My Kevin," he called the majority leader. Diminutive? Sure. A stamp of approval? Definitely. "I'll be all over the country," Trump said at that dinner, referring to the 2018 campaign. "Kevin, you'll get me all over. Where is our Kevin? You're going to get me all over the country, Kevin? And I'll be complaining every single trip. But I'm going to get there."

It was the kind of affirmation that almost every starry-eyed political hopeful dreams about. When you're young and on the campaign trail, hopping between stop one, stop two, and stop three—staying awake by guzzling Mountain Dew and eating Planters peanuts and dried fruit out of a blue plastic bag—you think of what it might be like if you got to Washington. Your first time walking onto the House floor. *Oh my goodness, it's so big.* But you belong. You won. Your first State of the Union—getting a glimpse of the man, grabbing his shoulder, you're on *his* team—he has no idea who you are, but you know who he is. You ran with him. Goddammit, you ran *for* him. The president of the United States. You told people that when you got to Washington, you'd be fighting in the trenches for him. You'd help him turn Washington upside down.

If you played your cards right, maybe you'd get a meeting with him. It wouldn't be just you and him, but you, him, and the other 230 members of your party. He might answer your question—if the leadership liked you and called on you. You'd take it, either way.

Maybe, some years down the road, you'd claw your way to being chairman of a subcommittee. Maybe one of your bills would get through the Senate, and you'd get invited to the signing ceremony. Maybe—just maybe—you'd get a handshake. A shout-out at the signing ceremony? Come on. Too much. You're a guy from a small town. You were a congressional staffer. You were a statehouse rat. You lucked into this. You—no way.

If you're a guy like Kevin McCarthy, you even didn't dream of this. No way. Not this stuff—it's too big. Way too big for a guy whose claim to fame was slinging deli sandwiches, winning the scratch-off California lottery on the second day it started, and hawking broken-down used cars. If you're Kevin McCarthy, you didn't dream of this stuff after what you'd been through. Not after walking out of a party election with your tail between your legs, confidence shot, unable to secure the speakership—a job all but teed up for you. Not after the rumors that you were unfaithful to your wife with a colleague. Hogwash, he told everyone. She had been by his side from day one.

That was a distant memory now. Past. Yesterday's news.

The president of the United States was now gushing over McCarthy in front of hundreds of filthy-rich donors and two hundred of his congressional colleagues. It seemed, at this point, that McCarthy could do anything.

So what the hell was he going to do? He often wondered that. Not too often, because he was always surrounded by people, consumed by interaction. But these days, it dogged him big-time. What the hell was Kevin McCarthy going to do?

As he hung up the phone with Ryan that morning, the question had become acute, because Ryan had not in fact created a power vacuum to be filled immediately. Instead, he had created a power vacuum that would come into being in nine months, after Election Day. If Ryan were to step down as Speaker now, in the middle of the Congress, McCarthy would run. Hell yes, he was ready. He thought he could put it together—if he had time. But Ryan staying on created as many problems for McCarthy as it solved.

Did Kevin want to be Speaker? Yes, he did. He lived for it. He loved the House. He was having fun—how could he not? He was friends with the president, pulling legislative stunts, making allies, punishing enemies—this was the kind of stuff the wide-eyed political neophyte lived for. Even in McCarthy's winter, after he dropped out of the Speaker race in 2015, he was still having fun.

But what if Republicans lost the majority after eight years? What if they squandered this 247-seat behemoth that McCarthy had built? The members he had recruited and cultivated—they'd be gone. Would he want to stay around? Could he go back to the minority, back to where he started? Offices would change. Staff would shrink. His job would change to protecting Donald Trump from impeachment, helping him with votes when he asked, and clawing his way back into the majority. That sounded a lot less appealing. But few around McCarthy expected he would be able to give it up.

STEVE SCALISE WAS WALKING toward the elevator to his office at around 7:45 when his cell phone rang. No caller ID popped up—it was either a telemarketer or the Speaker of the House. Telemarketers usually waited until nine.

"Steve-O," Ryan said, "I just really wanted to talk to you before the conference. I'm not filing for reelection."

Soon after Scalise made it to his office, his phone was ringing off the hook, as was that of his chief of staff, Brett Horton. Was it true? What were they hearing? And most important, people were already asking Horton and Scalise if the Louisiana Republican would challenge McCarthy for the top slot. Horton had close to twenty calls from people ranging from top aides to Republican lawmakers. He told everyone the same thing: "Steve is not challenging Kevin." But at the same time, his allies were openly acknowledging that Scalise was ready if McCarthy slipped up.

Perhaps sensing that staying on could cause more trouble than he expected, Ryan told McCarthy that he would leave the speakership if it would help ease the Californian's path to the gavel.

He put it in McCarthy's hands. "You make the decision," Ryan told McCarthy. "I give you my proxy to decide if you want to [become Speaker now] or not."

McCarthy said no.

They also discussed Ryan departing in September. But McCarthy thought that would be too late.

Ryan had started hearing criticism of his decision from some of those now coming into the loop. Patrick McHenry, the Republican chief deputy whip, thought Ryan was dead wrong.

"Look, I don't know whether this is sustainable," McHenry said when he finally got on the phone with Ryan that morning. "I completely disagree with your decision." A few moments later, though, McHenry quickly relented, saying he understood it was final.

Steve Stivers felt similarly. He'd also heard the rumor early that morning, but got the call in the eight A.M. hour. The news ruined his day and would immeasurably complicate his next six months. He thought Ryan leaving now looked like the ship's captain jumping off the ship. In fact, he thought, that was exactly what it was. "Mr. Speaker, are you sure?" Stivers asked Ryan. "Like, is there any way to change your mind?" Ryan said no.

Soon Stivers was sitting down with Ryan in person to quiz him about his intentions. He could not afford to lose the money Ryan brought in for the party. Would Ryan keep his schedule apace for the party and the super PAC?

"I don't want to leave early. I'm going to keep raising money," Ryan told him. "I'm committed to the NRCC, I'm committed to CLF, and I'm committed to the majority."

By eight-thirty A.M., Republican leadership offices were buzzing. McHenry got to the Capitol and quickly marched down to McCarthy's office with Scalise and both men's chiefs of staff. In one room was staff; in the other room, the members were going to meet privately.

Under the gaze of an abstract expressionist portrait of Abe Lincoln staring down from the wall in McCarthy's well-appointed congressional office, Scalise and McCarthy had the first of three conversations they would have that day. At all three, Scalise said he would not challenge McCarthy for the speakership. And yet after each one, Scalise's team continued to privately sow discontent with McCarthy and quietly doubt that McCarthy could win a Speaker's race.

The seating area in McCarthy's office was in front of a fireplace. At this first meeting, Scalise, notably, sat in McCarthy's seat, a large armchair closest to McCarthy's desk.

McCarthy's opening message was blunt: Ryan's retirement is a shock to the political system. We'll have to be strong to get through the rest of the year. We have to keep the majority—we can't be running internal party races at the moment. "Look, we had this meeting a few weeks ago," McCarthy said, referring to his come-to-Jesus meeting with Scalise earlier in the month. "We talked about being together. Is that still the case?"

"Yeah," Scalise said.

"Okay," McCarthy said, "we're all a team, which means I'm for you, you're for me. I'm for you, and you're for me." He pointed around the room at Scalise and McHenry as he spoke.

"Yes, yes," Scalise responded.

"Well, if that's the case," McCarthy said to Scalise, "then your staff needs to stop saying if I can't become Speaker, you're going to run. That undermines me. Are we clear?"

"Yes," Scalise said.

But Scalise wasn't committing to endorsing McCarthy publicly. His understanding was that they would all walk out of the room and say they were focused on keeping the majority, not endorsing each other. They had work to do.

The three men, their aides, and their armed police officers then headed to the nine A.M. party meeting in the Capitol basement to hear Ryan bid goodbye. What they saw spoke volumes about people and power in Washington: In 2015, when John Boehner announced he was going to resign, Republicans had lined up for nearly an hour. People begged him not to leave. The room stayed full. When Ryan announced his retirement, the room emptied quickly. Roughly halfway through the open mic session, the room was 20 percent full, by some estimates. In Trump's Washington, surprises wore off quickly.

McCarthy, meanwhile, had a busy day ahead of him. He was scheduled to be at the White House twice: once to see Trump sign a sex-trafficking bill, and again for dinner with Ryan, Mitch McConnell, and Senate Majority Whip John Cornyn.

Before the bill signing around eleven A.M., Trump pulled McCarthy into the Oval Office and asked him if he expected the Ryan announcement. McCarthy said no, he thought Ryan was going to run again in November, because that's what the Speaker had been saying to his colleagues and friends. Trump then bluntly asked McCarthy if he would want to be Speaker. McCarthy said yes.

McCarthy returned from the White House bill signing around noon, just in time for his one P.M. daily management meeting with Ryan and the leadership squad. The day was absolutely dizzying. The session itself was uneventful, but afterward staff departed the room, as did Cathy McMorris Rodgers, the number four House Republican, leaving just Ryan, McCarthy, Scalise, and McHenry.

"Pull the door closed. Let's talk," Ryan said to them. "I'm sorry I put you guys through this, but I'm not going to be dishonest, run, and know I'm not going to stay. We've got work to do and a leadership election down the road. We cannot let that interrupt our work. We've got a lot to do, so let's stay as a team. Steve, you're not going to run against Kevin. You guys would just cancel each other out."

The men shifted in their seats.

"Do we have this worked out?" Ryan asked the gang. He pointed to Scalise, McHenry, and McCarthy and asked again: "Do you have this worked out?" It was obvious what Ryan was asking: He wanted his leadership on the same page.

As they sat there in Ryan's opulent office—the same one that could belong to one of them someday—the tension was palpable. It seemed as if McCarthy was physically leaning out of the discussion. He wanted Scalise to weigh in in front of Ryan. Would he stop dogging McCarthy? Would he support his colleague?

Ryan put it into words: "Kevin's the guy, right?"

"Yeah," Scalise said for the second time that day.

The third time Scalise was urged to lay off McCarthy came later, at the White House dinner with McConnell and Cornyn. The dinner had been scheduled well before Ryan's bombshell announcement, but now the meal was entangled in the complicated McCarthy-Scalise relationship. Scalise was originally left off the invitation list; dinner was with the top two officials in each chamber, and Scalise was number three, a circumstance that habitually prompted Scalise's office to lodge a formal request for his attendance. But on this night, after the Ryan announcement, the White House reached out to McCarthy to see if, due to the developments, they should invite Scalise to dinner. McCarthy said yes, they should.

During the meal, the strong relationship between Trump and McCarthy was obvious. The president passed out a sheet showing that the generic ballot—voters' preference for a nameless Republican versus a nameless Democrat—was tightening. He had data that showed Democrats were up by just three or four points, practically a tie. That was a far cry from the twelve- to sixteen-point gap McCarthy had shown Trump and other Republican leaders at the Camp David meeting just a few months back.

"Go show that to your members," the president told McCarthy, to laughs.

After the meal, Trump and Pence pulled Ryan, McCarthy, and Scalise aside. No aides were present. Just five of the most powerful men in America, standing in perhaps the most famous building on earth, talking about the future of the Republican Party.

"Paul made his announcement today," McCarthy said. "We have a gentlemen's agreement. We're going to support each other to move up."

"Great," Trump said. "I'm for that."

Trump was unambiguous: no leadership fights. And no sniping at each other. This was a team.

Everyone was on the same page except Scalise. From his perspective, he was being bullied, put in a corner he didn't want to be in. Why did he have to endorse McCarthy now, when the focus should be on keeping the majority? *Ridiculous,* Scalise and his team thought.

On Thursday morning, just hours after the White House dinner, McCarthy tried once again to get a read on where Scalise was coming from. Why was he still saying one thing privately and another publicly? They sat down one on one in McCarthy's first-floor office, and McCarthy delivered a stark message.

"I've been through a lot of leadership teams," McCarthy told Scalise. "In this one, Paul and I never battle against each other. He trusts me to do everything. But I was in one with Boehner and Cantor, and it was uncomfortable. We can't start this way, or else we will not have a good relationship." The message was simple: His relationship with Scalise— blossoming for years—was quickly deteriorating, putting the entire party on the brink of implosion months before Election Day.

During a *Fox Business* interview later that day, Scalise sounded a bit more conciliatory, but he still did not endorse McCarthy: "I mean, I've never run against Kevin and wouldn't run against Kevin." Despite the confusion in the leadership circle about where Scalise stood, Ryan took the *Fox Business* comment as a step in the right direction, and the next day—Friday, April 13—Ryan pretaped an interview with Chuck Todd for that Sunday's *Meet the Press* in which he tried to throw some weight behind the door he thought Scalise was shutting.

"Do you have a preference? Kevin McCarthy? Steve Scalise?" Todd asked.

"I think we all believe that Kevin is the right person when it's all . . . We all think that Kevin is the right person," Ryan said.

"You say 'we all.' Are you speaking . . . ," Todd shot back.

"We all—our leadership team, I'm saying. I'm not saying every single person in Congress," Ryan said.

Todd saw what Ryan was doing and pressed him: "So Steve Scalise—it's your understanding that he believes that Kevin McCarthy should be the heir apparent, whether it's leader or Speaker?"

"That's right," said Ryan. "That's right." NBC blasted out the transcript just before three P.M. that Friday, with the headline MTP EXCLUSIVE: SPEAKER RYAN ENDORSES MAJORITY LEADER MCCARTHY TO BE HIS SUCCESSOR: "WE ALL THINK KEVIN IS THE RIGHT PERSON."

This sent Scalise into a tailspin. The "leadership team" thought Kevin was the right person? He hadn't publicly endorsed McCarthy. How dare Ryan do it for him!

Scalise called Ryan and asked him for a meeting. "Why are you putting words in my mouth?" Scalise asked Ryan in the Capitol. "That's not what I said."

"Well, we were in here, you were sitting right here—and I asked you, and I thought we were on the same page," Ryan said. Now he was legitimately confused as to Scalise's game plan. Was he actually going to challenge McCarthy? "You've told me twice you weren't going to run against him."

"Well, not exactly," Scalise said. "There is no race."

Scalise was playing a dangerous game by splitting hairs. Of course, there wasn't a race at that moment. But by saying he would run if McCarthy couldn't, and by declining to endorse his candidacy, he was giving members of the House an option: McCarthy or him. It was too cute by half, even for some of Scalise's closest allies.

"Even if you want this job, Steve, this is not the way to go about doing it," Ryan told Scalise privately. "Let the game come to you, if it ever does. I wasn't looking for this job, it came to me. And I ended up getting this job. That's the only way you're going to get it."

McCarthy, meanwhile, was forging ahead. "After this week, I'm just focused on how I can keep a majority," he said two days after Ryan announced his retirement, the same day Ryan's *Meet the Press* transcript was posted. "I'm not really worried about a leadership fight, to be honest with you. Maybe because I've been through the last one. I feel really secure where I'm at."

He had every reason to feel secure, because of the one powerful ally in his corner. By the time Ryan announced his retirement, it had become plain: McCarthy was Trump's guy. It had seeped its way into everything McCarthy did. Shortly after the February massacre at the Marjory Stoneman Douglas High School in Parkland, Florida, McCarthy had used a closed party leadership meeting to echo Trump's call for immediate legislation on guns. The Friday after Ryan's announcement, McCarthy's flight from D.C. to Denver had been delayed, meaning he would miss his connection to Bakersfield. What did he do instead? Stayed in D.C. and took a stroll with Stephen Miller, Trump's controversial senior adviser.

But McCarthy didn't want Trump's help, not with the speakership. *Stay out of the leadership race,* McCarthy secretly told the White House. People knew the pair were close, but that didn't need amplification. The last thing McCarthy wanted, when he finally reached the precipice of power, was to think it was because of someone else. He didn't want people voting for him because he was the president's guy.

But he did like being the president's guy.

14

STORMS BREWING OFFSHORE

CORRY BLISS HAD A KNACK for bringing in six- and seven-figure checks, and unlike many people in politics, he was permitted to receive them. During the 2018 election cycle, individual candidates running for office were able to accept contributions only up to $5,400, but Bliss, who ran the Congressional Leadership Fund super PAC, faced no such restrictions. By the second quarter of 2018, Bliss's donor list looked like a who's who of the upper echelons of American society: Hedge fund magnates Steven A. Cohen and Ken Griffin and Texas billionaire Paul Foster had all cut million-dollar checks.

But the couple that would keep the organization humming into election season was Sheldon and Miriam Adelson. Worth somewhere near $40 billion, the couple owned the Las Vegas Sands Corporation, a massive casino conglomerate that had revolutionized gaming in Nevada and Asia. They were longtime Republican donors and benefactors of CLF, exactly the kind of people you wanted around in a tough election cycle when you needed an ATM. So in the second quarter of 2018, with Republican coffers emptying as fast as they were filled, Bliss went with Paul Ryan and Jake Kastan to Las Vegas with a request for more cash.

Bliss, Ryan, and Kastan wanted to convince Adelson that he should continue spending heavily to keep the House. Ryan laid out his case: It was the House, not the Senate, that was in danger of flipping, and they needed cash to keep the losses to a minimum. But when it was time to ask for the $15 million checks—one from Sheldon, and another from his wife, Miriam—Ryan, Bliss, and Kastan left the room and allowed Norm Coleman, a former senator who served on the board of AAN, to make the ask. Federal law prohibited Ryan from asking for checks larger than the individual limit of $5,400. But they got what they came for: All told, the Adelsons contributed $50 million to CLF in the 2018 election cycle.

Bliss and Ryan were of one mind on much, but specifically on the expected political impact of the tax reform bill, which had passed a Congress thirsty for achievement at the end of 2017. Republicans had pushed all their proverbial chips in the middle, banking on this one legislative achievement to float them at the polls. Health care reform had fallen flat on its face. Entitlement reform was somewhere between a Republican pipe dream and political poison. And the grand infrastructure bill Steve Bannon had envisioned now shared his fate: gone and forgotten.

But despite the millions of dollars being spent, and the sunny public optimism, there remained an air of doom. Bliss was privately conflicted about whether the party could keep its House majority even after it passed tax reform.

"If we lose twenty-three seats, we won," Bliss said after tax reform was signed into law, a private sentiment for which he would have been excoriated if made public. "Seventy percent chance this year fucking sucks, okay? But if it's a tsunami, zero chance. We're in the between, in all the stuff I've seen. Meaning if it gets a little bit better, it'll be a tough year but we'll be okay, right? If it gets a little bit worse, we're fucked."

Kevin McCarthy privately shared Bliss's uncertainty. "There's a storm brewing offshore," he said in his office at the end of 2017. "The question is does it hit us head on, or pass us by."

House Republicans were in the majority, had been since 2011, and there were pluses and minuses that went with that. On the positive side, Paul Ryan and Kevin McCarthy had a massive fund-raising base, which they used to bring in big cash for the party. Ryan had the benefit of having been Mitt Romney's vice-presidential nominee, which opened up a whole world of donors who would never otherwise think about giving money to the House.

The minuses were plentiful, too, of course. Republicans were going to be judged on what they did—or didn't do—in Washington, and they were twinned to a president whose approval ratings were barrel-scrapingly low in places where it mattered. CLF's polling had Trump horribly unpopular in several key districts throughout the year. The critical question was whether candidates could create a narrative about their work in Washington that didn't include or completely ignored Trump.

Take Rep. Mike Coffman, for example. Coffman represented a suburban Denver district that was becoming more and more diverse, and more and more Democratic. Coffman had survived a number of tough races, including against a former Speaker of the Colorado House in 2014. However, he did it by focusing manically on local issues like the local Veterans Affairs hospital—a go-local tactic that operatives suggested to all Republicans. Coffman also picked on Trump when it was advantageous, and for good reason: In April 2018, internal party polling had Trump's favorables at just 38 percent in Coffman's district. Coffman was at 44 percent.

CLF's national polling had grown scary for Republicans. In April and May, 58 percent of independent voters said the country was on the wrong track, and the same percentage of voters in Democratic-leaning districts occupied by Republicans also said the country was on the wrong track. In the districts Republicans were targeting, 56 percent of voters said they disapproved of the president, and 46 percent strongly disapproved. Sixty percent of women disapproved of Trump, and voters were telling pollsters they would head to the ballot box to send a message to the president.

And congressional Republicans had completely belly-flopped when it came to voters' priorities. In May 2018—six months before the election—internal GOP polling showed voters' top priority was fixing the nation's health care system, which Republicans had failed to do.

Third-most important: public education and job training, which they had largely left untouched.

How about that tax cut? The one the GOP thought would put them on a glide path toward keeping their majority? Polling was dead even.

Unlike Dan Sena at the DCCC, Steve Stivers wasn't looking to gain seats—he was looking to hold on to the seats he had. Republicans were focused on the so-called Clinton seats—the twenty-five districts that Republicans held that Hillary Clinton had won in 2016. "Let's say we hold twelve of them," Stivers said in June, "and we pick up a seat or two—we don't have to pick up a lot—and we keep the field from growing where we have a lot of surprises. Like, there may be a surprise or two beyond the typical seat that everyone knows about . . . but as long as we avoid surprises, hold half the Clinton seats and pick up a couple of seats . . ."

It sounded like a bank shot at best.

Remarkably, even as Bliss and Stivers fretted, in the eyes of many Republicans the political mood was brightening in 2018. Sure, Democratic voter intensity had exploded following Trump's inauguration, but that energy had ebbed as time went on. The generic ballot was tightening. Republicans had methodically won a number of special elections—one in Montana and another in Georgia, before dropping one in Pennsylvania—which gave them hope that, while the climate was toxic, it wasn't impossible to win races. They saw positive data in primaries in California and Ohio, where more Republicans turned out to vote than Democrats. Plus, McCarthy was dumping tons of money into a ballot initiative in his home state aimed at repealing the gas tax. McCarthy knew the initiative would fail, but he thought it would bring Republicans out to the ballot box.

Republicans were also watching with bemusement as Sena and the DCCC sought to expand the playing field. They thought if Democrats were trying to compete everywhere, they would have to spend piles of money and pray for surprises. Stivers called the Democrats' strategy a "shotgun" theory. He thought if they spent money everywhere, Republicans would be able to spend heavily in competitive seats and narrowly keep the House.

Republicans deployed some fund-raising innovations for the first time in 2017 and 2018, techniques that helped them raise oodles more cash than ever before. McCarthy, Stivers, and Vice President Mike Pence collaborated to create a massive fund-raising outfit called Protect the House, a way to play off the star power of Pence and McCarthy to raise money for the country's most vulnerable House Republicans. Pence and McCarthy would walk into a room in a city like Houston, and a rich man like Robert McNair—the owner of the Houston Texans football team—would pay $371,500 to see the vice president and the majority leader. That money would then get split up and flow to vulnerable Republicans around the country.

It also helped McCarthy build chits with rank-and-file Republicans. One July day he sat in a collared golf shirt and khakis in his office, glasses on his nose, making phone calls to Republicans who were getting this cash.

"Come to my Protect the House thing tomorrow—Capitol Hill Club," McCarthy said into his iPhone. He was speaking to Rep. Brian Mast, a Florida Republican who had had both legs blown off in Afghanistan. Mast had a competitive South Florida seat and needed the money.

"I'm giving you $93,000 tomorrow. You have a late primary so you get the most of everyone," McCarthy told him. Mast won his primary and won reelection.

The committee was so successful that even some anti-Trump Republicans who were initially left out of the money pot at the White House's request—Reps. Coffman of Colorado, Curbelo of Florida, and Barbara Comstock of Virginia—were eventually brought into the fold.

But Stivers knew that even these bright spots cast only faint light in the darkness shrouding the Republicans' way to keeping the House. Money couldn't solve everything, and the GOP had serious policy concerns that kept sprouting up. There were two problems Republicans were acutely concerned about, which were in some ways self-inflicted. Health care premiums were expected to skyrocket in September, and Republicans were worried they didn't have a plan. And Trump's trigger-happy stance on tariffs was very concerning to GOP leaders in Washington. "I've had manufacturers in Ohio tell me the tariffs . . . completely or more than offset the positives of tax reform. That's how concerned a lot of manufacturers are right now," Stivers said.

Stivers faced a further challenge of getting nervous incumbents to shelter in place. Because of the political climate, and because so many Republicans were bone tired of Trump and unwilling to go into the minority again, there were a rash of retirements and a handful of resignations. On many occasions, Stivers was forced to beg Republicans not to retire, for fear that their successor would not be able to hold on to the seat. Rep. Fred Upton, an heir to the Whirlpool appliance fortune and a Michigan Republican in his thirty-first year in Congress, was hell-bent on leaving public life. When Stivers heard about Upton's plan to go back to St. Joseph, Michigan, he pleaded with him to stay on for the sake of the Republican Party. Upton eventually agreed.

Ryan's retirement left Stivers feeling kicked while he was down. Ryan was the Republican Party's biggest cash cow, and donors gave to him because he was the Speaker of the House. It was far less appealing to give to a lame-duck leader who would be history right after the election. Stivers hardly understood how Ryan could jump ship. When Stivers decided to take the job atop the party committee, he had sat his wife down and made sure she understood that it would lock him in through 2018.

"I just assumed everybody that runs for a leadership post does that with their family, but apparently not everybody does," Stivers said in the summer of 2018, clearly still peeved at Ryan.

Ryan had promised Stivers he would remain committed to raising money for both the NRCC and CLF, but almost immediately it became obvious to NRCC insiders that Ryan was siding with Bliss and not Stivers. That sent Stivers into a panic. If Ryan was fund-raising for the super PAC, it meant Bliss had control over the money and how it was spent. Stivers needed some money for the official party committee. To counteract Ryan's expected shift, Stivers began asking lawmakers to up their contributions to the party by 30 and 40 percent. He planned to enlist bundlers, lobbyists, and wealthy people across the country who would raise the House Republicans money. And he looked to sign contracts with a number of fund-raisers around the country to bring in cash on a contingency basis. Stivers was so worried, he wanted to offer some fund-raisers twice the commission if they convinced lapsed GOP donors to reengage with the party.

If all this wasn't enough to contend with, there was also Donald Trump. Forget the bombast, which Washington had become accustomed to, and which many voters clearly did not mind. Operationally, for Republicans Trump was a mixed bag: at times helpful, but on other occasions a train wreck. Stivers often spoke with the president and his staff as the GOP desperately tried to hold on to their majority. On a Sunday night in early 2018, Stivers's cell phone was ringing off the hook in his Columbus house. The caller ID was flashing "unavailable," so he ignored the call and continued to enjoy a rare sit-down dinner with his wife and their four- and eight-year-old children.

A few minutes later, he got a text message from RNC chair Ronna Romney McDaniel.

"The president is desperately trying to reach you," she said.

"Okay, well, it would've been nice if somebody would text me ahead of time and say, 'The president wants to talk to you.' What do you want me to do?" Stivers responded.

"Just call the White House switchboard," she said.

Stivers did, and he was patched through to Trump immediately. On a Sunday night, with no preparation, Stivers gave the president an update about the Pennsylvania special election, which Republicans would end up losing in an embarrassing fashion in March 2018.

After twenty minutes, Stivers said, "Mr. President, I'm sure you have better things to do."

Trump apparently didn't.

"Do you think Jim Jordan should run for the Senate?" Trump asked Stivers, who demurred. (During the January visit to Camp David, McCarthy had convinced Trump to try to push Jordan into the seat, a halfhearted effort to try to remove his biggest nag from Congress.)

Trump then started quizzing Stivers about the Ohio gubernatorial race, seen as one of the more competitive contests in the country.

"Should I endorse Jim Renacci?" Trump asked Stivers, referring to one of Stivers's congressional colleagues who was vying for the governorship.

"I don't think he's going to win, Mr. President," Stivers said. "If you want to do it, you can. Jim is a good man and a good friend of mine. But I just want you to know, he's not going to win that race even if you endorse him."

Renacci later dropped out of the gubernatorial race and launched a race for the Senate—at Trump's request.

Even though Stivers didn't always win with Trump, the two men had a growing rapport. Trump appreciated the statistics-laden updates that Stivers provided about elections around the country. Stivers wasn't always so upbeat about Trump. He had told *Politico* in 2015 that Trump's nomination "would be devastating to our attempts to grow our majority and would cost us seats." But the White House was, generally speaking, good to Stivers and did what he asked.

So in the spring of 2018, Stivers decided he would ask the president for a favor. Republicans were worried that Danny Tarkanian—a son of a legendary University of Nevada basketball coach and a six-time election loser in Nevada—was going to drop out of a primary race against a sitting Republican U.S. senator and run for the House. House Republicans were looking to avoid this at all costs.

Stivers heard about this gambit on March 16 and heard Trump was going to back it. He called the White House at nine A.M., hoping to speak to the president.

"I never call to talk to the president personally, but he told me, 'If you ever need anything, call,'" Stivers told a White House aide. "I need something pretty urgently, and I want to talk to someone. I really don't want him to push Danny Tarkanian into the race." Stivers told the White House he would find a way to get Tarkanian a job in D.C., if that was what he wanted, but he urged him to have the president call back immediately.

"If he's going to endorse Tarkanian for the House seat, he doesn't have to call me back," Stivers said before hanging up.

At 11:27 A.M. Trump tweeted: "It would be great for the Republican

Party of Nevada, and it's unity if good guy Danny Tarkanian would run for Congress and Dean Heller, who is doing a really good job, could run for Senate unopposed!"

Seconds after Stivers saw the tweet, Trump called him.

"Mr. President, I told Johnny DeStefano—I told your staff and the White House that if you were already going to do this, you didn't need to call me," Stivers told Trump. "I'm not calling to complain, I was just calling to give you advice, like you asked."

Trump told Stivers he liked Tarkanian, who was a fervent supporter of the president.

"Well, I understand, Mr. President, you already did what you've got to do, I'm not complaining to you, I just wanted to give you my advice," Stivers said.

Four days later, Trump appeared at the National Building Museum for the March Dinner, a massive NRCC fund-raiser that brought in $32 million for the party.

"NRCC chair Steve Stivers—a general," Trump said from the podium, referring to Stivers's National Guard commission. "I didn't even know about that. I'm impressed. I don't know if I like that or your political career better, but they're both very good. Thank you, General."

Trump had no problem praising Stivers publicly even as he made decisions that were crosswise with Republicans keeping the majority.

AS REPUBLICANS WERE STRUGGLING with their president, their fund-raising, and their political fortunes, Democrats were dealing with their own upheaval, in the form of challenges from the left. The Bernie Sanders wing of the party that emerged in the 2016 primary had taken root and was now supercharged by liberals furious with Donald Trump. Activists were pushing the party to the left, campaigning on free college tuition and health care for all. An entirely new crop of progressives were willing to take on veteran lawmakers—often old white men—who they believed were out of step with the future of the Democratic Party. The divide would have an unexpected effect on Democratic leadership.

In fact, it would overturn a succession that had once seemed almost a sure thing.

In the spring of 2018, Joe Crowley was fifty-six years old. He had been in Congress since 1999 and thought it was time for his next move. Crowley was two decades younger than any of the other top leaders, and he was frustrated. Many of his contemporaries had left the House to run for the Senate or state office, or to return to the private sector. Few of them said it, but House leadership was a passing dream for them. They weren't willing to wait for Pelosi and her leadership team to move on.

Crowley had pulled back from taking a shot at Pelosi in the wake of the 2016 shellacking, but now, with Democrats firmly stuck in the minority, he was growing restless in Trump's Washington. Pelosi and Hoyer were showing no signs of stepping aside. So behind the scenes, he and his staff had started to plot out how exactly he could move up the leadership ranks and pounce on a potential leadership vacuum if Democrats didn't win back the House in November.

On *Fox News Sunday* on April 8, Crowley publicly acknowledged what he had been mulling privately. He told Chris Wallace, "I would just wait and see what happened in terms of that, if Nancy Pelosi decided to run. But if Nancy Pelosi stays, I don't see a scenario by which I would challenge her for that position."

Privately, though, he was leaving all options on the table, including challenging Hoyer for the number one or number two slot. Such a move would be controversial. Hoyer and Crowley had long been allies in the House—Crowley had backed Hoyer's unsuccessful bid for whip in 2001—and that relationship at times had hurt Crowley with Pelosi.

When, Crowley wondered, would he get a chance to lead? When would he get to take the reins?

Crowley was biding his time but using it well. He had been in leadership now for five years. He had been vice chairman of the House Democratic Caucus and now served as chairman, a top slot. He had used the position to build support for his future ambitions, counseled Democrats looking to climb the leadership ladder, and served as a mentor for lawmakers just arriving in Washington. Crowley had long been a favorite among Democratic lawmakers for his affable nature, penchant for socializing, and comfort hobnobbing with elites as well as more middle-class Democrats. In 2018 Crowley wasn't explicitly asking for his fellow members to support him to be the next Speaker, but he had nonetheless emerged as the consensus pick of many Democrats: He was the fallback option if Pelosi had to go.

A big part of making a credible play for leadership was the ability to fund-raise for your colleagues. Even better was raising money for candidates as a way to curry favor even before people got into office. Debbie Wasserman Schultz, the aggressive Florida Democrat who had once been the next big thing before flaming out as chair of the DNC, gained notoriety as a candidate for doling out campaign checks even before she was sworn in. Crowley wanted to build a power base by stroking checks to candidates; at the moment he was focused on 2018 House races.

He knew he needed to step up his fund-raising game, regardless. There are a lot of creative ways that lawmakers use existing fund-raising laws to try to bundle loads of cash at one time. Crowley's was to set up a joint fund-raising committee, dubbed the Better Days Fund, as a way to raise massive amounts of cash for multiple candidates in one fell swoop.

Crowley thought that launching the fund-raising operation would raise red flags among Pelosi and her leadership team. They would immediately think he was looking to move up the leadership ranks. Pelosi's dominance in political fund-raising is unparalleled among House Democrats. For years she has brought in the vast majority of the tens of millions of dollars needed to fuel their campaign operations. It was one of the most convincing arguments her team had for why she should remain atop the leadership rungs despite being stuck in the minority. Now Crowley was raising his hand to show that he too could draw big dollars and share the wealth with the young crop of Democrats looking to get to Washington.

Crowley's inaugural event for Democratic candidates was March 1, and though it was held a stone's throw from Crowley's Queens congressional district, it felt like a world away. Crowley's team had rented out the swank Ides bar at the Wythe Hotel in Brooklyn's hip Williamsburg neighborhood. The venue featured navy lacquered walls, a long white marble bar, floor-to-ceiling windows, and a view of Manhattan.

Guests quickly filled up the venue, undeterred by the pouring rain. The packed crowd of thirty- and forty-something professionals in suits and dresses included a virtual who's who of local New York politicos: councilmen and -women from Queens, the Bronx, and the statehouse, along with Crowley's brother John (who goes by Sean), a lobbyist in Albany, and even some of Crowley's House colleagues. Crowley, wearing a dark suit and no tie, quickly commandeered the crowd, working the room before taking center stage. While he clearly had his eyes focused on a bid for top House Democratic leadership, he always tried to keep an eye on his political power base in the state. As he began his remarks, his New York fund-raiser, Walt Swett, surreptitiously handed him notes to make sure he thanked every local politician in the bar.

Once he finished his round of thank-yous, Crowley turned his attention to the reason they were all in Brooklyn that night: to hear his case for Democrats, and to see how much cash he could raise for the twelve candidates he was looking to bring to Washington.

"We're here [tonight] not just for the incredibly great weather or the view of the greatest city in the world. It's because there is a distrust in our nation," he said to the crowd. "People understand the future of our nation is what's at risk."

Building the narrative, Crowley quickly pivoted to a topic he liked to talk about more than just about anything: his upbringing in Queens. "I'm a kid from Queens. As I'm told, so is the president, but our lives could not be more different. The way we were raised, our values, the things that we care about, that I care about could not be more divergent from the experience of the president. And I think those of you who know me enough know what we're talking about."

Crowley liked to boast of his blue-collar background and highlight that he could be a particularly potent foil to Trump. He liked to say he grew up in working-class Elmhurst, while Trump grew up in Jamaica Estates, on the other side of the Long Island Expressway. Of course, while Crowley loved to talk about Queens, he had actually stopped living there quite a few years earlier. He had moved his primary residence to Virginia with his wife and three kids.

"It's the most important election of your lifetime," he said to the crowd. "You've heard that. Every election is the most important election of your lifetime, but this really is."

That night Crowley raised $900,000 for the twelve Democratic candidates who flew in for the event, including Abby Finkenauer of Iowa, Chuy Garcia and Brendan Kelly of Illinois, and Elissa Slotkin of Michigan. And this was just the beginning. He was heading to Cleveland, Seattle, and Chicago in April.

What Crowley wasn't fully aware of at that moment was that this election would be the most important one of *his* lifetime. While he was focused on his campaign inside the Capitol and on helping other Democratic candidates, his challenger Alexandria Ocasio-Cortez's upstart campaign was beginning to gain traction.

The Bronx-born community organizer, who was a member of the Democratic Socialists of America, was a unique political figure, younger than your average pol, still paying off student debt, and new to seeking political office. Her campaign exploded in May after she released an inspirational video that went viral. "Women like me aren't supposed to run for office. I wasn't born to a wealthy or powerful family. Mother from Puerto Rico, dad from the South Bronx. I was born in a place where your zip code determines your destiny," Ocasio-Cortez said in the video. "I'm an educator, an organizer, a working-class New Yorker."

She had a compelling bio. Although she had graduated from Boston University, Ocasio-Cortez had worked as a waitress and bartender to help out her mother. Her father had died from cancer, leaving behind bills that put her family home on the brink of foreclosure. Though Ocasio-Cortez had worked briefly for Sen. Ted Kennedy of Massachusetts while in college, she later switched to community organizing, something she highlighted on the campaign trail.

Ocasio-Cortez also was a vocal leader among a new crop of Democratic candidates who refused to take corporate money, something she regularly bashed Crowley for. As she painted Crowley as member of the old party establishment, Ocasio-Cortez quickly became a popular figure among high-profile Democrats like The Wing founder and CEO Audrey Gelman.

In many ways, Ocasio-Cortez embodied the leftward shift of the Democratic Party. Democrats had won a majority in 2006 because they toppled Republicans in purple districts. But in 2018, Democrats were challenging the tack-to-the-center strategy that had dominated their politics for a decade. Self-proclaimed socialists were running for and winning seats across the country. Rashida Tlaib, a Muslim woman from Detroit, had captured the Democratic nomination to fill the Detroit-area seat formerly held by John Conyers. Julia Salazar, a twenty-seven-year-old New Yorker, won a state senate seat after toppling longtime city politician Martin Dilan in a primary. The rise of the left in congressional politics was, in part, a response to Donald Trump's presidency; they wanted to abolish the Immigration and Customs Enforcement (ICE) agency, while the president was pushing for a physical barrier on the border with Mexico. They called for Medicare for All, a version of socialized medicine once seen as political suicide for Democrats. But the newly emerging left was also a challenge to the Democratic Party, seeing it as too closely tied to corporate interests and K Street.

Longtime politicians struggled to contend with the movement, Crowley perhaps chief among them. At every turn, his team discounted the work that Ocasio-Cortez and her campaign were doing. It started in the spring of 2018, when Crowley decided not to engage when Ocasio-Cortez started bashing him on Twitter. She regularly hit him for being a party boss, an establishment Democrat from the Hillary Clinton wing of the party, and for moving his family to the Washington suburbs—which proved a particularly potent attack.

"We have basically, on one side, a multimillion-dollar machine candidate that was never elected, who does not live in the district—he lives in Virginia, his children go to public school in Virginia," she said in an interview with the *Queens Courier*. "It's really kind of the pinnacle of someone who is a little out of touch, but very influential."

Ocasio-Cortez, meanwhile, portrayed herself as a champion of the people. She had a key ally in this respect: Sen. Bernie Sanders, the independent from Vermont, for whom she had been an organizer during the 2016 presidential campaign. She also raised her profile by traveling to Flint, Michigan, to call attention to the need for safe drinking water, and to the Mexican border to protest Trump's family separation policy.

She effectively criticized Crowley when he opted against attending one debate. When he sent a Latina surrogate to another, she took to social media. "In a bizarre twist, Rep. Crowley sent a woman with slight resemblance to me as his official surrogate to last night's debate," she tweeted. That led the *New York Times* editorial board to pen a piece on June 19, just days before the primary, calling out Crowley as an absentee lawmaker with the headline, IF YOU WANT TO BE SPEAKER, MR. CROWLEY, DON'T TAKE VOTERS FOR GRANTED.

Crowley's operation wasn't caught by complete surprise when Ocasio-Cortez gained traction. A poll Crowley commissioned in early 2018 had shown some troubling results: He was up by double digits, but his name ID was low despite being in office for nearly twenty years. He also faced a problem many incumbents were familiar with: low favorability. The second poll before the primary election had Crowley up by thirty-six points, but it surveyed only super-prime voters—voters who vote every election—and Ocasio-Cortez was attracting a massive number of first-time voters.

Despite doubling down on direct mail and voter outreach, Crowley couldn't get his numbers above the low fifties in the head-to-head race. Campaign finance rules hamstrung him: While Crowley, long known as a successful fund-raiser, had more than $1 million in his campaign account, more than half of that money had to be spent on the general election, not in this primary.

Crowley had plenty of fodder he could've used against Ocasio-Cortez, but his top New York campaign operatives decided to take the punches and not hit back. It wasn't just that Crowley didn't want to go dirty; he thought it would be a sign of weakness in D.C. if he was seen in a tight race against Ocasio-Cortez. He was supposed to be the next Democratic leader, not someone who had to fight for reelection.

PRIMARY DAY FOR Joe Crowley started just like his past ten had: He had a slew of public events across the district, grip-and-grin sessions to provide photo-ops for the local press and to thank voters and organizers who had worked on his campaign.

From the start, though, things weren't looking good. At the first stop, Crowley was slated to present an award for seniors, but Ocasio-Cortez's campaign was outgunning his operation. Her campaign had strategically set up volunteers at either end of the block going into the event, while Crowley had just a single volunteer outside. It was a sign of things to come: Everywhere Crowley and his team went across the district that day, there were Ocasio-Cortez supporters tabling at voting sites and wearing T-shirts emblazoned with her name.

This was the exact opposite of what Crowley's campaign staff had been telling him for months: that Ocasio-Cortez's shoestring campaign was going to show its weakness on Election Day, and his institutional support would drown her. But the signs were all around that this wasn't the case. Ocasio-Cortez's campaign had people blanketing polling sites; Crowley's team covered fewer than half of them. At eleven A.M. Crowley went to greet voters at a Bronx school, where he was met by an army of Ocasio-Cortez supporters on every block around the school, and big chalk drawings on the sidewalk saying "Vote Ocasio." Slews of volunteers at polling sites were hardly conclusive evidence for how the election would turn out, but it was emblematic of the festering problem Crowley's team had faced the entire campaign.

Crowley still thought he could win after the polls closed at nine P.M. Back at campaign headquarters, he was sitting downstairs with his friends and family watching the TV and following the race on Twitter. Around nine-thirty it became clear there was no coming back. Ocasio-Cortez had beat him by fifteen points, delivering a thorough rout that put her on track to be the youngest woman ever to be elected to Congress, at twenty-eight years old.

The seemingly invincible Queens party boss had gone down.

Quickly, his stunned team started talking about a concession speech; they did not have one prepared. His top aides, Kate Winkler Keating, Carlos Sanchez, and Lauren French, huddled in a side room to figure out what he should say.

Minutes later Crowley came upstairs and started hugging the staff and volunteers, apologizing to everyone. He told them it would "be okay" as he thanked them for supporting his campaign. He then walked over to what was supposed to be his victory party. With longtime staffers and volunteers dejected, some in tears, he took to the stage and dedicated his rendition of Bruce Springsteen's "Born to Run" to Ocasio-Cortez.

In true Crowley fashion, the night was hardly over. His entire team, emotionally shot, walked to an Astoria bar, drained beers, and commiserated about the once-unthinkable loss.

Crowley was there in body, but his mind and heart were in Maryland. His wife was in Annapolis with Cullen Crowley, their son, who would be entering the naval academy the next morning. At 9:45 P.M. Crowley called his wife, who said he should speak with Cullen. Cullen broke down. He had to report to the school just fifteen minutes later, after which time he would be forbidden to consume news. For two weeks, Cullen Crowley was without news. But time didn't change the results. Joe Crowley was out. His congressional career was over.

ON JUNE 28, TWO DAYS after his defeat, Crowley returned to Washington. It wasn't easy. He had spoken with Nancy Pelosi on election night, and she sounded distraught on the phone. Shocked.

Crowley arrived at the Capitol, his face scraggly with a gray beard, and his daughter, Kenzie, at his side. She was there to protect him, he told his staff and colleagues, and ideally, to stop him from crying.

On that day, Congress was voting on a bill by Mark Meadows to try to force the Justice Department to fork over investigative material it did not want to release, an outgrowth of the animus between Trump-aligned conservatives and the Jeff Sessions–run Justice Department. In normal times, Crowley would've been leading the charge for Democrats against what they considered Meadows's right-wing handiwork for the president. But instead, his head was hung low. The man who should've been the Democrats' next Speaker was now their sacrificial lamb.

Kenzie's presence at his side wasn't exactly steadying. Almost immediately, she started to cry. So did New York Democratic representatives Nydia Velázquez and eighty-year-old Nita Lowey.

Rep. Joe Kennedy slapped Crowley seven times on the back while they embraced. Rep. Michelle Lujan Grisham—a member of the leadership who would be the next governor of New Mexico—hugged and kissed Crowley. When Rep. Marcia Fudge, an Ohio Democrat hostile to Pelosi, saw them, she got in, and they all hugged together. The entire Democratic caucus felt his pain.

Crowley turned to see the children of Beto O'Rourke, the Texas Democrat who was looking to unseat Sen. Ted Cruz, and said, "Your dad is going to be a great president someday."

Steny Hoyer grabbed Crowley by the arm and looked at him as if he had just seen a ghost. Hoyer—Crowley's onetime mentor turned rival—had tried to get in touch with him on election night, but the call didn't go through. After Hoyer and House chaplain Pat Conroy said hello, Crowley walked into an area of the chamber called the Pennsylvania Corner, named after the Keystone State because for years its chief inhabitant was Jack Murtha, the burly Pennsylvania Democrat who chaired a key military spending panel.

Murtha's corner was now the province of the House Democrats who would have—had things gone as planned—been Crowley's base: white Catholic Democrats from the Northeast who were sick of Pelosi. Had Alexandria Ocasio-Cortez not upended Crowley's world, Reps. Bill Pascrell from New Jersey, Mike Doyle from Pittsburgh, and John Larson from Hartford could've been his most fervent boosters. Instead, they embraced him as if he were dying. It was Crowley's Irish wake.

Rep. Gerry Connolly of northern Virginia was a Democrat who was downtrodden. He hadn't committed to supporting Crowley in a leadership race, but he had seen the wisdom of his candidacy. He told anyone who would listen that the Democrats were dealing with a frightening new reality: There was no successor to Nancy Pelosi. "Now we have no Plan B," Connolly said.

Crowley's defeat quickly caused reverberations among his colleagues—"If Joe could lose, maybe we could too," they said. Pelosi tried to quell the growing concern in her caucus, arguing that Democrats shouldn't make too much of the loss. "They made a choice in one district. Let's not get yourself carried away," she said at a press conference on Capitol Hill. "It is all about that district."

But it wasn't just Crowley. Rep. Yvette Clarke, a New York Democrat who days before the primaries had said she was laughing at her challenger, won by just a few percentage points. And Ben Jealous, former head of the NAACP and an ally of Bernie Sanders, defeated a crowded Democratic gubernatorial primary field in Maryland.

Roughly 210 miles from Queens, another veteran, Rep. Michael Capuano, was facing a similar challenge. The ten-term congressman with a thick Boston accent who had represented the liberal wing of the Democratic Party for years was in the fight of his political career. Conventional wisdom among Democratic operatives was that Capuano, a sixty-six-year-old white man, wasn't in nearly as bad of a position as Crowley. He had seen this challenge coming for months. He wasn't running for leadership, he spent a lot of time back in his district, and he had long been a crusader of the left. Case closed.

But this time he faced Ayanna Pressley, the first black Boston city councilwoman, who positioned herself as an outsider who better represented the seventh district. After Ocasio-Cortez won, the press quickly focused on the similarities between the two women of color fighting longtime incumbents. But unlike Ocasio-Cortez, who was a relative novice in politics, Pressley had been involved in politics much of her adult life.

"If politics is like dog years, you know, I'm probably eighty right now," Pressley said in an interview while she wheeled around her Boston-area district. "I've been a Democrat proudly since I was in utero." Indeed, Pressley had interned for Joe Kennedy at twenty-two and went on to later work on his staff and as a senior aide to Sen. John Kerry.

Pressley had long been seen as a rising star of the Democratic Party—in 2015 Emily's List gave her their Gabrielle Giffords Rising Star award, and she'd served as a surrogate for former Massachusetts governor Deval Patrick and Sen. Elizabeth Warren and even Democratic presidential candidate Hillary Clinton.

Despite her extensive ties to the Democratic Party, Pressley quickly promised to be a "disruptive" presence on Capitol Hill. "If folks are going to be about the business of rolling back every civil right protection bit of progress that we've made, decades of progress," she said, "what I'm going to be focused on is fighting like hell to make it very hard for them—and very painful—every step of the way."

That rhetoric, and the fact that she was primarying a popular sitting Democrat, didn't earn her a lot of fans in the Democratic establishment. The Congressional Black Caucus PAC threw its support behind Capuano, and Emily's List opted to stay out of the House race altogether.

"I knew this was going to be lonely," Pressley said. "And so I don't take any of this personally. Again, it's not surprising, it is in keeping with sort of the cultural status quo and also people's long-standing history and relationships with a colleague—completely understandable."

But she wouldn't be lonely for long: Pressley won the primary.

15

THE DISCHARGE PETITION

ON MAY 9, FIVE POLITICALLY endangered House Republicans finally had had enough of Paul Ryan and Donald Trump's inability—or unwillingness—to deal with America's immigration crisis. So with very little fanfare or warning, they marched to the House floor and unleashed a shrieking legislative cry for help: They filed a rebel motion to start an immigration free-for-all on the House floor.

In normal times, the House is controlled by the majority's leadership on behalf of the party in power. In the first two years of Trump's Washington, Ryan, McCarthy, and Scalise decided, mostly in unison, what bills would come up for a vote, and which would die a slow death. Ryan and his predecessors made it a practice to allow consideration of only those bills that had the support of the majority of Republicans.

But over the years, there have been a few instances where large pockets of both parties wanted a bill to pass, but the leadership refused to accede to a vote. Overriding the leaders requires a break-the-glass tactic called a discharge petition. If the petition garners the signatures of the majority of the members of the House, a stalled piece of legislation will be brought to the floor. This had been successfully executed only twice in more than two decades: Republicans and Democrats filed one in 2015 to reauthorize the Export-Import Bank, a government-backed investment entity that had become a target of the right. And in 2002, lawmakers used the tactic to break the gridlock on McCain-Feingold, the landmark campaign finance reform bill.

The five Republicans who sparked the crisis in 2018 believed that finding a reasonable, humane solution to the immigration crisis was an urgent issue, and they thought Ryan and Trump were ignoring it. Of course, for these five, it wasn't only a policy imperative; it was also political. They represented some of the most Hispanic Republican-held districts in America. Reps. Jeff Denham and David Valadao were two physically towering Republicans from California's Central Valley; Reps. Carlos Curbelo and Mario Díaz-Balart were two Republicans from South Florida; and Rep. Will Hurd, a former CIA operative, represented the Texas-Mexico border. All five shared a goal: legal status for the more than one million undocumented immigrants who had been brought to America through no fault of their own.

The rules governing the petition were labyrinthine, but the upshot was this: If it was successfully executed, it would trigger a vote on *four* immigration bills: a Democratic proposal, which was likely to be the DREAM Act, legalizing most DREAMers; the hard-line proposal by Republican Bob Goodlatte, which the Freedom Caucus was pushing for; a proposal by Paul Ryan; and one pushed by Denham himself, which was the entire point of the petition. Denham's bill was called Hurd-Aguilar, named for the Republican Will Hurd and Rep. Pete Aguilar, a Democrat of California. Hurd-Aguilar, while bipartisan, was anathema to everything Trump had campaigned on: It extended DACA into perpetuity, gave a new pathway to citizenship, and did not include a dime for a physical barrier with Mexico. But if it was put on the floor, all Democrats and a pocket of Republicans could join forces to pass the bill, which would move bipartisan immigration legislation to the Senate while throwing the Republican Party into a tizzy.

If one wanted to understand the source of the gridlock that has kept Congress's approval ratings so low for so long, one need not look further than the crisis generated by the immigration discharge petition. What it showed was that a majority of the House wanted and was willing to pass progressive-looking immigration reform. The votes were there for

Hurd-Aguilar, a bipartisan bill approved by Democrats and pushed by a moderate Republican.

But its very bipartisanship was what doomed it. House Republican leadership thought the bill would be a massive political blow to the party, and they would not give a vote to something that a majority of the Republican members did not support. In fact, they would do everything they could to crush it. And in the process, the Freedom Caucus would compound the snub of majority will by using another important bill as a bargaining chip, one on whose passage depended the lives of millions of farmers and low-income Americans.

MUCH TO RYAN AND McCarthy's chagrin, the discharge petition immediately got momentum. After the original five Republicans signed on, another twelve quickly put their name behind the effort. It was stunningly quick work. If all Democrats got on board—which was a real possibility, since Hurd-Aguilar's aims had broad Democratic support—just twenty-five Republicans would be needed to force the series of votes.

The petition caused immediate alarm among House Republican leaders; they worried the party would be torn in two just months before Election Day. On May 10, Ryan, who long considered himself supportive of middle-of-the-road immigration reform, trashed the effort.

"I want to fix this problem," Ryan said. "So I would like to have an immigration vote before the midterms. But I want to have a vote on something that can make it into law. I don't want to have, you know, show ponies. I want to have actual law, and that means the White House has to be a part of this, and it's gotta be a bill the president can sign."

Six days later, on May 16, with eighteen Republicans and one Democrat already signed on to the petition, McCarthy took an even sharper tone. In a meeting with moderate Republicans, he put it this way: "If you want to depress intensity, this is the number one way to do it." Don't let Nancy Pelosi determine the party's future, he said. But Republicans weren't all too moved; Reps. John Katko of upstate New York and Dave Trott, a retiring Republican from Michigan, signed the petition that day. Five more Republicans, and the door could be opened.

At the same time, Mark Meadows was stewing. It had been months since he thought McHenry had promised him a vote on Goodlatte's hard-line immigration bill, and he had nothing to show for it. And now, suddenly, there was an effort afoot that might result in the House legalizing millions of undocumented immigrants. Sure, Goodlatte would come up for a vote if the discharge petition passed, but since the petition was a proxy for a vote on Hurd-Aguilar, Goodlatte would never stand a chance. "Too many promises made, and promises broken," Meadows said ruefully.

So he did what he did best: He caused mayhem. Late at night on Tuesday, May 15, Meadows called McHenry, who missed the call because he was already asleep. The next morning McHenry woke up to the news that Meadows had been calling about: The Freedom Caucus was going to withhold its votes for the farm bill, which was about to come to the floor, unless they got a vote on Goodlatte.

The farm bill might sound wonky, but it's one of the few bills Congress passes that has an immediate impact on people's lives. It sets food stamp law, and it deals with all sorts of social welfare programs, making it a critical part of America's safety net. When the farm bill doesn't pass, some of the policies could expire, with real consequence for those who depend on them. Because it included both food stamps and agriculture policy, it often passed with bipartisan majorities comprised of African-American Democrats and rural white Republicans. Politically, the bill was crucial to the GOP, because its majority was built in rural America—in places just like Jim Jordan's Urbana, Ohio.

In 2018 the farm bill's bipartisan passage was no longer assured. Republicans had taken the bill to the hard right by tightening work requirements for welfare programs. This was the stuff of conservative dreams but loathed by Democrats, who decided to uniformly oppose the bill, meaning Republicans would need all their votes to put it over the line.

Now Meadows—who actually supported many of the policies in the farm bill—was going to hold it up in exchange for a vote on Goodlatte's restrictive immigration bill. Meadows didn't believe the Goodlatte bill was as unpopular as McHenry told him it was a few months back, but the deputy whip wasn't lying: When Scalise returned from his surgery, he had whipped the bill, and found it had something around just one hundred supporters. *Fucking awful and a waste of time,* members of the whip organization thought, *but not surprising.*

Meadows and the Freedom Caucus didn't buy it. They decided to hold firm against the farm bill in hopes of cashing in their chit to get Goodlatte to the floor. The leadership was beyond frustrated. Republicans had been working on the policies in the farm bill for months, and now the Freedom Caucus was going to oppose it because of immigration concerns that were completely unrelated. But Meadows and Jordan chose the farm bill because, to their minds, it was a bill that needed to pass, so the leadership was likely to make concessions to get it across the finish line. In a feat of extrication, McHenry and Scalise had convinced half of the Freedom Caucus's members to peel away from Meadows and vote for the farm bill, but the other half (including Meadows, Jordan, and Scott Perry) were stubbornly unmovable, and without them the legislation was poised to fail—a major embarrassment for the GOP.

On Wednesday morning, facing no other options, McCarthy agreed to a vote on Goodlatte during the month of June. To his mind, it was a way for Republicans to pass the farm bill and place the immigration fight after June 5, when eight states, including California, would hold their primaries.

But that wasn't enough for Meadows and Jordan. By Friday morning, they were demanding a vote on Goodlatte immediately, without any canvassing of membership to gauge its chances. The leadership rejected the suggestion out of hand, but that quickly turned back on them—suddenly the members of the Freedom Caucus whom McHenry and Scalise had peeled away on the farm bill reversed themselves; now, they said, they were undecided. Many of them signaled that if Meadows voted yes on the farm bill, they would follow. But Meadows was hesitant to vote yes because he didn't want to be seen as less conserva-tive than Jordan, who was going to the mat on this issue, even though some of his constituents were people who might be hurt if the farm bill didn't pass.

Seeing that Meadows was the key, McHenry tried to bring him into the fold. Because of an unexpectedly high number of absences, McHenry knew that the Republican leadership needed only six more votes to pass the farm bill. The leadership tried to use the fact that it was so close to put more pressure on Meadows not to be the holdout. It made the stakes that much higher. A popular conservative bill would be going down because of him.

"Look, here's the deal," McHenry said to Meadows. "You and Perry vote yes, and then [Reps. Andy] Harris, [Matt] Gaetz, [Warren] David-son, and [Jody] Hice will follow."

"You only need six?" Meadows replied, shocked.

McHenry said, "We need six."

Meadows separately approached McCarthy and Scalise to see when they intended to bring up an immigration vote. Scalise said by June 25, and McCarthy said during the first week of June.

Noting the inconsistency, Meadows said he'd had enough. The lead-ership was playing cute on the Goodlatte vote once again, and it wasn't going to work. Meadows voted no and brought the massive farm bill down with him. Jordan, Perry, Davidson, and Gaetz voted with him. All told, 198 Republicans voted yes, and 30 voted no. All 183 Democrats opposed the bill.

Jaws dropped across the chamber in frustration and disbelief. As the bill went down, the Democratic minority was giddy. Republicans were dismayed. "You see that, Mark?" bellowed Rep. Mike Conaway of Texas, who had spent months putting the bill together. "I hope you're happy."

And Meadows had done nothing to slow down Denham and the rest of the fed-up five. By the time the farm bill went up in flames, 196 lawmakers had signed the discharge petition, placing it just 20 votes away from succeeding. The House was slowly building toward passing bipartisan immigration reform over the objections of its conservative wing and its leadership.

PAUL RYAN HAD HOPED that by now he would be able to escape Washington for a long weekend without being sucked back into the political vortex. He had scheduled some time away in Janesville because his son Charlie was graduating eighth grade, and he wanted to be there for it. But chaos was dragging him away from his family, again.

Ryan didn't need this. His speakership was coming to a close—he was just a few months from the end of his congressional career. And here he was, dealing with the same intractable issues and the same stubborn resistance that he'd hoped to break when he took the job. To his mind, he came to Washington to do *big things*. But here again was the game playing. The hostage taking. The intellectual dishonesty. The backstabbing. He had thought he would end all of it. And he was looking forward to not being a part of it anymore.

The House gaveled back into session on Monday evening, and Ryan decided to speak to his colleagues the very next morning, bringing him back to Washington a day earlier than he expected. Tension was blossoming in his ranks, and a narrative was building that the only reason Denham and the moderates had decided to file the discharge petition was that Ryan was a lame-duck Speaker. He needed to nip this insurrection in the bud.

"I wasn't supposed to be here today," Ryan said from the podium in HC-5, the party's basement meeting room. "Tonight is Charlie's eighth-grade graduation from our parish school. It's kind of a big deal at our church. I was just going to stay in Janesville and come up tomorrow. But after what happened Friday [with the farm bill], I wanted to be here today. I want to talk to this team."

The mood in the room was tense, not only because Ryan was laying the guilt on thick but also because the party was in open warfare. The growing popularity of the discharge petition and the real prospect that a Republican Congress was going to pass Hurd-Aguilar—

a Democratic-leaning immigration bill—was making conservatives and the leadership furious. Meadows had in return ignited the rage of moderates by blowing up the farm bill. Virtually everyone blamed the leadership.

"Last week we stopped being a majority," Ryan said. "Last week we got a taste of what being in the minority is like. It's not fun. And we cannot let it happen again."

The room was transfixed by Ryan, because for him this was atypical behavior. He was not one to lecture. He had to be brought kicking and screaming to confrontation. His leadership style was far more conducive to one-on-one sessions and debates about the merits of policy than admonishing members on the perils of misbehavior.

"Because everything we have," he continued, "control of the agenda, control of committees, the ability to enact policies that make this a better country—all of it relies on our ability to work together," he said. "We are a majority, or we are nothing."

At this very moment, Ryan said, a group of lawmakers were rallying support for a discharge petition, and the Freedom Caucus—which he did not mention by name—was "taking unrelated bills hostage," an allusion to the farm bill. "Not just taking hostage, but actually killing a bill that we've worked on for months, setting back one of our biggest policy priorities that we have been promoting for two years.

"Both of these are things you do when you're in the minority," Ryan continued. "And I promise you this, keeping this up is the quickest way to send us back to the minority. Good grief. And you know what is so puzzling and frustrating about all of this? This happens just as things are coming together for us. The economy is great. Our base is coming together and getting energized. People are more optimistic than they have been in decades."

Did they want to squander it all with infighting? Ryan asked. The room was silent.

Ryan told his Republican colleagues to "blame me if you want," that he was "happy to eat a lot of crap for this team." But he wanted respect, and at that moment, there was little of that being given. He urged Republicans to drop the discharge petition and allow the leadership to design a process in June that would set up votes on immigration bills.

"Look, we agree on most things, but there are always people in this room that don't agree on every issue," he said. "Those people are not your enemy. They are your fellow, equal partner in a Republican majority. We all have a heck of a lot more in common than we do with Democrats who could be running this place instead.

"I'm not on the ballot this fall," Ryan said. "But everything I stand for and everyone I believe in is. That matters to me. More than you can imagine. And I'm going to keep busting my butt to make sure next Congress we have a Republican Speaker. All I ask in return is that we don't let our divisions overcome us. And that we act like a majority should."

By the end of the next day, Rep. Erik Paulsen, an endangered Minneapolis-area Republican, signed the discharge petition. It was just thirteen signatures away from garnering majority support.

RYAN AND MCCARTHY'S PLAN to solve the immigration stalemate was a bit naive. As the signatures on the discharge petition continued to tick up, they decided to facilitate a series of conversations between moderates and conservatives, in the hope that they would somehow be able to bridge the giant chasm and come up with an immigration accord that could garner the support of 218 Republicans. But they quickly figured out that it was a waste of time.

In the room were members of the Republican leadership and conservatives like Jim Jordan, Mark Meadows, and Raúl Labrador of Idaho, coupled with Jeff Denham, Carlos Curbelo, and committee chairs like Mike McCaul of Texas and Bob Goodlatte.

Early on, members of the group discovered that they were deadlocked on one of the key components. Moderates needed a pathway to citizenship for DREAMers, while those like Jordan found that to be anathema. "Where I draw the line," Jordan said privately at the time, "is it cannot be a special pathway." In other words, he wanted people who had been in the United States illegally for decades to wait for their citizenship like everyone else.

"Look," Jordan said in the negotiating room, "we're going to give legal status to DACA individuals, but in exchange for that, we're going to do everything that this election was about. Border security wall, chain migration, visa lottery, asylum reform," he said, ticking off the list of highly restrictive immigration policies that had been key in the 2016 presidential campaign but would be unacceptable to a large swath of House Republicans—not to mention the more moderate Senate, which would have to clear anything the House passed for it to become law.

By early June, the talks had gone off the rails. The discussions had become so useless that Jordan left a few meetings early, once preferring to catch his flight home to Ohio rather than bang his head against a wall in a meeting with moderates. For a moment, conservatives in the group appeared to have scooted to the center, offering a visa for DREAMers that would put the undocumented on the road to citizenship, but as soon as that became public, the Freedom Caucus walked it back and said they had never made the offer.

Throughout his career, Paul Ryan wanted badly to pass immigration reform. But at this point, his main goal was to find something the House and Senate could pass and the president would sign. That, to his mind, was a deal that would trade DACA for the border wall. He had convinced Trump on several occasions to put off the fight for the border wall. But eventually Trump was going to stand firm, and Ryan believed it was better to find an agreement now than at the end of the year during a lame-duck session of Congress. Ryan was trying to push along this process in the House in order to pressure the Senate to get serious about immigration reform. What he really didn't want, though, was to pass an immigration bill that essentially gave Democrats the floor. That wasn't what the Speaker did. Convention would dictate it was bad political practice. But that's what would happen if he allowed the discharge petition to get 218 votes.

So Ryan, with McCarthy's help, desperately tried to keep the discharge petition from reaching the threshold. They were busy cutting deals, buying off people who otherwise would have supported it. Rep.

Dennis Ross of Florida got assurances he would get a vote on an agriculture guest worker program. Rep. Dan Newhouse of Washington State was assuaged by reassurances he'd have a vote on an immigration bill. By June 6, 215 lawmakers had signed on, only three short of victory. But Ryan and McCarthy were able to keep two more Republicans from signing on. They had squelched bipartisan immigration reform in the House.

As the last piece of the puzzle, Ryan placated the original five boosters of the discharge petition with the promise of a compromise bill. He understood the bind they were in, politically, and he knew something needed to be done to protect the DREAMers. But he tried to make them see it from his perspective. Let's do something for the DREAMers, he said, but let's do it in a bill that the majority of Republicans can support. If they let the discharge petition go, Ryan would allow a vote on this compromise bill that gave them what they needed.

On June 12, Ryan announced two votes: one on Goodlatte's hard-right legislation, and another on his compromise bill, which came to be known as Goodlatte II. The latter included wall money and, as Ryan had promised, a pathway to citizenship for DREAMers. For all the hassle Republicans were going through, neither bill would become law in the form the House was voting on—the Senate had little interest in the legislation. But Ryan was under the impression that Trump was in favor of the process, and he told his colleagues the president was "excited."

On June 19, Republicans would see how excited he was. Trump came to the Capitol, with plans to push Republicans to pass an immigration bill. But when he got into the room in the Capitol basement to talk to Republicans, the conversation was about almost everything but pushing the compromise bill.

Trump opened up by asking the audience if the media ever treated Barack Obama the way they treated him. Republicans said no. He called Meadows, Jordan, and Louie Gohmert "my warriors," and said he loved "my Peter," referring to veteran New York congressman Peter King. "Where is Trey Gowdy?" he asked, before answering himself: "Combing his hair," a reference to Gowdy's slick silver locks.

Only then did Trump talk about the border. He said the images from the country's southern border were "horrible," adding that "Ivanka came up and asked if there was anything I could do.

"It's a very sad situation," Trump said. "When they come illegally, we have to do something or they will keep coming. We have to get something passed. The public is watching." Did Ryan's compromise bill fall under the general heading of "something"? Perhaps.

"All the press does is show babies crying," Trump said. He urged Republicans to take action on an immigration bill: "I am with you one hundred percent. I am not going to leave you out in the wilderness." He was trying to tell Republican lawmakers he would not abandon them if they passed something.

But then it was back to other topics—many other topics. Trump said that Meadows told him he had his highest approval ratings since he was elected. ("I had to look it up," Trump said. "Because maybe I don't trust him.") He told Rep. Barbara Comstock, an endangered northern Virginia Republican, that she could "play it a little bit neutral with me . . . because you're going to win." He said that Kim Jong Un, the North Korean dictator, was a "great negotiator." He blamed over-burdensome highway regulations for making roads curvy, and he said, "If you're half stewed and driving on a curvy road, you'll crash." He asked Rep. Ron DeSantis how his campaign for Florida's governorship was doing and took credit for boosting DeSantis's poll numbers with a tweet. He baited Rep. Mark Sanford, who wasn't even in the room, with seemingly disingenuous praise for running a great race, even though Trump had practically sunk Sanford himself with a devastating last-minute takedown on Twitter. He promised that Republicans would pick up seats in the Senate, and he said the candidates running were "nicer than anyone in this room, saying amazing things about me. Saying I'm the greatest president ever." And he told Rep. Mario Díaz-Balart that he liked him more than his brother—presumably referring to the journalist José Díaz-Balart, with whom the president had sparred.

Finally, a few minutes later, Trump turned back to immigration. The "opposition" didn't want a wall, he said.

"We have an incredible, powerful strong base," Trump said. "They know we need border security. . . . Meadows, Louie, and Jordan fight for me like crazy, but I wanna help somebody who is not up by thirty-five." He was essentially saying that he thought the immigration reform that the House could pass would help moderate Republicans, not the hard right.

He closed with this: "I'm with you. I love you people. You're special people. You have the right idea, and I'm with you a thousand percent." Trump was behind them all the way. He never explicitly endorsed the immigration bill that Ryan was trying to pass, but the leadership took what they could get.

Just two days later, though, Trump imperiled the compromise bill: He asked on Twitter why the House was even bothering to try to pass it. "What is the purpose of the House doing good immigration bills when you need 9 votes by Democrats in the Senate, and the Dems are only looking to Obstruct (which they feel is good for them in the Mid-Terms). Republicans must get rid of the stupid Filibuster Rule—it is killing you!"

That day the House rejected the Goodlatte immigration bill, but it garnered a surprising 193 votes. Asked if the leadership had underestimated the bill, Jim Jordan said, "What do you think?"

Clearly exasperated, Jordan said, "One hundred and ninety-three votes—nineteen, twenty votes short of passing today? You bring it up in committee, you have the full debate, you pass it, it gains momentum, the president says 'That's the bill I want.' You don't think we could find nineteen, twenty votes? I think we probably could. . . . Where was the intensity on the whip effort for this bill? Imagine if we had one-tenth of the intensity of this bill that we had for the tax legislation." That was how Jordan viewed his immigration agenda: It was nearly as important as tax reform.

The next day, the president was back at it on Twitter. "Republicans should stop wasting their time on Immigration until after we elect more Senators and Congressmen/women in November," he wrote. "Dems are just playing games, have no intention of doing anything to solves this decades old problem. We can pass great legislation after the Red Wave!"

It was the second time he had dumped all over a bill that his party was trying to pass. The Republican leadership believed that the Freedom Caucus—specifically Meadows—had urged Trump to back away from it.

The president's dismissiveness had a numbing effect on House Republicans: Ryan's compromise bill was dying a slow death.

June 26 was a beautiful day in Washington, but in the Capitol, a sense of resigned dread had settled over House Republicans: Their immigration effort was going nowhere. On the floor, Raúl Labrador, the Idaho Republican in the middle of the immigration debate, chatted with Carlos Curbelo of Florida, but for the first time in weeks, they were alone. No members of leadership lingered by, waiting for an elusive immigration breakthrough. The immigration activity—the chats, the idea swapping, so frenetic in the last weeks—had gone silent. The private meetings between Meadows and Curbelo, between conservatives and moderates, were through.

At about noon that day, the president hosted roughly fourteen Republican members of Congress for lunch in the cabinet room. Notably, the guest list included Rep. Martha Roby, the Alabama Republican who had spent the 2016 campaign criticizing the president; Rep. Tom Graves, a Georgia Republican close to Kevin McCarthy; and Mario Díaz-Balart, who had spent the better part of the last several weeks trying to get to an immigration deal.

In the meeting, Trump again told Republicans they were destroying their party by not getting rid of the legislative filibuster—the much-hated sixty-vote threshold that stymied some of Trump's agenda.

The president said he loved both "compromise" immigration proposals—Goodlatte and Ryan's Goodlatte II—that the House had been considering, but he didn't want to foist a tough vote on the Senate. Some conservative Senate Democrats might vote yes, he said, but the no votes would pile up: John McCain, the Arizona Republican who was dying of brain cancer, would be absent; Jeff Flake, the Arizona Republican whom Trump called "Flakey," was sure to oppose the president; and "little Bobby Corker," the Tennessee Republican he had been feuding with, was an obvious tough spot.

The president then made clear the fight he was about to wage. He told the group he wanted $5 billion for his border wall.

"One point six billion is just a number someone came up with out of thin air," he said. "Two point two billion isn't much better. But five billion gets us a fifth of the way there."

The next morning, with Scalise on television saying Ryan's compromise bill was strong in building the border, Trump finally took to Twitter to endorse it:

> House republicans should pass the strong but fair immigration bill, known as goodlatte II, in their afternoon vote today, even though the dems won't let it pass in the senate. Passage will show that we want strong borders & security while the dems want open borders = crime. Win!

But it was too little too late.

"At this point . . . a lot of members have told constituents who have called their offices they're voting no," said one Republican involved in counting votes. "Hard to talk that back."

As predicted, the compromise immigration bill failed, falling nearly one hundred votes short of passage. As the bill was going down in fabulous fashion, Carlos Curbelo approached Parker Poling, the top aide to Patrick McHenry, the chief vote counter, bemoaning how the process had gone awry. He said there were elements in the bill that lawmakers could sell in moderate districts like his, and conservative districts like Meadows's. It had $25 billion for a wall. Status for DACA recipients. It would've gone nowhere in the Senate, but it would have been, in everyone's view, a start. With the bill tanking and the discharge petition abandoned, Curbelo and his cohort of desperate moderates would get no political relief.

On June 30 it came full circle. The president tweeted that he had never once lobbied for the House to pass the immigration bill. "I never pushed the Republicans in the House to vote for the Immigration Bill, either GOODLATTE 1 or 2, because it could never have gotten enough

Democrats as long as there is the 60 vote threshold. I released many prior to the vote knowing we need more Republicans to win in Nov."

That, of course, was not true. But once again, the immigration issue was left lingering with absolutely no closure in sight. Ryan had tossed bipartisan immigration reform to the side for Republican reform, and even with large margins in his chamber, the House GOP could not get it done.

16

LEFT AND CENTER

IT WAS JULY 20, AND BERNIE Sanders was riding high. First, his social-ist ally and former campaign organizer Alexandria Ocasio-Cortez had ousted Rep. Joe Crowley in June. Soon after, fellow traveler Ayanna Pressley upset Rep. Mike Capuano in Massachusetts. For a guy who had spent most of his political career in the Washington wilderness pushing policies that were never going to be embraced by establishment Democrats, the white-haired champion of the left had found a growing army of candidates willing to latch on to cherished causes he had been pushing for years. In Ocasio-Cortez, the seventy-six-year-old indepen-dent from Vermont had found an unlikely ally. They didn't have much in common. She was a Latina from Queens who was poised to be the youngest member of Congress. He was an old Jewish white guy who had spent decades toiling inside the Beltway. But the two self-described Democratic Socialists bonded in a call after her primary win. And now they were joining forces to barnstorm for candidates across the coun-try to try to re-create the magic that shocked the Democratic Party in her race.

Their first target: Kansas. Despite Trump winning the state by twenty points in the 2016 presidential election, Sanders and Ocasio-Cortez decided this was exactly the type of place where they wanted to flex their political muscle. So that was how, on that sweltering July day, Sanders found himself in front of a crowd of roughly four thousand people chanting "We love you Bernie!" as he ticked off issues important to him—Medicare for All, free college tuition, and a higher minimum wage—that had now become a near constant refrain among more progressive candidates on the campaign trail, much to the ire of congressional leadership.

Their call to arms was on behalf of James Thompson, a Democrat who had narrowly lost a 2017 special election against Rep. Ron Estes and was now once again challenging Estes for the seat. They were also planning to campaign that weekend for Brent Welder, a former Sanders delegate looking to oust Rep. Kevin Yoder, the Republican who had represented the Kansas City suburbs since 2011. It was the beginning of a busy campaign season for Sanders and Ocasio-Cortez in the run-up to the 2018 midterms. The two also campaigned for Abdul El-Sayed, a long-shot Democratic candidate for governor of Michigan, and Ocasio-Cortez lent staff to Kerri Harris, a challenger to Delaware Democratic senator Thomas Carper.

Yet for all the press that Sanders had garnered about moving the party to the left, and even as the optics of that day made the case for Ocasio-Cortez as exhibit A of his growing influence, the reality was more complicated. In terms of pure results, Sanders was hardly the kingmaker he seemed. While he excelled at garnering headlines, and perhaps even at changing public perception of socialist aims, his track record for influencing actual races was pretty abysmal. Sanders had been an early backer of Pete D'Alessandro, a former top aide to Sanders in his 2016 bid, in Iowa. D'Alessandro finished a disappointing third in the primary behind Eddie Mauro and Cindy Axne, who would go on to win the seat. And the Sanders-aligned group Our Revolution, which controlled the e-mail list from Sanders's 2016 presidential run, was mired in internal political problems in the two years since. A series of candidates it backed mostly fell short, including Tom Perriello in his high-profile primary in Virginia in 2017 against Ralph Northam, and Dennis Kucinich, in his gubernatorial bid in Ohio.

As Sanders was trying to flex his muscles outside the Beltway, he also looked to use his rise to national prominence on Capitol Hill, drawing more attention to issues he cared about and reframing the 2018 election cycle as a matter not just of opposing Trump but of laying bare the underlying tension in the Democratic Party. In the Democratic primary, Sanders had been the thorn in the side of Hillary Clinton for months, hanging on longer than anyone projected. Many Democrats still blamed him for weakening Clinton ahead of her unsuccessful general election bid. But that's not the way Sanders saw it. Long an independent in the Senate whose views on policy got little attention, now he had a platform, and he wanted to use it.

Perhaps no one bore the brunt of Sanders's newfound ambitions more than minority leader Chuck Schumer. Trapped in the minority for the foreseeable future, Schumer would have to accomplish the delicate yet essential task of maintaining Democratic solidarity when it came to close votes while also shoring up the handful of moderate Democrats up for reelection. In the January 2018 special election in Alabama, Doug Jones's defeat of Republican Roy Moore brought the balance of the Senate—when including the two independents who caucused with the Democrats—to just 51–49 in favor of the Republicans. And with Susan Collins and Lisa Murkowski known to vote with the Democrats on occasion, and John McCain's future presence in D.C. questionable, Schumer found himself in a situation where he could conceivably block Republican legislation under the right circumstances.

But that would mean holding Sanders to the center when he wanted to go left. And beyond Sanders, it would mean wrangling a caucus in which multiple members were already seen as, and in some cases acting like, potential 2020 presidential candidates. Almost every leader faces the challenge of building a coalition and keeping harmony within a party that encompasses a spectrum of views, but for Schumer in 2017 and 2018, the stakes were as high as they'd ever been, and the heat he got within his own party for even seeming to negotiate with Trump was practically enough to sear flesh. The process by which Schumer held things together reflected the maturation of a formidable political mind, a figure whose easily caricatured low-perched glasses and New York–ese belied his savvy and talent for bridging an increasingly fraught divide.

. . .

ON NOVEMBER 16, 2016, Schumer had finally ascended to the top of the Senate Democratic leadership. It was a long time coming. The son of an exterminator and a Brooklyn housewife, he had worked his way up from state assemblyman to House member to senator. His brash style and penchant for press hadn't always ingratiated him with colleagues, but Schumer was nothing if not a workhorse. He got a reputation early on for putting in long hours, and even once he was atop the party, he continued to travel each year to all sixty-two counties in New York. His ability to raise tens of millions of dollars for himself and his Democratic brethren and sistren didn't hurt him either.

Schumer graduated from Harvard, then from the university's law school, but he had never practiced law. Instead, at the age of twenty-three, he ran for the open state assembly seat in the section of Brooklyn where he grew up. Coming into office, he was an antiestablishment reformer, like many of his generation after the Watergate scandal. He quickly earned a reputation as an aggressive politician, one who rubbed some of the more traditionally minded elder statesmen the wrong way with his love of the camera and his willingness to take credit for things, deserved or not.

At thirty, he decided to run for Congress, and when he won, he became an advocate for public housing and tenants' rights. But he also moderated his positions, aligning himself with more centrist Democrats as he looked to run statewide. The move, which would eventually position him to pick off Sen. Al D'Amato, a Republican who had represented New York for eighteen years, would serve Schumer well for decades but created tension when the party's energy shifted to the far-left wing.

Like pretty much every member of Congress, Schumer had his quirks. He lived for more than thirty years in a run-down Capitol Hill townhouse owned by George Miller, a former Democratic member from California, sleeping on a mattress on the floor in the living room. Unlike most of his fellow senators, who were extremely wealthy—the Senate is known as the millionaires' club—Schumer ranked near the bottom when it came to personal wealth. Described by the *New York Times* as the "Yenta of the Senate," Schumer also had a long history as a matchmaker: More than two dozen of his staffers have married each other. And while most professionals have long forgotten how they scored on college admissions tests, Schumer often asks potential staffers, even those who may be ten or fifteen years out of college, how they scored on the SAT. Why? Because he had a perfect score, which he also likes to note. Still, that quirk downplays just how seriously Schumer takes his applicants' skills: He also shrewdly judges them based on their ability to handicap both Republicans and Democrats on where they are on the political spectrum, giving each member a number between zero and one hundred.

Schumer's quest to lead Senate Democrats was not assured of success. He had entered the chamber with a reputation for putting his self-interest ahead of the party's. And his sharp-elbowed tactics didn't always fit in with the more polished Senate, which placed a premium on decorum and seniority. But after the Democrats' wipeout in 2004, Harry Reid of Nevada assumed the reins of leadership from Tom Daschle, who had shockingly lost his race. Reid wanted Schumer to help lead Democrats out of the political wilderness by heading the Democratic Senatorial Campaign Committee. The job was a good fit for Schumer. Long a prolific fund-raiser, he could turn on the money spigot while also channeling his well-honed political skills on behalf of his colleagues. Over the next two election cycles, Schumer won back fourteen seats for the party, an impressive number by any count. In the process, he earned a lot of chits from the incoming Democratic senators for whom he had raised money and developed winning strategies.

During their time together in the Senate, Reid and Schumer were an odd couple. Over the years an unlikely friendship between the two grew, despite their polar-opposite personalities. Where Schumer could be loud and loved to be in front of the microphones, Reid, a former boxer, was a man of few words who wielded iron-fisted control over his caucus during his eight years as leader. His talent at arm twisting reached unparalleled heights as he successfully muscled Obamacare to passage through the Senate.

Reid continued to champion Schumer's ambition, creating the leadership position of Democratic vice chair in 2006 for Schumer as a way to give him a larger role in the caucus. Still, Reid's deputy, Dick Durbin of Illinois, also a close friend and roommate of Schumer's, was originally seen as the odds-on favorite to succeed Reid. Durbin had a much deeper reach with the more progressive senators. Yet Reid gave Schumer the ultimate parting gift in 2015 when, upon announcing his retirement, he endorsed Schumer to succeed him. By then, Schumer was in the pole position to win the leader slot largely due to the number of senators he had helped elect in 2006 and 2008, but without Reid's blessing, he would likely have faced a bloody fight against Durbin and Patty Murray of Washington State.

Schumer's ascent augured a new phase in relations between the parties. In an institution where manners and respect are at a premium, even in clashes of divergent views, Reid and Mitch McConnell's loathing of each other was palpable. When Schumer replaced Reid, he moved quickly to change that. On his first day on the job, he approached McConnell and said, "You and Harry didn't get along. In fact, you each thought each other were liars, but what I have found in life is most times when people think the other one is lying, it's misunderstanding." Schumer thought he could diagnose the problem: "Mitch, Harry had this habit of saying three words, and he thinks you understood the paragraphs in his head. And you have a habit of saying nothing. And so first, you passed each other like ships in the night, and second . . . the next phase was you thought each other was lying."

The two made an agreement early on to tell each other what they thought, which produced a fairly cordial relationship despite some bumps on the road—like when Schumer voted against the confirmation of Elaine Chao, McConnell's wife, to be the transportation secretary. "It's worked as good as it can be," Schumer said of their relationship. "Mitch is a very partisan, tactical man, but we've gotten along quite well, and he's quite candid with me, and I'm quite candid with him."

After enduring years of the tense back-and-forth between McConnell and Reid, pretty much everyone in the building was curious about how their relationship was going to work out. When Schumer was at the gym, he would often get questions from Republican senators about how it was going. After about three months of being asked every day how he was getting along with McConnell, Schumer told the GOP leaders, "Well, I'm getting along with him pretty well. He even laughs at my jokes," to which John Thune of South Dakota cracked, of the stoic McConnell, "How can you tell?"

Schumer also took a much different tack from Reid when it came to his vision for leading Senate Democrats. Reid had not been above throwing elbows at members of his own caucus. For instance, when Joe Manchin called Reid an "absolute embarrassment" when he criticized Trump after the presidential election, Reid shot back that Manchin was simply "running for a cabinet spot" in Trump's administration, *Politico* reported at the time. Schumer, meanwhile, in an early signal that he would support vulnerable moderates, backed Manchin's threat to shut down the government at the end of 2016 if the government funding bill didn't cover coal miner benefits. Reid, in his final days atop the Senate leadership, had declined to support the effort.

The move was a precursor to how Schumer planned to lead the Senate. He was hands-on but without the firm grip. He liked to check the temperature of his caucus all the time, often calling senators multiple times on the same issue through the week. He frequently bragged that he knew the cell phone number of every single Democratic senator by heart, even reciting them to reporters.

Schumer wanted to fashion his leadership tenure in his own inclusive style. That meant two big changes. He was going to open the tent and let senators of all political stripes onto his leadership team. Shortly after the 2016 election, he began recruiting the most liberal and the most conservative members of his caucus to join him. He wanted Elizabeth Warren and Bernie Sanders to serve as vice chairs. He brought on Amy Klobuchar of Minnesota as steering committee chair, and Joe Manchin of West Virginia as Democratic policy and communications committee vice chair. A senator's decision to join Schumer's team wasn't always easy. Being in leadership could be perilous for senators from both sides of the political spectrum; leaders tend to be unpopular, and being too close to them can provide fodder for future political opponents.

Schumer wanted his ten-member leadership team to meet every Monday evening the Senate was in session. His strategy wasn't just about bringing the team together. It was also a recognition that it's a lot harder for senators to publicly complain about the leadership's strategy and decisions if they are brought in on the front end. The meetings also gave senators an opportunity to weigh in directly with Schumer, so they could be heard on an issue even if he didn't ultimately agree with their way of seeing it. "They're my second family," Schumer said. "Whatever the problems are for the week, and sometimes longer term, I discuss it with them. And sometimes I have ideas. And, sometimes I don't, but we blend." That blending continued on Tuesdays, when he tapped a larger group of twenty senators to continue to refine the message, followed by a lunch that day, and a Thursday lunch meeting with the entire caucus. "The key has been unity of our caucus, which is amazing," Schumer said.

Yet that unity was tested right from the start of the new Congress in 2017, when Sanders saw his first opportunity to use his newfound sway on the occasion of a vote on prescription drug importation. Sanders had long been frustrated by how expensive it was for Americans to purchase drugs. He believed the pharmaceutical industry was living high on the hog while people living paycheck to paycheck were subsidizing its bottom lines. And one didn't have to look far to see that people in other countries paid much less for the same drugs. Drug prices were also a very popular issue among the electorate. A Kaiser poll in 2015 found that 72 percent of Americans supported allowing the importation of prescription drugs. Sanders also had an odd bedfellow in the fight—Donald Trump had campaigned in favor of importation during his presidential bid.

So on January 11, just eight days after the new Congress came into session, Sanders made his move, sponsoring a largely symbolic amendment that would allow cheaper drugs to be imported from Canada. He, along with Amy Klobuchar, another champion of the issue, introduced the amendment as part of a seven-hour "vote-a-rama" on the Republicans' budget resolution that would make way for the GOP's push on repealing Obamacare. The drug importation measure had no chance of becoming law, but it would force senators to take a position on one of the most high-profile issues in health care, and it also could signal the future of drug price reform.

Democrats had long called for lowering the price of prescription drugs, but they had no unified position on how exactly to deal with the issue. Many Democrats had taken money from Big Pharma for years, and some had concerns over whether Sanders's measure did enough to ensure that imported drugs would be safe for public consumption. Unsurprisingly, the pharmaceutical industry was staunchly opposed.

Sanders and Klobuchar took to the Senate floor, urging their colleagues to stand up and support the measure. Sanders even referenced Trump as he pleaded with his colleagues for their support. "With a Republican president-elect telling the truth that pharma is getting away with murder," Sanders said, "will the Republicans, will all the Democrats have the guts finally to stand up to the pharmaceutical industry and their lobbyists and their campaign donations and fight for the American consumer and end the disgrace of having our country pay by far the highest prices in the world for prescription drugs?"

Shortly after eleven P.M., the amendment came up for a vote. It had already been a long night in the Senate. Hours had ticked by as issue after issue was brought up and discussed and voted on. As their colleagues came into the chamber to vote, many of them in their late seventies and eighties, Klobuchar and Sanders milled about talking with senators as they hawkishly watched the vote tally. Schumer, who voted for the measure, was on hand as senators like Chris Murphy, Elizabeth Warren, and others filed in. The amendment failed 46–52, with thirteen Democrats voting against it.

The vote sparked outrage among the party's Bernie wing. Twelve Republicans had supported the bill, including Ted Cruz, meaning that a more unified Democratic front could have put it over the top. Sanders seized the moment, coming out aggressively against those who voted against the amendment. The next day he poured salt into the wound, putting out a statement criticizing his colleagues who had opposed it. "The Democratic Party has got to stand up to the greed of the pharmaceutical industry," he said. "It is not acceptable that the five biggest drug companies made $50 billion in profits in 2015 while nearly one in five Americans cannot afford the medicine that their doctor prescribes."

The reaction from Bernie supporters was swift—Reddit threads and websites like Jezebel castigated Democrats for what they perceived as siding with the drug industry. Cory Booker, the New Jersey Democrat whose name was often bandied about as a possible 2020 candidate, faced the most heat from progressives who were upset that he hadn't gotten in line with Sanders.

Sanders pushing the issue even when it had no chance of passing caused a major problem for Schumer. Heading into 2020, he needed to keep an eye out for vulnerable Democratic moderates: Claire McCaskill, Heidi Heitkamp, and others faced what already looked to be strong headwinds against their reelection bids. They were, out of necessity, hard noes on this issue.

Just two days later, the issue flared up again during a regularly scheduled Friday meeting of Democratic Senate chiefs of staff. The meeting, which was typically a pretty vanilla walk-through of the previous week, got hot, as chiefs of staff to senators like Heitkamp, Tom Carper of Delaware, and Martin Heinrich of New Mexico gave voice to widespread frustration with Sanders. The rhetoric was particularly heated since most of the Democrats in the room were still pissed off about the 2016 election and blamed Sanders for wounding Clinton during the primary.

Afterward Schumer tried to play the role of peacemaker, bringing together Sanders and the senators who were upset with him. Sanders refused to apologize but said he wasn't doing it to purposely hurt his colleagues. Schumer also wanted to send a subtle signal that Sanders, who was now in charge of Senate Democrats' outreach, needed to be a team player. He seemed to get the hint: Sanders would later work with Booker to introduce a modified bill that would lower the cost of prescription drugs by allowing importation. Yet Sanders's involvement in the prescription drug vote was emblematic of the larger problems Schumer would face over his first two years as minority leader.

Of course, Schumer and his colleagues were often united by their new common foe, Donald Trump. But Schumer could never stay fully focused on battling Trump, so long as he had to keep a close eye on the factions within his caucus. By March 2018, he had another problem on his hands: Elizabeth Warren. Despite keeping his colleagues together to vote against and ultimately tank Republicans' long-held goal of repealing Obamacare, he couldn't keep them together when it came to Wall Street.

Warren, long a vocal critic of big banks and opposed to bailouts after the 2008 financial crisis, trained her fire on her fellow Democratic senators over a bipartisan bill that would ease some of the regulations that were forced on the banks as part of the bailouts. Called the Economic Growth, Regulatory Relief, and Consumer Protection Act, the bill was the first overhaul of the financial system since Dodd-Frank passed amid the financial crisis. It exempted smaller banks from rules that were focused on stopping risky behavior, and it increased the level for which banks were considered "systemically important." Warren, who believed the banking system needed to be strictly regulated in order to prevent another financial collapse, derisively referred to it as the Bank Lobbyist Act. She retweeted *Politico* reporter Victoria Guida's list of all the Democrats who supported moving forward debate on the bill: "Senate Republicans voted unanimously for the #BankLobbyistAct. But this bill wouldn't be on the path to becoming law without the support of these Democrats. The Senate just voted to increase the chances your money will be used to bail out big banks again."

Warren wasn't finished going after her own team. It's hard to underscore how poorly it goes over when a lawmaker tries to raise money by attacking a colleague in the same party, but that's exactly what Warren did. The same day as her tweet, she sent a fund-raising e-mail criticizing everyone who supported the bill, including the sixteen Democrats who were "with the big banks." Two days later she was sticking to her guns on *Medium*. "Saying Democrats are helping to roll back rules on big banks doesn't make me the most popular kid on the team," she wrote. "But Massachusetts didn't send me here to fight for big banks. The people of Massachusetts sent me here to fight for them."

The whole thing left a bad taste in the mouths of some of her colleagues. It wasn't just the fund-raising e-mail; as with Sanders and prescription drugs, Democrats worried that Warren's outspoken criticism of her colleagues could hurt them on the campaign trail. Joe Donnelly of Indiana, for example, told Warren her criticism was damaging him back home. Nobody wanted to seem soft on big banks, but moderate Democrats were looking for ways to show they could be effective and work across party lines. Heidi Heitkamp, the number one most endangered Senate Democrat, had long wanted to ease the burden on community banks and credit unions—a big issue in rural North Dakota. She saw this bill as her vehicle, but now Warren was burnishing her own progressive credentials at Heitkamp's expense. Things blew up that Friday in a meeting of Democratic senior aides, with Warren's team refusing to back down. Heitkamp got so angry, she sent back a contribution that Warren had made to her campaign.

Right in the middle of Warren's campaign against her fellow Democrats, Schumer called her into his office. He didn't tell her to knock off her campaign against the legislation, but he did ask her to focus her ire on the substance of the bill instead of her fellow Democrats' support for it. It was classic Schumer, trying to guide his fellow members without throwing down the hammer.

It was also a bit of personal calculation. The bill put Schumer in an awkward place. Many progressives already viewed him skeptically as being too close to Wall Street, and while he eventually came out to oppose the bill, along with most of the liberal flank of the party, it took him a while to get there. He would barely talk about it with reporters and hadn't whipped votes against it. The reason: Ahead of the midterms, he had to contend with moderates who were frustrated by the lack of bipartisan accomplishments.

Ultimately, on March 14, sixteen Democrats and independent senator Angus King voted in support of the measure, which passed 67–31. And as Warren riled up progressives across the country on the issue, moderates didn't hesitate to throw her under the bus. "I think people in North Dakota don't care what Elizabeth Warren thinks," said Heitkamp in an interview in *The Atlantic*.

Schumer's problems with the progressives in the party were hardly limited to the Senate chamber. As campaign season kicked into high gear that summer, the party's energy was squarely positioned in its activist wing, visible in the charged crowds for Sanders and Ocasio-Cortez. The growing calls for abolishing ICE, establishing Medicare for All, and other progressive policies that had just a few years ago been laughed off were now making headway into the mainstream of the party. It meant that the challenges Schumer faced in keeping the party united were likely to grow rather than shrink.

Nowhere was Sanders's infiltration into the Democratic bloodstream more clear than in Chicago during the DNC's summer meeting in August. Two years before, during the 2016 presidential primaries, Sanders had railed against the DNC, calling the system "rigged" for Clinton and against himself. Now key Democratic operatives from around the country were taking up his mantle, voting to dramatically reduce the power of superdelegates in the presidential nominating process. The reforms included ending the system that allowed superdelegates the first opportunity to vote on the nominating ballot for the presidential primary, encouraging open primaries, rewarding states that had same-day voter registration, and increasing oversight into the DNC's finances. Sanders called the reforms "an important step forward" for the Democratic Party, which was rich since Sanders still was not a member of the Democratic Party. In fact, the reforms were an important step forward for him, an independent—they would make it much easier for him to claim the Democrats' mantle in 2020.

17

GOING NEGATIVE

AS THE DOG DAYS of summer 2018 set in, the House went out with a whimper.

The August recess is typically a time for politicking, not governing. Mitch McConnell, always open to political mischief, said he was going to keep the Senate in session over the summer to work through presidential confirmations. He was also trying to pass government-funding bills to prevent a shutdown. And he had his second Supreme Court nominee to confirm, this time Brett Kavanaugh, an appeals court judge with two Yale degrees. Not to mention, Republicans didn't mind that Senate Democrats would be in Washington, not on the campaign trail trying to win their races.

But the House had little on its schedule, and its members were eager to get out of town. Paul Ryan and Kevin McCarthy were planning to hit four states on a fund-raising swing that would bring in millions for the party. Ryan even relaxed his longtime ban on fund-raising in the Hamptons, heading to the tony Long Island enclave to collect cash with his wife, Janna, by his side. Jim Jordan, who had recently announced his candidacy for House Speaker, was planning to keep a busy schedule in Ohio, but he made time to go to Indiana, where his son was settling in as a wrestling coach at Indiana University.

Before they left town, Republicans badly needed a jolt of momentum. Democrats were walloping them. The signs of a coming electoral drubbing were everywhere. On July 18, the DCCC announced it had raised $15.2 million in June, almost double the Republicans' paltry $7.7 million. Getting beaten that badly in the money game when you held the White House, House, and Senate was a downright embarrassment, and McCarthy felt it. Even worse, the Democrats' plan to swamp the electoral map seemed to be working; they were threatening in places where history suggested they had no business competing.

Some kind of shakeup was needed. So on July 24, a few days before the House would head out of town for the summer, McCarthy invited the entire House Republican Conference to the Eisenhower Room at the Capitol Hill Club for an ass-kicking session. The invitation wasn't optional. And two days later, when members arrived at the appointed time, they found the room's chairs were arranged classroom style, sending a not-too-subtle message: McCarthy was going to lecture and everyone else was going to listen.

The lecture was not subtle, either: Their eight-year-old majority—one of the largest Republican majorities in American history—was slipping away. The fear that McCarthy had articulated to President Trump at Camp David back in January was becoming a reality.

"We have to correct our actions. We need to change now," McCarthy told the group, as he fired up a forty-one-slide presentation. (McCarthy never missed an opportunity to put together a killer slide presentation.) "I'm concerned. I wanted to talk to everyone before August recess. I couldn't let you leave town without talking about this."

A GAME PLAN TO FIGHT BACK flashed across the screen.

McCarthy's first slide showed the stunning hole Republicans were in: The GOP was losing independent voters by a whopping twenty-two points. Most professional pollsters assume the vast majority of self-identified independent voters are in fact right-leaning Republicans, which meant the party was in for a historic defeat. Trump had *won* independents in 2016.

McCarthy's data, blaring forth from slide after slide, showed that

Republicans had made a massive miscalculation. They had bet their majority on tax reform, summoning every last bit of legislative capital to push through the tax bill, yet polls were now showing that just 22 percent of people cared about economic issues, a drop from nearly 71 percent eight years earlier. They were in charge, and people were worried about Washington's dysfunction. They couldn't pass an immigration bill, and six times as many people were concerned about immigration than when they took the majority. And 8 percent of voters said they were concerned about Donald Trump—something the party never had to contend with.

All these numbers made it plain: Republicans were completely screwed.

McCarthy's solution was for the party to adopt a massive messaging shift, one that would come to define the 2018 election cycle: That morning he urged the dozens of Republicans gathered to forget the positive message on the economy that the GOP had publicly been touting. Instead, he implored them to go sharply negative on the issues that mattered the most: safety, and Democrats' efforts to turn America toward socialism, destroy health care, and raise taxes. Why? Because his data showed that it worked, that's why. McCarthy pointed out that positive messaging moved independent and college-educated women an average of 10.3 percent, while negative advertising moved them 13 percent.

Armed with data from the NRCC and other Republican political entities, McCarthy outlined a new strategy: attack, attack, attack. To win over swing voters and centrist Democrats, they should attack "government controlled, one-size-fits-all health care." To win Republicans, "government-run" and "government takeover" should be the new watchwords. Never mind that Republicans had been in complete control of Washington for two whole years and were still walloping Democrats for their health care plan, a now-eight-year-old law that the GOP could not find the courage or the votes to repeal.

McCarthy then urged them to attempt to say in public something many Republicans couldn't say with a straight face: that Democrats—who controlled not one slice of government—were the dysfunctional ones who were gumming up Washington. It was Democrats, McCarthy said, who had introduced articles of impeachment and who opposed a whole bunch of bipartisan measures like VA reform and disaster relief.

Another slide showed images of Nancy Pelosi and Mike Bloomberg, the two rich elderly Democrats who were raising piles of money to put the party back in control. This was the image Republicans wanted to sear into the brains of Americans: Putting Democrats in power in the House was akin to handing over the keys to San Francisco and New York liberals.

All this message-shifting meant nothing, though, if Republicans kept losing at the most important game: the cash race. Money is like oxygen for politicians, and Republican lawmakers were beginning to feel like they couldn't breathe. This brought McCarthy to his next big point. "We need to close the gap," he said. "Republican leadership has transferred $64.6 million. And we'll do more. The president is going to have a fund-raiser for us," he announced. "Who wants to come up— who is ready to help the team?"

Eight people immediately lined up behind a microphone at the center of the room pledging between $50,000 and $1 million. McCarthy had hinted to his friends that they should be ready to stroke checks, and they were.

All told, McCarthy raised $10 million that day. He knew it wouldn't be nearly enough.

THE 2018 ELECTION CYCLE was becoming damned expensive for Republicans. A single 2017 House race in Georgia between Democrat Jon Ossoff and Republican Karen Handel had cost the NRCC and CLF a combined $12 million—a stunningly high amount for a short special election in red America. A race in the sleepy suburbs of Pittsburgh had cost more than $8 million.

In late July, Republicans found themselves with their wallets out once again. The previous fall Pat Tiberi, a slick but understated congressman from Columbus, Ohio, had announced he would forgo reelection and leave office in early 2018. It was a jolt to Republicans, because Tiberi had been seen as a D.C. lifer, a member of Congress since 2001. His departure triggered a special election in Ohio's twelfth district. This should have been an insanely easy seat for Republicans to defend. The district included the upscale suburbs of Columbus and stretched into rural and exurban environs that were friendly to Trump, who had won it by eleven points in 2016. Tiberi had won his last three elections with more than 60 percent of the vote. The seat had been in Republican hands continually since 1983 and for all but two years since 1939. Instead, the Republicans found themselves in a too-close-for-comfort mess that was bleeding their coffers.

When a safe Republican seat like this opens up, there's always sure to be a bloody primary, and Ohioans got one for the ages. D.C. Republicans, including Stivers and the NRCC, supported Troy Balderson, a fifty-six-year-old state senator with a perpetually unkempt head of hair. Balderson had been in state government for nearly a decade and was seen as a safe bet. But once again, the Freedom Caucus clashed with the party establishment over whom they should support. Mark Meadows and Jim Jordan—who represented a nearby district—supported Melanie Leneghan, a local politician who branded herself a "businesswoman, a pro-life Christian and a proud supporter of President Trump." "We need a real conservative in Congress," she said at the end of a campaign ad that showed her bowing her head in prayer.

Things got rough between Leneghan, Balderson, and seven other candidates. Balderson won by just 775 votes, triggering a recount. Leneghan went to court, claiming that officials in Muskingum County, Balderson's home and political base, had tampered with ballots before the recount. The litigation went nowhere, but the long battle took its toll on Balderson's campaign accounts; he advanced to the special election to face Democrat Danny O'Connor starved for cash.

O'Connor was a baby-faced thirty-one-year-old who had only recently won an election to be the recorder of Franklin County, which includes Columbus. He was a particularly good candidate for the Democrats, young and telegenic. He swore up and down he would not vote for Nancy Pelosi for Speaker—sharp politics in a district where Republicans had Pelosi's approval rating pegged between 26 and 28 percent.

The race remained close, even as both O'Connor and Balderson made missteps that were akin to cardinal sins in their parties. Balderson told the *Columbus Dispatch*'s editorial board he would be open to raising the retirement age for Medicare and Social Security, which gave Democrats a chance to hit him for being an entitlement-busting Republican who was willing to throw Grandma off a cliff. O'Connor got bullied on MSNBC by Chris Matthews into saying he'd support "whoever the Democratic Party puts forward" for Speaker, a characterization that most certainly included Nancy Pelosi. But nothing helped either candidate break away in the polls.

On August 4, three days before the election, Balderson got some much-needed last-second help: Donald Trump dropped into Lewis Center, Ohio, to stump at Olentangy Orange High School. Lewis Center is in Delaware County, which is a suburb of Columbus. Stivers had suggested that Trump stump for Balderson in Mansfield, a more distant, rural town, where there was less awareness of the race and where Trump could have more impact. The White House disagreed.

Trump opened the rally, unsurprisingly, by talking about himself. "Remember these guys on television saying over and over again, 'You cannot win unless you get the great State of Ohio,' we got the great State of Ohio," he told the crowd. "Remember they used to say, 'Trump can't get it because it all goes through Ohio.' They didn't know we were going to win by a lot—we won by a lot. Eleven. We won by a lot." Quickly, it became clear that the goal of the rally was less about Balderson specifically than about reminding voters of the power and excitement of Trump. He first mentioned Troy Balderson's full name nearly eleven minutes into the seventy-five-minute rally.

"Right from the beginning, Troy Balderson, he is the guy," Trump said. "He is the guy that's going to do things, and you are going to be very surprised. You know, they're talking about this blue wave. I don't think so."

The way Trump viewed the election was clear: Because he was there in Ohio, stumping for Balderson, then Balderson would turn into a loyal ally in Washington. Trump was in Ohio to give himself another soldier who would beat the drum against the establishment in D.C.

"There's only one choice in this election, that's vote for Troy Balderson, he's going to help Mark Meadows . . . he's going to help Jim," Trump said, referring to Jim Jordan. "He's going to help everybody."

During the rally, Trump called Jordan to the microphone, which sparked "Speaker of the House" chants, something that could not have pleased Kevin McCarthy. Trump didn't try to tamp down or encourage the chant. He stood there, soaking it all in.

Possibly Balderson could have been spared a close shave in a "safe" Republican district if he had had the full-throated endorsement of Ohio's Republican governor. But Donald Trump's presence in the White House made that a problem, too. The governor was the exceedingly popular John Kasich, who loathed Trump and was thus hesitant to get involved on Balderson's behalf because he felt the candidate was too closely tied to the president.

As the sitting Republican governor, Kasich was universally expected to put his weight behind Balderson, so his silence was astounding. It gave O'Connor an opening, and he jumped on it, running a thirty-second ad that featured women saying they had voted for Kasich for governor but this time they would support O'Connor. Kasich remained silent, withholding his endorsement as the ads blanketed the Ohio airwaves, which allowed voters to think O'Connor was the rightful heir to Kasich's down-the-middle, truth-talking political identity.

Balderson needed validation. The governor went back and forth with his advisers, and finally he made it clear to Balderson he was not going to endorse him if he was going to go to D.C. and support Trump and the Republican leadership down the line. Balderson assured Kasich that he was already distinguishing himself as a separate entity from Trump and would stand up to the president when it came to his trade wars, national security policy, and separating kids from their families at the border.

Locked in a desperately tight race, Balderson's campaign had a laundry list of things it hoped to get from Kasich, including a statement of support, a video, and a campaign appearance. Kasich delivered Balderson his endorsement on July 26 but refused to cough up the rest. This wasn't good enough for Balderson's boosters—they wanted more. Through emissaries, Corry Bliss used the prospect of a Democrat taking the seat to twist Kasich's arm into recording an ad, which even then the governor's people insisted could be used only as a digital spot. "On August 7, we're going to elect a new member of Congress," Kasich said in the ad. "Troy shares our commonsense values on the important issues that face us today. Troy Balderson has my vote, he should have your vote too."

Before long, contrary to what Kasich's team believed was the agreement, the ad started airing on television. Kasich was furious. His team let the Balderson campaign know that Kasich felt "set up." At 10:14 A.M. on July 31, John Weaver, Kasich's top political adviser, sent an e-mail to people in the governor's inner circle, saying, "I thought we agreed the ad would run on targeted digital only?" The e-mail included a link to a *Columbus Dispatch* story with the headline KASICH BACKS BALDERSON IN NEW TV AD FOR SPECIAL ELECTION. After getting assurances that the ad was coming down immediately, Weaver woke up the next day to find it was still running, which led him to surmise that Bliss was slow-rolling taking it down. This further infuriated the governor's team.

When Kasich's camp finally got hold of Bliss, they said they wanted the ad taken off the air. Bliss said no and told Kasich's team to feel free to complain to the press. With less than a week before the election in a close, hotly contested race, there was no way he was giving up such an urgent piece of ammunition for Balderson. Making little headway with Bliss, an emissary for Kasich then called Steve Stivers that weekend before the election. Stivers, who was at a swimming pool with his young children, angrily replied that he would be happy to go on television to explain that John Kasich had cost Balderson—and the Republican Party—the election.

As the TV ad continued to run, Kasich's strategy confounded political insiders. Why would he endorse someone who was rallying with Donald Trump? On August 3, Ron Brownstein—a writer for *The*

Atlantic—e-mailed Weaver, wondering what they were up to: "How Kasich gets into the position of possibly throwing the lifeline to Balderson, when a Balderson defeat would be powerful evidence of Trump effect on the party that would likely create more space for your critique of the party's direction under Trump?

"Aren't you working against your own long term interest by trying so hard to prop up Balderson, despite his embrace of Trump-like themes?" Brownstein continued. ". . . Won't the message, if he wins, be that Trump-ism can survive a suburban district and therefore the party doesn't need to reconsider it? Discuss?"

Aides suggested that Kasich not engage in these kinds of questions.

Days later, though, the governor got his revenge. Appearing on ABC's *This Week,* he revealed that in a private conversation, Balderson had told him he had never invited Trump to the August 4 rally. Trump had merely shown up, Kasich said. It was technically true, of course, because Balderson did not know the president. Stivers had made the ask and coordinated with the White House. But Kasich publicly embarrassed Trump and Balderson. Payback is a bitch.

SPECIAL ELECTION DAY IN Ohio was Tuesday, August 7—a sunny, hot day with rain clouds looming over the flatlands. The modest, sleepy midwestern district had attracted quite the lineup of political celebrities of late. Aside from Trump, Vice President Mike Pence had visited to stump for Balderson. Kevin McCarthy had been there with Steve Stivers. While McCarthy was on the ground, President Donald Trump dialed him to say hello and wish him well. Rob Portman, Ohio's junior senator, had chipped in. And in the days before the election, Joe Biden—the former vice president and potential 2020 contender—recorded a robocall to urge voters to get out to the polls for O'Connor.

The race also attracted an unbelievable amount of Republican cash; it was a remarkable drain in a district they never thought they'd have to defend. CLF spent $3.1 million on everything from television advertising to door knocking. The NRCC spent $1.3 million. Even the RNC kicked in half a million dollars.

And yet despite Republicans' massive spending advantage, Democrats seemed to have the better vibe on the ground on Election Day. Balderson just couldn't seem to get out of his own way. The night before polls opened, he thought it wise to tell a crowd of supporters—and reporters—that "we don't want somebody from Franklin County representing us." Franklin County, where O'Connor lived, was the district's most Democratic and vote-rich county. When the comment reached Washington, party operatives who had poured money into the district just shook their heads. In a race that was within three points, why insult anyone who could vote?

If there was one day that was emblematic of the campaign and the quality of the candidates, it was Election Day. Around noon, Balderson arrived at Genoa Baptist Church, a polling location, to mingle with voters who just might help send him to Washington. Despite the opportunity to win a vote or two, he was stiff and awkward. He was surrounded by two aides, who physically shielded him from questions. "Thank you for coming out today," he said to one voter, who clearly had no idea who he was. After all of four minutes at the church, Balderson was gone, leaving behind a trail of voters and reporters. Later that day he visited a group of volunteers and spoke to them for twenty-four seconds.

O'Connor, visiting his own campaign headquarters in Columbus, was fired up. "You are the most important people in the United States right now," he told the enthusiastic crowd. "Honest to God. It's not people sitting in boardrooms. It's not people making decisions about mergers and acquisitions. It is you, the people, who have taken this up and have decided that democracy is something that's worth fighting for. That our country is something worth fighting for. This group, and everyone else who is with you knocking in different parts of this district. You are the backbone of our country right now. You are fighting for something great. We need you, let's go do it, thank you."

At 7:35 P.M. the first totals began to come in: O'Connor had an 80–19 lead in Franklin County, his political base. Insiders on both campaigns had expected that, because of a significant lead the Democrats built in early voting. But the lead continued to seesaw. At 9:43 the crowd let out an audible sigh when CNN showed the race knotted at 49.7 percent. At

9:56 Rep. Joyce Beatty, Columbus's Democratic congresswoman, stood before a crowd and said she was excited to get a partner in Congress. Less than an hour later, though, Beatty was giving a thundering but defeated speech, imploring voters to come out again in November to give O'Connor another try.

Balderson won by fewer than 2,000 votes. Appearing at a Double-Tree hotel in Newark, he thanked the president while appearing almost frozen with confusion as to what to say about him. "It's time to get to work," he concluded. "Over the next three months, I'm going to do everything I can to keep America great again."

Keep America great again?

If Republicans had to fight this hard to hold a seat in a district that Donald Trump won by eleven points, they were in big trouble.

THE MORNING AFTER BALDERSON'S eke-out win, the U.S. attorney for the Southern District of New York—a man handpicked by Donald Trump—announced he was indicting Rep. Chris Collins, a Republican from upstate New York who had been Trump's first supporter in Congress. Collins was a slight man, skinny and short, with a head of thinning hair and cheap black shoes that made him look like an insurance salesman. But his flimsy look belied a different reality: Collins was one of the richest members of Congress, with assets in the tens of millions of dollars.

Collins had come into Congress with a massive pile of stock in Innate Immunotherapeutics, an Australian company that had been working on what it expected to be a groundbreaking multiple sclerosis drug. Collins was on the company's board, in addition to sitting on the congressional committee that regulates the pharmaceutical industry. Senators are not allowed to sit on the board of publicly traded companies, but that rule didn't apply in the House, and there was nothing specifically banning him from legislative work that could benefit the company.

In January 2017 Collins's holding in the company was worth between $25 million and $50 million. The stock was too good to keep to himself. Collins started telling people about the company, and though it's not clear whether he discussed it with his House Republican colleagues, some of them started investing their own money into the company. Rep. Markwayne Mullin, an Oklahoma Republican, bought between $100,000 and $250,000 of stock. Rep. Doug Lamborn, a Colorado Republican, poured in between $15,000 and $50,000 of his own money. Rep. Michael Conaway, the former chair of the Ethics Committee from Texas, bought as much as $30,000 of stock.

Collins's fatal mistake came on June 22, 2017, at about 6:55 P.M. He was at the annual White House picnic when the CEO of Innate e-mailed him to tell him that the drug had failed a key clinical test.

"I have bad news to report," the e-mail began. "Top-line 12 month data . . . show no clinically meaningful or statistically significant differences in [outcomes] between [the drug] and placebo."

Fifteen minutes later Collins and his son, Cameron, played phone tag before connecting at 7:16 P.M. for six minutes. During that conversation, prosecutors say Collins told his son about the failed drug test, and the next day Cameron dumped more than 16,000 shares. All told, Cameron Collins dumped nearly 1.4 million shares of stock, saving himself nearly $600,000. Cameron Collins also told friends and family members, who themselves dumped the stock.

Rep. Chris Collins was charged with eleven criminal counts, including lying to an FBI agent, wire fraud, and securities fraud. He pleaded not guilty and vowed to fight the charges. "The charges that have been levied against me are meritless," Collins said during a news conference in Buffalo. "And I will mount a vigorous defense in court to clear my name. I look forward to being fully vindicated and exonerated." Collins said he would no longer address the charges and would run again in November.

Nancy Pelosi used the incident to open a new line of attack on Republicans: They were not fit to hold public office. "The charges against Congressman Collins show the rampant culture of corruption and self-enrichment among Republicans in Washington today," she said in a news release from San Francisco. Democrats had a compelling case, and Pelosi urged the DCCC to pick up this mantle. The president's campaign manager Paul Manafort was on trial. The president himself was involved in an investigation. And one of his closest allies in Congress was under indictment.

"OUR POLICIES ARE WORKING, the economy is surging, and recent polling is starting to reflect that."

So read an e-mail from Kevin McCarthy to House Republicans on August 9, two days after the special election in Ohio. McCarthy was inviting everyone to a "Protect the House" conference call that would serve as a follow-up to the terror-inducing meeting in the Eisenhower Room just two weeks earlier. If this new message seemed like night and day from the grim slideshow projections of the earlier meeting, it was because McCarthy was looking at new numbers that showed a totally different race, one that looked much better for House Republicans. "If you were in the field a few weeks ago, your poll would likely look very different than if you were in the field today," he wrote.

McCarthy ran the call the next day from Hawaii, where he was vacationing with his family. Stivers was in Ohio, where he was still cautiously gleeful about dragging Troy Balderson across the finish line. McCarthy's aim for the conference call was to give his colleagues an update on the political climate—and to share a bunch of good news. What he had begun to understand was that the race was too volatile to take any single poll as gospel. One day you might be down by over ten on the generic ballot, but two weeks later you could be down just one. As far as McCarthy could see, the race was shifting, tightening. Polls were looking better, and Donald Trump had set the date for his big-time fund-raiser for House Republicans on September 27 in Washington. The media had all but written Republicans off, and McCarthy wanted to try to realign House Republicans' thinking, to the extent he could.

"I understand what the media is trying to write, but what is happening out there today is fundamentally different than what I am reading," he said on the call. "What's happening right now is I see the press, they're trying to psychologically change what is happening out in the field." In fact, it made sense that the media was skeptical of the Republicans' political position. They had just barely squeaked by in the Ohio race, and all available evidence was that they were going to get smoked in November. But McCarthy had good news, and he didn't mind knocking the media to frame it.

McCarthy said the latest internal party numbers were better for the GOP. In January, he said, Democrats had a thirteen-point advantage on the generic ballot. "My personal belief is that it needs to be [a six-point Democratic advantage] or less for us to keep the majority," McCarthy said. "When we departed two weeks ago, it was D plus seven. Do you know what the latest numbers just came back? D plus *three.* . . . That is the exact same spot that we were in on the day before the election in 2016. And y'all know what happened in 2016. Not only did we win the presidency, we kept the majority." Sure, Trump was also not on the ballot in 2018, and this was only August, far enough out from Election Day for the climate to shift once again, but this call was as much a pep talk as it was a strategy session.

Why had the polls moved over these two weeks? While it would have been nice if the cause had been Republicans' pointed, powerful arguments to voters, McCarthy knew the real reason, as did Stivers and John Rogers, the NRCC executive director, who was also on the line: Republicans were out of Washington and out of voters' minds. The American public had turned sharply against the inhabitants of the capital city, and that was mostly attributed to the chaos that Trump stirred. Republicans were forced to respond to his every utterance. When they were at home, they got a reprieve, and their poll numbers shot up.

But McCarthy had another reason for arranging this call: He wanted to sharpen the knives of Republicans' attacks on Democrats as the campaigns headed into the home stretch, to fine-tune the shift toward going negative. "We need to remind people, because remember, not one Democrat voted for the tax cut bill," McCarthy said, explaining part of what he viewed as a winning political argument under Donald Trump. McCarthy said that women beat men 71 percent of the time, underscoring how difficult it would be to keep the House with so many female Democratic candidates. "What people are really worried about, [is] dysfunction. They don't want their government to be dysfunction[al]. They don't want their government taken over by Democrats just to create dysfunction.

"Let me walk you through some when it comes to what they want to do on health care," McCarthy said. "Health care is going to continue to rise. But what they are trying to do with government-controlled health care . . . And you can say that." McCarthy was urging Republicans to offset the political damage caused by the rise in health care premiums by accusing Democrats of trying to nationalize health care.

"Government-controlled health care," he continued. "It costs up to thirty-two trillion [dollars]. It forces every American into the same government-run health care. That means if you have employee-based health care—that goes away. Requires new taxes on the middle class and seniors to pay for it. It will end Medicare as we know it, and it takes away people's employer-based coverage. . . . This is the issue you want to talk about and what the Democrats are out there saying. They've got more than a hundred Democrats signed onto that bill, co-sponsoring it."

After Stivers cheered members over Balderson's Ohio win—evidence that Republicans were not down and out—John Rogers chimed in to say that the NRCC had seen in polling that voters did not view Democrats as a legitimate alternative to Republicans. The Democratic Party, he said, was drifting leftward and being overtaken by "radical leftists" who wanted to impeach the president.

"I think the impeachment points are very important," Rogers said. "What our focus groups are seeing is that if you think that the government is dysfunctional, and then add impeachment to the mix of that. They think that multiplies the dysfunction by a million and then nothing will get done from that point on. And I think it's really important that we highlight that distinction."

McCarthy jumped back in. "So you have the issues to talk about: government-run health care, that the Democrats want to do. They want to abolish ICE, they want to impeach the president. Those are the three main issues of why they want to take over the government."

A new election message was set.

"I'm going to tell you, history, wind is in our face," McCarthy said. "And what they're writing is not true. We can win this thing. I've been through a lot of fights in my time, but I've played my politics like I play my sports: It's all contact. We're going to win this thing."

IT DIDN'T TAKE LONG for the Republicans' burn-the-House-down strategy to become evident on airwaves across America. Gone was the idea that they were going to run on the tax bill or on any positive message. It was now all fear, all the time.

Corry Bliss's CLF started running television ads that Democrats decried as racist, dog-whistling spots aimed at scaring the hell out of Americans. In Ohio's first district—a seat anchored around Cincinnati—CLF ran a spot linking Aftab Pureval, who is Indian and Tibetan, to Libyan strongman Muammar Gaddafi and the 1988 Lockerbie bombing.

"He worked at a D.C. lobbying firm," the narrator in the ad said. "But worse than Pureval's lies, is his hypocrisy. Pureval's lobbying firm made millions from helping reduce payments owed to families of Americans killed by Libyan terrorism. Selling out Americans? Aftab Pureval can't be trusted."

White & Case, the firm where Pureval worked as an antitrust litigator, represented Libya, but he did not work on this case. The Libyan government settled in 2008, when Pureval graduated law school.

CLF ran another spot in upstate New York against Antonio Delgado, who once was a rapper named "A.D. The Voice." Delgado rapped in 2006, more than a decade ahead of the election. He also picked up degrees from Colgate and Harvard Law and was a Rhodes scholar. CLF's ad said, "Delgado admits he'd bring the same ideals to Congress, saying 'Listen to the content of the lyrics my mission is clear.'" Delgado said his raps dealt with injustice and misogyny, and "the ideals are the same, and there's the same desire to serve," according to AllOtsego.com, a local news site.

Bliss bought completely into the negativity messaging. His view was that in 2018 Trump was so unpopular that, if Republicans didn't tarnish

Democrats beyond recognition, they would get wiped out. Republicans had to frighten white, college-educated voters in order to win. If that meant tying a man to his ten-year-old rap album, or linking a lawyer to work he never did, so be it.

The Republican operatives who were involved in these ads felt like they got flak for attacking a Democrat, but no one ever complained when Democrats attacked Republicans. Democrats would run the same ad, they said. Still, pushing the envelope like this was not out of character for CLF's president.

"When I was young, I was raised in a more rural area," said Stivers. "I trained a lot of horses, and some horses just can't be trained. Corry Bliss would be one of those."

ON AUGUST 11—THE DAY AFTER the McCarthy call and eighty-seven days before Election Day—Rep. Chris Collins unexpectedly said he would forgo reelection. It seemed like a curious decision. Collins seemed unlikely to lose even with the insider trading charges pending. New York's twenty-seventh district, which he had represented since 2013, was the Trumpiest district in the Empire State. Collins had won with 67 percent of the vote in 2016, and 71 percent in 2014. Trump himself won the district by 24 points.

But something strange was swirling in the political air. A private poll after the indictment found the district was swinging wildly toward Democrats. The poll showed that a generic, nameless Democrat was beating Collins by eighteen points.

Ten days after that, the Justice Department indicted Rep. Duncan Hunter for allegedly spending a quarter-million campaign dollars on personal expenses, like trips to Italy, golf shorts, and food. He blamed his wife—his friends said he was in an unhappy marriage. Hunter also said the forces that took him down were the same ones that were dogging Donald Trump.

"This is the new Department of Justice. This is the Democrats' arm of law enforcement, that's what's happening right now," Hunter said to a local ABC station in California. "It's happening with Trump, and it's happening with me."

On that same day, a jury found Paul Manafort guilty, and Michael Cohen accepted a plea deal. This was all a gift to Democrats, who were looking to make this election about chaos and corruption. Republican leaders were privately praying that Trump would not pardon either man. By this point, they knew that it would take something drastic and unforeseen to change the calculus in November.

18

THE SECOND SEAT

ON JUNE 27, 2018, roughly one year and three months after the Senate confirmed Neil Gorsuch, Donald Trump called Mitch McConnell. They were speaking frequently at this point, but this discussion was very pointed: The president wanted to know if McConnell thought Justice Anthony Kennedy would step down from the Court. It was a fair question. Kennedy was eighty-one and the Court's second-oldest justice. Trump was itching for another big-time court pick. He had seen crowds go crazy over the Gorsuch nomination and thought another justice would give him a bump.

McConnell said no, he didn't think so. But then just hours later, Kennedy delivered a letter to the White House saying he would step down. The president and the Senate majority leader hopped back on the phone. How about that, they said.

McConnell had his own ideas about who should take the seat. He liked Amul Thapar, a forty-nine-year-old Michigan native of Indian descent who had a federal judgeship in McConnell's home state of Kentucky. Thapar got an interview, mostly out of deference to McConnell, but was passed over.

Trump is known to float lots of ideas to friends and colleagues, and it is, at times, difficult to separate his serious ideas from musings. In that vein, at various points during Trump's internal deliberations about whom to nominate to the bench, the president privately raised the prospect of tapping Merrick Garland—the very man McConnell had blocked from even getting a hearing. It's not clear how serious Trump was, and McConnell was unaware of the musings. Told of it months later, McConnell let out a belly laugh and said, "That would've been a tough sell." Sen. Charles Grassley, who chaired the Senate Judiciary Committee, said Trump couldn't have been serious.

The White House sought out McConnell's input about another candidate: Brett Kavanaugh, a U.S. Court of Appeals judge on the D.C. Circuit. Kavanaugh had all the markings of a man who would be the twinkle in Trump's eye. He had two Yale degrees, and with a mop of well-kept hair, he looked the part of a Republican justice. He was well connected in Washington: He counted White House counsel Donald McGahn as a close friend, and his stint as the staff secretary in George W. Bush's White House had put him in close contact with all sorts of D.C. insiders. Rob Portman, the Ohio senator, was a friend. So was Joel Kaplan, the head of Facebook's public policy team.

McConnell thought highly of Kavanaugh but warned the White House that he would be a tough confirmation. Democrats, he told McGahn and the president, would try to get their hands on every piece of paper that Kavanaugh touched during his stint in the Bush White House and during his time working for Ken Starr, the man who spent the better part of the 1990s probing Bill Clinton's indiscretions.

Meanwhile, Mike Davis—the Gorsuch booster who had shepherded his man onto the high court—had moved to Washington. He helped set up Gorsuch's office at the Supreme Court in 2017, then took a job in the Capitol working for Grassley. Davis was now in charge of all judicial nominations on Grassley's Judiciary Committee—processing them, vetting them, and ensuring the trains ran on time—which made him the critical linchpin in McConnell's quest to remake the nation's courts. The Judiciary Committee had a methodical process: Every other Wednesday, it cleared four or five district judges and at least one circuit court judge.

Davis thought absolutely nothing of Kavanaugh. To Davis and some other Republicans in D.C., Kavanaugh was a loser whose only constituency was blond wives who spent their summers at country club pools in Bethesda, Maryland. Kavanaugh was the twenty-fifth choice of twenty-five, Davis told colleagues in the Capitol and at the White House. He took to calling Kavanaugh "Bushy, swampy, chiefy," meaning he was seen as a Bush acolyte who had spent his life in the "swamp" of Washington and was too similar to John Roberts, the chief justice who disappointed conservatives by voting to uphold the Affordable Care Act. Kavanaugh, Davis was known to say, would be conservative "95 percent" of the time but would abandon conservatives on the 5 percent of cases that mattered.

Davis and other Judiciary aides were also concerned that Kavanaugh would be outed as a partier—a frat boy of sorts. He had no constituency, Davis told friends. He wasn't a fire-breathing conservative or an anti-abortion warrior. Grassley's inner circle was hoping the White House would nominate someone like Amy Coney Barrett, a judge with virtually no paper trail who could sail through the confirmation process. Grassley himself was not concerned about Kavanaugh's credentials and judicial outlook, but he shared McConnell's worries about the challenges his paper trail could present.

Davis was unsuccessful in trying to torpedo Kavanaugh. And McConnell and Grassley's concerns about his paper trail seemed to not matter. In fact, they were ignored. On July 9, 2018, Trump announced he would nominate Kavanaugh to the Supreme Court. Senators were bused from the Capitol to the White House for the ceremony, at which Trump called Kavanaugh "a brilliant jurist with a clear and effective writing style, universally regarded as one of the finest and sharpest legal minds in our time." Trump also noted that Kavanaugh went to Yale for undergrad and law school.

The next day, July 10, Kavanaugh came to the Capitol with Vice President Mike Pence and Don McGahn to meet with McConnell and Grassley. McConnell said Trump had made an "outstanding nomination." Afterward Kavanaugh met with Grassley. McGahn spied Davis in the room and approached him to say hello, but Davis wanted to get a message across about this nomination. "The ball's on the tee," he told McGahn. "Don't fuck this up."

Schumer and top Democrats knew once Kavanaugh was selected as Trump's pick it was going to be an uphill battle to block his confirmation. Much of Dianne Feinstein's judiciary committee staff, besides her committee staff director, Jennifer Duck, were very green and had little experience in the high-profile, hand-to-hand combat that was about to ensue in the most heated Supreme Court battle in recent memory. Feinstein's team quickly recruited Laurie Rubiner, a twenty-year veteran Democratic staffer who had served as chief of staff to judiciary committee member Sen. Richard Blumenthal of Connecticut, to come back to Capitol Hill on a short-term basis.

From the beginning, Rubiner sat down with chief counsels and members to try to make sure Democrats were more strategic than they had been during the Gorsuch nomination. When Gorsuch testified, senators had frequently repeated each other's questions and not used their time to develop specific lines of inquiry. Gorsuch got through the confirmation hearing essentially talking in generalities; Democratic committee members couldn't pin him down on anything. They couldn't get him off topic or rattle him at all.

Addressing these issues meant managing a complicated bunch of personalities. For starters, each of the senators on the Judiciary Committee typically thinks he or she is the smartest member in the room, which is why they seek out the plum committee slot. There were also three senators—Amy Klobuchar of Minnesota, Cory Booker of New Jersey, and Kamala Harris of California—who were taking a serious look at running for president. That meant there was a chance they would use the high-profile hearing to play to the cameras, increase the buzz about a potential 2020 bid, and get the pundits opining on whether they came off as presidential.

Schumer himself was extremely engaged throughout the process, regularly looking to Max Young, a former aide who temporarily came back to work on the Kavanaugh nomination, as his eyes and ears. It wasn't necessarily surprising that Schumer would be deeply involved in such a high-profile Supreme Court fight, but it was also a tacit acknowledgment of concern among Democrats about Feinstein's age and her ability to effectively push back on Republicans and manage the competing interests of junior members of the committee.

As Mitch McConnell predicted, the fight over Kavanaugh's documents was fervent. Senate Democrats on the Judiciary Committee asked for all documents from the Bush White House years—every single piece of paper that had gone in and out of the White House. They rebuffed requests to limit the search by terms, such as "Guantánamo Bay" or "Abu Ghraib." Committee Republicans immediately said no, they would not ask for every single piece of paper produced in the Bush administration. That would've been more than 10 million documents, far more than the committee could handle. Republicans were concerned that Democrats would ask for all Kavanaugh's records as staff secretary, a request that would've produced 1.1 million records, to which Republicans said they would've had to accede. If Democrats went this route, Republicans believed they would've had to wait until 2019 to confirm Kavanaugh. But the Democrats didn't make the request.

During this back-and-forth on documents, Grassley's staff asked Don McGahn if he would be willing to call Dianne Feinstein, the ranking Democrat on the Judiciary Committee, to explain what records the White House was willing to give up. McGahn didn't bother to reply to the request.

Democrats felt like they were fighting with one arm tied behind their back. Grassley's team was playing dirty, from their perspective, upending the process of document production and limiting the scope so that many of Kavanaugh's records were not accessible. But they did not have recourse. One of their biggest challenges was getting reporters and the public interested in a process fight over access to pieces of paper. "People's eyes glazed over," one top Democratic staffer recalled. John Podesta and Todd Stern wrote an op-ed to try to press Democrats' case, but it didn't help much. It was August. Nobody was paying attention. Republicans said they were willing to allow "keyword" searches, but Democrats didn't see that as much of a compromise because Grassley's team had final veto power over what words would be used.

The tug-of-war between Grassley's and Feinstein's teams hit a breaking point after the Republicans tasked Bill Burck, President George W. Bush's personal lawyer, to prescreen documents. Grassley's team e-mailed Feinstein's office and summoned them to a meeting with Burck to tell them about the arrangement. Democratic staffers were stunned. Typically documents were reviewed by the nonpartisan National Archives and Records Administration, so they can be scanned for any national security and personal information before release. But Republicans wanted Kavanaugh seated by October 1 for the start of the next Supreme Court session, so the typical process, which is very time-consuming, wasn't going to work for them. The problem for Democrats was that since the documents were not screened by the National Archives, they were termed "committee confidential," which meant only people with clearance on the committee could see them.

Democrats grew increasingly frustrated with the constraints. They hadn't found a silver bullet that would take Kavanaugh out, but there were documents on issues like warrantless wiretapping that they would have liked to flag for reporters. They believed those documents could have hurt Kavanaugh's confirmation chances.

Eventually the committee settled on 500,000 of Kavanaugh's records. Grassley's team had twenty-four lawyers working day and night sifting through the documents on Relativity, an electronic document review system. Grassley's staff set up computers in his office and enlisted staff to stay around the clock so senators could review the records. Not a single Democratic senator showed up, and at Kavanaugh's confirmation hearing, Cory Booker of New Jersey made a show of releasing some of these records, only to be told that the records had been made public overnight.

That was pretty much how the first four days of confirmation hearings went: Democrats tried to tarnish Kavanaugh, with little success. Sen. Kamala Harris postulated, without evidence, that Kavanaugh might've been in touch with a law firm that was representing the president, but that line of questioning fell flat. Kavanaugh seemed like he was well on his way to the Supreme Court.

Until September 12. That day *The Intercept*, a left-leaning publication, dropped a bombshell: "Democrats on the Senate Judiciary Committee have privately requested to view a Brett Kavanaugh–related document in possession of the panel's top Democrat, Dianne Feinstein, but the senior California senator has so far refused, according to multiple sources familiar with the situation," they wrote. "The specific content of the document, which is a letter from a California constituent, is unclear, but Feinstein's refusal to share the letter has created tension on the committee, particularly after Feinstein largely took a back seat to her more junior colleagues last week, as they took over Kavanaugh's confirmation hearings with protests around access to documents."

On September 13 Feinstein referred the letter to the FBI. But it had been leaked: the *Washington Post* and the *New York Times* reported that it contained allegations of sexual misconduct against Kavanaugh dating to his high school years. Three days later, on September 16, the *Post* reported the allegation: that Kavanaugh, as a high school boy, had drunkenly assaulted a woman named Christine Blasey Ford in a home in a Maryland suburb of Washington.

The *Post*'s Emma Brown was the first to speak to Ford. "While his friend [Mark Judge] watched, she said, Kavanaugh pinned her to a bed on her back and groped her over her clothes, grinding his body against hers and clumsily attempting to pull off her one-piece bathing suit and the clothing she wore over it. When she tried to scream, she said, he put his hand over her mouth. 'I thought he might inadvertently kill me,' said Ford, now a 51-year-old research psychologist in northern California. 'He was trying to attack me and remove my clothing.'"

Democrats quickly shifted gears to try to shame Grassley and McConnell into holding a hearing. For his part, Grassley later said he knew immediately that he would need to hold a hearing when he read the story in the *Post*.

It was as if a bomb had been dropped, a wrench thrown in Mitch McConnell's plans. All of a sudden, it looked as if Kavanaugh might be the next prominent figure to fall in the wake of the #MeToo movement. Democrats called on the president to rescind the nomination.

McConnell, however, was steely—some opponents said insensitive, or out of step with the times. To him and his fellow Republicans, it appeared as if Democrats were dropping this now because nothing else had worked to discredit Kavanaugh. It was absurd, he felt, to think that this late-breaking document leak wasn't a calculated move. "The people who would've been inclined to do that would've been the people who had access to it," said McConnell, "which would've been either Judiciary Committee staffers on the Democratic side, or the lawyers who'd been apparently recommended to her by them. So it was like an eleventh-hour drive-by shooting. But a very sensitive subject."

Still, McConnell thought Ford needed to be heard. And he knew Kavanaugh was dying to be heard because his whole reputation was on the line.

But now there was definitely nervousness among Republicans about Kavanaugh's nomination. People approached Trump telling him that he had to pull it. "There were many people that said that," Trump later recalled. "'Cut him loose, President, cut him loose. It's killing you.'" Even Grassley wondered to himself whether the president would stick with Kavanaugh.

McConnell said that not a single senator approached him suggesting the White House pull the nomination, but on September 21 Trump called the majority leader, feeling him out about how committed he was to Kavanaugh's nomination. McConnell's response: "I'm stronger than mule piss." McConnell echoed the remarks publicly. During a speech at the Value Voters Summit, comfy confines for a Republican leader, McConnell vowed to "plow right through" the nomination.

Two days later, though, it got worse. *The New Yorker*'s Ronan Farrow and Jane Mayer published a story about Deborah Ramirez, a classmate of Kavanaugh's from Yale. Ramirez said Kavanaugh had waved his penis in her face during a party in New Haven. Kavanaugh, again, denied the allegations in a private phone call with Senate Republican staff. But now alarm was growing among top White House and McConnell aides.

At that point, the Judiciary Committee decided that they needed to investigate every single claim that came into their office. They went into rapid-response crisis mode. Grassley had an eighteen-lawyer oversight and investigation staff, which was tasked with springing into action each time an accusation came in. If an accuser requested confidentiality, they were going to honor that, but if not, they decided to make the claim public. And each time an allegation came in, the committee called Kavanaugh through his attorney and asked about the specifics of the alleged incident.

September 23 was Davis's forty-first birthday, and it wasn't a particularly fun one. On that day, Grassley announced that Ford and Kavanaugh would testify that Thursday, September 27, at ten A.M. And at 7:33 that night, Davis was sitting in his Capitol office when the provocateur lawyer Michael Avenatti started tweeting. Davis didn't know who Avenatti was—Davis is the kind of guy who wouldn't know who Avenatti was and would brag about it—but the tweet caught his eye.

"I represent a woman with credible information regarding Judge Kavanaugh and Mark Judge," Avenatti wrote. "We will be demanding the opportunity to present testimony to the committee and will likewise be demanding that Judge and others be subpoenaed to testify. The nomination must be withdrawn."

Nine minutes later Davis e-mailed Avenatti: "According to your Tweet from 7:33 P.M. E.T. this evening, you claim to have information you consider credible regarding Judge Kavanaugh and Mark Judge. Please advise of this information so that the Senate investigators may promptly begin an inquiry."

A bit more than an hour later, Avenatti responded by e-mail with a litany of suggestions for the Judiciary Committee, including asking Kavanaugh if he ever "targeted" any women for sex or rape at house parties. Moments later Davis saw that Avenatti had posted his e-mail on Twitter, and thought, "This guy is a total clown. He is manna from heaven." Davis figured that Avenatti's involvement made the entire investigation a circus and would help discredit allegations against Kavanaugh. Many Democrats on the Judiciary Committee would come to feel similarly.

The next day Senate Republican leadership aides convinced the Kavanaugh team that he needed to make his case on television. He was getting crushed in the media, and in Trump's Washington, one had to make one's case on cable news—preferably Fox News. So the White

House offered Kavanaugh to Martha MacCallum, one of the cable network's stars. Kavanaugh sat for the interview with his wife, Ashley, by his side.

"Thank you both for sitting down with me today," MacCallum said. "What made you decide to speak out before the hearing on Thursday? Judge Kavanaugh?"

"I am looking for a fair process, a process where I can defend my integrity and clear my name," Kavanaugh said. "And all I'm asking for is fairness and that I'd be heard in this process."

Fair process? Republicans on the Hill thought. *How about saying, "I didn't rape anyone!"* The performance was panned, internally. And senior Capitol Hill aides thought Kavanaugh's nomination was hanging by a thread.

AS THE KAVANAUGH SAGA was unfolding, House Republicans saw their political fortunes unraveling. The next morning, September 25, the elected leadership—Ryan, McCarthy, Steve Scalise, and their deputies—repaired to the Capitol Hill Club for a closed briefing with Steve Stivers. The leadership usually met in Ryan's office and discussed the legislative plan for the week. But that wasn't necessary on this Tuesday. They needed to talk about their dire political state with the chairman and staff of the NRCC.

Good news was hard to come by almost anywhere on the electoral map. Rep. Luke Messer, the Indiana Republican who served as the vice chair of House Republicans, raised the problems that his fellow Hoosier Rep. Jackie Walorski was having. She was beginning to show signs of struggle in her district, which Trump had won with 60 percent of the vote. Rep. Doug Collins, a Georgia Republican, said his colleague Rep. Rob Woodall was having a tough time in his district, which Trump had won by six points, with 51 percent of the vote. Rep. Pete Sessions, the House Rules Committee chairman who'd once run the party's campaign apparatus, said Republicans—including himself—were struggling even in deep-red Texas. And because Beto O'Rourke—a Democrat—was giving

Sen. Ted Cruz a tough run in the Lone Star State, Democratic turnout was expected to be through the roof, Sessions told the group.

In the face of all this, the NRCC's John Rogers was unusually optimistic. He pointed out that the generic ballot, which had favored Democrats by fourteen points the previous week, was down to eight points in some surveys. No one was buying it. How about *New York Times*/Siena College polling, which showed Republicans struggling across the country, in places like the Deep South, the Midwest, and California, multiple people in the room asked Rogers.

Rogers explained it away with some novel reasoning. Those polls were taken on Fridays, he said, and polls conducted on Fridays favored Democrats. The explanation made Rogers the butt of endless jokes that week within the GOP leadership.

Stivers asked the two dozen or so aides in the room to leave so he could have some time alone with the elected officials. He was increasingly under fire for Republicans' political positions, which was—of course—not his fault. But on this day, Stivers needed to beat a drum that these men by now had become tired of hearing: The party was in dire financial straits, and members of the Republican leadership needed to cough up more cash. Stivers put a figure on it: The half-dozen Republicans in the room needed to raise another $3 million in the forty days before Election Day.

Stivers said he would kick in more, as did McCarthy and Scalise. In this group, and in Congress generally, people liked to hoard their campaign cash, but this was no time to pad coffers.

"If we lose the majority," Stivers warned, "and anybody has a million-dollar carryover balance, they should be ashamed of themselves, and people will notice."

But there was one person who couldn't guarantee he was going to cut another check: Paul Ryan. Stivers had asked the Speaker's staff if he would be willing to stroke a check for another few million dollars. It was a reasonable ask: Ryan no longer needed the money, since he wasn't running for reelection. But Ryan's staff balked. They couldn't even hold on to the Speaker's money: Because of his decision to retire in the middle of the congressional term, Ryan had to be ready to return more than $1 million in contributions he had received, exactly what Stivers didn't need to hear. In Ryan's team's view, he had already raised piles of money for the party.

Throughout the election cycle, McCarthy and other top Republicans had been telling their rank-and-file members that if you don't like the political climate today, wait until tomorrow, and it might improve. Little did they know, the political climate was about to be shaken up once again in a way they never expected.

AS THE HOUSE REPUBLICANS were scrambling to replenish emptying coffers, the Senate Judiciary Committee was preparing for the Ford-Kavanaugh hearing. Grassley and the rest of his Judiciary Committee members knew the optics were going to be tough for the GOP. Grassley didn't want to repeat the mistakes of the Clarence Thomas hearing: men hammering away with questions at a female victim. Every single Republican member of the committee was a white man. Many of them were old. Republicans thought they might consider hiring outside counsel to question Ford, so Davis and the committee interviewed thirty candidates in the course of a week. Many turned them down, but one was willing: Rachel Mitchell, the deputy county attorney in Maricopa County, Arizona, and the chief of a division that investigates sex crimes. Grassley vetted Mitchell with Arizona Republicans and found that people thought highly of her.

Democrats felt like the situation was spiraling out of control. Republicans were releasing all allegations against Kavanaugh, credible or not, to the public unless the accuser requested confidentiality. The Republican strategy: sunlight was the best disinfectant. But Democrats had scant ability to keep up, and they felt like the wilder accusations made the whole situation seem less rooted in reality. Adding insult to injury, Grassley's team was controlling who would testify at the hearing. For context: There were scores of witnesses during the Anita Hill hearing. This time, Republicans allowed just Ford and Kavanaugh.

On September 25, Michael Avenatti sent Davis a sworn testimony by a woman named Julie Swetnick, who said she knew that Kavanaugh and his friend Mark Judge had spiked the punch at parties during their high school years and facilitated gang rapes. At 7:42 A.M. on September 26, Avenatti released the sworn statement and his correspondence with Davis on Twitter.

It took until later that day to pull together the information and lawyers necessary to bring Swetnick's allegations to Kavanaugh by phone, and Judiciary staff didn't reach Kavanaugh until after eight P.M. that night, little more than sixteen hours or so before he was to appear before the committee. Worse, Grassley's aides forgot to e-mail Kavanaugh the allegations beforehand, and it was the committee's impression he was hearing them fresh. While they were on the phone, Kavanaugh exploded.

"Judge Kavanaugh, Michael Avenatti has publicly posted fifteen allegations from Ms. Julie Swetnick. Do you know Ms. Swetnick?" a Judiciary Committee aide asked Kavanaugh on the call.

"No," Kavanaugh replied. "Don't know her."

"Okay," the aide said. "Ms. Swetnick raises several specific allegations related to house parties that occurred in the Washington, D.C., area from 1981 to 1983. I'm going to ask you about some of her claims. Ms. Swetnick claims that she observed you being overly aggressive with girls during these house parties. Did you ever become abusive or physically aggressive with women at house parties between 1981 and 1983?"

"No, and she's lying," Kavanaugh said, growing increasingly frustrated. "She was supposedly at Gaithersburg High School. I don't know. I don't know her. I don't know anyone like her. This is just total B.S."

"She also alleges that you fondled girls without consent between 1981 and 1983. Did you fondle girls without consent between 1981 and 1983?" the Judiciary aide asked.

"No, she's lying," Kavanaugh said. "I don't know her. I didn't—we didn't hang out. I didn't know people from Gaithersburg High School, which is way out 270," Kavanaugh said, referring to I-270, the highway that stretches northwest from Washington to Gaithersburg, Maryland.

"This is a joke. She supposedly—how old is she? She's supposed—like class of 'eighty? Give me a break. This whole thing is a farce," Kavanaugh said angrily.

"Okay," the aide said. "Moving on to some of her additional allegations. Did you grab girls without consent at parties between 1981 and 1983?"

"No," Kavanaugh said.

"Did you press girls against your body without their consent between 1981 and 1983?"

"No," Kavanaugh said.

"Did you attempt to shift a woman's clothing to expose her breasts or genitals without her consent at a party between 1981 and 1983?"

"No," Kavanaugh said.

The interview continued in a similar fashion for roughly twenty minutes—the committee's Republican aides asking if Kavanaugh was a sexual assailant, and him replying no, seeming to grow more infuriated with each question. When Kavanaugh walked into the Dirksen Senate Office building the next morning, he was still steaming.

That morning, September 27, was as charged as Washington could possibly imagine. Pulling off a hearing of this consequence in the tough political environment of the Trump era required acrobatics of sorts. Kavanaugh was kept on one side of the building, in a meeting space controlled by the Senate Finance Committee. Ford was kept in the Democratic staff's office. Capitol Police cleared the hallway, to ensure the two would never meet.

By then, Democratic senators and staff had grown frustrated with how cautious Feinstein and her chief of staff, Jennifer Duck, were being when it came to Ford. Other Democrats on the committee had little to no interaction with Ford and her team before she appeared before the committee. They didn't know what she was going to say in her opening statement, or what lines of questioning would be fruitful. Feinstein's people would say they were acting appropriately, but other Democrats were desperate for a plan of attack.

Grassley had been similarly shut out. His staff had been e-mailing

Ford's attorneys, trying to set up a meeting between the chairman and Ford, but her legal team kept putting him off. Finally, as he was about to enter the hearing room, Grassley's staff got an e-mail from Ford's team inviting him to pay her a visit. It was a friendly conversation—at least from Grassley's point of view. He promised her a dignified hearing. Looking back on the interaction, Grassley said he wanted Ford to know that "I don't have horns."

The hearing they got was unlike anything in modern American politics. For hours, Ford painstakingly detailed a sexual assault that she said was at the hands of Brett Kavanaugh and his friend Mark Judge during their teenage years.

"I am here today not because I want to be," Ford said, her voice quivering. "I am terrified. I am here because I believe it is my civic duty to tell you what happened to me while Brett Kavanaugh and I were in high school."

Ford's testimony was absolutely wrenching, and the hearing room—and indeed, the country, which was watching live on cable TV or over the Internet—was completely enrapt. It was as if the Capitol were frozen. McConnell cleared his schedule to watch it on a flat-screen television in his office. Other senators were watching live or had the entire session taped for further review.

For many, the most gut-wrenching part of Ford's testimony was an exchange with Sen. Patrick Leahy, the seventy-eight-year-old Vermont Democrat who once chaired the panel.

"What is the strongest memory you have," Leahy asked, "the strongest memory of the incident, something that you cannot forget? Take whatever time you need."

"Indelible in the hippocampus is the laughter, the laugh—the uproarious laughter between the two, and their having fun at my expense," Ford said.

"You've never forgotten that laughter," he said. "You've never forgotten them laughing at you."

"They were laughing with each other," she added.

"And you were the object of the laughter?" Leahy said.

"I was, you know, underneath one of them while the two laughed, two friend—two friends having a really good time with one another," Ford replied.

After three hours, Ford's wrenching testimony ended. McConnell picked up the phone in his office and dialed the White House. "Well, it's halftime," he told the president, keenly aware about how visceral and believable Ford's testimony was. "Let's see how we feel at the end of the game."

Ford's testimony will forever be remembered for its raw emotion—a woman who lived for more than thirty years, bearing the scars of a teenage sexual assault. Kavanaugh's portion of the day will be remembered for a different kind of raw emotion: anger.

The hours that morning had not burned off any of Kavanaugh's rage. And when he sat down, it boiled over.

"This confirmation process has become a national disgrace," Kavanaugh said. "The Constitution gives the Senate an important role in the confirmation process, but you have replaced advice and consent with search and destroy. . . . This whole two-week effort has been a calculated and orchestrated political hit, fueled with apparent pent-up anger about President Trump and the 2016 election. Fear that has been unfairly stoked about my judicial record. Revenge on behalf of the Clintons. And millions of dollars in money from outside left-wing opposition groups."

At the White House, Vice President Mike Pence was watching Kavanaugh with aides, including Kellyanne Conway. "We're back in the game," he said. Grassley thought Kavanaugh's anger saved his nomination.

After Kavanaugh's testimony, McConnell called Trump back. "Both of us felt he had done well. And there was no further discussion of withdrawing the nomination."

TURMOIL NOTWITHSTANDING, Trump was going to make good on his month-old promise to help get House Republicans some cash. Later that evening the president headed to the Trump Hotel—naturally—to take part in the $15 million fund-raising event organized by Kevin

McCarthy. The event, held in the presidential ballroom, was to feature a roundtable for lawmakers and Trump, a photo line, and a small private dinner for five- and six-figure donors and elected officials. The White House nixed the roundtable with lawmakers—and stripped cell phones from everyone attending the dinner portion of the evening to ensure the utmost secrecy.

Before the fund-raiser officially began, McCarthy filmed a campaign video with Trump for Protect the House, after which members got in line with donors to shake the president's hand. But this was all a warm-up for the most noteworthy part of the evening—Trump's hour-plus-long riff about politics, policy, sports, and culture. Trump really let it fly.

Trump conceded that he had watched the vast majority of the Ford-Kavanaugh hearing, and he called it "brutal," "painful to watch," and "tough to watch." But he said Kavanaugh "knocked it out of the park." The president said there were three undecided Republican senators—Jeff Flake of Arizona, Susan Collins of Maine, and Lisa Murkowski of Alaska—and though he never publicly acknowledged any kind of Plan B on Kavanaugh, that night he told the crowd that if two of these senators voted against the nominee, he would have to go "back to the drawing board."

For many in attendance, Trump's most memorable riff of the evening was his recounting of his May 2017 trip to Saudi Arabia.

I don't know which trip was better, Trump said, China or Saudi Arabia. In China they had closed the Forbidden City for him, but he thought Saudi Arabia was "way better." Trump recounted how an aide had approached him to say that, per Saudi custom, he should bow when he met King Salman. Trump told the crowd that Obama had bowed, and so he told the aide he would refuse to do it. He then described how the aide told Melania Trump that King Salman would not shake her hand if she extended it. Receive, that's what they call it, Trump said. They will not receive your hand, he said, mimicking the aide's warnings.

Trump built up to his punch line. When I landed, he said, they tell me the king is waiting on the tarmac. I say, that's pretty good—for Obama he was waiting in the palace in the air conditioning. He was waiting on the tarmac for me. And it was 115 degrees out! That's a cool day in Saudi Arabia, and he's on the asphalt tarmac for me. So, I get off the plane, I shake his hand, I don't bow, and Melania offers her hand. Remember, they told us "He will not receive your hand." He grabs her hand, and kisses her, mwah, mwah, mwah. And I go, hey, King, lay off, that's enough—three kisses! The room was uproarious. Video footage, in fact, showed that the king did not kiss Melania, but the two did shake hands.

So, we had a good meeting, Trump recalled, and I said, "King, if we leave—if our military leaves, Iran is going to take you over in two weeks. You got $2 trillion here. All you guys got 747s."

Trump then started talking about the donors. By the way, he said, you all flew here on Gulfstream 650s, right? That's the size of one inch of a 747. And the sultan of finance has a 747, the king has one—you're poor if you don't have a 747. So I said, "King, you have $2 trillion in the bank, we're going to need $4 billion to protect you or else we'll pull out." The king says, "Well, this has never happened before, I don't understand it." I said "Yeah, I know, we're sorry, but we're going to need $4 billion."

Those schmucks, Trump said, seemingly referring to the Saudi royal family.

The president finally got around to one of his favorite punching bags: the State of California. They were allowing illegal immigrants to vote, Trump ranted. California had sanctuary cities—municipalities where undocumented immigrants could live. And how about Maxine Waters, the Los Angeles–area Democrat who had particularly sharp words for the president?

And now, Trump said, California was ready to elect a governor from San Francisco—the city's former mayor, Gavin Newsom.

"Kimberly," he said, calling out to Kimberly Guilfoyle, his son Don Jr.'s girlfriend, "you know him, right?"

There was some awkward, tepid laughter around the room. Guilfoyle had been married to Newsom from 2001 to 2006.

THE NEXT MORNING THE Senate Judiciary Committee was scheduled to vote on Kavanaugh's nomination and send it to the floor. It was an incredibly important moment that would put Kavanaugh one step closer to the Supreme Court. Just before nine-thirty A.M. on September 28, Jeff Flake announced that he would vote to advance Kavanaugh from the committee. But something happened on his way to the hearing: He was accosted in an elevator for several minutes by women who said they were victims of sexual assault. Aides on the Judiciary Committee had to call the Capitol Police to help Flake extricate himself from the elevator.

When he finally got to the committee room, Flake looked sullen. He eyes were drifting downward. His face was tense. Sen. Chris Coons, a Democrat from Delaware with whom Flake was close, suggested that they pause the hearing for one week to allow the FBI to investigate further.

Flake tapped Coons on the shoulder, and asked him to join him in the anteroom, a private space off the committee hearing room. Flake told Coons that he was having trouble voting to confirm Kavanaugh at the moment, and he believed the process was tearing the country apart. A one-week extension to allow the FBI to conduct a further probe made sense, he told Coons. But Flake expressed concern that Democrats would try to delay a vote indefinitely.

Coons and Flake remained in the back room for more than an hour, talking about the probe. Squeezed into a tiny phone booth, they called Chris Wray, the FBI director, and got a call back from Rod Rosenstein, the deputy attorney general. Rosenstein warned them that the probe was unlikely to turn up much more, but one week was enough time to complete an additional background investigation. Former president George W. Bush called Flake, pressing him to stand down. Staff reached out to Mitt Romney—like Flake, a Mormon—to see if he would be willing to talk to the Arizona Republican, but the call did not happen.

Flake agreed to advance Kavanaugh out of committee, but he said he would not support the Supreme Court nominee on the Senate floor unless there was an additional FBI investigation.

That afternoon McConnell got involved. He controlled the Senate floor, and it was his decision whether to delay the vote to allow a further FBI background check. McConnell invited the eleven Republicans on the Judiciary Committee, plus Susan Collins and Lisa Murkowski, to a small, red-walled conference room off of the Republican leader's personal office. He knew he didn't have the votes, but he thought he might get them by negotiating the scope of the further FBI investigation. Unless he could satisfy Flake, Collins, and Murkowski, he couldn't win, a circumstance that was frustrating and infuriating other Republicans. Davis took to calling Collins, Murkowski, and Flake the "cupcake caucus," a nod to the fact that they weren't marching in lockstep with the party.

"If we're going to move the goalpost here," McConnell told the group assembled in his office, "what do we need to look at?" After an extensive conversation, the group decided on the parameters of the investigation. It could last only seven days. Investigators could talk to anyone mentioned by Christine Blasey Ford, to Deborah Ramirez, and to anyone Ramirez mentioned. And they decided that they would not permit the FBI to talk to Michael Avenatti or anyone he was representing. McConnell said Republicans plainly "were not interested in Avenatti, or anybody Avenatti came up with." He called Don McGahn in the White House counsel's office to relay the parameters.

The FBI followed McConnell's orders. Avenatti never heard from them; nor did his client Julie Swetnick. Democrats immediately blamed the White House for stymieing the investigation, but it was McConnell who had set the ground rules.

Keeping the time frame fixed to a week was critical. McConnell didn't want to let the episode drag out further for two reasons: Kavanaugh's prospects were worsening with time, and if he was voted down, McConnell wanted to try to squeeze in another nomination before the end of the year.

During that week, as the Senate waited for the FBI report to wrap up, McConnell spoke to the president on several occasions. But during one call, McConnell told Trump that he should prepare a fallback option if Kavanaugh were to fail.

"I said, 'You know, you've talked to a lot of people in the course of making this decision,'" McConnell said he told Trump. "'If we don't get there, we need to pop another one quickly, so we can still sandwich this in between now and the end of this year.'" Trump, for his part, said he would not have viewed pulling Kavanaugh's nomination as a defeat. He would've immediately chosen someone else and pushed for their approval.

By Thursday, the FBI probe was over, and the report arrived on Capitol Hill for a final look. Because of an agreement between the Senate and the White House forged during the Obama administration, committee aides couldn't make copies of the report. Instead it was kept under lock and key in a secure Intelligence Committee room. Wavering senators said that the report showed no new information, and McConnell quickly decided it was time to schedule a vote for Friday.

Retrospectively, Grassley said he believed the additional FBI probe helped Republicans lock down the votes they needed. "It looked like we were making one last chance to be sure, and if we hadn't done that, we wouldn't have gotten the fifty votes we had," he said.

And then, all eyes in the Capitol became transfixed on Susan Collins and Lisa Murkowski. The two women were seatmates on the Senate floor and close politically and personally. Murkowski came from a political family—her father had represented Alaska in the Senate for twenty years and was the state's governor from 2002 to 2006. And Murkowski was mostly unafraid of her base: In 2010 she had lost the GOP nomination, only to win the seat in a write-in campaign. The political class in her state was wary of Kavanaugh because of a series of judicial decisions considered controversial by Native Americans. That political dynamic was highlighted on September 20, when Alaska's governor and lieutenant governor publicly opposed his nomination.

Collins, meanwhile, had been in the Senate since 1996 and voted for every Supreme Court nominee in her tenure, regardless of the party of the president. Throughout the entire process, Collins and Murkowski were cagey about which way they would vote, and McConnell had limited visibility into their thinking—they were holding their cards close to the vest.

But Davis took it upon himself to try to sway them. *This is your guy, he's a squish,* he said to each of them separately. *I tried to take him out and I failed.* Davis told them that Trump would nominate someone far more conservative if Kavanaugh didn't get the votes.

Meanwhile every Democrat besides one had said they would vote against Kavanaugh. Sen. Joe Manchin, up for reelection in West Virginia, a state Trump won by forty-one points, was seen universally as a yes vote, but he got a warning from Trump during a private phone call.

"Don't vote yes if you're going to be the winning vote," Trump said. "I don't want your vote."

Because of the Senate's arcane and, at times, frustrating rules, there were two rounds of votes. The only vote that truly mattered was the cloture vote, which was held on Friday, October 5. Manchin entered through the Democratic cloakroom but immediately left when the clerk started calling the roll.

"Mrs. Collins," the clerk said.

"Aye," she said, rising from her seat.

McConnell sat in his customary seat—in the front row of the chamber—with his left leg crossed over his right, his face resting on his right hand. A few minutes later they called Murkowski's name.

"Mrs. Murkowski," the clerk said.

"No," she said quietly, her eyes locked straight ahead. The roll was already read, and Manchin was nowhere to be found. At 10:44—ten minutes after he had first walked in the chamber—Manchin reappeared and gave a thumbs-up, all but cementing Kavanaugh's place on the Court. (Oddly enough, the entire chamber had to wait for Sen. Tom Carper of Delaware, a Democrat who had never been seen as a yes vote. Carper was running late.)

After the vote, Davis ran into Collins dining with Murkowski at Bistro Cacao on Capitol Hill. Murkowski said sympathetically, "I know how hard you worked."

"There's no hard feelings," Davis said.

The next day, a Saturday, the result was all but assured, but nevertheless Republicans had one last vote to clear to send Kavanaugh to the Supreme Court. The Capitol was flooded with protesters—thousands of people were on the east side of the building. In the chamber, with Mike Pence presiding over the vote, people were carried out, screaming "Where's my representation?" Jeff Flake voted yes and immediately left the chamber.

In the lead-up to the vote, Davis pleaded with Grassley to stay in Washington to do a victory lap. Appear on the Sunday shows, Davis said—this is a big deal. Grassley would not commit. He was notorious for going back to Iowa at the first chance he had. He had missed one vote in thirty-six years of service—and that was in 1992, when the state was under feet of water. Davis trailed Grassley to the floor that day so the two would be able to sit together for the confirmation. As soon as Grassley cast his yes vote, he left for the airport, to get back to Iowa.

MITCH MCCONNELL CELEBRATED Kavanaugh's confirmation with a toast in his office suite. As the festivities wound down, a McConnell aide passed around an alcoholic shot they called "mule piss," a reference to McConnell's remark about the strength of his resolve to confirm Kavanaugh.

The Senate majority leader later said he thought Ford was trustworthy. But he said Kavanaugh was a good man—and losing this nomination had never been an option. McConnell was, he claimed, in the results business, figuring out what was achievable and how to get there. Don't overclaim what might be achievable. Work on the things that you know you've got a chance of getting a result on. Do it in a consistent, dogged way.

It was a remarkably bloodless perspective, especially in light of the situation: A man accused of serial sexual assault had just been elevated to the Supreme Court. Republicans were the subject of constant protesting. The Capitol looked like a 1960s-era war protest.

Trump looked back on the episode and admired McConnell's resolve. "Mitch McConnell never wavered an inch either," he said. "We work with others, but we were up there strong and I give Mitch a lot of credit for that because he was under the same pressure that I was."

To hear McConnell tell it, the episode wasn't nearly as wrenching for him as it was for some of his colleagues, or for many Americans. "I think what the Democrats misunderstood was that there are a lot of mothers who have sons in the country," McConnell said. "And they hadn't thought fully through that this wasn't gonna just be a total game changer." Ultimately, the entire affair impacted McConnell in a way that was remarkably consistent with his chief drive: winning. "That dramatic week, every speech I made—Monday, Tuesday, Wednesday, Thursday, Friday, and Saturday—was carried live on all the cables from beginning to end," he recalled. "I decided to try to frame this about two things. One, the presumption of innocence. And two, the assault of the angry mob. And CNN did a poll, and they factored out the Republicans, and my approval rating went from thirty to sixty-two. I'd never had an audience like that before. So all of these Republicans who are constantly told by radio talk show hosts and others that I'm a villain got to see a sort of different side.

"So that's how it impacted me," McConnell said. "I know it won't last. But for the moment, I'm a rock star."

19

OCTOBER

"HEY, WHEN DO YOU GO on TV?" Steve Stivers said into his cell phone. It was nearly October, and he was sitting in his office at the NRCC on Capitol Hill, the Kavanaugh hearing playing behind him on television. "Good. Do you see how many points your opponent has? Two thousand points this week." Stivers was telling Rep. Bob Gibbs, a fellow Ohio Republican, that his opponent was spending enough money on television to potentially alter the course of the race.

Gibbs was running against Ken Harbaugh, a Democrat who was turning heads. Harbaugh was branding himself as a tough-talking, truck-driving political disrupter, something like Donald Trump. Stivers was trying to get Gibbs to understand that Harbaugh was flooding the airwaves and that he needed to catch up. He knew that Gibbs, who had comfortably won his previous four contests, could be in trouble if he didn't step up his campaigning. Gibbs's central Ohio district was Republican, but in a year like this, with a highly polarizing president in the White House, he could easily lose. He was a cookie-cutter candidate who was spending no money on television. He was easily forgettable.

What was worse, Gibbs didn't seem to realize how dire his condition could become. He was sitting on money that Stivers thought he should be spending. "You got money, get on TV. You can't take it with you," Stivers said to him. "How much on TV? A million? Too late. Figure out how to add at least another week of broadcast. You might have even started sooner rather than later just to remind them who you are." Harbaugh was running advertisements featuring his daughter, Lizzie, who needed four surgeries before the age of four, in order to make Gibbs look heartless for taking contributions from big insurance companies. "Yeah, your wife is going to see a lot of these ads," Stivers told him. "Tell her to get used to it."

On multiple calls and conversations each day, Stivers reminded the rank and file that this wasn't like any other year, but by early October, he could actually say it with a spot of enthusiasm. The GOP was convinced that the Kavanaugh episode was energizing their base and closing the yawning enthusiasm deficit with Democrats. The economy was clicking, the jobless rate was low, and North Korea had stopped testing its nuclear weapons—that's how Republicans saw the political climate as they approached Election Day.

By his polling, Stivers saw twenty to thirty races that were within the margin of error, meaning control of the American government was down to a jump ball. He was feeling modestly good, which helped ease the stress of being under attack by his colleagues for his spending decisions—he had put nearly $5 million into northern Virginia to help prop up Barbara Comstock, a former campaign operative who was struggling in the blue Virginia suburbs. Republicans questioned the huge expenditure on one race that seemed like a long shot for the party. Stivers had thought if he poured money into tight races, Democrats would follow suit and be kept from expanding the playing field, but that strategy was being tested by the massive amounts Democrats were raising: $21 million in September alone, compared to the $12 million the Republicans brought in. Still, Donald Trump's approval rating was ticking up slightly, giving the party hope. Trump was interested to know how he could help his party retain the House, and Stivers suggested he go to "West Virginia again and again," one of the deep-red states where Trump was exceedingly popular. Republicans didn't want the president anywhere near tough races.

"This election is not going to be about Trump," Stivers said. "It is about making sure we get our voters out, and that we convince our voters." That meant helping voters understand the choice in front of them and showing them what the other side really looked like. Asked to sum that up in one sentence, Stivers said, "*Maxine Waters* would be two words."

In early October, Paul Ryan said he thought the House was going to flip to Democrats, but he also believed the Kavanaugh hearing more or less erased the enthusiasm gap. By the end of the month, he was feeling better about his party's prospects. "I think we're basically at jump ball right now," he said. "I think we're going to have a majority. We're going to have an eight-to-ten-seat majority, or they're going to have an eight-to-ten-seat majority. It's somewhere in between, is the way I see it."

Over at the DCCC, Dan Sena had a completely different view. In October 2018 he and his colleagues thought the political universe was shifting dramatically toward Democrats. Cash was pouring into races across the country—mostly thanks to billionaires like Mike Bloomberg, who were funneling massive sums of money into television ads in races nationwide. Donald Trump seemed to want to talk about everything besides the booming economy.

Employing a well-worn sports metaphor, Sena liked to say October was the fourth quarter of the election, and he liked the score as the clock was winding down. The DCCC was spending money in eighty districts from Florida to California, Washington State to New York.

From a political perspective, almost everything in Donald Trump's presidency had gone well for Democrats. The Republicans' tax bill was not the boon they had thought it would be; in fact, it was, on the whole, unpopular. Democrats cruised through a series of primaries, helping thirty-nine of their forty-one top-tier candidates get the nomination. And they had successfully branded their opposition as power hungry and out of touch with everyday Americans.

Their theory of the case—build a massive battlefield, and be ready to fight everywhere—had been validated. Sena told anyone who would listen about his goal to stretch Republicans thin, make them spend piles of money, and get ready for unexpected political opportunities. They had done all three. Republicans' hope that they could spend heavily in thirty districts and fortify their majority was looking naive.

And here the Dems were, in October, painting America blue. They forced Republicans to spend money in Michigan to defend Rep. Fred Upton, the three-decade veteran of Congress whom Stivers had begged not to retire, and to help Rep. George Holding hold a seat in the deep-red middle of North Carolina. Republicans had to abandon Rep. Mike Coffman in the diverse suburbs of Denver and Rep. Mike Bishop in Michigan, two traditionally Republican seats. Rep. Kevin Yoder, who represented some of the upscale Kansas City suburbs, called Steve Stivers both a "fucking idiot" and a "fucking liar" when the party pulled its financial support for his candidacy.

Democrats were a month away from Election Day and well positioned to break Trump's stranglehold on power. They weren't yet saying it publicly, but Dan Sena, Ben Ray Luján, and Nancy Pelosi were cautiously optimistic that Democrats would finally find their way out of the wilderness.

Still, Sena wouldn't let himself get too excited. He had been shocked before. Every time he walked into his office at the DCCC, he passed a sign that he'd taped to his door: "71%." It was the odds the political handicapping site FiveThirtyEight had given Hillary Clinton of becoming the forty-fifth president in late 2016. For Sena, it was a nagging reminder of the post-traumatic stress that Democrats throughout Washington felt from losing that election, and of the need to stay level-headed about the party's prospects for regaining some power.

So he continued to push forward with his plan. In the weeks leading up to the election, he commissioned focus groups in Orange County, California; a Des Moines–area district; and central New Jersey, all Republican-held seats the Democrats were trying to flip. He wanted to make sure their message was on point in the closing days.

Employing their cash advantage, the DCCC continued to pour money into competitive districts. No one was advertising on the radio in Republican congressman Carlos Curbelo's south Florida district, so the Democrats flooded the airwaves. Meanwhile Republicans were scrambling to shore up more seats they never envisioned having to protect, such as a deep-red Charleston, South Carolina, district that Republicans had held since 1981.

Sena had long been convinced that Trump would use immigration in the closing days of the election to rev up his base—he called that tactic Trump's "shake the snow globe" moment, a reference to his desire to confuse the political landscape. Multiple Democratic candidates in tough races across the country had ads prepared to insulate themselves from immigration-related attacks.

Sena also wanted to secure the integrity of the vote. He called campaign managers and top operatives in the twenty-seven most competitive races in America, walking them through how to make sure all their ballots were counted, and how to ensure that counties and states were following election laws. This election was going to be close, he thought. Democrats could not afford a flub. The DCCC made plans to fly its West Coast campaign operation to Washington the day before the election. Sena wanted to make sure that, when the results started rolling in, he had staff in his office who were living on West Coast time. There were going to be late-night decisions, Sena thought, and he wanted fresh minds to counsel him on where to deploy lawyers and staff in case of recounts.

As Election Day grew near, Sena knew he had won seventeen or eighteen seats—just a few short of the majority.

Still, he was cautious. "I think if we had to bet today," he said in mid-October, "we take the House by a seat or two. I don't think it's changed. I've felt that way for a year."

OCTOBER WAS, IN ALMOST every sense, the truest battle for the future of Trump's America. The way Republicans explained it was jobs versus mobs, conservative stewardship of government versus an endless stream of investigations. In sum, it was a fight for the continuation of Trump's agenda versus a mandate for its screeching halt.

Congress was out of session the entire month, and Kevin McCarthy and Steve Scalise were crisscrossing America, campaigning for endangered incumbents and raising cash for the final push to November 6.

But something else was also occupying their minds: their own futures. No matter what happened in October, a leadership race awaited, and McCarthy and Scalise would both have decisions to make. Scalise had publicly made it clear that he would not run against McCarthy for House Speaker if Republicans won the majority. But privately he was promising that he wasn't going to lift a finger to help McCarthy get the job. And while no one had publicly asked him if he would challenge McCarthy for minority leader if Republicans lost the House, he was still considering it. It had been the subject of chatter in his office for some time. "I think we'll hold the majority. And if we don't—I don't know what our conference is going to be like if that happens," he said. "If we don't get there, I think we gotta look and see what we look like."

The potential impact of such a scuffle between Scalise and McCarthy was serious, if only because of the two men's differing relationships with Donald Trump. McCarthy was a fierce ally, but he also had the ability to translate Trump, and the tendency to temper his instincts. When Trump veered too far to the left (siding with Democrats on immigration reform) or to the right (flirting with ideas from the Freedom Caucus), McCarthy brought him back to center. McCarthy had the relationship with Trump, and the legislative know-how. He had the potential to be the Trump-aligned Republican that Speaker Ryan could never be and, quite frankly, never wanted to be. Scalise, meanwhile, tended to fall in line behind the president's priorities and helped build coalitions to accomplish what he wanted to get done.

As Scalise let on that he was open to challenging McCarthy if Republicans lost the majority, his staff was hard at work planning to make it happen. How could McCarthy lead the party when Republicans in California were losing across the board? Scalise's allies asked. Won't the party want to go in a new direction? With McCarthy, Scalise, and Jim Jordan all vying for minority leader, could Scalise topple McCarthy in a second round of voting? Scalise allies were trying to figure that out.

McCarthy, meanwhile, was fighting off existential doubts and beginning to grapple with his own political mortality. Whether or not he knew about Scalise's plans, he knew for sure that if Republicans kept the House, he would have a tough slog toward the speakership—the same death march he had faced last time, where he'd have to stiff-arm the conservatives while trying to keep his own integrity intact. And if they lost, it would mean another stint in the minority, something with which he'd yet to fully come to terms. His closeness to the president could be put under the microscope, and the idea that Trump was a political liability would come to the fore. McCarthy's identity had become so wrapped up in Donald Trump, it was tough to see how he'd survive with the president down and out. Eight years had passed since McCarthy led Republicans from the political ashes in 2010—did he want to commit to doing it again? He was now fifty-three and a bit skeptical that he had the same fire in the belly.

Still, if Republicans somehow ended up in the majority, McCarthy was going to seek the speakership. He wouldn't drop out, as he had last time. When pressed, he had to admit that he still got a high from this work. And for all he had accomplished in the House, he'd never been able to call the shots. Walking away from that opportunity—well, he just couldn't do it.

In the meantime, though, there was a majority to fight to keep.

TRAVEL WITH MCCARTHY IS exhausting. By this time of year, the road routine had become quite familiar. He woke up in his hotel somewhere in America, unfailingly on time, and got into a Chevy Suburban. He did a few events and was whisked by motorcade to an airport. The SUV took him onto the tarmac, where he climbed aboard a jet to be ferried to the next city, where he would do it all over again.

McCarthy's big October journey was through the Lone Star State. Texas was truly Republicans' ATM, the one place they could always count on if they needed cash. The state has money both old and new, and from the West Texas border town of El Paso to the metropolises of Houston, Dallas, San Antonio, and Austin, there are donors who are tickled by a big-name politician coming to visit, and are more than willing to help the GOP in good times and bad.

In mid-October, with the party's political fortunes stuck somewhere in the middle, McCarthy found himself in Texas, hat in hand, raising money for Protect the House. On the tenth of that month, his chartered jet—a white-and-blue Gulfstream G200 with a cream-white interior—ferried him to El Paso, where he went straight to get a private tour of the U.S.-Mexico border. The visual was so good that McCarthy hired a political ad firm to film him there for a campaign spot, urging voters to vote Republican so Congress could build Trump's wall, which McCarthy had introduced legislation to fund.

After a quick shower, McCarthy changed into a suit and headed to Anson 11, a restaurant owned by billionaire Republican donor Paul L. Foster, to talk to seven wealthy local donors who had opened their wallets for him.

Throughout the day, and during the lunch, McCarthy tugged on his suit, as if it were a bit too formal for campaign season. He could small-talk with the best, but his purpose here—as it was behind closed doors across the country—was to give an extremely blunt assessment of the political climate, along with a critical, if questionable, piece of analysis: Republicans could, in fact, keep the House majority. The spectacle over Brett Kavanaugh's nomination to the Supreme Court was, he told his lunchmates, a political boon to the GOP. A donor who hadn't given to the party in years told McCarthy he was ready to cut a $100,000 check because of Kavanaugh, McCarthy said. He was getting a lot of mileage out of Kavanaugh at these lunches. "The thing that disturbed me the most," he said to the table in El Paso, "was watching people pound on the Supreme Court door."

"Oh, that was unbelievable," said one female attendee.

"Democrats had us on intensity by ten points," McCarthy told the group in El Paso. "It's narrowed to two over Kavanaugh. . . . But the more important thing, we saw the approval rating of the president has ticked up a few points, which makes a big difference. If he moves anywhere from three to five points in approval between now and the election, we'll be gold."

Part of McCarthy's election-season message was that coastal liberal billionaires were looking to hijack the country and the government on behalf of Democrats. Tom Steyer, Mike Bloomberg, and their hundreds of millions in campaign contributions were a constant hobbyhorse. George Soros was pouring money in for Democrats. This message was paying dividends with Republican donors.

What would happen if the Democrats won? McCarthy was asked. This was a fat pitch over the middle, one McCarthy inevitably used to paint an apocalyptic portrait of America if Democrats were able to get control of government again.

"If they win, and you watch that Senate hearing," McCarthy said, referring to the Kavanaugh hearing, "that's what two years would be like. It'll just be chaos. It'll be oversight. It will be just bringing people in. They don't have an agenda, so it won't be an agenda passing. It'll just be undermining, which I'm fearful of."

"We want you to be the next Speaker," an attendee said. "Can you make that happen?"

"We're going to make sure Republicans keep the majority. However this election turns out, it's going to be a very close margin. I'm going to make sure Nancy Pelosi is not the next Speaker. I think if the Democrats win the majority, she's the next Speaker."

It was a line McCarthy used almost everywhere he went: that Pelosi would be the Speaker of the House if Republicans didn't come out to vote. It was less a prognostication than a rallying cry. If Pelosi was unpopular generally, she was deeply unpopular with Republican donors and downright loathed by Republican donors in Texas. The mere visage of the San Francisco liberal atop the House was enough to pry open Republicans' wallets.

This was McCarthy's life that week, spinning out the message on Trump's great economy, and the terrifying prospect of Nancy Pelosi's Democrats, to donors across Texas. By the time he reached his third stop in two days—Austin on Thursday, October 11—he had so fully internalized this message that he nearly let it get away from him. At an event with wealthy business leaders at the members-only Headliners Club on the twenty-first floor of the Chase Tower, McCarthy was wheeling through his political talking points—good economy, Trump was getting results overseas, and Republicans still had a prayer—until he got to his closing anecdote. The campaign trail, at times, could be like a time warp, an insulating bubble inside which one loses connection with reality. Which was why it was so stunning that McCarthy, standing in Austin less than one month from Election Day, tried to present himself and his party as welcoming of immigrants.

McCarthy told the story of a painting he has in his office in D.C.: Steve Penley's modern re-creation of Emanuel Leutze's iconic 1851 canvas *Washington Crossing the Delaware*. McCarthy pointed out that Leutze could never have known what that scene truly looked like, since it had happened nearly a hundred years before he completed the work. Washington, McCarthy said, was depicted in a ceremonial uniform—probably not true to history. He looked like a man who had never lost a battle, but at that point, of course, he had never won one.

"But I want you to see who is in the boat," McCarthy said: a Scottish man, a black man, a woman, and a Native American. "I can't tell you historically who was in that boat," he said to the lunch crowd, nibbling on enchiladas. "But I know to Emanuel—who was a young immigrant in America—that's who he pictured to be in the boat living here." Two days after he'd pitched a bill to spend $23 billion on a border wall and filmed a campaign ad at the border, urging voters to help him build it, McCarthy was extolling the virtues of a diverse America.

IT WAS SATURDAY, OCTOBER 13, and for Nancy Pelosi, that meant Philadelphia and Madeleine Dean, who was on the ballot in Pennsylvania's fourth congressional district. For Pelosi, it was another city, another candidate, another day of raising more money to make her way out of the political wilderness. It was nine A.M., and her hotel, the Ritz-Carlton, was not serving breakfast, so she found herself in a bright-pink tailored dress, eating a Siggi's yogurt and a banana in a basement-level food court, musing about the movement she had helped foment.

"You know, the president calls us an angry mob, but we're on a mission," Pelosi said, as she dug into the yogurt, which had been brought by an aide. Indeed, Pelosi was on a mission—an almost decade-long mission that seemed to be finally nearing its completion. She was once again on the brink of power. In her quest to achieve it, for herself and her party, she was hitting thirty cities in thirty-one days. And despite what Republicans said, Pelosi wasn't limiting herself to the liberal coasts—she was everywhere.

Her closing message, what she wanted to sear into the minds of voters in the four weeks before Election Day, was this: *Is your member of Congress working for you or for the donors and special interests that have flooded Donald Trump's Washington?* Democrats would do the opposite, she suggested their campaigns say. *Democrats will fight for what's best for the district. They'll protect health care, Medicare, and Social Security; slash middle-class taxes; and work to raise wages.* Much like Donald Trump, Pelosi and the Democrats were trying to make this election about politicians swimming in the swamp versus a political movement working for the people.

Pelosi wasn't under any illusions that Democrats' return to power was going to be easy. She knew the races would be close, that five or six hundred votes either way could make the difference. Twenty-five thousand votes could determine which party controlled the government. "Every race is a fight, fight, fight for the values of our country," she said.

Pelosi would repeat this mantra time after time as she campaigned in downtown Philadelphia and later in the suburbs for Dean, the woman poised to succeed embattled longtime party boss Rep. Bob Brady, who had announced his retirement in January.

The Commonwealth of Pennsylvania was a microcosm of what was happening across the nation: Women were ascendant, which fit neatly into Pelosi's designs. Pelosi was the woman, in the year of the woman, booting Republicans out of power and bringing Democrats back into the majority to face off against a president who was seen by women as a failure. It was a "watershed moment," Pelosi told a group of roughly fifty women at a campaign event for Dean and Mary Gay Scanlon, another Pennsylvania congressional candidate. "What a time for Pennsylvania to make up for lost time in such a way," she said. "Nothing is more wholesome in America than the increased participation of women."

Women, of course, were carrying Democrats toward power, and Pelosi had been a trailblazer in that respect. When she came to Congress in 1987, there had been twenty-four other women in office. In 2019 there would likely be at least a hundred. Pelosi had been a mother of young children when she got into elective politics in the mid-1980s; her youngest daughter, Alexandra, had been in high school. "Opportunity came, and I was ready," she said. She asked her daughter if it would be okay for her to run, explaining that she would have to be in Washington several nights a week. Alexandra told her mom to "get a life."

"Get a life" was the kind of reaction that a lot of Democrats had when Pelosi hung on after losing the majority in 2010. Yet here she was, an über-wealthy grandmother of nine still grinding every day on the road, giving House floor speeches, counting votes, and listening to moaning from unappreciative Democrats.

During the first week of October, Pelosi sat down with Luján and Sena for a "soup-to-nuts" briefing about the state of the Democrats' quest to take back the House: where Democrats were spending money, how they were spending it, and what their prospects were for November 6. Pelosi, of course, had the right to know; she raised roughly fifty cents of every dollar the DCCC took in.

She had to admit that she liked what she saw. A few days later, on October 9, Luján and Pelosi scheduled a conference call to let all Democrats in on the secret: Democrats were on the brink of regaining control of the House of Representatives. Most of the 193 Democrats joined the call that morning, a sign of intensity rippling across the party as the election neared. Pelosi kicked it off, saying that the fight for the majority would be a close one, and it was important for Democrats to close out strong. Luján methodically walked Democrats through just how far the party had penetrated into Donald Trump's Republican Party. In Utah, Ben McAdams, the Democratic mayor of Salt Lake County, was leading Republican congresswoman Mia Love by one point. It was the first time McAdams had been running ahead of the two-term incumbent.

Many candidates who were running had not even been in public office when Pelosi was last in charge. But Pelosi had doggedly stayed the course. And despite the odds, she and her allies always seemed to envision her triumphant return to power.

Republicans, of course, were salivating at that prospect. At every stop on Kevin McCarthy's Texas fund-raising tour, they tried to turn the entire political climate into a referendum on Pelosi. Pelosi's aides and allies said there was never any evidence that she was more unpopular than any other congressional leader, but Republicans laughed at that and continued to run ads claiming that generic Democratic candidate X was going to go to Washington and vote with San Francisco liberal Nancy Pelosi. She was the embodiment of everything Republicans loathed. Pelosi's team believed the criticism smacked of sexism.

"You don't run away from a fight," Pelosi said of the attacks. "You do not let everybody mischaracterize you. You do not let the Republicans choose the leader of your party. Why are they after me? I'm a legislative virtuoso, and I get the job done."

It wasn't just Republicans she was standing up to. She had tuned out the dissenters in her own party, many of whom openly questioned whether it was time for new blood. During this campaign season, some two dozen Democratic candidates said they would vote against Pelosi as Speaker, but she challenged her doubters with a work ethic that bespoke the behavior of a twenty-eight-year-old, not a seventy-eight-year-old. They could criticize her age (which they did) or her progressive politics (which some tagged as the reason they were in the minority), but Pelosi didn't much care, and she didn't let the negativity get in the way of pursuing victory: Quietly, she nudged her donors to contribute even to candidates who preferred she stay away.

"My heartbeat," she said, "is member impact. Member impact. Member impact." She tapped her fist to her chest, mimicking a heartbeat.

Most politicians like to feign humility. Pelosi did not, certainly not as she approached the pinnacle once again. She was, in her mind, the only person who could do what she could do. The only one who could beat Republicans. The only one who could raise the piles of cash she did. "I beat them in every fight because I'm a dazzling fund-raiser," she said. "I mean, really, people just respond.

"This is going to sound so arrogant, but I have to tell you this. Everywhere I go people say to me, 'Why didn't you ever run for president?' Or 'Why don't you run for president?'" Pelosi said. "I love to legislate. I just love it. I love to see, understand what the priorities of the person, what the priorities of the region, how you bring it together and in a way that has sustainability over time."

But as October dragged on, and Pelosi became more aware that her party would likely take power, she began musing about what that might look like, and when her end might come. In an interview in Miami with Mark Z. Barabak—the *Los Angeles Times*'s San Francisco–based political reporter—Pelosi said she would be a "transitional" leader. She didn't say what that meant, or how long that transition might be. But she was keenly aware that the time to pass the baton was coming shortly. She wanted to, at least she said she did. But no one, so far as she could see, was ready to raise the money she could raise. No one was ready to legislate like she could. For Pelosi, the sign that the baton should be passed would be the emergence of someone who could step up to take it from her.

"It isn't up to me to say, 'You're next,'" she said. "Nobody said that to me. In fact, they were like, 'Who said you could run.' . . . That was the attitude."

Pelosi was using October to give shape to her projected majority. It would be historic. Only one other Speaker, Sam Rayburn, a Democrat from Texas, had held the speakership, lost it, then wielded the gavel again. As she had in 2007, when she first became Speaker, Pelosi wanted to kick off the 116th Congress in 2019 by unveiling a campaign finance reform package as the first bill Democrats would pass. "We have to put one good day in front of another and the opportunity to present our 'For the People' agenda—lower health care costs, bigger paychecks, cleaner government," she said.

The one thing Pelosi was hesitant to discuss throughout her October travels was her leadership team. She didn't want to talk about whether Steny Hoyer of Maryland and Jim Clyburn of South Carolina, both in their upper seventies, would remain. She made clear they'd have to fend for themselves. "I don't know what you mean by 'my leadership,'" she said, rebuffing the idea that they were a single unit. "They never would have identified themselves that way." She said she had "no idea" whether they'd stay together.

But as Pelosi wheeled around the country, her mind also drifted to Trump. When Trump was a real estate executive in New York and Pelosi a newly anointed Speaker, he had sent her a note, saying she was "the best." These days they didn't have much of a relationship, and if her party won the majority—and she the speakership—they would be each other's foil. It was clear she was energized by the president.

Pelosi, though, was keenly aware of the pitfalls that came with Trump in the White House and Democrats in control of Congress. When Barack Obama was president, Republicans had endlessly hounded him with investigations, and many observers thought the Democrats risked political blowback if they were perceived as overzealous in pursuing Trump. But Pelosi was already priming the pump, swearing that Democrats would never impeach the president unless it was bipartisan and promising a tight investigative operation. "I'm not having any pound of flesh club that says we're going to do with them what they did to us," she said.

Still, she anticipated gaining little cooperation from Trump. He was a bit of a fraud, she seemed to think, and unlike her, not interested in the details. When Pelosi passed her landmark legislation, the Affordable Care Act, she said she had been sleeping just four hours a night because she was poring over the details so she could be ready to answer any question. Trump? He hardly knew the top lines, so far as she could see. They had cut one deal, a simple accord to prevent a government shutdown, and that seemed like ancient history now. "Even when he agrees to something, he doesn't agree to something. So why?" Pelosi said of Trump.

Pelosi considered herself a legislative guru—one of the finest strategists in the history of the republic, in fact—and from that vantage point, the president was a boor with little finesse and barely any understanding of public policy. She had chased him on infrastructure only to get kicked over to Gary Cohn, who was soon gone. Sixteen months later she got what she saw as a pathetic little excuse of a plan before Trump finally reneged on it all. "In the campaign, he said he was going to negotiate 'like crazy' for lower prescription drugs. 'Like crazy' turns out to be not at all," she said. "He keeps talking about these promises he made. Promised to build the wall, he has to build the wall. He promised the Mexicans were going to pay for it—how silly is that?" Infrastructure, taking on Big Pharma, his claim that Mexico would pay for his border wall—everywhere Pelosi looked with the president, she found disappointment.

But she didn't talk much about him on the campaign trail. It was part of the strategy she and the Democrats employed nationwide: Trump spoke for himself, so Democrats should speak about what they cared about. Pelosi, for her part, always paraphrased Ronald Reagan. "The vital force in America's preeminence in the world is every generation of new immigrants who come to America, and when we fail to recognize that, we have failed to be preeminent in the world," she would say, invoking the fortieth president's final speech. Her strategy: weaponize the lionized Reagan as the antithesis of Trump.

At the end of October, Pelosi was in New York and made an appearance on CBS's *Late Show with Stephen Colbert*. It was there she said Democrats would win the House.

"How are you feeling about the next six days?" Colbert asked.

"Well, let me say this," Pelosi said. "Up until today, I would've said, 'If the election were held today, we would win.'"

"What happened today that changed that?" Colbert said in his famous deadpan.

"What now I'm saying is, we will win," Pelosi said to applause. "We will win, we own the ground, we're not yielding one grain of sand."

AS THE DAYS COUNTED down to Election Day, Steve Scalise fully inhabited the new identity born from his shooting and his near full recovery: survivor. He was fearless and confident—exceedingly so, confident not only in his own abilities but in his convictions. He was more optimistic, with more energy than he'd had in months. He walked through a crowd like a man who had just risen from the dead. Onlookers went slack-jawed. *We are praying for you,* they told him. *I can't believe you're* *here, looking so healthy,* they said. "I appreciate the blessings," he'd respond.

Scalise arrived in Peoria, Illinois, on October 16 to begin a week-long fund-raising swing that would take him across the Midwest, down to South Carolina, to Florida, and eventually to New Orleans. On the trail, Scalise was much more fluid than McCarthy, more of a natural speaker. They'd hit the same topics, the stuff of conservative, red-meat applause lines: Pelosi would be a disaster as Speaker, Trump had been a genius to nominate Brett Kavanaugh (*and the crowd goes wild!*), and liberals were out of touch. But Scalise went bigger, spun it harder, and took more liberties. At one point in Peoria, he posited without evidence that John Kerry, the former secretary of state, had been busy drinking wine in Geneva and Paris while he cut international accords. If McCarthy was fond of numbers, statistics, and anecdotes, Scalise loved imagined stereotypes. He told crowds that Nancy Pelosi "doesn't go to swing districts" during election years, and instead stayed camped in "Washington or San Francisco." It wasn't true, but this kind of talk made the crowd howl. "They don't support the same radical, leftist, socialist values that they're talking about," Scalise said of swing district voters. "They wanna see this great economic growth continue."

That was the argument Scalise was making: The money in your pocket. The values. The America you believe in. It'd all be gone if voters gave control to Democrats.

One of Scalise's last stops that week was at the Naperville Marriott outside Chicago for his old rival Peter Roskam, the man he had beaten to become GOP whip and begin his rocket-like ascent to the top echelon of the Republican Party. A few years earlier Scalise and Roskam were rivals. Scalise's visit now was a sign of both how far he had come and just how badly he wanted to win the majority and gain allies.

Roskam emerged from a side entrance of the hotel to greet Scalise, who was sitting in his SUV. It was a brisk Wednesday, late in the afternoon, and Roskam walked over to talk to Scalise through the car window as Capitol Police stood guard around the vehicle. Trump's approval rating was lagging in the district, Roskam told Scalise, but he was finding modest success at painting his opponent, Sean Casten, as a tax-and-spend liberal who was out of touch with the moderately conservative leanings of the Chicagoland district.

There was a brief moment of silence, and then Roskam spoke up. "Hey," he said to Scalise, who was looking down at his iPad. "Look in my eyes."

Scalise looked up.

"Thank you for coming," he told the man who had booted him from leadership. "I appreciate it."

That night a few hundred donors gathered in a ballroom at the Marriott to hear Scalise and Roskam speak together. It was at an event like this where a guy like Scalise could make his mettle. A few minutes onstage could give Roskam tens of thousands of dollars, and if Roskam were to win, it could buy Scalise loyalty for a lifetime.

Scalise took the stage and immediately whipped out a check for Roskam from his jacket pocket and held it in the air. "They call this a battleground district, but is there anyone left to vote for the other guy?" Scalise said as the crowd applauded. "He has no idea what's coming in twenty days.

"If Pelosi becomes Speaker again, in just a few months, guess what?" Scalise continued. "They can reverse what we have finally started to do. Are you going to let that happen?"

"No!" the crowd yelled.

"You're going to send Peter Roskam back," Scalise said.

Scalise had the crowd in the palm of his hands. They were videotaping him on iPhones. They were standing along the walls that lined the ballroom. They were there for him, Steve Scalise. And Scalise was there for Roskam, but most important, he was there for the majority. And he was there for himself.

In between campaign stops, Scalise secretly slipped back into Washington for a dinner with his top advisers where they discussed the potential of a coup against McCarthy. There were eerie similarities to 2016, when the Freedom Caucus had met to consider overthrowing

Paul Ryan days before the election. This time, instead of a bunch of lawmakers meeting in an apartment, Scalise gathered his staff at Del Frisco's Double Eagle, a steakhouse in the glitzy CityCenter complex located in downtown D.C.

Brett Horton was there, with a small clutch of other Scalise staffers. Over bottles of red wine and steak, they discussed the scenarios under which they might launch a run against McCarthy. Horton, whom Scalise trusted the most, frequently played devil's advocate to Scalise's impulses. Other aides were more insistent that he should challenge McCarthy. Scalise listened and nodded his head, and was noncommittal about what he might do. But as he left, he was more skeptical he would go for McCarthy's jugular. He knew if he missed, his career would likely be over.

On October 26, eleven days before Election Day, Scalise was forced to a decision point. A text popped up on his phone from McCarthy. The majority leader was getting press inquiries about Scalise flying to Washington to have a meeting about a challenge to his leadership. The Del Frisco's dinner had leaked.

Caught out, Scalise responded, "WTF." He wrote that the media was reveling in stirring up drama between the top two Republicans. McCarthy told Scalise that *Axios* reporter Jonathan Swan—the same reporter who broke the news of Paul Ryan's retirement—was inquiring about the dinner. Scalise responded that his staff begged Swan off the story, and pointed out that the media refused to write any stories about unrest in Pelosi's ranks. We will keep the majority, Scalise typed, and the stories will stop. Scalise said he wasn't even at Del Frisco's—he had been at the Trump Hotel.

He then asked if he could call McCarthy, but McCarthy didn't immediately answer. When McCarthy and Scalise finally got on the phone, the Louisianan stuck to his guns: the press is trying to pit us against each other.

But McCarthy wasn't buying it. For months, maybe almost a year, the tension had been bubbling between the two. Now it was less than two weeks before Election Day and Scalise was still plotting against him. McCarthy was tired of it. *Run against me,* McCarthy told him, *I've had it. I don't want to take this shit anymore. I've been on leadership teams where the top two leaders don't get along, and I won't do it again.*

If there was a moment for Scalise to step up and admit to the challenge, this was it. But Scalise assured McCarthy he wasn't running against him. Scalise was fearless—but not that fearless. He didn't want to take the chance. He was going to wait. He had waited before.

That didn't mean the issue was put entirely to rest. After the McCarthy call, Scalise's inner circle began wondering who had betrayed him.

20

ELECTION DAY

THERE WAS NO OCTOBER SURPRISE per se, but the month before the election brought a lot of strange behavior from the administration. The president first said he was going to get a tax bill passed before Election Day, even though Congress was out of session, and the Republican leadership had no idea what he was talking about. A caravan of Central Americans was making its way toward the border, with footage that was played on repeat on Fox News, and even though most experts said the group was months away from reaching the border, Trump assigned five thousand troops there, even flirting with closing the border completely. He later said he might send fifteen thousand troops, making it a more active U.S. engagement than the war in Afghanistan.

A series of pipe bombs were sent to Democratic leaders like the Clintons and the Obamas, to George Soros, and to former CIA director John Brennan. A man opened fire in a synagogue in Pittsburgh with the express intent of killing Jews—he succeeded, murdering eleven.

And in the final days of October, the age-old tension between Ryan and Trump bubbled back to the surface. Donald Trump told *Axios*'s Jonathan Swan that he was considering undoing the Fourteenth Amendment by executive order. The Fourteenth Amendment, of course, made anyone who was born in the United States automatically a citizen.

This drove Ryan absolutely crazy. His party was fighting for its life in the suburbs, and here Trump was saying he could unilaterally rewrite the Constitution. The Speaker was campaigning in Kentucky with Andy Barr, and immediately spoke to his advisers about how they might respond. They ruled out a news conference and a written statement, deciding instead to address the issue on a local radio show.

On air, Ryan said that "you cannot end birthright citizenship with an executive order." He thought he was making a factual argument: that the president, obviously, could not rewrite the Constitution. That's not how American government worked. The president fired back on Twitter. "Paul Ryan should be focusing on holding the Majority rather than giving his opinions on Birthright Citizenship, something he knows nothing about! Our new Republican Majority will work on this, Closing the Immigration Loopholes and Securing our Border!" The irony, of course, was that Ryan was well versed in immigration law, and he gave the interview during a campaign stop for an endangered Republican lawmaker.

That afternoon, Ryan and Trump had a heated phone conversation. *Why are you popping me?* Ryan asked the president. *Because you just did it to me!* Trump responded.

"We are six days out from the election, and you're scaring the crap out of suburbanites who see you thinking you can rewrite the Constitution," Ryan told Trump. "You can't do that." The yelling went on for a while; the president was angry with Ryan and unleashed on him for criticizing him publicly. Trump went on for so long that Ryan finally had to say: "Are you finished? Can I talk now? Can I say something?" After Ryan explained his viewpoint, the president agreed that they should move on.

Meanwhile, on October 31, Halloween, Kevin McCarthy was driving through the mountains of California. He had finally broken out of his rut. He was almost certain that Republicans were going to lose the House, but—and this was new—he felt okay about it. There was little he could do. He saw a bounce in poll numbers across the board after the caravan of migrants started getting airtime, but after mail bombs and the violence, Republicans fell back to earth.

Six days ahead of Election Day, McCarthy finally felt like he was going to stick it out and help lead the House GOP to the majority in 2020. His mind was already drifting to whom he would recruit to run. Democratic candidates who were winning in 2018 had no record, no votes to use against them, but many of them were going to come in and immediately cast a ballot for Nancy Pelosi as Speaker. "They are going to break their fundamental promise," McCarthy said.

McCarthy had been calling his colleagues, drumming up support for his minority leader bid. He was far ahead of everyone, he said. "I've got one more swing at this before redistricting," he said, referring to winning back the majority. "If you sit back and look, tell me who else is best prepared to run this thing?"

ELECTION NIGHT 2018 WAS a strange one in Washington. Democrats were almost certainly going to take the House majority, and Republicans were going to keep their hold on the Senate, but so much uncertainty lay ahead for the American political system and the stability of the U.S. government. The lame-duck session of Congress was mere days away, and President Trump was almost certain to take an unflinching stand for his border wall. If Democrats were indeed successful, Pelosi would try to claw her way back to the speakership. And, come 2019, the security blanket of an all-Republican Washington would be ripped from the president, forcing him to do business with the enemy.

Nancy Pelosi had touched down in Washington and was ready to take a victory lap. It was a stunning moment for the Californian. Despite the doubters and the haters—and there were many—she was on the brink of bringing her colleagues back to power at a most opportune time for her party.

And Pelosi was feeling good. Early in the day, she and her daughters got their hair done in a Georgetown salon before heading to the DCCC for a photo op. After posing for photos, Pelosi took a few questions and told reporters she was "one hundred percent" confident Democrats would win back the majority: "It's just a question of [what] the size of the victory is."

Pelosi was making calls ahead of the election results to wish candidates good luck. Then she headed to the swanky Joe's Stone Crab to hold court with some of her top donors and backers, like lobbyists Steve Elmendorf and Vin Roberti, and with progressive leaders like Nancy Zirkin—people she had worked with for decades. The luncheon was just the type of classic back-scratching that Pelosi was so good at. She spoke for nearly two hours as she confidently walked her guests through the electoral map, laying out her predictions about who would win in districts from coast to coast.

As the lunch wrapped, Pelosi made a brief detour from her Election Day responsibilities. Just like she did in 2016, Pelosi went to visit a friend. This time, she went with two of her college roommates to Georgetown to visit a grieving widow of one of their friends from their days at Trinity University. Pelosi was a master of the small stuff.

And just as it did two years ago, Pelosi's motorcade headed to Shirlington—a neighborhood in Arlington, Virginia—to do an interview on *PBS NewsHour* with Judy Woodruff, a television host she had known for years on an outlet she was comfortable with. Predicting victory once again, Pelosi said the election was about "making government more accountable by having integrity in government, overturning some of their corruption in the Republican Congress and in the administration."

That evening, she headed to the Democratic victory party at the Hyatt Regency. The VIP room at the hotel was one of two nerve centers in the Democratic universe; the other was the DCCC headquarters, where Dan Sena and Meredith Kelly were spending most of their evening. Pelosi was the main attraction in the back rooms of the hotel area, which was filled with roughly 150 people, all Pelosi loyalists: former staffers, donors, advocates, and top officials from the labor community.

Kevin McCarthy was also in Washington, having returned to spend the evening at NRCC headquarters on Capitol Hill. He knew the majority was all but lost and wanted to be in D.C. with his team. Steve Stivers was there too, having taken a late-afternoon flight back to D.C. to watch with his staff. He was holding out hope. He had sketched out a scenario—both on paper and in his head—in which Republicans kept the House. He thought the GOP could keep its California losses to an absolute minimum, win southern Florida seats, and hang on to a few seats in Illinois.

McCarthy and Stivers watched together from the war room at NRCC headquarters, where they viewed county-by-county results on an overhead screen. Paul Ryan was at his campaign office in Wisconsin for one last election night get-together. Steve Scalise was holding his own gathering in New Orleans.

Truth be told, there wasn't much to do on election night other than watch, wait, and make phone calls. One battle the committees had to wage was on television. The DCCC's Meredith Kelly had been in touch with all the television networks laying out what a good night, great night, and exceptional night looked like for Democrats. None of those calculations included Kentucky's sixth district, where the DCCC assumed that Rep. Andy Barr, the Republican incumbent, would prevail against Democrat Amy McGrath. Yet that was one of the first races where the results would come in, and the television networks were transfixed by it.

At 8:11 P.M., McCarthy texted Barr, writing, "Hang in there, you are going to win. The Republican precincts haven't come in yet." When Barr finally won, McCarthy was elated and Democrats were deflated, despite ample warning from the party committee. But their mood brightened just moments later when Democratic challenger Jennifer Wexton beat Rep. Barbara Comstock in northern Virginia, denying Stivers his $5 million prize.

Meanwhile, Mitch McConnell was at the National Republican Senatorial Committee's headquarters next to Union Station in D.C. He was holed up in the party committee's conference room, which had been outfitted to display three large-screen TVs showing the three major cable networks. They were playing Fox News aloud, of course. Close aides and confidants piled into the room talking while McConnell stayed focused on the TV. The stakes couldn't have been higher. His whole agenda hinged on keeping the majority. Over the past month, polling showed a groundswell of activity among Democrats in House races, but it was unclear if that would bleed over into the Senate. The map still had key unknowns. Polling in Tennessee, for example, showed a supertight race. Arizona was unclear, too.

Around the same time Barr won, Indiana Republican Senate candidate Mike Braun's campaign notified McConnell's team that Braun was on the verge of victory. A few minutes later a Braun staffer texted Josh Holmes, McConnell's former chief of staff and political adviser, a photo of Braun on the phone with Sen. Joe Donnelly, who was calling him to concede the race. McConnell called Braun to congratulate him on his victory, telling him he couldn't wait to get him up to Washington.

The night continued to go well for McConnell. Soon afterward Ward Baker, the former head of the Senate party committee who was now working on Marsha Blackburn's race in Tennessee, called Holmes. Polls in the days leading up to the election had Blackburn and Democrat Phil Bredesen, a moderate, running neck and neck. But Ward was calling to say they would win by a large margin; he had Blackburn on the phone, and she wanted to tell McConnell how appreciative she was of all of his help in the race. As McConnell waited out the results, NRSC executive director Chris Hansen and Sen. Cory Gardner, who was running the committee, came in periodically to give updates on key counties and states. With Indiana and Tennessee in the bag and then Kevin Cramer defeating Heidi Heitkamp in North Dakota, the night was looking good.

The cheerful mood at McConnell headquarters did not extend to House Republicans. At 9:33 P.M., Fox News unexpectedly said it was projecting that Democrats had won the House of Representatives. This sent McCarthy into a tizzy. He immediately called Fox News chairman Rupert Murdoch to complain. Polls were not closed yet in California, and McCarthy was concerned that calling the House so early would keep voters at home.

For her part, Pelosi didn't appear nervous. Diane Dewhirst, her deputy chief of staff, was accompanied at the Hyatt that night by her son Robby, who had been just five years old in 2006 when he accompanied his mother to the election night party that preceded Pelosi's first speakership. Now he was more than six feet tall—a visual reminder of how long it had been since first she was Speaker.

Meanwhile, at the DCCC, Kelly and Dan Sena stayed calm. Like much else in this cycle, election night was going perfectly according to plan. The early signs were good: Democrats knocked off Rep. Carlos Curbelo, who had tried to push through the immigration discharge petition, in Miami, and Donna Shalala won a South Florida seat that had been held by Republican Ileana Ros-Lehtinen for three decades.

By 9:47 P.M., three races in Illinois were starting to look good. Democrats could see the blue wave rippling across America.

Sena and Kelly had been forced to look at the landscape methodically. They had no choice. It was how they approached the cycle—all the spending decisions, message shifts, and late-stage race investments. But at this point, race after race was coming in, and they felt confident. Sena had his eye on the races with Curbelo, Comstock, Rep. Mike Coffman, and Rep. Will Hurd. If Democrats won three of those, he thought, they would have the majority.

Kelly had a different view. Her barometers were New York's eleventh district, and Virginia's seventh. And at just before nine P.M., in the eleventh, Democratic challenger Max Rose toppled Rep. Dan Donovan in the Staten Island and Brooklyn–anchored seat that Donald Trump had won by ten points. Early in the summer, Rose told the DCCC that Republicans would look away and he would be able to snatch the seat. Rose won by six points.

Virginia's seventh was even sweeter. That was the seat held by former House majority leader Eric Cantor, and later by Freedom Caucus firebrand Dave Brat. Abigail Spanberger, a former CIA operative, edged out Brat by a shade less than two points.

Sena and Kelly were watching two sets of races, but both were seeing the same result: Democrats were capturing the majority. By eleven o'clock, it was time to celebrate. Sena sent a DCCC aide to Harris Teeter, a local supermarket chain, to buy three dozen bottles of three-dollar champagne. He walked Ben Ray Luján, the DCCC chair, out of the building so he could get to the celebration at the Hyatt. On the way out,

Sena put his arm around Luján and said, "I told you this was all going to work." Kelly personally told Pelosi the DCCC believed Democrats had won back the majority.

The brutal eight years—the wilderness, the empty press conferences, being shut out of negotiations—it was all over. The last two had been especially bruising: Trump was president, Pelosi was the punching bag. But she was about to become the puncher. She took to the stage at roughly eleven-thirty, in front of a raucous crowd of celebrating Democrats, to announce it was a "new day in America."

"Today is more than about Democrats and Republicans. It's about restoring the Constitution's checks and balances to the Trump administration . . . but more than anything, it's about what a new Democratic majority will mean in the lives of hard-working Americans."

As Pelosi left the stage, an aide handed her a cell phone. It was President Trump, who had just watched her speech on TV and now was on the phone acknowledging her call for bipartisanship. He told her they could work on an infrastructure bill together. Vice President Pence, standing mere feet from Trump, listened in as he made the call. Pelosi thanked Trump but could barely hear him over all the noise and celebration.

At Senate Republican headquarters, the biggest reaction of the night came when Missouri was called for Josh Hawley, who knocked off Claire McCaskill. Cornyn fist-pumped. McConnell gave him a high-five and said, "We are going to be setting the agenda again next year."

McConnell ended his evening with congratulations to his staff, and a warning. The election was not even hours old, and he was already worrying about money. Republicans had succeeded in keeping the Senate, but they had a huge deficit when it came to online fund-raising, and that gap could prove deadly in future elections. McConnell didn't waste any time. He was already about to set a plan in motion to try to close the gap, scheduling a meeting with top Republican lobbyists and donors the very next day, to task them with figuring out how Republicans could get on par with Democrats in the online-small-dollar-fund-raising game.

The depth of the electoral rout that night was stunning. Some of the star players in Trump's Washington fell. Curbelo and Reps. Jeff Denham and David Valadao of California all lost after spending much of the Congress trying to strike an immigration compromise. Rep. Mia Love, the Utah Republican who stood up in a private meeting and rebuked the president for calling African countries shitholes, lost her seat.

Rep. Peter Roskam—whom Steve Scalise had tried to save—got smacked by a Democrat who ran against Roskam's votes to repeal Obamacare and pass Trump's tax bill. Rep. John Culberson, Republican of Houston, had been castigated by Corry Bliss for not raising enough money, and perhaps he should have heeded the warning: Culberson lost his seat, which had been held by the GOP since 1967, when George H. W. Bush won his first elective office.

Pelosi left the Hyatt around 1:15 A.M., exhausted yet elated. Her party had seized victory, but she still had a slog ahead of her if she wanted to once again grasp the Speaker's gavel.

21

THE SPEAKERSHIP

NANCY PELOSI WASTED ABSOLUTELY no time. Less than twenty-four hours after Election Day, she was in her office, personalizing a note to each returning member of her party. It was a painstaking process, taking lots of time and effort, and it slowed her productivity. But these personal touches were the mark of Nancy Pelosi.

"Congratulations on your victory and for being a part of an historic and exciting new Democratic Majority," the text of the computer-typed letter read. "Your wisdom and leadership will be essential to our efforts in the months ahead."

Using a blue felt-tip pen, Pelosi used cursive to hand-write the recipient's name over the typed greeting. Below her signature—"Nancy," in rounded lettering—she jotted a personal note.

"Lois," she wrote to Lois Frankel, a Florida Democrat who had just won reelection to her seat without opposition, "I would be honored by your support. N." Pelosi's staff scanned the letters into the computer and e-mailed them out with the subject line "Personal Correspondence from Leader Pelosi."

But the note to Frankel arrived at the wrong inbox. At 7:48 P.M. on Wednesday, November 7, Rep. Bill Foster, a gangly-looking physicist from a Democratic district west of Chicago, got the message in his Gmail account. The irony was especially delicious because, for the past several weeks, Foster had been part of a ragtag crew of Democrats looking to do away with Pelosi.

Foster had been brought into the "NeverPelosi" fold by Rep. Ed Perlmutter of Colorado, a Democrat from Denver's western suburbs who was first elected in the giant class of 2006. Even though Perlmutter had supported Pelosi's bid for Speaker in previous years, he was a skeptic of the California Democrat, if a reasonable one. Pelosi and Perlmutter maintained a friendly and professional relationship. And Foster and Perlmutter were buddies. They frequently grabbed dinner together in Washington, and Foster's friends and allies knew that when Perlmutter asked him to do something, he did it.

The way the anti-Pelosi crowd saw it, it was time for new leadership. Now. Not next year, not in two years, but now. Pelosi was in her late seventies, and the party was getting younger. It mattered little to the agitators that Democrats were ascendant, or that Pelosi was the most skilled and powerful figure in the party. She had become a liability, they thought. Candidates across America had run against her, or said openly on the campaign trail that they needed new leadership. The resistance to Pelosi wasn't geographically confined. Candidates ranging from Rep. Conor Lamb outside Pittsburgh to Rep. Abigail Spanberger, newly elected from Richmond, had said they planned to vote against Pelosi. The signs were everywhere. Pelosi needed to go, her opponents said. Pelosi's team maintained they weren't worried about the dissenters, but they kept a careful watch on who came out against Pelosi and how aggressive they were.

Foster and Perlmutter were backed up by a pocket of dissenters, all with histories of opposing Pelosi. There was Rep. Seth Moulton, a Massachusetts Democrat who had recruited and donated to fellow military veterans running for office. Moulton was a bit of a loner in the House Democratic Caucus, but he thought he had gained the loyalty of the cadre of young vets who were elected in no small part based on his campaign largesse. Moulton himself had been a Marine captain in Iraq who worked closely with David Petraeus. Pelosi, during her tenure as minority leader and later as House Speaker, had been one of the chief critics of the war in Iraq. Moulton had also knocked off John Tierney, a Pelosi loyalist who had once employed Pelosi's daughter Christine as his chief of staff, in a 2014 Democratic primary. Rep. Kathleen Rice, a Democrat from the Long Island suburbs of New York, was another staunch anti-Pelosi force. She was a take-no-prisoners prosecutor during nine years as district attorney of Nassau County. Rep. Tim Ryan of Ohio was again involved, just two years after failing to knock Pelosi off as Democratic leader.

The anti-Pelosi effort had started with a dud. In October, members of the group had tried to push for a change of party rules to force the candidate for Speaker to earn 218 votes in the first round of party voting, instead of a simple majority. It would allow Democrats to try to toss Pelosi aside in a closed meeting instead of publicly on the House floor during the official vote. But many of Perlmutter's colleagues thought it foolhardy to drag the party through drama before the election, so they tabled their plan until November.

Still, they quietly plotted. They didn't have a candidate they wanted for the speakership, but their strategy was to starve Pelosi of the 218 votes she needed on the floor to be Speaker, and to hope that someone else would emerge. At one point, they even discussed nominating Michelle Obama—technically, the Speaker of the House did not have to be a member of Congress.

PAUL RYAN'S REFLECTION on a private party conference call about the electoral beating his party suffered was this: "I think we can all say that this was not the way everyone was predicting."

In fact, many people had been predicting it. Almost everyone, really: television pundits, political prognosticators, pollsters, and journalists. The conventional wisdom had been wrong in 2016, and Republicans thought it would be wrong in 2018, but it was on the money. Blue wave. Smackdown. Trump slump. Call it what you want, but Republicans were yesterday's news.

The severity of the Election Day bludgeoning was only beginning to dawn on Republican leaders. Some of their best colleagues—the ones who actually tried to get things done—were gone, victims of an electoral climate that had never come their way.

Did Ryan have regrets? No, not really. Not publicly or privately. He looked back at governing with Donald Trump and saw the congressional session as one of the most productive of his lifetime. He wasn't disappointed that he was unable to notch entitlement reform. To his mind, Congress had rebuilt the military, rewritten the tax code, and passed a whole pile of legislation he thought would be good for America.

"I think every single one of us should hold our heads high," Ryan said on the Republican conference call. "Because we made an incredible and lasting contribution to this country. This last session of Congress is one of the most productive sessions in Congress in our lifetimes. We packed into this session what normally would take three or four Congresses to pass. So I think we should all be extremely proud of what we've been able to accomplish."

The voters had clearly felt otherwise.

But Ryan was heading home to Janesville within a matter of weeks, and this was someone else's problem. That someone else was Kevin McCarthy, who was also on the line and would be the man to clean up the mess. McCarthy knew it was coming and was prepared to take control.

"I came to Congress in 2006, in the year Republicans lost the majority," McCarthy told his House Republican colleagues on the call. "They're putting back the exact same team in their leadership. It's like a scary movie. They're back. You got Pelosi, you got Steny, you got Clyburn. Average age is seventy-nine. We can win this back in . . . two years. I think our first goal is to move America forward. Our next goal is to win the majority back."

After the drubbing, Steve Stivers announced what most assumed: He would not seek another term atop the NRCC. McCarthy was already thinking about just who would run the party committee: Rep. Tom Emmer of Minnesota, supported by Parker Poling, Patrick McHenry's chief of staff, as executive director. McCarthy had designs on the Congressional Leadership Fund moving on from Corry Bliss and hiring Dan Conston, a thirty-three-year-old Republican operative who had worked extensively with the party's richest and most powerful donors. Bliss would head to FP1, a Republican consultancy, which worked on two dozen races for CLF and AAN. Bliss had given FP1 millions of dollars of business; now FP1 had given Bliss a job.

On the conference call, some Republicans were itchy to give the leadership a piece of their mind. They were now out of power, and beginning to grapple with that new dynamic. Rep. David McKinley, a Republican from West Virginia, urged Ryan to put a bill on the floor that would show that Republicans cared about insuring people with preexisting health conditions, an effort, in McKinley's mind, to rebut a central Democratic talking point in the 2018 campaign. Ryan said he thought that was unnecessary. Rep. Ted Yoho, a Florida Republican, urged his party's leadership to dive right back into immigration by passing an agricultural visa overhaul.

Then Rep. French Hill piped up. Hill, an Arkansan who had previously run a bank, had been in the House since 2015. He pleaded with the leadership to host "some smaller group discussions" with Republicans about shifting to the minority. Some would have to shed staff, because their budgets would shrink under Democratic control. Many Republicans, including himself, had never been in the minority before.

Republicans were, indeed, getting ready for a new world. Later that week, McCarthy would trounce Jim Jordan in a race for minority leader. McCarthy got 159 votes, Jordan 43, making the mess officially McCarthy's to manage.

As for Stivers, he was going back to being a rank-and-file member of Congress, out of the leadership and mostly out of the drama. At the end of the day, Stivers thought there was really nothing he could have done to help Republicans keep the House majority. The die was cast, he said. Traditional Republican voters had essentially been free agents in 2018. They didn't show up, or they voted for Democrats, or for Republicans.

In Stivers's view, the White House's late-in-the-game immigration gambit—caravans coming, military at the border—was designed to save the Senate, which mostly came down to contests in deep-red states, at the expense of maintaining the House majority. "I don't think it was intentionally meant to hurt the House, but they didn't care what the impact was on the House.

"Once [voters] decided they weren't all in and they weren't hip with the agenda, all we could do is change course, which we didn't do," Stivers said. He added, "It's hard to do with a president that's driving the train."

WHEN THE HOUSE RETURNED to Washington on Tuesday, November 13, Pelosi was in her element. No longer a bogeyman from San Francisco, she was a powerful D.C. leader who held enormous sway for newly elected members of the House. She hosted a lunch for all new Democrats at Osteria Morini, a restaurant on Washington's southwest waterfront with floor-to-ceiling glass and pricey northern Italian cuisine. Later that evening Pelosi attended a cocktail party for newly elected lawmakers in the Rayburn Reception Room, a high-ceilinged event space adjacent to her office and mere feet from the House floor. Scores of reporters stood outside, craning their necks to get a peek.

Ryan and McCarthy were there, moving through the crowd of Democrats who had just snatched their majority. At one point, Ryan eyed Alexandria Ocasio-Cortez, the twenty-nine-year-old Democrat who was the star of the new class. "Hey, I know you," he said with a big smile on his face. "I'm Paul." Ocasio-Cortez smiled and shook his hand.

By this time, the Perlmutter effort against Pelosi—the group had now become known as the "rebels"—had grown more complex and intricate. The rebels had advanced to actual hand-to-hand combat: Perlmutter, Moulton, and Rice were pushing people to add their names to a letter pledging to vote against Pelosi.

"We promised to change the status quo, and we intend to deliver on that promise," they wrote in the missive, which was being passed throughout the membership on a iPhone app. "Therefore, we are committed to voting for new leadership in both our Caucus meeting and on the House floor."

The group dragged its feet in making the letter public, wanting to maximize the signatures first. At one point, Perlmutter was keeping a handwritten whip list, and the group was talking on text chain about who would reach out to whom. Soon the effort got so serious that staff became involved and professionalized the operation—they digitized the list and began divvying up whipping responsibilities based on regions and who had donated to whom. In its early phase, the group wanted Pelosi to commit to stepping down as Speaker after two or three months. Pelosi and her staff privately scoffed at such demands.

The letter infuriated Pelosi's allies, because when it came to winning the speakership, she didn't have a huge margin of error; at this point, she could lose roughly seventeen Democrats. And Pelosi herself angrily dismissed it. It was difficult to imagine that people would want to dump Pelosi after Democrats had won nearly forty seats. Would they have done this to a man? her allies asked.

On November 14, Democrats headed to the Capitol Visitors Center for their first meeting since Election Day, and the mood was celebratory. They gave a standing ovation to Ben Ray Luján, the New Mexico Democrat who as DCCC chair had just won the majority for the party. There was applause for Michelle Lujan Grisham of New Mexico, Jared Polis of Colorado, and Tim Walz of Minnesota, all of whom would become governors in 2019.

Then Pelosi got up and got a standing ovation before she spoke. "Every place I went in the last week or so," she said, "they said 'Thank you for saving our country.'" It was typical Pelosi: soaring rhetoric lined with ego. She told the crowd that this win was far more important than the one in 2006 because "there is far greater urgency"—a clear reference to Donald Trump. Then she began laying out her priorities for the new majority. Insist on bipartisan initiatives, she said, so we can get as many results as possible. Income disparity, she said, is a top priority. CEOs once made forty times what workers made; now they made four hundred times, she explained.

"Thank you for saving our country," Pelosi said to the crowd. "Each and every one of you."

Not everyone was feeling as magnanimous. Moments after the meeting ended, Tim Ryan stepped outside and was immediately swarmed by reporters. Ryan had run against Pelosi in 2016 and was seen by some as the leading candidate to run against her again. The dissenters, though, understood that a challenger to Pelosi could not be a white male—not this year, not this time. Ryan wanted Rep. Marcia Fudge, a fellow Ohio Democrat, to run. He said his crew had a "significant" number of votes, which would eventually be enough to topple Pelosi. Moulton said the same.

"We're here to help the incoming members who have made these commitments during their campaign," Ryan said. "They should not be asked to walk the plank on their first vote, break the promise on their first vote."

Pelosi had absolutely no patience for any of it. As she exited the caucus meeting, she was asked about the challenge to her speakership, and she said, "I will be Speaker of the House no matter what Seth Moulton says."

The next day House Democrats met again, and the rebels received a painful blow. Perlmutter tried to offer his motion to raise the internal vote threshold to nominate Pelosi but was shut down—by a freshman. Katie Hill, a newly elected California Democrat, stood up in the closed party meeting and said that the freshman class was not interested in internal strife. With that, the momentum was turned, and the motion was soon killed.

Later that day, November 15, Pelosi headed to a Capitol studio to give her weekly press conference. Much of her senior staff came to watch. They were feeling confident. Danny Weiss, Pelosi's chief of staff, was giddy while talking to Dick Meltzer, her policy director, in the back of the room. Weiss suggested to Meltzer that, when it was time for leadership elections, they reverse the process by which the Speaker vote normally came first. Instead, they should find someone in the Democratic Caucus to motion to elect Pelosi in the private party vote last, after all the other positions in the leadership had been filled.

"Clear out the underbrush," Weiss whispered to Meltzer. "Save the best for last."

The confidence was well placed. On November 16, Pelosi had one of several marathon days of meetings with incoming lawmakers. She was booked like a barber, one aide observed. Each meeting was sched-uled for twenty minutes but frequently went longer. While Pelosi was in a meeting with one lawmaker, the next sat outside her door, while others waited in a conference room and in a spare office in the back. Pelosi didn't bring up her bid for Speaker but rather talked to each law-maker about his or her priorities and what they wanted to do in D.C. If someone brought up the race, she discussed it, but she didn't foist it on anyone.

As these days of wall-to-wall conversations passed, it seemed like her opposition was melting away. These personal conversations were having an effect. New members came to the dawning realization that she had immense power, the ability to raise cash, and the uncanny knowhow to get things done in Washington. Haley Stevens, a newly elected Democrat from Michigan, told reporters that she didn't say no to Pelosi. Mikie Sherrill, a New Jersey Democrat endorsed by Moulton, would not say a word upon leaving, seemingly shocked that reporters could trail her wherever she went in the Capitol.

Pelosi also met with Marcia Fudge that day, a meeting that was bro-kered by Rep. Elijah Cummings, a fellow member of the Congressional Black Caucus and an ally of both women. Fudge was still considering Ryan's encouragement to run against Pelosi, and in the meeting, Pe-losi described what she had to do as Speaker. Constant travel. Endless fund-raising. Fudge left the meeting saying she would have to take the holiday to think about it. Four days later, in the middle of the holiday recess, Fudge said she would support Pelosi. (Tim Ryan, meanwhile, eventually told Fudge he didn't think she could win. Fudge thanked him for the honesty.)

But with every step forward, there was a bump back. On the same day as the Fudge meeting, Rep. Ron Kind of Wisconsin met with Pelosi in her Capitol office. If you're not going to step aside, Kind said, what is your plan to leave? Pelosi had no interest in laying that out. Kind did not announce which way he would vote, and it was clear that Pelosi had yet to satisfy all her potential opponents.

The rebels, meanwhile, were getting ready to release their letter. On November 16, as Pelosi was working through her first whirlwind day of meetings, they met in a row house near the Democratic Club and decided Rice would be the television spokeswoman for the group, and that everyone else would avoid the cameras. (Moulton didn't listen and appeared on TV to speak out against Pelosi, much to everyone's chagrin.) On November 19, the Monday of Thanksgiving week, the rebels finally made the letter public. It had sixteen signatories—practically enough to block Pelosi from winning the speakership. Aside from Foster, Moulton, Rice, and Ryan, it included a few Democrats who simply could never support Pelosi because their districts wouldn't allow it: Anthony Brindisi, an upstate New Yorker who had snatched a Republican district; Joe Cunningham, who had won Mark Sanford's South Carolina seat; and Ben McAdams, who had won a deep-red Utah seat.

But many of the other signers were gettable for Pelosi. Why? Because not a single person was saying they would actually challenge her for the speakership. With Fudge on the sidelines, there were no candidates besides Pelosi. *You can't beat somebody with nobody,* her allies kept saying. It allowed Pelosi to lock up wobbly dissenters. For example, one letter-signer, Buffalo Democrat Brian Higgins, had a long-standing gripe with Pelosi over how her staff had handled a Medicare reform bill he wanted a vote on; years ago Pelosi had shoved the issue off to an aide, and Higgins felt shortchanged. In November, after Higgins had signed on to the letter, Schumer called him and told him to get together with Pelosi. Pelosi promised Higgins she would make him a part of negotiations over a possible infrastructure package in the new Congress, and a consideration on the Medicare bill, which would make the program available for people older than fifty.

Another signer, Rep. Stephen Lynch of Boston, got assurances from Pelosi that "working families" would be a focus in the next Congress. He dropped off the letter and Pelosi was another vote closer to the speakership.

THE PERSON WHO SEEMED to want Pelosi to be Speaker more than anyone else was sitting in the Oval Office. Donald Trump told Pelosi—and frankly, anyone who would listen—that he believed the California

Democrat deserved the speakership, and he was offering to make it happen for her. On November 17, he tweeted: "I can get Nancy Pelosi as many votes as she wants in order for her to be Speaker of the House. She deserves this victory, she has earned it—but there are those in her party who are trying to take it away. She will win!" It was a shaky proposition, to be sure, because it was hard to imagine that after a dozen years and hundreds of millions of dollars spent lambasting Pelosi, Republicans would somehow be interested in supporting her. Trump thought he would be able to get the "strongest, toughest, meanest person out of the Freedom Caucus" to do him "a favor" and vote for Pelosi. "When they say yes, everyone would know it was okay," he said. Members of the Freedom Caucus laughed nervously at this idea and dismissed it.

Sitting in the Oval Office in late November, Trump said a lot of people thought it was "the coolest thing" when he offered to help her.

"Look, she actually deserves it," Trump said. "She's been there. She deserves it. Now, does it get goodwill? Maybe, maybe not. I'm not sure if it gets goodwill, but if she needed the votes, I would be able to get her the votes very easily."

Pelosi, for her part, did not want Trump's help, and there was mounting evidence she didn't need anyone but herself. While the rebel group continued to try to garner support, Pelosi picked off vote after vote.

The so-called Problem Solvers Caucus was causing Pelosi problems. The group, led by Rep. Josh Gottheimer, a New Jersey Democrat, and Rep. Tom Reed, a New York Republican, had given itself the name, which was curious because in its years of existence it had not solved a single problem. But the group fashioned itself nonpartisan and served its leaders' political interests: Gottheimer was a Democrat in a Republican seat, and Reed enjoyed the optics of crossing party lines. Their beef wasn't with Pelosi in particular, although some members had grumbled about her. They wanted to make the Congress work better, and they proposed a slew of internal procedural measures they thought would do that.

Gottheimer privately got phone calls from Bill Clinton, for whom he once worked as a speechwriter, and Chuck Schumer, urging him to come to a deal with Pelosi. On November 28, Pelosi agreed to a series of reforms to win their votes.

That day Democrats held their internal party elections, which Pelosi was assured to win. Her candidacy was nominated by Rep. Joe Kennedy III, a Massachusetts Democrat who was the grandson of Bobby Kennedy, and by Rep. John Lewis of Georgia, the civil rights hero. Kennedy said in his speech that he had heard from Republicans that Paul Ryan was not "half the leader" Pelosi was. "No person," Kennedy said, "is more aptly suited . . . to move our country and our party forward." Pelosi had no opposition and became the party's nominee without a sweat.

Meanwhile there was progress on the rebel front, at least according to Moulton. Moulton had told Rice and Tim Ryan that they had a meeting scheduled with Pelosi. *Pelosi wants to meet with us?* members of the group thought. *That's progress. Maybe she realizes she needs our votes.*

Ryan was standing in the caucus election meeting just feet from Rice and Moulton when a Pelosi aide approached them. The aide looked at Rice and said, "The leader would like to meet with you at twelve-thirty." Rice said okay, then turned to Ryan, seeming slightly surprised, and said, "Should we go?"

"Yes, it's the leader, you have to go," Ryan said.

"Do you want to come?" Rice asked him. Ryan said he didn't need to go but ended up going with them anyway.

When Moulton, Ryan, and Rice entered the room, Rice looked at Pelosi and said, "Thank you for calling this meeting."

"I didn't ask for this meeting," Pelosi shot back. It was Moulton who had asked Pelosi for the get-together, but somehow he never told this to Ryan and Rice. In the meeting, Moulton told Pelosi that Democrats needed a Speaker they could be proud of. Ryan told Pelosi that he remembered when she was Speaker: "I know how capable you are, this is not about skill, it is about our brand."

But Pelosi brushed aside the concerns, saying she was already raising money for the freshmen, and their political future was her top priority. The meeting was practically useless, and the three rebels left without a scintilla of hope that Pelosi would accede to their demands that she leave Congress or agree to a date-certain departure. But Ryan, now tied closely with Moulton and Rice, left knowing he had to keep an eye on them because they needed to cut a deal, and quickly. Pelosi wasn't going anywhere, and, by this point, Ryan seemed to realize that.

Little did they know, Pelosi had for weeks been deep in conversations with Perlmutter, the ringleader, about helping him find an off-ramp. Perlmutter and Pelosi were friendly. Her inner circle viewed the Coloradan as a reasonable adult, unlike Rice and Moulton, whom they considered loud-mouthed amateurs. Pelosi and Perlmutter had been speaking privately since Thanksgiving and there were hints that they had developed a deep rapport, including a hug the two exchanged after Pelosi spoke at a meeting of New Democrats.

The two discussed lots of options for keeping Pelosi in power while limiting her tenure, including term limits for committee chairs, but they dropped that idea, cognizant it would ignite fury in the Congressional Black Caucus, which, by and large, hated term limits. Bill Foster came up with a construct that could work: term limits on members of the leadership. The limit would be constructed so Pelosi could feasibly have two more terms as Speaker, from 2018 to 2020, and then one more term if she garnered approval by two-thirds of Democrats. For Pelosi, it was an acknowledgment that she was nearly eighty and would not serve in public office forever. Members of the rebel group had heard murmurs that Pelosi would use the 2020 Democratic convention to retire and try to pass her seat to her daughter.

On December 13, Pelosi and Perlmutter huddled on the House floor after a vote series. Most House members had dispersed. For weeks now, Perlmutter, Moulton, Rice, and Ryan had been trailed by reporters and flooded with questions about whether they would support Pelosi. But now Pelosi and Perlmutter were secretly cutting a deal. Pelosi slipped him a piece of paper with her statement agreeing to the term limit proposal. They retreated from the middle of the House floor to the cloakroom, an adjacent private space, where he gave the statement his okay.

A bit later Perlmutter showed her his own statement. It had a passing reference to Mitch McConnell. Pelosi asked that he remove it. "Why even bring him into it," she said.

With that, Pelosi notched the speakership. Moulton said he would vote for her, as did Foster and most of the other rebels. Her victory was won by attrition. She ground down both sides—the veteran dissenters and the young NeverPelosi'ers—with persistence and skill. She was helped by the fact that she had no opposition and was up against a group of lawmakers who lacked know-how and savvy. In the end, the rebels found it easier to follow Pelosi than Moulton and Perlmutter. Pelosi was also helped by Tim Ryan, her former foe, who saw that they needed an off-ramp and tried to help steer the group toward a deal. That deal allowed both the rebels and Pelosi to declare victory: Pelosi would get at least one more term as Speaker, and the rebels got to claim that they had limited her tenure. Steny Hoyer had been vehemently opposed to term limits for years, and was angry with Perlmutter for proposing the agreement and with Pelosi for accepting it. One more Pelosi victory at Hoyer's expense.

On December 19, Ryan was on the House floor when Pelosi approached him. When he lost the speakership to Pelosi in 2016, she had barely said a word to him afterward. This time was different. He had helped paved the way for her victory.

"Thank you," Pelosi said to Ryan. "I really appreciate what you did."

PELOSI'S PATH TO THE speakership was also helped by the leadership team that materialized around her. It was diverse, both regionally and ethnically, but perhaps more important, it was young. The Congressional Black Caucus had Jim Clyburn, a veteran South Carolinian, as the Democratic whip (Rep. Diana DeGette of Colorado dropped her challenge early on), but forty-six-year-old Ben Ray Luján of New Mexico became assistant speaker, a job that had not existed in the Republican majority and lacked clear definition in the emerging Democratic majority. The Democratic Caucus chair was Rep. Hakeem Jeffries, a forty-eight-year-old black New York City congressman. And Rep. Cheri

Bustos, a lawmaker from a Trump-won district in Illinois, took the helm of the DCCC. The young, diverse leadership team helped take the pressure off Pelosi and Hoyer, both white and in their upper seventies. And for Democrats who had campaigned saying they would elect younger leaders, they had done it—even if Pelosi was still on top.

But much of the focus for the party's future immediately centered on Jeffries. He was a charismatic speaker, young, good-looking, and unafraid of brawling. He had a safe Democratic district anchored in Brooklyn, and he had already traveled the country on behalf of Democrats seeking election. When Joe Crowley lost his race to Alexandria Ocasio-Cortez, it was a useful reminder to Jeffries that he had to stay rooted in Brooklyn despite his higher ambitions.

Sitting in his office in August, well before he was elected to be the number three in the House Democratic Caucus, he had already begun to consider a run for leadership. He was taking stock of the Democratic Party and didn't see the massive leftward shift that others were describing.

"At the end of the day, I think it's important not to overstate the notion that we're in the midst of a so-called hard-left revolutionary moment," Jeffries said. "Where exactly is the revolution beyond a particular shocking result that occurred in a district anchored in Queens in the Bronx?" He did call Ocasio-Cortez—the star of the new Democratic class—a "smart, charismatic candidate who did a phenomenal job," but he urged caution in concluding too much from her victory, "one race," a primary challenge, in which "twenty-eight-thousand people voted."

To Jeffries's mind, House Democrats had the chance to be a big-tent party, with room for moderates and centrists. "At the end of the day," he said, "I think the Democratic Party has to decide, do we want to be Internet celebrities, or do we want to govern?" He had incredibly sharp words for Trump, with whom he had no relationship. He called him the "birther in chief" and the "Grand Wizard of 1600 Pennsylvania Avenue."

.   .   .

AT THE END OF December, the vibe in Washington immediately began to change. Pelosi announced she would create a new special committee to tackle climate change, something that would've been unheard of in Republican Washington. Democrats began preparing gun control legislation, bills to protect voting rights, and legal strategies to protect the Affordable Care Act. Individual Democrats even began envisioning impeaching Donald Trump, much to the leadership's chagrin. It was as if the entire town had been turned on its head overnight.

In January, Trump's Washington truly started glowing Democratic blue. On January 2, the day before the House officially flipped, the Italian embassy hosted a glitzy party honoring Nancy D'Alesandro Pelosi as the next Speaker of the House. She hadn't yet officially won the vote on the House floor, but it didn't much matter. The who's who of the Democratic elite were there to celebrate her. Bill and Hillary Clinton attended—the embassy was down the street from their Washington mansion—as did John Kerry. Tony Bennett, the ninety-two-year-old Italian American singer, sang "I Left My Heart in San Francisco," in honor of the next Speaker and her adopted hometown.

The official proceedings in the Capitol began around noon on January 3. It was a striking scene: The Republican side of the chamber was almost all white and male. The Democratic side was diverse, teeming with women wearing bright-colored dresses and jackets and excited to take power. Ocasio-Cortez, wearing a bright white suit, sat among her new freshmen colleagues. Joseph Kennedy of Massachusetts handed out blue pins that said MADAME SPEAKER. He was sitting next to Kathleen Rice, who didn't appear as excited as he was to be in the House chamber. Seth Moulton mostly hung out in the back, leaning on the metal rails at the rear of the gargantuan room.

Around twelve-thirty, with the floor buzzing with action, Mark Meadows made a beeline for the Democratic side of the chamber to see some of his colleagues. Meadows was out of power but not out of ideas. He still had the ear of the president, and he wanted to be his link to the Democrats. Despite his burn-the-house-down attitude, Democrats liked him and found him charming and a bit amusing—as if he were in on the joke. After approaching a clutch of CBC members, he made his way toward the middle of the chamber, where he found Ocasio-Cortez and congratulated her on becoming a member of Congress. He told her he had sent her some North Carolina peanuts as a welcome gift. He then told her he was starting a podcast, where Freedom Caucus members would debate members of the Progressive Caucus, and her inclusion was important to him. They bade farewell, promising to stay in touch.

At 12:42 P.M., Hakeem Jeffries was at the microphone getting ready to nominate Pelosi as Speaker. The speech was rousing and highlighted that this man was among the next generation of House Democrats. Pelosi had "rescued our economy" in the Obama years, she had saved the automobile industry, and had "provided affordable health care to more than 20 million Americans." And she was just getting started, Jeffries said with gusto.

"Nancy Pelosi is a woman of faith," he said. "A loving wife, a mother of five, a grandmother of nine, a sophisticated strategist, a legendary legislator, a voice for the voiceless, a defender of the disenfranchised, a powerful, profound, prophetic, principled public servant. And that's why we stand squarely behind her today. Let me be clear—House Democrats are down with NDP—Nancy D'Alesandro Pelosi, the once and future Speaker of the United States House of Representatives." (Jeffries seemed to be referencing the early-1990s hip-hop song "O.P.P.," which stood for "other people's" private parts.)

Like much in the House of Representatives, the floor election for Speaker is a bizarre affair. The clerk reads the name of each member, and members shout their choice from their seats. Some members had fun with it: Rep. Steve Cohen of Tennessee bellowed that Pelosi was "the woman who would make America great again" before voting for her. Rep. Veronica Escobar, a Democrat from El Paso, voted for "No Walls" Pelosi.

Of course, a pocket of Democrats voted against her. Reps. Jim Cooper of Tennessee and Elissa Slotkin of Michigan voted "present," which did not count their vote for any individual. Rep. Jeff Van Drew of New Jersey voted no, which was not an option, so they switched his vote to present. Some conservative Democrats cast creative votes: Rep. Anthony Brindisi of New York cast his vote for Joe Biden, and Rep. Kathleen Rice voted for Stacey Abrams, the Democrat who had lost the governorship of Georgia and was not even a member of the House.

Ocasio-Cortez voted for Pelosi, as expected, as Republicans booed and hissed, but her vote for Pelosi had never been in doubt. Shortly after she beat Joe Crowley, Pelosi had lunch with her in San Francisco. Pelosi's charm offensive began early.

When the clerk called on Pelosi to vote for herself, she missed the announcement because she was surrounded by two grandchildren. They called her name a second time, and her granddaughter grabbed her hand and jumped up and down yelling "Pelosi!"

After all the votes were cast, Pelosi won with 220 votes, a close victory but a win nonetheless. After she took the gavel, she invited the children and grandchildren of elected lawmakers to surround her in the Speaker's chair. The racially diverse crowd of dark- and light-skinned boys and girls celebrated with the first woman Speaker, who became only the second person to return to the speakership in a half century. The battle with Donald J. Trump was officially joined. Unofficially, though, it was already raging.

22

SHUTDOWN

IT WAS AS IF MARK MEADOWS were watching a political car crash in slow motion. In November, when House Republicans lost their legislative majority, it rendered him a bit player in Donald Trump's Washington and forced him to reimagine his role as a key go-between on Capitol Hill. Then in late November and early December, a more paralyzing fear began to creep into his mind: Republicans were going to fold and keep government open without delivering on the president's promise to fund the border wall with Mexico. Unthinkable. Unconscionable. He had to stop it. *How could Republican leadership end this two-year stretch by giving up on Trump's wall?* They needed to move swiftly.

So in mid-December, Meadows and Jordan started plotting. They had both been talking to the president, urging him to stand firm come December 21, when the Department of Homeland Security and a smattering of other government agencies' funding ran dry. They thought they were getting through to him, but the president was always susceptible to other opinions. This time the pair was going to amplify their message in any way they could.

They employed all the lessons they had learned in Trump's Washington. Beginning on December 17, the House Freedom Caucus booked its top lawmakers on Fox News programs to urge the president to use the funding deadline to extract money for the border wall. They were talking to him on the phone and in person, but putting the message on the president's preferred cable network was a surefire way to get his and others' attention. And on December 19, with the cold winter darkness setting in over Washington, Meadows and Jordan scheduled a thirty-minute block of time on the House floor to thunder against the weak-kneed stance of those who might give up the fight.

"I rise today to encourage my colleagues to stay in the fight to make sure that we help this president deliver on a promise he made years ago," Meadows said in a mostly empty chamber, Jordan sitting behind him, head down as he looked at his prepared remarks. "I'm sad that tonight we're here and we're on a backdrop of a potential government shutdown. But really what it is is more a function of the fact that we have not done our job like we should've done already.

"The president," Meadows continued with gusto, "many, many months ago, said that he would not sign another funding bill unless we gave him wall funding. So what did this House do? It passed a bill to fund the Department of Defense, and passed a short-term [funding bill] and they said, 'You know what? We're going to have that fight, but we're going to have that fight after the midterms.' Mr. Speaker, it's after the midterms. And we're here with a number of my colleagues tonight to say that we're ready to fight on behalf of all the freedom-loving Americans to make sure that we have secure borders. And that never again do we have to worry about terrorists and drug traffickers coming across our southern borders."

IN 1996 BILL CLINTON was president, the House and Senate were controlled by Republicans, and Washington decided it needed a fence on the border with Mexico. Section 102 of a massive spending bill called for fourteen miles of fencing, "starting at the Pacific Ocean and extending eastward." Congress decided to spend $12 million on this barrier, and Nancy Pelosi and Chuck Schumer were among the 370 yes votes in the House of Representatives.

A decade later, with Republicans controlling all branches of government, Congress did it again, authorizing even more border fencing in New Mexico and Texas. Pelosi voted no, but Schumer and Hillary Clinton voted yes. After Pelosi became Speaker, with George W. Bush in the White House, her House approved "reinforced fencing along not less than 700 miles of the southwest border where fencing would be most practical and effective."

So by the time Donald Trump took office in January 2017, just short of seven hundred miles of fencing had been constructed along the nearly two-thousand-mile border with Mexico.

Put plainly, the scuffle over Trump's border wall was a big fat fraud.

In one sense, Trump's request that Congress approve a physical barrier on the border with Mexico was not abnormal or even radical. In fact, it was in line with what Congress had approved for decades: a physical barrier so the United States could gain "operational control" of the nation's porous southern border. Yet that request also belied the reality of the barriers that already existed, barriers that almost certainly had contributed to the steady decrease in illegal immigration along the border.

For Democrats, refusing Trump wall money made little practical sense in the context that virtually all the leadership had at one point or another approved money for a physical barrier at the border. All agreed on the need for better border security and had voted again and again to fund it. Now they had taken a firm stance against money for a barrier. In the trillion-dollar-plus budget of the United States, there was almost no difference between the $1.6 billion they were willing to give Trump and the $5 billion they were set on denying him, but for Democrats, this money had become an uncrossable moral bridge.

The wall was no longer a wall. Conceived as a campaign rallying cry, it had become a symbol, a political cudgel that divided both parties. The substance of whether the United States needed a new barrier on its southern border mattered little. The prospect of building the wall became a binary: supporting it meant you were with Trump, and if you were against the president, you were against the wall.

The way Trump allies saw it, the construction of the wall was imperative on almost every front. It was a policy imperative; they believed there was a crisis unfolding on the southern border, and a new barrier was the only way to stop it. They thought it was a political imperative as well: This was a promise that the president made as a candidate, one that his supporters had latched on to. But most important, perhaps, they believed that Trump needed to win this fight to establish his dominance over the burgeoning Democratic majority.

As he entered divided government, Mark Meadows believed that finally this was Donald Trump's hill to die on. "It's a symbol of the dysfunction of government overall, and it's bigger than just the wall, and it's why the two sides are dug in," said Meadows, who had urged and supported the president's firm line during the shutdown. "It's who's going to decide what happens in the next two years under this administration. So it's bigger than the wall. . . . If Nancy wins, she controls the next two years, and she knows it. And if Nancy wins and she controls the next two years, the president knows that. . . . We're trying to figure out who's going to be the most powerful person in Washington, D.C., and bottom line is, it's either going to be Nancy Pelosi or it's going to be Donald J. Trump. And that's what this comes down to."

THIS LEGISLATIVE CRISIS CAUGHT no one by surprise. The president had talked unendingly about the idea of building a physical barrier on the border with Mexico. But Paul Ryan had repeatedly convinced him to put off the fight. That summer, when Ryan had quashed the discharge petition in an attempt to pass a DACA-for-wall bill, he had hoped to start a conversation with the Senate that might finally lead to Trump's goal, but he was unsuccessful. In the lead-up to the 2018 midterm elections, Republicans thought a confrontation over the border wall would split their party and could portend losses in suburban districts, where a focus on building a barrier was a losing political issue. Safety? Fine. Border wall? No thanks.

But in December 2018, with Republican Washington taking its last gasp and Democratic D.C. rearing its head, the president was ready to take the plunge. And when he did, he relished the fight, summarily refusing the traditional legislative off-ramps that politicians take in the middle of governing crises. He finally fully lined up with backbench bomb throwers, pushing aside the Republican leadership as it tried to get him out of the mess.

The skirmish had started in earnest in September 2018. A few months before Election Day, Congress passed two large-scale funding bills that kept much of the government operating through 2019. One funded most of the government—including the Pentagon—through the 2019 fiscal year, and the other funded the Department of Homeland Security (DHS) and a smattering of other agencies through the end of 2018. Why separate the Pentagon and DHS? They knew that President Trump would try to use the DHS funding bill to build his border wall with Mexico before he lost his iron grip on Washington. And if the president sparked this legislative calamity, they wanted to limit the damage.

On November 27, during an interview in the Oval Office for *Politico,* Trump laid out his demands: He wanted at least $5 billion for his wall and more money for border security. And, contrary to what his political advisers and the congressional leadership told him, Trump had come to believe that the fight was a political plus for him. "I don't do anything . . . just for political gain," Trump said. "But I will tell you, politically speaking, that issue is a total winner." Washington had trouble gauging how seriously to take his saber-rattling; he had done it so many times before, only to back down when urged by so-called adults in Washington.

George H. W. Bush's death on the last day of November forced Congress to shove off the funding deadline to December 21, just in front of the Christmas break. But the president wanted to get a jump start on the negotiations, so he invited Chuck Schumer to the White House for a December 11 Oval Office meeting. One of the White House's strategies—they had many, none of them proven or good—was to split Pelosi and Schumer, to pit them against each other. Depending on the day and the mood of the White House aide to whom one spoke, they might try to argue that either of the Democratic leaders was more likely to make a deal. But Pelosi and Schumer were not novices, and they took steps to make sure they were twinned at the hip. They met or spoke almost daily, and their chiefs of staff were in close communication.

When Schumer got the invite from the president, he asked Pelosi to come along.

The Democrats had already given the president options to circumvent a shutdown. One was a stopgap funding bill for all seven government agencies until September 2019. That would keep the government open at 2018 spending levels, with no increases for any agencies across the board. Another was to pass six of the new, negotiated spending bills, alongside a stopgap that would kick the deadline for DHS into 2019. In the matrix of Washington options, this one made sense. It would give a man who considered himself the ultimate deal maker time to make a deal with Schumer and Pelosi, two Democrats he had a history of cutting deals with. But Trump's allies didn't like it, because they were cognizant that "punting," in Washington parlance, was a useless strategy when Democrats would soon control the House.

Another option from the Democrats was to pass all seven outstanding spending bills, a package that would boost Trump's border funding from $1.3 billion to $1.6 billion. Of course, this was far short of the $5 billion he was demanding, but it was a funding increase over the previous year, and it would give the president something to brag about. It would also have the benefit of removing the threat of a shutdown for ten months. Plus, Democrats said Trump hadn't even spent the money Congress had allocated in 2018 for border security. Trump said he liked to pay contractors *after* they completed a task.

Schumer called each member of his Senate Democratic Caucus to tell them that they could not let Trump get $5 billion. It was too much money, and the Democrats didn't believe the president needed it, not to mention that the symbolism of acceding to Trump right after his party got slammed at the ballot box was politically unwise, to say the least. Democrats saw this standoff as a low-risk proposition. Seventy-odd percent of the government was already funded. And if the government did shut down on December 21, two weeks later a Democratic House could reopen it without allocating any money for the wall.

"There's an endgame," Schumer said in an interview days before the White House meeting. "January 3, Nancy is going to pass a [funding bill] without the wall, and we will be all for it, and it will be Mitch

McConnell keeping the government closed." He added: "We believe we have the upper hand."

Schumer was right. And on December 11, the world got to see that. Pelosi and Schumer went to the White House for a meeting with the president, and true to form, Trump allowed cameras to stay in the room. Schumer and Trump bantered about the wall, and then Trump, as was his custom, rambled about everything from the wall to the so-called immigrant caravan (he said he had stopped it by putting troops at the border) to his desire to not shut the government down. Pelosi mostly sat there quietly, observing.

Then the president asked if she would like to say something.

"Well, thank you, Mr. President, for the opportunity to meet with you, so that we can work together in a bipartisan way to meet the needs of the American people," she said. "I think the American people recognize that we must keep government open, that a shutdown is not worth anything, and that you should not have a Trump shutdown."

Trump was caught off guard. "Did you say Trump?" he asked. "I was going to call it a Pelosi shutdown," he said in an aside to Schumer.

"You have the White House. You have the Senate. You have the House of Representatives. You have the votes. You should pass it," Pelosi said.

"No, we don't have the votes, Nancy, because in the Senate we need sixty votes, and we don't have it," Trump said, expressing his long-held frustration that it took well more than a simple majority to clear legislation in the Senate. Pelosi and Schumer doubted aloud that Trump could even get a bill with $5 billion for his wall through the House. That stuck in the president's craw.

Before long came the moment that would leave Republicans grimacing. Badgered by Schumer over who would be responsible if the government shut down, Trump decide to own it. "You know what I'll say?" he said. "Yes. If we don't get what we want one way or the other, whether it's through you, through a military, through anything you want to call, I will shut down the government, absolutely."

"Okay, fair enough," Schumer replied. "We disagree. We disagree."

"And I'll tell you what, I am proud to shut down the government for border security, Chuck, because the people of this country don't want criminals and people that have lots of problems, and drugs pouring into our country," the president said. "So I will take the mantle. I will be the one to shut it down. I'm not going to blame you for it. The last time you shut it down, it didn't work. I will take the mantle of shutting down, and I'm going to shut it down for border security."

Pelosi returned to the Capitol that afternoon a bit whiplashed about her appearance with the president. "The press is all there!" she said to a meeting of the House Democratic policy and steering committee. "Chuck is really shouting out. I was trying to be the mom. I can't explain it to you. It was so wild. It goes to show you: You get into a tinkle contest with a skunk, you get tinkle all over you.

"But the fact is we did get him to say, to fully own that the shutdown was his," she continued. "That was an accomplishment."

Mike Pence had lunch with senators in the Capitol, and when he returned to the White House, he told Trump that lawmakers were thrilled with his Oval Office performance. That was not exactly the case. There was griping in all quarters. The meeting had been a smashing success for Democrats and an undeniable train wreck for Republicans; there was near unanimity about that on Capitol Hill, even among many of the president's aides.

The president had a different view. After the meeting, Trump told Paul Ryan that the "ratings were great. This is why I was so good at *The Apprentice*," he said.

"There are ratings for this stuff?" Ryan asked, seemingly baffled by the remark.

"There are ratings for everything," Trump said.

JUST OVER A WEEK LATER, as Mark Meadows was on the House floor exhorting Republicans to keep a stiff spine, his fears of a GOP fold were coming to fruition on the other side of the Capitol dome. Mitch McConnell was preparing a bill to fund all of the government through February 2019. This would be a way to avoid a shutdown, and it had the added benefit of disrupting the early days of Pelosi's speakership with a wall crisis—a skirmish Republicans thought they could win. McConnell's decision to pass the bill was publicly viewed as a positive development. He wouldn't waste time passing something that stood no chance of becoming law, so it looked like Congress would avoid a shutdown and get home for the Christmas holiday. Before McConnell put it on the floor, his chief of staff, Sharon Soderstrom, spoke to Jonathan Burks, Ryan's chief of staff, and delivered a hopeful message: This was a done deal. Ryan didn't call McConnell. He didn't need to. There was no drama this time around.

Meadows didn't like any of this. *Why in God's name would Republicans have more leverage once Democrats took back the House?* he thought. *Start the fight now.* After he got off the House floor, he headed to the Capitol Hill Club with Jordan and fellow Freedom Caucus stalwart Scott Perry of Pennsylvania. They were there to meet Mick Mulvaney, their old colleague who had recently been named acting White House chief of staff, for a bite to eat. But whether they planned it or not, the private club meeting became the jump-off point for the longest shutdown in American history.

Here's what Meadows thought: If McConnell was able to pass his package to keep government open, the House would have a stark choice. They could pass it, keep government open, and go home for the holidays having not funded the president's border wall. This would avoid a shutdown—almost always a top prerogative for leadership—but the bill would pass with mostly Democratic votes, an embarrassing end to all-Republican Washington. Or they could have the fight.

At around ten P.M., a few blocks away on Capitol Hill, McConnell did exactly what Meadows predicted: He took up the funding bill in the Senate, with little fanfare. The Senate was ready to give up.

"All in favor, say aye?" said Sen. Jeff Flake, the Arizona Republican who was presiding over the chamber. Ayes rang throughout the chamber. "Those opposed, no. The ayes appear to have it. The ayes do have it, the motion is agreed to."

They passed the bill by voice vote, a rare method of passing a piece of legislation without a single senator having to cast a recorded vote. It showed just how uncontroversial this was in the Senate. As the bill passed, senators were scattered across the floor, chatting, seemingly ready to go home for the holiday.

But before he let them go for the evening, McConnell delivered an ominous message: "For the information of all senators, there are no more roll call votes tonight," he said. "We will still be in session tomorrow. We have to see what the House does with what we just sent them." McConnell had heard that there was unrest in the Republican ranks in the House, so he wasn't going to let anyone go home until the bill had cleared the other chamber.

Then, with one phone call, the situation started spinning out of control for McConnell and Ryan. Kevin McCarthy called Ryan with very bad news. He had spoken to Trump and got the sense that he was getting cold feet about supporting the spending package. The president had been watching cable news—Fox, mostly—and was getting lambasted. Another big-ticket spending bill with no wall money. That was the narrative Meadows and Jordan had teed up, and it worked: That's what the president was hearing and seeing.

Then Ryan got a call from Trump himself and heard the bad news straight from the president's mouth: Trump told Ryan he was getting beat up on cable television, didn't like it, and was turning against the spending plan McConnell was pushing.

Ryan had little patience for this type of bullshit. You always suffered somewhere for making big decisions. He'd been a darling of the right wing before he became Speaker and gave that up when he got into leadership. *That's just what leaders do,* Ryan thought. You take the flak and move on. Trump, in Ryan's view, was never able to do that. He never got to the point where he made the tough decision, took the darts, and moved on. The president talked about it—he could do what no other president could do, Trump boasted—but it was just talk.

"That's how this always works," Ryan told him. He explained that a compromise bill to keep government open would, indeed, anger the talkers on Fox News, but they would eventually get over it. At this point, Ryan was four days away from the end of his congressional career, and he was looking to get out of the building without a high-impact legislative fight. The Speaker tried to explain to Trump that a shutdown was not in his interest, but he wasn't making much progress. "There's no endgame," Ryan said of shutting the government down. "You'll just help the Democrats."

"OK," Trump said. "Let's just talk in the morning."

Ryan hung up the phone, feeling a bit better. Sure, the president was wobbly, but Ryan was proceeding as planned. He was going to instruct the Rules Committee to begin preparing for their hearing, which was the first step to getting the government funded. At 10:44 P.M., Rules announced an 11:00 P.M. meeting.

But back at the Capitol Hill Club, Meadows and Jordan were stirring up trouble. This was the moment, they were telling Republicans: The party should finally have the fight it had been waiting for for two years. *Build the wall!* Remember that? Jordan and Meadows did. And they were going to hold Trump to it. Mulvaney, a Freedom Caucus man at heart, began wheeling around the club, expressly threatening that the president might veto the package. "Why would he sign it if it didn't have a majority of the majority?" Mulvaney asked a group of lawmakers including Rep. Greg Walden, an Oregon Republican who chaired the powerful Energy and Commerce Committee. It was clear that night that Meadows and Jordan were getting traction, and that those looking for a quick and clean end to this fight were in for a long slog.

Sometime after 10 P.M., Meadows looked at his cell phone, where he received a message that the Senate had cleared the bill. "A profile in courage," he said to Mulvaney sarcastically, referring to the voice vote.

Some of the House Rules Committees' members were at the Capitol Hill Club and heard Mulvaney's threats of a presidential veto, and they relayed that information to the committee's leadership. Almost immediately, the committee—which Ryan, as the Speaker, controlled—got cold feet. They canceled their eleven o'clock meeting. By eight minutes past midnight, they went into recess subject to the call of the chair. In the Capitol, this is called "going into blue screen," because the televisions in the Capitol switch to a blue screen while the party in control tries to figure out its next move. The Freedom Caucus and Trump's new chief of staff had outfoxed Ryan and McConnell, and paralyzed Congress.

McConnell was prescient to keep his senators in D.C. By the next morning, the entire party sounded like Meadows and Mulvaney. In a closed full-party meeting, House Republicans burst into revolt. President Trump was under the impression that it was just the Freedom Caucus that was opposed to the Senate package, but it was immediately clear that Meadows's brush fire had spread far and wide. Republicans wanted to fight.

Rep. Steve Womack of Arkansas, chair of the House Budget Committee, quoted John Stuart Mill: "War is an ugly thing, but not the ugliest of things: the decayed and degraded state of moral and patriotic feeling which thinks that nothing is worth a war, is much worse." Rep. Roger Williams of Texas, a former car dealer who usually fell in line with leadership, stood up and quoted Dutch Meyer, the former head football coach at his alma mater, Texas Christian University, who said, "Fight them until hell freezes over, then fight them on the ice!"

Meanwhile, Ryan and McCarthy walked into the meeting with what they thought was a manageable goal: try to convince just half of the GOP membership to vote for the Senate-passed bill. But it was abundantly clear the game had slipped away from them. McCarthy told his colleagues that Trump's request for $5 billion in wall funding could not pass the House, but they just booed and hissed at him. Now, it seemed, the leadership was in a jam—the Senate bill wouldn't cut it.

As his fellow Republicans raged, Paul Ryan's phone rang. It was the president. Ryan stepped out of the meeting and into a small office next to the party's Capitol meeting room to take the call. It was as if his conversation with Trump from the night before had picked up exactly where it left off: Trump was once again telling Ryan that he was getting killed on television.

Again? Ryan was pissed. He knew that Meadows had gotten to the president. Look, he told Trump, "this is some Fox News people, this is some Freedom Caucus guys and that's it." Ryan wanted Trump to see that the opposition was limited. "What's your endgame?" Ryan quizzed him once again. "How do you get out of this? It's like you're shooting yourself in the foot." Ryan tried to make the case to Trump to push off this fight until February 2019. He urged the president to sign the package and then spend the next two months building the case for an immigration deal that would trade DACA protections for a big border wall. He and McConnell separately had been trying to explain to Trump that when Pelosi took over, he would have no leverage over her at all. But it was all falling on deaf ears. Without Trump's support, this package would fail, and the government would plunge into a shutdown. Moreover, in Ryan's final days of Congress, Mark Meadows would win and Paul Ryan would lose.

Back in the closed meeting, Meadows was emboldened—and he was damn sure feeling validated. He felt confident that his strategy of pushing the president to take a stand was getting a seal of approval from his colleagues. "If you think we are going to fight in February, and we're going to win, it defies logic," he told the House Republicans. "Most of you have been told, we are going to fight the next time. Let me just tell you, it's a lie. If we don't fight today, we will have no better position than today."

Ryan hung up the phone with the president after forty-five minutes, having made no headway. He didn't bother going back into the meeting room where Republicans were still chatting. At that point, he knew the president was dug in; the dynamics would need to shift drastically to save the party and the country another shutdown.

Toward the end of the meeting, Meadows's phone rang. The caller ID showed "unavailable," so he knew it was the president. He slipped into an adjacent kitchen to take the call. Trump told Meadows he had spoken to Ryan and got the impression that it was just the Freedom Caucus—Ryan called them the "Freedom guys"—that was opposed to keeping the government open, not a broad spectrum of Republicans. Meadows told the president that Ryan wasn't being straight with him. Fresh out of the uproarious meeting of Republicans, he said that it wasn't just the Freedom Caucus anymore—there were many Republicans who didn't want the president to back down on the wall.

Fine. The president had a new idea. Trump asked Meadows and the Republican leadership to the White House and told the Freedom Caucus leader to bring ten other Republicans with him. Trump didn't want only right-wing conservatives, but rather a group that was representative of the entire party. So Ryan and Meadows headed down Pennsylvania Avenue for the White House. The noon meeting was so hastily scheduled that some of the invitees didn't make it because they did not get the message quickly enough.

That meeting between Trump, Meadows, Jordan, Ryan, and McCarthy neatly encapsulated the forces pushing and pulling Trump in the first two years of his presidency: Meadows and Jordan were conservatives who wanted a fight, while Ryan and McCarthy tended to focus on developing strategies with a chance of success. Meadows was always fixated on the idea that in a long, protracted showdown, Democrats would get nervous and want to negotiate. Jordan thought some version of that, too, but he also believed that Trump was the ultimate salesman and that he would be able to sway opinion in a crisis. Ryan, McConnell, and McCarthy instinctively knew that shutdowns were dumb, and the party should avoid them at any and all cost.

Before the group gathered, Ryan and Trump had a short chat in the Oval Office, but it was mostly perfunctory. The president was eager to get in the room with the larger group, and he refused to discuss the standoff with Ryan at length. Ryan got the sense that the president had made up his mind.

In the Cabinet Room, Trump gave absolutely no doubt about what he was thinking: If it doesn't have border security, he said, I'm not going to sign it. Of course, *every* bill under consideration had more than $1 billion in border security but not the billions he wanted for *his* wall. Throughout the meeting, Trump vacillated between policy, politics, and grievances. He was still complaining about the fact that Pelosi and Schumer doubted that the House could pass the $5 billion he wanted for his wall. He seemed to want the House to do it for the explicit reason of proving them wrong.

By then, Trump was fixated on calling the wall a "steel slat barrier," or SSB. He was envisioning not a concrete barrier but a series of spiked poles, which, he told the group, were harder for grappling hooks to grab hold of. Rep. Barry Loudermilk, a Georgia Republican, lightly joked with the president that " 'build that steel slat barrier' doesn't have the same ring as 'build that wall.' " But there were serious political implications at play as well. Rep. Ann Wagner, a Missouri Republican, told the president that the skirmish over the border wall created a tricky political situation for her suburban St. Louis seat, which she had just won by a narrow four points.

Jordan, who desperately wanted this fight, warned the president that it wouldn't be easy. "Once you're in it," he said, "the best part of it is taking a stand and fighting. The worst part is you can't cave."

Shahira Knight, the president's liaison to Capitol Hill, tried to yank the conversation back to reality, saying the House should pass something that could muster sixty votes in the Senate. She suggested $1.6 billion for border security—that was in the Senate's bill. But Meadows immediately shot back that Republicans should fight for the $5 billion the president was demanding. Through most of the conversation, Ryan remained silent.

By the end of the meeting, one thing was clear: The president had sided with Meadows and Jordan, two rank-and-file congressmen, over the Speaker of the House and the Senate majority leader. He wouldn't sign the bill without billions of dollars for his border wall. It was a stunning coda to a gobsmacking two years. The government was headed for a shutdown, and no one—including the president, Meadows, and Jordan—had any idea how to get it back open again.

After the meeting had ended, Ryan, McCarthy, and their chiefs of staff quickly decided to go to the microphones set up on the White House driveway to announce the president's veto threat. They wanted to speak before Jordan and Meadows got a chance to say anything publicly. They feared the Freedom Caucus duo would pour gas on a smoldering fire and make the situation worse, if that was possible.

"The president informed us that he will not sign the bill that came over from the Senate last evening because of his legitimate concerns for border security," Ryan said, calling the meeting with the president "productive." "So what we're going to do is go back to the House and work with our members. We want to keep the government open. But we also want to see an agreement that protects the border."

Ryan still thought there was a slight chance Trump would back down after a short blink of a shutdown, and hoped that passing $5 billion in funding might convince the president to relent. They also explored another option: The Speaker and Shahira Knight pressed the senior White House staff to have Trump issue what's called a "pocket veto." A pocket veto is when the president ignores a bill Congress has passed for a period of ten days. After that, the bill becomes law without the president's signature. This way Trump would get the optics of a shutdown without the prolonged pain. Trump was not open to the suggestion.

The play for House Republicans was now obvious: They'd put a little elbow grease into it. The House would pass the $5 billion wall funding bill. In Ryan's mind, he had no choice. He was certain Trump was going to veto the current bill, and he wasn't going to force his members to take a tough vote on a piece of legislation that would only be met with a presidential veto.

But did Ryan have no choice? This moment was, essentially, the end of his career, in which he had long held himself out as a responsible steward of government in an era when government could easily go off the rails. And there was an easy way to try to do his part to keep this situation on the rails: He could have passed the Senate's bill with Democrats, almost all of whom would have voted for it. That would have dared Trump to issue a veto. There was even a precedent; on his way out in 2015, John Boehner had "cleaned the barn," working with Democrats to pass thorny but necessary legislation that his own party wouldn't back. But Ryan didn't do that. Instead of passing the Senate bill and possibly avoiding the shutdown, the obvious solution to many of his colleagues, Ryan agreed with Trump and didn't put the bill on the floor. He was convinced Trump would veto it, and didn't want to fracture the Republican Party on his way out of Congress. And so the responsible steward of good government would end his speakership with the government shut down.

JUST BEFORE EIGHT O'CLOCK that evening, the House made good on the president's promise, passing a bill with $5 billion for the border wall. Moderate Republicans, throwing caution to the wind, voted to approve the measure. Most of them brushed it off, saying it was an effort to keep government open. But it was a stunning moment: Forty-two days after the party had lost more than three dozen House seats, it was passing legislation to approve a $5 billion border wall with Mexico.

The next day, December 21, the government would shut down at midnight, absent some congressional action. After a useless meeting between the Senate Republicans and Trump, during which the president mostly complained about the sixty-vote threshold, McConnell put the House bill on the floor. He knew it wasn't going to get close to passage, but he had to prove to the president that the $5 billion was not feasible. Plus, from a procedural point of view, on the off chance there was a last-second legislative deal, he would have a live bill on the floor to take up.

McConnell held the vote open for hours, allowing senators to travel back to Washington after having just left for the holidays. (Sen. Brian Schatz of Hawaii said he landed in Honolulu, only to get on a return flight hours later.) "How was your Christmas?" Dick Durbin asked Jeff Flake with a chuckle—the two had been away from the floor for only a few hours. Most senators were pretty grumpy, forced to hang around in Washington during the holiday season. McConnell, Cornyn, and Murkowski were wearing red pins that said SENATE CRANKY CAUCUS.

Around five-forty-five, Democrats and Republicans reached a procedural agreement that would allow the Senate to proceed to the House's $5 billion wall bill but not pass it, a way to ensure there would be a bill on the floor in case of a last-minute deal.

Flake was quite blunt about how he viewed the House's $5 billion offer: "There is no path forward for the House bill."

As the Senate went through its machinations, Pence, Mulvaney, and Jared Kushner came to the Capitol. Few were heartened by their presence. Mulvaney, of course, had been stoking the shutdown flames. The group bounced around from the House to Senate, from Schumer's office to an office Pence kept on the House side of the Capitol, in search of common ground. They found none.

At one point, Meadows and Jordan huddled with Lindsey Graham and put Kushner and Trump on speakerphone. Graham pitched his BRIDGE Act, a bill he had authored with Durbin. It would've given

DREAMers a temporary reprieve from deportation if they agreed to pay a fine to the government. In exchange, Graham pitched the idea that Democrats might agree to $5 billion in border funding. It would've been a tall ask for Democrats, and it never gained steam.

It was at this point that Kushner got more involved in trying to solve the shutdown. He seemed to view himself as uniquely qualified to break legislative logjams, although there was scant evidence that that was the case. Kushner had played a central role in passing a bipartisan criminal-justice reform bill, and appeared to relish his work on that front. But, to longtime aides on Capitol Hill, this wasn't the triumph he seemed to think it was, since Democrats were always yearning to rewrite the nation's incarceration laws. Just before the shutdown set in, Kushner told Ryan, McCarthy, and Scalise that he wasn't focused on the immigration standoff because he was "distracted with criminal justice reform." But now that reform was done, he expected to make short work of it. *I'm on it,* he told Ryan. *I can quickly fix it.*

After Jordan and Meadows exited that meeting in the Capitol, Meadows was swarmed by reporters. Jordan hung a step or two back on his cell phone, briefing Fox News host Sean Hannity on the talks and what conservatives might be able to accept. Promising to call Hannity again later, he hung up and told reporters that $1.6 billion would never be enough border funding for conservatives. "It's gotta be more than that," he said. He wasn't at all worried about the president caving under pressure. "The president knows how important this is. He campaigned on it. The president has been fighting the whole time."

When the clock hit midnight, the shutdown was under way.

BY THE NEXT MORNING, Saturday, the crowd in the Capitol had thinned out. The negotiating slowed a bit. McConnell opened the Senate at around noon, wearing a red sweater under his sport coat, and red socks, which he showed off on the floor by raising his foot and pulling up his pant leg.

"I have on a red sweater this morning in the hope that Christmas is not too far away from all of us, including the members of Congress," he said from the floor. He explained that he had left a live bill on the floor in case Democrats and the president came to a deal. Otherwise he had extricated himself from the legislative process. After the president threatened to veto his bill, in his view, the negotiation needed to be completed by Chuck Schumer. "We pushed the pause button until the president, from whom we will need a signature, and Senate Democrats, from whom we will need votes, reach an agreement."

McConnell was issuing a not-so-subtle suggestion that Trump sit down with Schumer to cut a deal. But in fact, the president did the opposite. He invited hard-line Republicans like Matt Gaetz, Jordan, and Meadows to the White House for lunch with Graham and Sen. Richard Shelby of Alabama. Those looking to get out of the shutdown thought it was a sign Trump was beginning to work to soften the conservative agitators. Conservatives said Trump wanted Shelby—an establishment figure—to recognize just how serious the right wing was. Whatever the strategy, Trump came out of the lunch emboldened.

"The president was nice, and he seemed to be exuberant at lunch," Shelby said upon returning to the Capitol. He was then asked by the crowd of reporters if the government would be closed for the next several days.

"Could be," Shelby said. Asked why he said that, Shelby replied: "Reality."

SHELBY WAS RIGHT. The shutdown—which Trump had boasted he would own—quickly became intractable. Nearly one million people, some of the president's staff included, worked without pay for weeks on end. Inside the White House in the beginning of 2019, some top aides began to fret: they were logging long hours, had not received a paycheck since before Christmas, and were being asked to support a president who had shut down the government against the advice of his party's elders. Some of the top administration staffers were worried they would not be able to pay for their children's day care if the shutdown dragged into February.

For the first time in American history, Congress began a new session—complete with a transition of power in the House—with a big chunk of the government unfunded. By January, the federal funding gap had come to define Trump and his presidency. The president boasted how he had hardly left the White House over the holidays save for a quick trip to Iraq and Germany, and he criticized Congress, which was still controlled by Republicans, for being out of town. Trump didn't use the holiday lull in Washington to build the case for his wall; instead, he stayed cloistered in the White House, out of public view. The White House quietly seemed to take joy in spreading the message that Pelosi was in Hawaii, where she spent Christmas with her family.

Trump no longer needed to be egged on by Meadows and Jordan; the shutdown mantle was his. In the early stages of the crisis—late December and early January—the president seemed to revel in the stand he was taking. Meadows was in regular touch with Trump, but his role was to give him a read of where things stood on Capitol Hill. The president's spine no longer needed stiffening. Aides in Trump's White House, members of his inner circle and staffers tasked with advancing his legislative agenda, continued to try to imagine a deal that would allow the president to declare victory and end the shutdown, but the president refused.

Pelosi, meanwhile, had a remarkably clear point of view: she was newly empowered, and was not going to give the president a single dime for his border wall. It wasn't only her policy preference, but it was the unambiguous view of her Democratic majority, which had been elected promising to oppose Trump on every front, including on his immigration policies.

"We're not doing a wall," Pelosi said firmly on January 3, standing feet from the House floor. "So that's that."

Pelosi brought that position to the White House for a January 4 meeting with the president, her fellow Democratic leaders, and the Republican leadership. Pelosi had been in close touch with Schumer, and they had a unified message: once Trump agreed to open the government, they would begin to negotiate on a border security package. In fact, Pelosi's first act as Speaker was to pass a bill to reopen the government, but

Mitch McConnell declared it dead on arrival in the Senate. He didn't even bring it up for a vote. Of course, Democrats' demand that Trump reopen the government *before* negotiations ran contrary to the basic strategy of a shutdown. Trump closed the government in a gamble that his position was the one that would win the day. Part of Republicans' thinking behind inducing this legislative crisis was that the Democrats' position—not a single dollar for the border wall—was completely unsustainable, and that Pelosi and Schumer would blink.

They were all about to put that theory to test.

The January 4 meeting was two hours long, but it was not terribly productive. Trump told Pelosi that he watched her on television all the time, and rapped Rep. Rashida Tlaib, a newly elected Michigan Democrat, for declaring that Congress should "impeach the motherfucker," referring, obviously, to the president. Trump asked Pelosi if she too was aiming to impeach him, and the Speaker said no, that wasn't what this meeting was about. Mick Mulvaney, who only a few weeks before had been encouraging the shutdown, urged compromise, but the president angrily shut that idea down. It was clear that Trump was having a tough time reconciling with the effects of a shutdown: he said the furloughed workers were on "strike." The meeting ended with the two sides deciding they should get some staffers together for a negotiating session. But Trump, once again illustrating his unfamiliarity with government, asked Vice President Mike Pence to captain the weekend sessions, which would put the man second in line to the presidency in a room with a bunch of mid-level Capitol Hill aides.

Perhaps unsurprisingly, the sessions, which happened over the first weekend of 2019, did not bear much fruit. Participants were struck by how many aides the White House had gathered—more than fifty, by several estimates—which made the sessions unconducive to deal cutting. Kushner began speaking more regularly in these meetings. In one, he marveled at the fact that it costs the government $750 per day to keep an undocumented child in the United States. They might as well put them up at the Four Seasons Hotel in Georgetown, he quipped. He also said he was bringing a businessman's mind-set to the border talks.

The border needed more money because people were trying to cross it more often, he said. He brushed aside concerns about cost, and said the federal government should spend whatever it needs on security.

The meetings left Democrats and Republicans alike bewildered. How, they thought, could they come to a deal with a White House that was so scattershot in its thinking? How could the president put his trust in a neophyte like Kushner?

Watching the president during the shutdown was a bit like watching someone at a control panel who had no idea what any of the buttons did. He had lots of tools at his disposal, but couldn't seem to use any of them effectively. On January 8, he gave an Oval Office address to the nation, and polls showed it barely moved public opinion. On January 9, during a visit to a Senate Republican luncheon he spent much of the time discussing foreign affairs. He said he got along better with tough guys than with Democrats; senators figured he was referring to international strongmen like North Korea's Kim Jong Un. And once again, the president switched positions on what kind of wall he was seeking, saying he was open to steel slats but thought they looked a bit too much like Venetian blinds. He expressed anger that the Senate had not been able to repeal Obamacare in 2017—"someone let us down," he said of the deceased John McCain—and he complained that Pelosi and Schumer had been afforded television time to respond to his Oval Office address. Then the president returned to his comfort zone: talking about Republicans' electoral triumphs. He said that he helped get newly elected Republican senators like Kevin Cramer of North Dakota and Marsha Blackburn of Tennessee elected. He remarked that the GOP did well in Georgia—"the governor," he said, referring to Republican Brian Kemp, "did better than Oprah." (Oprah campaigned for Stacey Abrams, who lost the Georgia governor race to Kemp.)

"We beat Oprah," Trump told Republican senators nineteen days into a government shutdown.

Later that day, the president invited the leadership to the White House for a 3 P.M. meeting. Trump tried to test Pelosi, who was remaining incredibly steely during the showdown. *If I agree to open the government,* Trump asked, *would you give me money for the border wall?* Pelosi said no, and the president immediately stormed out of the meeting, an act Democrats likened to a temper tantrum.

The White House desperately tried new tactics to break the stalemate, which, by January 12, had officially become the longest shutdown in history. Urged in part by Kushner, they dialed centrist Democrats to see if they could ratchet up the pressure and force a break with their leadership. It was a complete waste of time; many of them wouldn't even accept a meeting with the president. On January 15, in a House Democratic Caucus meeting, Pelosi joked to Steny Hoyer that maybe rank-and-file members should go to the White House, so they "can see what we've been dealing with."

"They'll want to make a citizen's arrest," Pelosi joked.

As the shutdown dragged on, Washington slid deeper into crisis. The Coast Guard was not getting paid. Museums were shuttering. Agencies were operating on a shoestring budget. Food inspections were slowing. There were even concerns about the integrity of the nation's airspace due to shortages at the Federal Aviation Administration. Pelosi started becoming concerned about the safety of the State of the Union, which was scheduled for January 29. Unpaid Secret Service agents would be charged with protecting almost the entire U.S. government in the Capitol. So she penned a letter to Trump, saying they ought to find another date. Trump was peeved, and the next day, he responded in kind, canceling military transportation for a Pelosi trip to Brussels and Afghanistan.

While newly elected freshmen Democrats were keeping a straight face publicly, some were starting to fret privately. Pelosi and Hoyer began hearing from the rank and file that maybe it was time to negotiate in good faith by putting some money on the table for a border wall. But Pelosi wouldn't budge.

Mitch McConnell watched all this from the sidelines, offering few words after Trump rejected his funding plan in December. When McConnell saw Pelosi pull the State of the Union invitation, and Trump canceled her trip to a war zone, the Senate majority leader understood that the standoff had devolved. The two sides were relying on stunts, which meant there was no chance they would negotiate. McConnell was losing a bit of leverage as well, as senators were talking, looking for their own way out of the crisis.

It was time for McConnell to get off the sidelines. He called Trump on Thursday, January 17, and urged him to draw up a proposal of his liking to end the shutdown. McConnell said he would schedule it for a floor vote. Out of nowhere, Pence and Kushner materialized at McConnell's office for a meeting about an immigration package that Kushner said was the result of conversations with Democrats. Trump would propose limited protections for DREAMers and refugees from troubled countries in exchange for $5.7 billion for his border wall, which Kushner posited was a compromise position after a slew of meetings with Democrats. One only had to be vaguely familiar with the previous decade of immigration politics to know that Democrats would not vote for this plan, but McConnell vowed to press ahead, hoping to break the stalemate. (Trump laid the plan out during a Saturday address from the White House, where his administration inexplicably billed the plan as a framework that would end the shutdown.)

On January 24, McConnell was true to his word: he put Trump's bill on the floor for a vote, and Schumer offered a clean short-term funding bill at the same time. Both failed. In an embarrassment to the president—and, more acutely, to Kushner—the Democratic proposal, which included no money for the border wall, got more votes than Trump's proposal.

In the Capitol, frustration blossomed. The shutdown had reached thirty-five days, and Republicans hadn't extracted anything from Democrats. After the pair of bills failed, McConnell got on a private conference call with the president, Mulvaney, Pence, Kushner, and Stephen Miller. "What was the last month for?!" Kushner huffed. He was advocating for further negotiations with Democrats, confident that he could convince them to craft a large-scale immigration deal if Congress could reopen government and give him some breathing space. Needless to say, it was difficult to find anyone on Capitol Hill who shared in his optimism.

By this point, the government was near a breaking point. Nearly one million government employees were going without a paycheck. Airports were beginning to close security checkpoints because Transportation Security Agency officers were calling in sick. Air-traffic controllers were being forced to slow traffic into the largest airports because they were short staffed. The infrastructure that kept America safe was slowly beginning to crack, and polls were showing that the American public would hold Republicans responsible.

It was time to end the shutdown. Desperate not to lose face, Trump thought he had ways to act unilaterally. The president again considered declaring a national emergency. On the private conference call, Trump asked Miller if an emergency declaration would be considered a victory with the party's base. Trump was privately told by some of his aides that he could even open the government by executive order—something that had not been tried before, and that many doubted would work. McConnell didn't like the president's go-it-alone strategy, but was skeptical of reopening government and entering into negotiations with Democrats.

"They will screw us," McConnell said on the call.

McConnell had already sprung into action, looking to enact what Trump was willing to sign. After the votes had failed, McConnell held court on the floor with Republican senators, whispering about strategy. He also began meeting with Schumer in his Capitol office. The two discussed reopening the government for three weeks while Republicans and Democrats entered into formal negotiations—something for which Schumer was advocating. This was a deal that the White House had rejected multiple times over the previous few weeks, because opening the government without wall money represented an unambiguous cave to Democrats. But Trump had put McConnell in a bind. The majority leader privately told the president that his Senate Republican colleagues were buckling, and he did not know how much longer he could keep government shuttered. It was McConnell's way of telling the president that the shutdown needed to end.

On January 25, Trump went to the Rose Garden and said he'd reopen the government without a dime for the wall. He would agree to the plan McConnell and Schumer had been discussing: government would open for three weeks to allow negotiations between Democrats and Republicans. Congress, his aides said privately, would have one more chance to get a deal. If it failed, he would declare a national emergency and attempt to build the wall on his own.

Bluntly, Trump himself seemed sick of the shutdown, and his White House knew it was losing.

"My fellow Americans," Trump said, with much of the Cabinet watching from the edge of the Rose Garden. "I am very proud to announce today that we have reached a deal to end the shutdown and re-open the federal government. As everyone knows, I have a very powerful alternative, but I didn't want to use it at this time. Hopefully it will be unnecessary."

It was shocking. Everyone knew there was no deal, and the president was caving. He had decided to buckle to Democrats, giving them exactly what they asked for after a month-long crisis. Republicans got nothing. Zero. Trump had decided to end the shutdown without getting a dime for his border wall. Pelosi and Schumer never blinked.

But they never really had to. Paul Ryan and Kevin McCarthy had been right when they told Trump that there was no endgame to a shutdown. Once Trump had owned it on camera in the Oval Office with Schumer and Pelosi, he made himself the locus of all the pain that would follow, and responsible for all the damage the shutdown would cause. Democrats were never going to give him the money he wanted for the border wall, so Trump had no chance for victory. Short of agreeing to a deal without wall money, which he could never do, there was no way to shift responsibility onto the Democrats. Trump would take all the heat. Pelosi and Schumer needed only to close their ranks and wait for him to boil.

The "Freedom guys," Meadows and Jordan, were dispirited. After all those weeks of standing firm, Trump had caved and allowed Pelosi to best him. Not only did the president bend to her insistence that he postpone the State of the Union, he opened the government back up so negotiations could resume, just as Pelosi and Schumer had asked.

"They're more concerned with stopping the president than helping the country," said Jordan. "So much so, they won't even vote for what they voted for before. Go figure. That's where they're at. I don't know how to get around that other than just keep at it and debate, and see if we can ultimately win."

Wins, though, looked scarce for Trump in what had quickly become Pelosi's Washington. Democrats were already revving up their investigations, dreaming of impeachment and stopping Trump in his tracks.

"No one should ever underestimate the Speaker, as Donald Trump has learned," Schumer said in the Capitol, shortly after the president's remarks. "But I also think in addition to that . . . our Democrats stayed totally unified."

In the hours after Schumer spoke, Congress ended the shutdown with absolutely no fanfare. McConnell took to the Senate floor, where Florida's newly elected Republican Sen. Rick Scott and Democratic Sen. Sheldon Whitehouse were the only two onlookers. The bill passed by voice vote with just three people on the Senate floor. The House followed suit later that day.

THIS WASN'T HOW TRUMP envisioned the story ending. In the middle of the legislative crisis, the president had vowed to fight for his border wall for as long as it took.

But weeks before funding expired, just after Election Day, the president had seemed almost giddy at the idea of working with Democrats. Here was his sales pitch: Republicans liked him so much that he could get away with working with Democrats to "do things that are good for the public."

"It really allows me to do things that are proper and right," Trump said, claiming a Republican approval rating in the low nineties. But his patience wasn't unlimited. Trump said Democrats needed to make a choice: either they would investigate him, or they could legislate with him, but he would not do both.

"I could go down fifteen different tracks if I want, but I wouldn't do that," he said. "Why would I do that? So, they've got to choose one or the other."

But the shutdown showed that there was a figure in Washington bigger than Donald Trump: Nancy Pelosi. In many ways, Pelosi was

Trump's polar opposite. Like Trump, she had skeptics in her ranks, but unlike the president, she was able to win them over, and awarded loyalty in return. She didn't twist in the wind. Sure, she was flawed, gaffe prone at times, unpopular and grating for many Democrats. But much like McConnell, Pelosi picked a goal and pursued it with steely resolve, never leaving the members of her party wondering whether she'd be with them the next day. Pelosi wasn't wowed by Trump, or wooed by his flourishes. She stood up to him, and didn't back down. This was new for the president, since Republicans had spent the previous two years tending to his whims and catering to his concerns.

The shutdown revealed another great paradox of Donald John Trump. He often bragged about how big of a Republican he was, but he always seemed taken by the other party and its leaders. He cut deals with them, often projecting that he was willing to abandon the set of principles that got him elected in pursuit of bipartisan achievements, before being yanked back by his party. Deep inside, Trump seemed to know Democrats had something that Republicans, and, more acutely, he, was always struggling to find: unity.

"They're lousy politicians, they're lousy on policy, they got the worst ideas in the world, but they stick together," Trump said of the Democrats in late November, just weeks before the shutdown. "And the Republicans do not stick together as well, okay? There's no question about it. And I respect them for that, and I tell the Republicans that. I say, 'These people stick together. Even if it's bad, they stick together.'"

23

"JUST NOT WORTH IT"

CONGRESS WAS ON THE DOORSTEP of Christmas, but Nancy Pelosi was dressed as if she were going to a funeral. The House of Representatives was moments away from voting to charge Donald John Trump with high crimes and misdemeanors—the first step toward removing him from office—and, if you listened to Pelosi, it seemed as if it were the last place she wanted to be and the last thing she wanted to do. It was December 18—almost one year to the day removed from the longest government shutdown in American history—and Pelosi was presiding over the House, her boisterous, large, and ideologically diverse Democratic Caucus arrayed in front of her in the chamber, readying to take a vote the Speaker had long vowed to avoid, a vote she warned could return Republicans to power.

Pelosi never leaves things to chance. Her office staff famously orders flowers with stunning regularity to ensure that there's always a floral pop in her quarters. Her aides make sure to dress to the nines when she's in Washington, ever wary of catching Pelosi's eye for the wrong reason. The seventy-nine-year-old weaves in and out of crowds at the Capitol with the precision of a fleet-footed football running back as she meets with Democrats, keeping them in line as she has done since ascending to the Democratic leadership in the early 2000s.

So it was not by chance—it couldn't be—that the one sartorial flourish on Pelosi that day was a pin festooning her chest. It was a mace: a shaft attached to a globe, topped by an eagle. Pelosi had told friends she thought it was one of a kind, until she started seeing it pop up on others at events of hers around the country. The actual mace represented by the pin was an important symbol of perhaps the most important institution in America: the United States Congress. Every day, the mace is placed on a dedicated stand next to the Speaker. It's carried with care, handled only by a clerk wearing white gloves. The shaft looks like one piece, but it's actually thirteen rods bound together, symbolizing a message that Pelosi frequently preaches: Through unity comes strength. On rare occasions throughout American history, the mace has been taken from its stand and presented to a member of the House as a message that they were out of line.

It was fitting that the Speaker of the House—at the pinnacle of her power, sharper and stronger than ever before—had that mace as the one piece of sartorial contrast on what she termed a sad and somber day. She had acted as the physical manifestation of the mace for much of 2019, binding together the increasingly divergent elements of her party. If Pelosi could be described as anything, it would be a proud Capitol Hill institutionalist, someone who believes in Congress as an equal in representative government. But in that vein, she did everything in her power to avoid initiating the impeachment proceedings. She didn't much care for Trump, but she thought that seeking to remove the president would tear her party, and her country, asunder. She worked hard to maintain unity, using phone calls and face-to-face conversations, public proclamations and private tongue-lashings. But after months of this, Pelosi had finally relented. Of course, she knew impeachment was risky, but, as she liked to say, the time found her.

"In the darkest days of the American Revolution, Thomas Paine wrote, 'The times have found us.' The times found them to fight for and establish our democracy," Pelosi intoned, standing feet from the Speaker's suite on September 24. "The times have found us today, not to place ourselves in the same category of greatness as our founders but to place us in the urgency of protecting and defending our Constitution from all enemies, foreign and domestic. In the words of Ben Franklin, to keep our republic."

TO BE FAIR, PELOSI publicly and privately said she believed the republic was at significant risk. She was disgusted by the Trump administration, concerned about the democracy that she had helped foster and safeguard. Trump, of course, had little concern or care for Pelosi's Washington and the norms and standards she upheld, something that became clear to many in Trump's dealings with Ukraine and its leader, Volodymyr Zelensky. In Pelosi's eyes—and in those of many elected Republicans and Democrats—Trump had used the machinery of the federal government to hold back aid from Ukraine in exchange for an investigation into Burisma, a corrupt state oil company. The catch, as it became clear, was that what Trump really wanted was an investigation into Joe Biden and his son Hunter, who held a high-paid seat on Burisma's board. The elder Biden, of course, was the leading Democratic candidate gearing up to take Trump on. The evidence of this attempted quid pro quo was stunning; it included a whistleblower complaint from a member of the Trump administration who heard the president on a call with the Ukrainian president—a call during which Trump asked for an investigation—and reported it to his superiors. To Pelosi, and indeed to many Democrats and Republicans, the evidence was abundantly clear: Trump had used his office to strong-arm a foreign leader into launching an investigation of a political rival.

It was this charge—of abusing the office of the presidency and obstructing the subsequent congressional inquest—on which Pelosi's House was readying to render judgment that Wednesday, on the eve of the Christmas holiday. Every single Democrat save longtime conservative Minnesota congressman Collin Peterson voted in favor of charging President Trump with a crime. (One congressman, Jeff Van Drew of New Jersey, left the Democratic party because of impeachment. Another, Jared Golden, voted for one charge and against another.)

Pelosi didn't celebrate, and she didn't linger. She immediately moved on from kicking Trump in the stomach to delivering him victories. The

United States' new trade deal with Mexico and Canada, which was Trump's top priority, passed the House easily. Pelosi's Democrats then passed a massive government funding deal, giving the president domestic and international wins. Pelosi was frequently quizzed about why she was ready to hand the president victories shortly after voting to charge him with crimes. They were separate issues, she replied. Plus, when it came to impeachment, she couldn't say it enough: She didn't want to do this. Her hand was forced. This may have been true, but the road that brought her there was bumpy, the atmosphere was windy, and the situation showed just how much Trump had disrupted not only his own party but the Democratic Party as well.

WELL BEFORE THE DECEMBER vote, Nancy Pelosi had thought long and hard about impeachment and had come to a blunt conclusion that she was always happy to share: Trying to remove Trump was a bad idea. In fact, it was a really bad idea. It was also useless, because it would help Trump and bolster his political standing. The House would impeach him, charging him with high crimes and misdemeanors, and then the issue would move to Mitch McConnell's Senate, which would almost certainly acquit him, something the forty-fifth president was sure to use in his 2020 re-election campaign as a seal of approval from the nation's legislature.

Armed with a mountain of data and evidence, the House Democratic leadership went into overdrive hammering home that sharp message: We should not, under almost any circumstances, impeach President Trump. Democrats, the leadership said, had been delivered from the wilderness in the 2018 midterms and into power in order to fix health care policy, lower prescription drug prices, and create jobs, not to impeach the president of the United States. Sure, internal party polling consistently showed that the public wanted Congress to hold the president accountable, but it did not want overtly political lawmakers to try to overturn the will of 60 million voters. Aides to Pelosi and other Democratic leaders quietly spread the word that they had seen poll results showing that if they impeached Trump, their presidential nominee would likely lose the 2020 race for the presidency, and Democrats would lose their hard-won House majority.

It wasn't a stretch to believe that there was peril in going too hard at Trump. In 2018, many of the same voters who put Trump in office had turned around and voted for a Democrat. Pelosi's new majority was built in places like the suburbs of Richmond, Virginia; in Oklahoma City; and in Charleston, South Carolina—long bastions of modern-day conservatism. Those areas were now represented by Democrats. And the theory went that, in those districts, voting to remove Trump was akin to signing your own political death warrant.

So Pelosi, an expert reader of political moves and forecaster of political winds, proposed a lofty standard that would have to be met to proceed with impeachment: Democrats and Republicans together would have to support it. In the meanwhile, the Democratic majority would investigate, legislate, and litigate. Her edict was deflating to many Democrats, who thought she was slow-walking the inevitable. Their concerns were further heightened in March, the third month of Pelosi's robust Democratic majority, when she told the *Washington Post Magazine* bluntly that she was "not for impeachment."

"This is news. I'm going to give you some news right now because I haven't said this to any press person before," Pelosi said in the interview. "But since you asked, and I've been thinking about this: Impeachment is so divisive to the country that unless there's something so compelling and overwhelming and bipartisan, I don't think we should go down that path, because it divides the country. And he's just not worth it."

Just not worth it.

Still, impeachment was the Democrats' forbidden fruit. They couldn't stay away from it; they couldn't stop talking about it and wondering when it might become a reality.

The fulcrum of much of this chatter was Jerrold Lewis Nadler of New York. Jerry, as he's known, is a short, stout man with the kind of old-fashioned New York accent out of a period movie. He had been elected to the House in 1992, when the previous occupant of his seat had a heart attack one day before the Democratic primary. Nadler had been involved in New York City politics since 1977, when he was elected to the state house in Albany. His district includes most of the West Side of Manhattan—from Columbia University to the southern tip of the island—but it stops at Eighth Avenue, missing Trump's residence by just a few blocks. Even so, Nadler and Trump were hardly strangers— the two had tangled over some of Trump's developments in Manhattan in the 1980s.

On impeachment, Nadler, too, started out being cautious, seemingly influenced by Pelosi's proclamations. In November, shortly after Democrats took the majority, he went on MSNBC's *Morning Joe* to say that a "partisan impeachment" would "tear the country apart." "You don't want half the country to say to the other half for the next thirty years, 'We won the election. You stole it from us,'" Nadler said on the morning show. The evidence, he opined, must be "so clear, of offenses so grave, that once you've laid out all the evidence, a good fraction of the opposition, the voters, will reluctantly admit to themselves 'They have to do it.'"

As with everything, Pelosi approached impeachment with steely resolve. When Democrats began clamoring for proceedings after Robert Mueller's report was released, Pelosi shut them down. "We can investigate Trump without drafting articles," she said in a private party call on April 22. She vowed to "uncover the truth," yes, but impeachment was a bridge too far. But through May, the pressure continued to build, including in Pelosi's inner circle. During a meeting in her plush office suite, the large leadership team she built turned against her. Joe Neguse, a Coloradan elected in 2018; David Cicilline of Rhode Island; and Jamie Raskin, a Marylander with a pair of Harvard degrees, told Pelosi it was time to give up the act and push toward impeachment. *Politico* reported that Steve Cohen, a Memphis Democrat, complained that Bill Clinton had been impeached for sex, but Trump was "raping the country."

Slowly, the pressure on Pelosi grew. Jim Clyburn, the South Carolinian who was the number-three Democrat, said publicly that Trump would be impeached. In a closed-door party meeting two days later, Pelosi implored Democrats to keep an eye on the courts, where Democrats were making progress toward getting Trump's tax records. But her caucus grew more and more restive, and the meeting grew confrontational, as lawmakers stood up and bucked Pelosi's cautious stance, suggesting they impeach the president.

Many Democrats were confused by what they saw as Pelosi's mixed messages. She didn't want to impeach Trump, but constantly said she would like to see him imprisoned and that he was engaged in a "cover-up." Given that view, they wondered, how could Pelosi not want the president impeached? There was a remedy for the behavior Pelosi was describing, Democrats said, and it was charging him with high crimes and removing him from office. This dynamic led to flare-ups, including with Jerry Nadler, who now believed that it was crucial to move toward impeaching the president. Democrats didn't have to commit to charging Trump, but Nadler wanted the House to open an investigation to see what exactly they would find. The division between Pelosi and Nadler was obvious among Democrats, and infuriating to many.

Such division was not evident on the Republican side of the aisle. In fact, if anything had come of Republicans losing their majority, it was unity among their ranks. After Republicans had spent much of the past two years at one another's throats, the party's leadership had calmed. Paul Ryan's retirement had helped. His turbulent relationship with Trump had turned so sour and distrustful that simply reshuffling the deck had a seismic impact on the mood in the GOP.

Nowhere was this more evident than in the evaporation of the wariness with which people viewed Kevin McCarthy, now the number-one Republican leader. Steve Scalise, who had considered challenging McCarthy, was now his loyal deputy, their arms locked in the fight to protect the president of the United States and earn back the House majority. McCarthy had even made peace with Jim Jordan, who had challenged McCarthy for the top Republican slot. McCarthy first gave Jordan the top position on the Oversight Committee, the House's top investigatory committee. Then, when Trump needed defending on the Intelligence Committee, he shifted Jordan to that panel for reinforcements.

By September, the schism between Pelosi and Nadler was the defining characteristic of the House Democratic Caucus. In early September, *Politico* reported that at a meeting with Nadler and his staff, Pelosi angrily accused him of being far more aggressive than almost any other

Democrat on removing the president. "And you can feel free to leak this," she told them, according to the *Politico* report.

But Pelosi could hold out only so long. By late September, reports emerged that the president had threatened to withhold badly needed military aid from the Ukrainians unless they initiated an investigation into Joe Biden and his son Hunter. These reports were later bolstered by the whistleblower complaint, and by a transcript that the president himself released, showing that, indeed, he did ask the Ukrainians for an investigation. Pelosi was in New York attending a dinner in conjunction with the annual United Nations General Assembly, which Trump would address later that week, when she finally turned the corner. Seven freshmen Democrats with national security backgrounds had penned an op-ed in the *Washington Post* calling for impeachment proceedings. The very people Pelosi was trying to protect were essentially saying they no longer needed protection. In a way, Pelosi was now politically untethered, free to go at Trump's jugular. Shortly after she got back to Washington, she made the statement supporting the inquiry. Trump's allies complained that Pelosi had embraced impeachment while Trump was at the UN to embarrass him.

THE DEMOCRATIC CAUCUS HAD its firebrands. There was Al Green, the Texas preacher who had made impeaching Donald Trump his chief legislative priority. In the maiden days of the Democratic majority, Green had bucked the Democratic leadership and offered articles of impeachment, mostly centered on the president's business dealings. Michigan's Rashida Tlaib, one of the many women ushered in in 2018, made news early in the majority when, in her first days in Congress, she said she wanted to "impeach the motherfucker."

But Pelosi relied on Adam Bennett Schiff to guide the party through the stormy waters of removing a president from office. Schiff was a bookish fifty-nine-year old whose district stretched from West Hollywood north through the Hollywood Hills. He is unassuming, short and thin with receding hair. As a Californian, he was close and loyal to Pelosi. Many California Democrats saw Schiff as a prime candidate for the Senate when Dianne Feinstein, who would turn eighty-seven in 2020, eventually left her seat. Schiff was up for the task. He was a Harvard-trained lawyer who had clerked for a federal judge and worked for the Department of Justice as a young attorney. He was viewed as responsible and even-keeled. His staff was filled to the brim with talented, experienced attorneys. Daniel Goldman, Schiff's top adviser, was a Yale and Stanford Law graduate who had worked in the Justice Department's Southern District of New York, perhaps the most important district in the United States. (Schiff met him in a television green room.) Pelosi tapped Schiff to lead the investigation instead of Nadler—a move seen internally as a commentary on her lack of trust in Nadler.

Schiff's impeachment investigation, though, turned into a political food fight. Lawmakers viewed evidence and spoke to witnesses in the Capitol basement, in a secure room that is typically used for sensitive conversations. But Republicans turned that into a political liability, saying that Schiff was hiding in the basement, out of sight of the American people. Republicans, including Steve Scalise, protested outside the room, trying to highlight what they saw as a sham investigation.

It didn't work. By November 2019, the Trump administration was collapsing on itself. Schiff's Intelligence Committee held a series of high-profile hearings, in which senior officials in the Trump administration testified that the president had, indeed, withheld aid to Ukraine in order to secure an investigation of the Bidens. Schiff ended each day with a speech to wrap up the testimony, given extemporaneously. Soon he became such a frequent target of Trump's that he was afforded a police detail, an exceedingly rare circumstance for a rank-and-file member of Congress.

Trump was seen by some Republicans as completely bungling the impeachment process. He was unable to hold a consistent position for more than a day or two. Depending on which day you found him, he might say he wanted his entire administration to testify or he wanted no one to participate in what he termed a partisan sham. Sure, he had his defenders—including Jim Jordan and Devin Nunes—but he blocked key figures in his administration from testifying. Democrats threatened to go to court to compel testimony, but instead, Schiff simply vowed he would impeach the president on charges that he had obstructed Congress.

THE VOTE TO IMPEACH Trump was called for December 18, the last week of the 2019 congressional session. Democrats rang up Trump on two charges: obstruction of justice and abuse of power. The debate stretched for hours on the House floor, and got quite contentious. About eight hours into the debate, Lee Zeldin, one of the few remaining New York Republicans, took to the floor and aimed his fire at Schiff.

"In closed-door interviews, Schiff was prosecutor, judge, jury, and witness coach," Zeldin said, seemingly seething with disdain for Schiff. "Every day, he loved getting Americans drunk on his favorite cocktail, three ingredients: cherry-picking leaks, withholding key facts, and misstating evidence."

"It's a total Schiff show," Zeldin said. Schiff, who was sitting on the other side of the House chamber, ignored this and stared straight ahead. When Zeldin wrapped up, he stood up and laughed.

A few minutes later, it was Jim Jordan's turn. The president's closest allies, like Jordan, Mark Meadows of North Carolina, and John Ratcliffe of Texas, each got three minutes to speak, compared to the one minute that many other Republicans got.

"Madam Speaker," Jordan said, while shuffling yellow pages torn from a notepad, "the Democrats forgot two key things: forgot about facts, and forgot about fairness. Four facts will never change. We have the transcript: no quid pro quo. We have the two guys on the call, who've repeatedly said there was no pressure, there was no pushing. We have the fact Ukraine didn't know aid was held up at the time of the phone call, and most importantly, Ukraine took no action, no announcement of investigation, to get the aid released. But Democrats don't care."

"This is really about—the president's been driving these guys crazy because he's getting things done," Jordan said. "He's doing what he said he's gonna do, he's having results, taxes have been cut, regulations reduced, unemployment at its lowest level in fifty years, the economy growing, Gorsuch and Kavanaugh on the court, out of the Iran deal, embassy in Jerusalem, hostages home from North Korea and a new NAFTA agreement coming tomorrow. But guess what, when you drain the swamp, the swamp fights back."

Jordan closed with this: "We are less than eleven months away from the election. Let the American people decide who should be president. Let the American people decide."

Before the American people could decide, Congress did—and did so overwhelmingly. The abuse-of-power article passed with 230 votes, all of the Democrats along with Justin Amash of Michigan, who left the Republican Party to become an independent. The obstruction article passed with 229 votes; Jared Golden, a freshman Democrat from Maine, voted against the obstruction charge.

And with that, the president retreated to his Florida home. Trump had missed his Christmastime vacation in 2018 because of the government shutdown, a legislative entanglement during which he misjudged Pelosi's resolve to starve him of the money he so badly desired to build his border wall. Now, in 2019, as the president sat at Mar-a-Lago between golf rounds and dining with pals, he tweeted sixteen times about Pelosi.

Trump got ammo from Pelosi in January, when the Speaker decided to withhold the impeachment articles in a bid to try to convince Mitch McConnell, the Senate majority leader, to allow witnesses to testify in the trial. McConnell preferred a process similar to how the Senate had impeached Bill Clinton in 1999: The managers would present the impeachment case, and witnesses could be called if a majority of senators were in favor. Democrats wanted witnesses guaranteed.

McConnell quickly solidified support, and essentially told Pelosi to scram. It left Pelosi exposed; she was holding the impeachment articles, without an ounce of leverage over McConnell. Democrats got frustrated with Pelosi, urging her to transmit the articles to the Senate so the trial could get underway. But nearly each Democrat who criticized Pelosi later walked back their critique. Nancy Cordes, a veteran Capitol Hill correspondent for CBS News, asked Pelosi on January 9 if she was going to hold the articles indefinitely.

"No, I'm not holding them indefinitely," Pelosi said, looking down at some papers during her weekly news conference. "I'll send them over when I'm ready, and that will probably be soon. . . . We want to see what they're willing to do, and the manner in which they will do it."

The next day, having seen nothing from the Senate and receiving no guarantees from McConnell, Pelosi sent a letter to her colleagues, saying the play was over. McConnell didn't guarantee anything—he didn't have to.

"I am very proud of the courage and patriotism exhibited by our House Democratic Caucus as we support and defend the Constitution," she wrote. "I have asked Judiciary Committee Chairman Jerry Nadler to be prepared to bring to the Floor next week a resolution to appoint managers and transmit articles of impeachment to the Senate. I will be consulting with you at our Tuesday House Democratic Caucus meeting on how we proceed further."

THE FITTING CODA AT the sunset of the first term of Donald John Trump's presidency was the announcement that Mark Meadows—his staunchest defender, close adviser, and friend—was quitting Congress. Meadows, like his two dozen colleagues in 2020 and four dozen in 2018, was plainly sick of serving, bored by the job he once cherished. He was in the minority, which was no fun, especially for a rabble-rouser like him. He didn't know what he would do, but after eight years of causing trouble in the Capitol, he was ready for a new challenge. He wouldn't be returning to North Carolina, the state he represented in the House. Meadows was planning to stay in Washington, where he was looking to take a job in the Trump White House or in the private sector, where he surely would cash in on his relationships with the president and Republicans in Congress.

"Obviously, I've looked at this as a temporary job," Meadows said, leaning back on a brown leather chair just feet from the House floor, as Washington was in the throes of the impeachment debate. "Every year it's a decision whether you want to run again. The hardest thing for me was the timing of this, because the president's accomplished so much."

But what had he accomplished? The tax bill Republicans pushed through with the help of Meadows turned out to be more of a liability than a benefit. Trump had become the third president ever to be impeached; Democrats could hardly stand him. They revolted at his foreign policy and were disgusted with his personality and sick of his policies. Suburban America, which had made up the bulk of the Republican electoral coalition for the past two decades, had abandoned the GOP. The Republican Party of yesteryear—small government, sober leadership, and responsible and consistent foreign policy—was hardly recognizable. By the beginning of 2020, it seemed as though the public had responded: Polling showed every major Democratic candidate within striking distance of beating the forty-fifth president, despite an economy that seemed unstoppable.

Yet to people like Meadows and Jim Jordan, the president was without fault. They publicly fawned over him. He moved the American embassy in Israel to Jerusalem, got out of the Iran deal, passed tax reform, and, in their estimation, restored American prestige abroad.

For those reasons, Meadows—much like Jordan—remained loyal to Trump. He saw him as a kindred spirit, a troublemaker who at once hated the political establishment but was so eager to be a leading part of it. Never was their alliance so close and so critical to Trump than during impeachment. Meadows frequently found himself at the White House, slinking in to see Trump, Mick Mulvaney, and Jared Kushner, dispensing advice and offering insights. His commitment knew no bounds. The relationship, though, was not without hiccups. One time during the impeachment process, Meadows drove overnight from North Carolina to take part in a deposition, only to have the White House block the person from being deposed.

"The biggest thing and the hardest decision for me is that when they're in the fight, you enjoy staying in the fight," Meadows said wistfully. "And so this is not me shrinking away from a fight. In fact, it's just going to be continuing to fight in a different capacity."

ACKNOWLEDGMENTS

FOR MANY YEARS, WE TOYED with the idea about writing a book about Congress, an institution we have spent much of our professional lives observing, studying, and writing about. We don't have a rooting interest in any party, but we do have an interest in how legislators exercise power. We've been fortunate to watch this process up close for roughly a decade, and with this book, we've tried to capture the essence of the nation's legislature.

This book was a labor of love, and we're extraordinarily grateful for the sources who opened up to us, giving us countless hours of their time. We appreciate their candor and honesty. Sometimes they thought we were irritating, but more often than not they understood we were trying to chronicle an interesting period in American history.

Thanks to our employer, *Politico*. We began at *Politico* in 2009 (Jake) and 2011 (Anna). When we came on board, it was a start-up. Now it's a global news behemoth with more than six hundred people across America and Europe. Thanks to Robert and Dr. Elena Allbritton for all their support.

We owe tremendous gratitude to Carrie Budoff Brown and John Harris. They've given us the honor of captaining the newsroom's flagship product, *Playbook,* as well as the latitude to work on this book for two years. Patrick Steel, *Politico*'s CEO, has also been very supportive of us.

Politico's best-in-business Capitol Hill team is our family. To call John Bresnahan our friend would be like calling the Yankees his occasional hobby. Bres is sometimes our big brother, other times our parent, but is always one of our closest friends. Burgess Everett, Heather Caygle, Kyle Cheney, Nolan McCaskill, Marianne LeVine, Sarah Ferris, Laura Barrón-López, and Melanie Zanona are the best in town and sources of constant support. Mike Zapler has been a great editor for us. We are also appreciative of *Politico*'s Alex Isenstadt, Eliana Johnson, Brad Dayspring, Heidi Sommers, Sudeep Reddy, and Paul Volpe, and our extended family of *Politico* alumni, Manu Raju, Seung Min Kim, Rachael Bade, Marin Cogan, and Alexis Williams.

What can we say about our editor for this book? Kevin Doughten of Crown took a chance on two first-time authors and helped us turn our reporting and stories into a book. He is patient, kind, smart, and exceedingly good at what he does. We appreciated when he pushed us—and if you know us, we don't get pushed easily. It was amazing to see his mind work. At Crown, we'd also like to thank David Drake, Annsley Rosner, Jon Darga, Christine Tanigawa, Jessica Heim, Elizabeth Rendfleisch, Penny Simon, Julia Bradshaw, Rachel Rokicki, Kathleen Quinlan, and Julie Cepler. Molly Stern, the publisher of Crown when the book was acquired, was very supportive of this project.

A big thank-you to our eagle-eyed fact-checker Hilary McClellen. Creative Artists Agency's Rachel Adler and David Larabell are invaluable advisers.

—JS and AP

CARRIE BUDOFF BROWN STARTED as my newsroom mentor in 2010 and was my White House counterpart when I was the House leadership reporter during the John Boehner years. She taught me how to think as a reporter, and to write with purpose and confidence.

Jim VandeHei—the cofounder of *Politico* and the chief at *Axios*—

and John Harris hired me when I was a dumb twenty-three-year-old. I'm appreciative of their friendship as a dumb thirty-three-year-old.

Bob Costa, Paul Kane, and James Hohmann of the *Washington Post*; Mark Leibovich, Jonathan Martin, Maggie Haberman, and Carl Hulse of the *New York Times*; Katy Tur, Kasie Hunt, Frank Thorp, Garrett Haake, Alex Moe, and Dylan Byers of NBC News; Jesse Rodriguez of MSNBC; CNN's Hadas Gold and Phil Mattingly; CNBC's Kayla Tausche; *HuffPo*'s Matt Fuller; and *The Atlantic*'s Elaina Plott put up with my professional and personal craziness all the time. Costa also deserves plaudits for always indulging our shared passion of seeing live music wherever in the country it might be. A smart man told Katy Tur and me never to read the reviews. I'm going to try to listen to him.

Dan Klein, Ian Wishingrad, Phil Kaminski, Jeremy Waldstreicher, Mike Forrest, Adam Wallace, Dan Conston, Adam Elias, Alex Makler, Alex Hornbrook, Dani Greenspan, Mosheh Oinounou, Andrew Snow, Josh Green, Ryan Callas, Gary Freilich, Luke Russert, and Jonathan Fayman are dear friends and family. I lean on them through everything.

Anna has been my best friend and writing partner. It's hard to imagine a better one of either.

To Mom and Dad, Corey and Molly and Kate, Grandma and Grandpa, Lynn, Dennis, Jamie, Julia, Wendy, Peter, and family—thank you doesn't begin to express my gratitude. To the Beren-Jefferson clan—thank you. To the people who are no longer with us, I hope we made you proud.

And to Irene and Ryder Sherman: I love you. You are my rock. Irene, you made this book possible. Thank you for your patience and love. All I do is for you.

—JS

I CAME FROM NORTH DAKOTA to Washington a wide-eyed woman with bleach-blond hair and a nose ring and waitress shoes in my suitcase (in case the whole journalism thing didn't work out). Thankfully, *Legal Times*'s Eva Rodriguez and later Jim Oliphant believed that I had the chops, or could develop them, and put me on the lobbying beat. I can't thank enough the people—many who prefer to remain nameless—who spent time helping me understand how Washington really works.

Along the way, so many editors and reporters have been in the trenches with me. Charlie Mitchell, Ted Goldman, Kate Ackley, Emily Heil, Elizabeth Brotherton, John Stanton, Darren Samuelsohn, Robin Bravender, Jessica Brady, Tarini Parti, Dave Levinthal, and Lauren French—you all made me better. Erin Billings, Kate Hunter, and Jackie Kucinich—we started as colleagues but now have become lifelong friends.

At *Politico*, Jim VandeHei took a chance on me. Craig Gordon and Laura McGann taught me how to lean in and write what I know. Carrie Budoff Brown has been an amazing colleague and friend, generously allowing me to lead the *Women Rule* platform and host the *Women Rule* podcast. Never have I felt more blessed to have such an amazing group of women standing with me. Thank you to the entire *Women Rule* community.

I couldn't ask for a better friend or writing partner than Jake.

Annie Hall and Brendan Leary, Ryan Triplette, Annie Brady Perron and Jay Perron, Jay Driscoll, Victoria and Michael Logsdon, Katie and Alan Ahlrich, Kathleen Pessolano, Anne and Scott Hetz, Marissa Mitrovich, Lauren Cozzi, Megan Muske, Liz Kaderli, Elizabeth Sullivan, Sarah Goldthwait, Nathan Soland, Tim Lim, Andrew Kovalcin, Robb Watters, Nancy Margaret and Andy Adler, Edith Gregson, and Lanier Hodgson, you are more than just friends. You have become my family.

To my mother, Joyce: Your unwavering belief in me has allowed me to achieve more than my wildest dreams. Lynn, Leah, John, Rachel, Leo, and Neha—thank you for always being there for me. To my niece and nephews, Adeline, Deven, and Kiran, and goddaughter, Eleanor, I hope I make you proud one day.

And to Patrick. I couldn't have written this without you. Your support and selflessness throughout this process has been invaluable.

—AP

INDEX

AAN. *See* American Action Network

Abrams, Stacey, 371, 393

Access Hollywood video, 21–23, 30–31, 135, 148

Adelson, Miriam and Sheldon, 234–35

Aden-Wansbury, Casey, 138

Affordable Care Act. *See* Obamacare

Aguilar, Pete, 255

Alexander, Lamar, 88, 210

Amash, Justin, 3, 15, 166, 181, 188, 410

American Action Network (AAN), 60, 65, 67, 117, 358

American Health Care Act. *See* Obamacare repeal efforts

Angus, Barbara, 156

The Atlantic, 290–91

Avenatti, Michael, 309, 313, 320

Axne, Cindy, 271

Bacon, Don, 67, 68

Bade, Rachael, 219, 222

Bailey, David, 106

Baker, Ward, 350

Balderson, Troy, 286–93, 295, 297

Bannon, Stephen, 45, 49, 176, 180, 235

Barr, Andy, 63, 346, 349

Barrett, Amy Coney, 303

Barthold, Tom, 168, 171

Barton, Joe, 127, 139

Beatty, Joyce, 293

Benghazi investigation, 102–3, 105

Bennet, Michael, 210

Berry, Tim, 104–5

Biden, Hunter, 402

Biden, Joe, 51, 71, 291, 371, 402

bipartisanship, 76–77, 91, 153, 186, 194, 255–56, 260–61

   Trump's dealings with Democrats, 111, 123–25, 127, 129–32, 187, 194, 197, 209–12, 377

birthright citizenship, 345–46

Bishop, Mike, 328

Blackburn, Marsha, 350, 393

Black Caucus. *See* Congressional Black Caucus

Black, Diane, 164, 172

Bliss, Corry, 65–68, 154, 219, 234–35, 237, 239, 290, 298–99, 353, 357–58

Bloomberg, Michael, 286, 327, 333

Blumenthal, Richard, 4, 304

Boehner, John, 5, 36, 66–67, 97, 113, 114, 133, 218, 221

Boehner, John (*continued*)
   allies and staff, 5, 65, 156, 181
   and Democrats, 14, 44, 216, 387
   Republican critics and challengers,
      14, 17, 18, 101, 102, 188–89,
      206–7
   and Trump, 49
Booker, Cory, 52, 279, 304, 306
border-adjustment tax proposal, 45,
   155–56, 158
border security funding, 129,
      130–31, 196–200, 263, 268, 377,
      386, 392. *See also* border wall;
      immigration and border security
border wall. *See also* government
      shutdown crisis (2018–2019);
      immigration and border security
   and the 2018 discharge petition
      effort, 263
   background, 373–74
   bills with funding for, 216, 264,
      268–69, 386, 387–89
   bills without funding for, 49, 110,
      213, 255, 382–86
   Democratic views and positions,
      129, 209–10, 211, 340, 391, 394,
      397
   Freedom Caucus views on, 29, 187,
      190, 213, 263, 372–73, 375, 382
   McCarthy campaign ad, 332
   as a political symbol, 374–75, 377
   and the tentative 2017 deal with
      Democrats, 130, 131
   Trump's calls for/language about,
      130, 131, 156, 190, 216, 265,
      268–69, 374–76, 385, 393
Bork, Robert, 71
Brady, Bob, 37, 335
Brady, Kevin, 94, 151, 152, 156
   and tax reform, 156, 158, 162, 163,
      165, 170, 172
Brat, Dave, 128, 351
Braun, Mike, 350
Bredesen, Phil, 350
Brennan, John, 345
BRIDGE Act, 388–89
Brindisi, Anthony, 363, 371
Brown, Emma, 307
Brown, Sherrod, 52, 147
Brownstein, Ron, 290–91

Buck, Brendan, 16, 25, 26, 28, 214,
   218, 220
Burck, Bill, 306
Burisma, 402
Burks, Jonathan, 118, 214, 218,
   379–80
Burr, Richard, 184
Bush, George H. W., 353, 376
Bush, George W., x, 36, 44, 106, 306,
   319
Bush, George W. administration, 8,
   72, 153, 302, 305
Bustos, Cheri, 367–68
Buzzfeed, 138

Callas, George, 156–57
campaign finance, 2–3, 59–60,
   66, 69–70, 98, 244. *See also*
   Democratic fund-raising;
   lobbyists; Republican
   fund-raising
campaign finance reform, 255
Cantor, Eric, 36, 97, 98, 128, 153, 191,
   207, 221, 222, 351
Caplin, Glen, 147
Capuano, Michael, 251, 252, 270
Carper, Thomas, 271, 279, 322
Carswell, G. Harrold, 70
Casten, Sean, 342, 353
CBC. *See* Congressional Black
   Caucus
CBO (Congressional Budget Office),
   83–84
Cernovich, Mike, 138
Chaffetz, Jason, 103
chain migration, 195, 197, 199, 200,
   201
Chao, Elaine, 71, 275
Charlottesville incident (2017),
   117–18
Chávez, Dennis, 57
China, 123, 129, 151–52, 317
Cicilline, David, 405
Clarke, Yvette, 252
CLF. *See* Bliss, Corry; Congressional
   Leadership Fund
Clinton, Bill, 178, 345, 364, 369, 373,
   405, 410
Clinton, Hillary, 14–15, 33, 34, 35,
   253, 345, 369

Benghazi investigation, 102–3, 105
border security Senate vote, 199, 374
2016 campaign and election loss, 11, 27–30, 33, 58, 102, 103, 237, 272, 279, 328
Clyburn, Jim, 119, 139, 142, 338, 357, 367, 405
CNN, 7, 20, 79, 105, 106, 192
Cochran, Thad, 51–52
Coffman, Mike, xi, 236, 238, 328, 351
Cohen, Michael, 300
Cohen, Steve, 370, 405
Cohen, Steven A., 234
Cohen-Watnick, Ezra, 182
Cohn, Gary, 48, 118, 129, 176, 179–80, 339
and tax reform, 158, 160, 161, 171–72
Colbert, Stephen, 340
Coleman, Norm, 235
Cole, Tom, 204
Collins, Cameron, 294
Collins, Chris, 293–95, 299
Collins, Doug, 310
Collins, Susan, 89, 147, 169, 171, 210, 272, 321
and the Kavanaugh vote, 317, 319–20, 321
Comey, James, 35
Comstock, Barbara, 238, 265, 326, 349, 351
Conaway, Michael, 259, 294
Congress, 1–9, 44, 50–55, 183. *See also* House of Representatives; Senate; *specific members of Congress*
bipartisanship in, 76–77, 91, 153
post-Trump changes and relationships, 7–8, 9–10, 44–50, 55, 181–82
Congressional Black Caucus, 39, 41, 60, 119, 139, 142, 253, 366, 367
Congressional Budget Office (CBO), 83–84
Congressional Leadership Fund (CLF), 60, 65, 67–68, 154, 227, 234–35, 239, 291, 298–99, 357–58. *See also* Bliss, Corry
Connolly, Gerry, 251–52

Conston, Dan, 357–58
Conyers, John, 138–41, 142–43, 146–47, 247
Coons, Chris, 145, 210, 319
Cooper, Jim, 370
Cordes, Nancy, 410
Corker, Bob, 267
Cornyn, John, 3, 155, 172, 175, 210, 229, 230, 388
corruption. *See* misconduct; Russia investigations; *specific individuals*
Costa, Robert, 80
Cotton, Tom, 52, 82–83, 99
Covey-Brandt, Alexis, 114, 115
Cramer, Kevin, 350, 393
criminal justice reform, 389
Crowley, Cullen, 250
Crowley, Joe, 38, 40, 43, 119, 120, 128, 142, 143, 243–46
2018 primary loss, 246, 248–52, 368
Crowley, Kenzie, 250, 251
Cruz, Ted, 89, 251, 278, 310–11
Culberson, John, 353
Cummings, Elijah, 362
Cunningham, Joe, 363
Cuomo, Chris, 192
Curbelo, Carlos, xi, 238, 255, 262, 264, 267, 268, 328, 351, 352–53

DACA (Deferred Action for Childhood Arrivals), 116, 119–20, 124–26
DACA recipients (DREAMers). *See also* DREAM Act; immigration and border security
deportation concerns, 124
status protections for, 124–26, 128–32, 187, 195–201, 204, 205, 209–13, 262–69, 388, 395
D'Alesandro, Thomas, Jr., 36
D'Alessandro, Pete, 271
D'Amato, Al, 273
Daschle, Tom, 274
Davidson, Warren, 259
Davis, Mike, 72, 73, 302–4, 309, 312–13, 320–23
Davis, Tom, 6
Dawsey, Josh, 201

DCCC. *See* Democratic fund-raising

Dean, Madeleine, 334, 335

debt limit, 113, 195

debt limit extension/hurricane aid bill (September 2017), 110–29
  background, 112–14
  and the DACA repeal, 119, 120, 124, 124–26
  Democratic views, 115–17, 119–20, 124–26
  House vote, 128–29
  Republican strategizing and proposal, 118–19, 120–23
  White House involvement, 110–11, 114–15, 119, 120–25, 127–28

Deferred Action for Childhood Arrivals. *See* DACA

deficits. *See* debt limit *entries;* national debt

DeGette, Diana, 367

Delgado, Antonio, 298

Democratic Congressional Campaign Committee (DCCC). *See* Democratic fund-raising

Democratic fund-raising and campaign spending, 56–64, 119, 244–46, 274, 326. *See also* Sena, Dan
  DCCC leadership and funding, 56–58, 59–60, 367–68
  DCCC's midterm preparations, 57–59, 60–64, 143–44, 237, 284, 327–29, 336–37, 351
  Pelosi's fund-raising, 2, 33–34, 40, 60, 244, 337

Democratic leadership. *See also* Pelosi, Nancy; Schumer, Chuck; *other leadership members*
  concerns about impeaching Trump, 403–4
  current team, 367–68
  term limits proposal, 366–67

Democratic National Committee (DNC), 282

Democratic Party. *See also* elections; *specific individuals*
  post-2016 leftward shift in, 242–43, 247–53, 270–72, 277–82, 297, 368
  2008 election gains, 96

  2010 midterm losses, 36, 97–98
  2018 superdelegate rule changes, 282

Democratic Senatorial Campaign Committee (DSCC), 119, 274

Denham, Jeff, 255, 260, 262, 264, 353

Dent, Charlie, 7, 208

DeSantis, Ron, 188, 265

DesJarlais, Scott, 97

Dewhirst, Diane, 350–51

Díaz-Balart, José, 265

Díaz-Balart, Mario, 255, 264, 265, 267

Dilan, Martin, 247

discharge petitions, 254–55
  2018 petition on immigration reform, 254, 255–57, 259–62, 263–64, 375

diversity visa lottery, 195, 199, 200, 201, 263

DNC (Democratic National Committee), 282

Donnelly, Joe, 74, 157, 210, 281, 350

Donovan, Dan, 54, 351

Doyle, Mike, 251

DREAM Act, 124–25, 255

DREAMers. *See* DACA recipients

DSCC (Democratic Senatorial Campaign Committee), 119, 274

Ducey, Doug, 91

Duck, Jennifer, 314

Duke, David, 100

Dunn, Brendan, 157, 158, 167–68, 170

Durbin, Dick, 114, 119, 120, 125–26, 195, 196, 275, 388

Economic Growth, Regulatory Relief, and Consumer Protection Act, 280–81

elections of 2008, 96

elections of 2010, 17, 36, 79, 97–98, 113–14

elections of 2016. *See also* Clinton, Hillary; Russia investigations; Trump, Donald J. — candidacy and campaign
  Democratic results and reaction, 32–36, 38–39, 58–59, 61
  Republican results and reaction, 25–31

elections of 2018. *See also specific candidates*
Democratic preparations, 57–59, 60–64, 143–44, 237, 242–43, 284, 294–95, 327–29, 334–37, 351
Democratic primaries, 63–64, 237, 246, 248–53, 327
Democratic priorities after, 403
election day and results, 347–53, 393, 404
October 2018 developments, 325–44, 345–46, 358–59
Republican concerns about, 173–74, 177–80, 230–31, 235–36, 237, 284–86, 310–12, 326–27
Republican messaging and advertising, 285–86, 296–99, 325–27, 329, 332–34, 336–37, 341
Republican preparations, 64–68, 175–80, 234–42, 283–86, 310–12
Republican reactions to results, 356–59
Republican strategy session (Camp David), 175–80, 240
Ryan's retirement and, 67, 217, 219
Trump and, 64, 174–78, 236, 240–42, 316–18, 326–27, 329, 332, 341–42, 346
Trump's responses to, ix–xii, 352, 393
voter attitudes and priorities, xi, 236–37, 284–85, 296, 297, 298–99, 311
elections of 2020:
Democratic hopefuls, 52–53
impeachment concerns and, 403–4
presidential polling, 412
elections, special. *See* special elections
Ellis, Michael, 182
Ellmers, Renee, 101, 104, 105, 225
Elmendorf, Steve, 8, 348
El-Sayed, Abdul, 271
Elshami, Nadeam, 114, 116–17, 118, 123
Emanuel, Rahm, 36
Emily's List, 253
Emmer, Tom, 357
entitlement reform, 21, 177, 235, 288, 357

Enzi, Mike, 157, 172
Epshteyn, Boris, 48
Escobar, Veronica, 370
Eshoo, Anna, 3
Estes, Ron, 271
European-American Unity and Rights Organization, 100
Export-Import Bank reauthorization, 254–55
Eye of the Tiger PAC, 98

Facebook, 61
Farah, Alyssa, 29, 159, 172
Farenthold, Blake, 149
farm bill (2018), 257–59
Farrow, Ronan, 308
Faso, John, 81
FBI, 35, 182, 307, 319–21
Federalist Society, 21, 73
Feinstein, Dianne, 52, 195, 198–200, 304, 305–7, 314, 408
Finkenauer, Abby, 246
Fire and Fury (Wolff), 176, 180
Flake, Jeff, 52, 93, 107, 169, 171, 267, 380, 388
and the Kavanaugh nomination, 317, 319–20, 322
Flynn, Michael, 181
food stamp funding, 257
Ford, Christine Blasey, 307–8, 309, 312, 314–16, 320, 323
Ford, Gerald, 71
Foster, Bill, 354–55, 363
Foster, Paul L., 234, 332
Fox News, 28, 49, 166, 183, 231, 243, 345, 350. *See also* Hannity, Sean
Kavanaugh interview, 309–10
McCarthy's 2015 appearance, 102–5
and the 2018–2019 shutdown crisis, 381, 383
FP1, 358
Frankel, Lois, 354
Franken, Al, 135–38, 143, 144–49
Franks, Trent, 148
Freedom Caucus, 17–18, 181, 188–89. *See also* Jordan, Jim; Meadows, Mark; *other specific members*
and the Balderson-Leneghan primary, 287

Freedom Caucus (*continued*)
  and Boehner, 14, 16–17, 18
  and immigration/border policy,
    186–87, 190, 203, 216, 257–60,
    262–63, 266, 267, 372–73
  and the January 2018 funding bill,
    202–3, 204, 206–9, 212–13
  and McCarthy, 18, 102, 103, 104,
    223
  and Obamacare repeal, 78, 82, 84,
    85, 86, 89
  and Pelosi, xii, 364
  and Ryan, 13–15, 17, 18–19, 28, 29,
    219–20, 342–43
  and tax reform, 45, 158–63, 172
  and Trump, xii, 29, 45, 48, 49, 53,
    54–55
  and the 2018–2019 shutdown
    crisis, 372–73, 375, 380, 382–86,
    389–91, 397–98
Frelinghuysen, Rodney, 54, 128
Fudge, Marcia, 41, 251, 361, 362

Gaetz, Matt, 259, 390
Gallego, Ruben, 36, 41
Garcia, Chuy, 246
Gardner, Cory, 52, 99, 350
Garland, Merrick, 71–72, 74, 302
Gibbs, Bob, 325–26
Gillibrand, Kirsten, 145–46, 147
Gingrich, Newt, 28, 72, 113
Gohmert, Louie, 152, 264, 266
Goodlatte, Bob, 201, 262
Goodlatte I immigration bill, 201,
  207–9, 255, 257–59, 264, 266,
  268–69
Goodlatte II (Ryan immigration bill),
  255, 264–69
Google, 61
Gorsuch, Neil, 45, 48, 72, 73–74, 301,
  304
Gottheimer, Josh, 364–65
government funding and shutdowns,
  112–14, 181, 218. *See also* debt
  limit extension/hurricane aid
  bill; government shutdown crisis
  (2018–2019)
  January 2018 shutdown, 202–13
  March 2018 omnibus bill, 216
  September 2018 funding bills, 376

  2016 threat, 276
  2017 developments, 49, 195
  2019–2020 funding bill, 403
government shutdown crisis
  (2018–2019), xii, 372–99
  background, 376–77
  Democratic views and
    negotiations, 377–78, 389–90,
    391–94
  final funding legislation, 398
  Freedom Caucus and, 372–73, 375,
    380, 382–86, 389–91, 397
  House rebellion and first funding
    bill, 380–89
  impacts of, 390–91, 394, 395–96,
    397–99
  post-shutdown negotiations,
    391–95, 396
  Senate bills and negotiations,
    379–81, 382, 395, 396
  Trump and, 372–73, 375–76,
    378–79, 381, 383–99, 410
government spending. *See* debt limit;
  national debt; *specific spending
  programs*
Gowdy, Trey, 103–4, 182, 184, 264
Grace, Stephanie, 100
Graham, Lindsey, 90–91, 210,
  388–89, 390
Grassley, Chuck, 52, 72, 131, 197–98,
  302
  and the Kavanaugh nomination,
    303, 305–8, 312–16, 321, 323
Graves, Tom, 267
Gray, Jim, 63–64
Green, Al, 407
Greene, Lauren, 149
Green, Gene, 3
Griffin, Ken, 234
Grijalva, Raúl, 125
Grisham, Michelle Lujan, 251, 360
Grothman, Glenn, 204
Guilfoyle, Kimberly, 318
gun control legislation, 233, 369
gun violence, 92–93, 105–9, 233,
  345
Gutiérrez, Luis, 125, 190, 191

Halpern, Hugh, 5
Handel, Karen, 286

Hannity, Sean, 28, 78, 85, 102–3, 106–7, 389

Harbaugh, Ken, 325, 326

Harris, Andy, 259

Harris, Kamala, 52, 53, 304, 306

Harris, Kerri, 271

Hastings, Alcee, 41

Hatch, Orrin, 7, 52, 157, 158, 172

Hawley, Josh, 352

Haynsworth, Clement, 70

health care and health insurance, 178, 238, 297, 358. *See also* Medicaid; Medicare; Obamacare
  prescription drug policy, 277–78, 339–40
  progressive proposals, 247, 271, 282, 297

Heinrich, Martin, 279

Heitkamp, Heidi, 74, 123, 279, 281, 350

Heller, Dean, 242

Hice, Jody, 259

Higgins, Brian, 363

Hill, Anita, 312

Hill, French, 358

Hill, Katie, 361

Hispanic Caucus, 126

Hodgkinson, James T., 93, 106

Holding, George, 328

Holmes, Josh, 350

Horton, Brett, 94, 106–8, 179, 226–27, 343

House Freedom Caucus. *See* Freedom Caucus

House of Representatives, 53–55. *See also* Congress; House speakership; *specific members and legislative topics*
  the Benghazi investigation, 102, 103, 105
  growth of support for Trump's impeachment, 401–7
  sexual misconduct and, 133–35, 138–43, 146, 148, 149
  State of the Union address, 54, 394, 397
  Trump impeachment investigation and hearings, 407–9
  Trump impeachment vote, 400–401, 402, 409–10

House Speakership, 18–19, 54. *See also* Boehner, John; Pelosi, Nancy; Ryan, Paul
  Crowley's interest in, 243–44
  election rules and procedures, 18–19, 40, 356, 361, 370
  Freedom Caucus challenges, 13–15, 17, 18–19, 28, 29
  the mace as symbol of, 401
  McCarthy's aspirations and 2015 bid for, 18, 101–5, 222, 226, 228–32, 330–31

Hoyer, Steny, 33, 212, 243, 251, 338, 357, 367, 394
  and immigration reform, 195, 196, 197, 201, 212
  and Pelosi, 38–39, 40, 110, 338, 357
  and the 2017 debt limit extension/ hurricane aid bill, 114, 115–16, 119–20, 125–26, 129

Hunter, Duncan, 299–300

Hurd-Aguilar immigration bill, 255–56, 260–61

Hurd, Will, 255, 351

hurricane aid, 118, 121. *See also* debt limit extension/hurricane aid bill

ICE, 247, 282, 297

immigration and border security. *See also* border security funding; border wall; DACA; DACA recipients; DREAM Act
  birthright citizenship, 345–46
  calls for ICE abolishment, 247, 282, 297
  chain migration, 195, 197, 199, 200, 201, 263
  and the December 2017–January 2018 shutdown threats, 195, 202–13
  Democratic positions and proposals, 130, 195, 196, 198–99, 201, 205, 209–12
  Democrats' hopes of working with Trump, 111, 123–25, 129–32, 197
  diversity visa lottery, 195, 199, 200, 201, 263

immigration and border security
(*continued*)
Freedom Caucus and, 186–87, 190,
203, 216, 257–60, 262–63, 266,
267, 372–73
the Goodlatte bill, 201, 207–9, 255,
257–59, 264, 266, 268–69
House discharge petition, 254–57,
259–64, 375
Hurd-Aguilar proposal, 255–56,
260–61
January 2018 White House
roundtable, 194–201
October 2018 developments, 345,
358–59, 378
public opinion about, 285
reform efforts before Trump's
election, 190–91
Ryan bill (Goodlatte II), 255,
264–69
sanctuary cities, 201, 318
and the 2017 debt limit extension/
hurricane aid bill, 110, 111, 115,
116, 119, 120
and the 2018 midterms, 329, 332, 334
Immigration and Customs
Enforcement (ICE), 247, 282, 297
impeachment. *See* Trump, Donald J. —
impeachment
infrastructure programs and
spending, 179–80, 235, 339
Inhofe, Jim, 52
The Intercept, 306–7
Isakson, Johnny, 145
Issa, Darrell, 4, 127

Jackson Lee, Sheila, 139
Jealous, Ben, 252
Jeffries, Hakeem, 128, 367, 368, 370
Jindal, Bobby, 94, 95
Johnson, Lyndon Baines, 136
Johnson, Ron, 12, 13, 22, 24, 89, 90,
169, 211
Jones, Doug, 272
Jones, Walter, 104
Jordan, Jim, 4, 53, 185–93, 240. *See
also* Freedom Caucus
and immigration/border policy,
186–87, 190, 216, 257–59,
262–63, 266

leadership aspirations, xi–xii, 29,
283, 330, 358
and McCarthy, 104, 110, 188, 192,
240, 358, 406
and Obamacare repeal, 82, 84
and Ryan, 15, 18–19, 29
and tax reform, 159, 160, 162, 172
and Trump, xi–xii, 54–55, 159,
191–92, 216, 264, 289, 412
and Trump's impeachment, 408,
409–10
and the 2018–2019 shutdown
crisis, 372–73, 382, 385, 386, 389,
390, 397
Judge, Mark, 307, 309, 313, 315–16
judicial appointments, 9, 21, 45, 68,
70, 71–74, 302. *See also* Gorsuch,
Neil; Kavanaugh, Brett

Kaine, Tim, 210
Kaplan, Joel, 302
Kasich, John, 289–91
Kastan, Jake, 27, 66–67, 218, 234–35
Katko, John, 205, 256–57
Kavanaugh, Brett, 72, 283, 301–10,
312–24
background and nomination of,
302–4
Democratic opposition, 304–8,
312, 314, 322
final confirmation, 316, 317, 318–43
political impact of confirmation,
326, 327, 332, 341
sexual misconduct allegations
and Ford's testimony, 307–10,
313–16, 318–21, 323
Kelly, Brendan, 246
Kelly, John, 129, 160, 207, 210
Kelly, Meredith, 57–58, 61, 348, 349,
351, 352
Kemp, Brian, 393
Kemp, Jack, 16, 153
Kemplin, Stephanie, 145
Kennedy, Anthony, 301
Kennedy, Joseph, III, 251, 252–53,
365, 369
Kennedy, Ted, 51, 246
Kerry, John, 252, 341, 369
Khosla, Jay, 157, 163, 167–68, 170, 171
Kihuen, Rubén, 143

Kim Jong Un, 265, 393
Kind, Ron, 42, 362
King, Angus, 210, 281
King, Peter, 54, 163, 264
King, Steve, 131
Kline, John, 96
Klobuchar, Amy, 52, 276, 277, 278, 304
Knight, Shahira, 387
Kronquist, Tim, 218, 221
Kucinich, Dennis, 271
Kushner, Jared, 47, 174, 388–89, 392–93, 395, 412

Labrador, Raúl, 15, 195, 262, 267
Lamb, Conor, 355
Lamborn, Doug, 294
Lance, Leonard, 163
Lankford, James, 52, 99
Larson, John, 39, 251
Lawrence, Brenda, 137
Leahy, Patrick, 315–16
Lee, Chris, 133
Lee, Mike, 23, 89
legislation. *See specific topics, bills, and sponsors*
Leneghan, Melanie, 287
Lewandowski, Corey, 8
Lewis, John, 365
lobbyists and lobbying, 5–7, 134, 149, 153
Lofgren, Zoe, 128
Lomonaco, Jeff, 136
Long, Billy, 87, 220
Lott, Trent, 6
Loudermilk, Barry, 385
Love, Mia, x–xi, 205, 336, 353
Lugar, Dave, 6
Luján, Ben Ray, 58, 61–62, 63, 143, 328, 336, 351–52, 360, 367
Luntz, Frank, 102
Lynch, Mike, 114, 115, 129
Lynch, Stephen, 363

McAdams, Ben, 336, 363
MacArthur, Tom, 81, 86, 89, 163, 166
McCain-Feingold campaign finance bill, 255
McCain, John, 48, 75–77, 89–91, 167, 267, 272, 393
MacCallum, Martha, 310

McCarthy, Kevin, 2, 27, 28, 93–99, 223–24, 225
after the 2018 elections, 406
campaigning and fund-raising by, 1, 238, 283–84, 286, 291, 311, 316–17, 329, 331–34, 341
at the Camp David retreat, 176–80, 240
Ellmers affair allegations, 101, 104, 105, 225
and the Freedom Caucus, 18, 102–4, 110, 188, 192, 223, 240
and immigration/border policy, 191, 195, 197, 199–200, 256, 258, 259, 263–64, 332, 334
and Ivanka Trump, 173–74, 174–75, 224
and the January 2018 funding bill, 208, 209, 225
and Jordan, 104, 110, 188, 192, 240, 358, 406
leadership aspirations and positions, 18, 98, 101–5, 222, 226, 228–32, 330–31, 347, 358
and Ryan's retirement, 219, 221, 223–33
and Ryan's support for Trump's candidacy, 23, 28
and Scalise, 93–99, 108, 109, 222, 223, 227–32, 330–31, 342–44, 406
and tax reform, 164, 169–70, 172
and Trump, xi, 19, 54–55, 179, 196–97, 199, 224–25, 229–32, 291, 330–31
and the 2017 debt limit extension/hurricane aid bill, 121, 128
and the 2018–2019 shutdown crisis, 381, 383, 384–86
and 2018 midterm concerns and preparations, 173–74, 177–78, 235, 237, 283–86, 295–98, 310–12, 346–47
and 2018 midterm results, 347, 350, 357
McCaskill, Claire, 279, 352
McCaul, Mike, 262
McClintock, Tom, 81
McConnell, Mitch, 51, 69–76, 204, 229, 230, 275–76, 283

McConnell, Mitch (*continued*)
  at the Camp David retreat, 175, 177
  and the January 2018 funding bill,
    210, 211
  and judicial appointments, 70,
    71–74, 301–3, 307–8, 316, 319–24
  and Obamacare repeal, 22, 75, 76,
    83, 88–91
  and tax reform, 157, 158, 162, 167,
    169, 171, 172
  and Trump, 45, 46, 47, 49, 89, 90,
    118
  and the Trump candidacy, 22–23
  and Trump's impeachment trial,
    410
  and the 2017 debt limit extension/
    hurricane aid bill, 121, 123, 127
  and the 2018–2019 shutdown crisis,
    377–82, 388–92, 394–96, 398
  and the 2018 midterms, 177,
    349–50, 352
McDaniel, Ronna Romney, 221, 240
McGahn, Don, 72, 73, 302, 303–4,
    305, 320
McGrath, Amy, 63–64, 349
McHenry, Patrick, 99, 151, 206–8,
    257, 258, 259, 268
  and Ryan's retirement, 214, 221,
    227–28, 229
McKinley, David, 358
McSally, Martha, 195, 204
Manafort, Paul, 294–95, 300
Manchin, Joe, 47, 74, 276, 322
Mast, Brian, 238
Matthews, Chris, 288
Mattis, James, 181, 216
Mayer, Jane, 308
Meadows, Mark, 53, 188–89, 250–51,
    369–70. *See also* Freedom
    Caucus
  and immigration/border policy,
    132, 191, 216, 257–60, 262, 266,
    267, 372–73
  and the January 2018 funding bill,
    202–3, 204, 206–9
  and Obamacare repeal, 78, 82,
    84–87, 89
  retirement from the House, 411–12
  and the Speakership, 13–15, 18–19,
    29, 105

  and tax reform, 158–63, 169–70,
    172
  and Trump, 48, 54–55, 159, 202,
    216, 264, 265, 384, 412
  and Trump's impeachment, 409
  and the 2018–2019 shutdown
    crisis, 372–73, 379, 380, 382–83,
    384–86, 389–91, 397
media, 69, 77, 295–96. *See also* social
    media; *specific stories, media
    outlets, and journalists*
  the #MeToo phenomenon, 135
  Trump and, 47, 49, 264
Medicaid, 82, 84
Medicare for All, 247, 271, 282, 297
Medicare reform. *See* entitlement
    reform
Meeks, Gregory, 128
Meet the Press, 139–41, 231–32
Meltzer, Dick, 129, 361
Menz, Lindsay, 138
Messer, Luke, 310
#MeToo, 135. *See also* sexual
    misconduct
Meyer, Dutch, 383
midterm elections. *See* elections of
    2010; elections of 2018
Miller, George, 273
Miller, Stephen, 45, 233, 395
Mill, John Stuart, 383
misconduct, 293–95, 299–300. *See
    also* sexual misconduct
Mitchell, Rachel, 312
Mnuchin, Steven, 48, 121, 122,
    127–28, 129, 158, 195
  and tax reform, 158, 160, 161, 163,
    171–72
Moore, Gwen, 212
Moore, Roy, 137, 148, 162, 272
Moran, Jerry, 89
Moulton, Seth, 36, 40, 41, 355–56,
    359–63, 365–67
MSNBC, 82, 288, 405
Mueller investigation, 181, 183–84,
    294–95, 300
Mullin, Markwayne, 189–90, 294
Mulvaney, Mick, 15, 84–85, 121, 123,
    127–28, 188, 412
  and the 2018–2019 shutdown
    crisis, 33, 388, 392, 395

Murkowski, Lisa, 89, 172, 272, 321, 388
   and the Kavanaugh vote, 317, 319–20, 321, 322
Murphy, Chris, 52, 75, 278
Murphy, Tim, 134
Murray, Patty, 275

Nadler, Jerrold, 404–5, 406, 408, 411
national debt, 113–14, 128, 153, 163. *See also* debt limit; tax reform
National Republican Congressional Committee (NRCC), 15, 59, 60, 117, 227, 291, 348, 357–58. *See also* Stivers, Steve
   and the 2018 midterms, 64, 65, 67, 68, 237–42, 296, 297, 310–12
National Republican Senatorial Committee (NRSC), 48, 349–50
Neal, Richard, 162–63
Neguse, Joe, 405
Nehlen, Paul, 20
Newhouse, Dan, 264
Newsom, Gavin, 318
The New Yorker, 143, 308
New York Times, 66, 182, 248, 307
Nixon, Richard, 70
Northam, Ralph, 271
NRCC. *See* National Republican Congressional Committee; Stivers, Steve
NRSC (National Republican Senatorial Committee), 48, 349–50
Nunes, Devin, 181–84, 408

Obama, Barack/Obama administration, x, 36, 61, 96, 106, 153, 196, 317, 339, 345. *See also* DACA
   and Congressional leadership, 14, 44, 102, 160, 215
   Garland nomination, 71–72, 74, 302
   and government funding crises, 112, 113
Obamacare (Affordable Care Act), 32, 77–80, 84, 91, 113, 166–67, 274, 339, 369
Obamacare repeal efforts, 17, 77–87, 204, 220, 303

CBO analysis, 83–84
   failure and its impact, 164–65, 235, 236
   in the House, 79–82, 83–87
   individual mandate repeal, 167–69
   in the Senate, 48, 49, 74–77, 82–83, 87–91, 118, 280
   Trump and, 45, 75, 77–82, 85–89, 91, 393
Obama, Michelle, 345, 356
Ocasio-Cortez, Alexandria, 246–50, 270–71, 282, 359, 368–71
O'Connor, Danny, 287–89, 291, 292–93
O'Neill, Tip, 153
O'Rourke, Beto, 251, 310–11
Ossoff, Jon, 286
Our Revolution, 271

Paine, Thomas, 401
Pascrell, Bill, 251
Patrick, Deval, 253
Paul, Rand, 63, 80, 89
Paulsen, Erik, xi, 262
PBS NewsHour, 34–35, 348
Pelosi, Alexandra, 336
Pelosi, Christine, 32, 356, 366
Pelosi, Nancy:
   in the aftermath of the 2016 election, 32–43, 58, 61–62, 64
   background, 34, 335–36
   and Bush (George W.), 36, 44
   on the Chris Collins charges, 294
   and the Conyers misconduct allegations, 139–41, 142–43
   and Crowley, 250, 251–52
   as a Democratic fund-raiser, 2, 33–34, 60, 244, 337
   first term as Speaker, 32, 36–37, 355–56
   and Hoyer, 38–39, 40, 110, 338, 357
   and immigration/border policy, 123–26, 129–32, 195, 373, 374, 391
   and the January 2018 funding bill, 205
   and Obama, 215
   political skills and methods, 33–34, 339, 348, 354, 361–62, 367, 398–99

Pelosi, Nancy (*continued*)
  public opinion about, 62
  reelection to speakership (2019), x,
    370–71
  Republican views of, 286, 288, 333,
    336–37, 341, 357, 364
  resistance to her election as
    minority leader, 32–33, 38–43
  resistance to her reelection as
    Speaker, xii, 338–40, 354–56,
    359–68
  retirement thoughts, 32, 37
  and Scalise, 96, 106
  second term as Speaker, 401
  and Trump, xii, 37–38, 43, 123–25,
    339–40, 352, 363–64, 392, 399
  and the Trump administration's
    post–2018 midterm legislative
    agenda, 402–3
  and Trump's impeachment,
    400–407, 410–11
  and the 2017 debt limit extension/
    hurricane aid bill, 110–11,
    114–17, 119–27
  and the 2018–2019 shutdown
    crisis, 375, 377–78, 379, 391–92,
    393–94, 397, 398–99, 410
  and the 2018 midterms, 64, 286,
    288, 328, 334–40, 347–48, 350,
    352, 353, 360
  and the 2019 freshmen, 361–62, 365
Pence, Mike, 20, 30, 31, 159, 179, 181,
    188, 230, 291
  and the Kavanaugh nomination,
    303, 316, 322
  and Obamacare repeal, 75, 80, 82,
    87, 91
  and Ryan, 12, 221
  and tax reform, 160–61, 171–72
  and 2018–2019 shutdown crisis,
    379, 388, 392, 395
  and the 2018 midterms, 238, 352, 353
Penley, Steve, 334
Pergram, Chad, 166
Perlmutter, Ed, 41, 355, 356, 359–60,
    361, 366–67
Perriello, Tom, 271
Perry, Rick, 47
Perry, Scott, 15, 258, 259, 380
Peterson, Collin, 402

Petraeus, David, 355
pharmaceutical industry, 278–79,
    293, 339–40
  Chris Collins's ties and
    indictment, 293–95, 299
Planned Parenthood, 81, 82
Podesta, John, 305
Poling, Parker, 208, 268, 357
Polis, Jared, 360
Politico, 3, 146, 147, 219, 222, 280, 376
polls. *See* public opinion
Pompeo, Mike, 19, 181
Portman, Rob, 66, 170, 291, 302
Posey, Bill, 49
prescription drugs, 277–78, 339–40
Pressley, Ayanna, 252–53, 270
Price, Tom, 82, 83
Priebus, Reince, 20, 22, 26, 49–50
Problem Solvers Caucus, 364
Progressive Caucus, 370
Protect the House, 238, 295–97, 317,
    332
public opinion:
  about Kavanaugh, 305, 323–24
  about the 2018–2019 shutdown,
    393, 396
  of Congress, 8–9, 112
  of Trump, 46, 236, 265, 285,
    298–99, 326, 332
  Trump on polls, 174, 178
  2017 voter opinions, 62
  2018 voter opinions, 236–37, 284,
    285, 296, 297, 311
  2019–2020 voter opinions, 412
Pureval, Aftab, 298

Ramirez, Deborah, 308, 320
Raskin, Jamie, 405
Ratcliffe, John, 409
Rayburn, Sam, 338
Reagan, Ronald, 153, 340
Reed, Tom, 364
Reid, Harry, 57, 74, 274–75, 276
Renacci, Jim, 97, 240–41
Republican fund-raising and
    campaign spending, 342,
    352. *See also* Congressional
    Leadership Fund; elections
    of 2018; National Republican
    Congressional Committee

Ryan's retirement and, 219, 221,
223, 227, 239, 311–12
Trump at September 2018 fund-
raiser, 316–18
Republican leadership. *See also*
McCarthy, Kevin; McConnell,
Mitch; Ryan, Paul; Scalise, Steve
2018 minority leader contest, 358
tensions/competition between
Scalise and McCarthy, 93–99,
108, 109, 222, 223, 227–32,
330–31, 342–44
the Young Guns, 96–97
Republican National Committee
(RNC), 291
Republican Party. *See also* elections
of 2018; National Republican
Congressional Committee;
Obamacare repeal efforts;
specific individuals
post-2018 midterm unity, 406
2008 election losses and the
"Young Guns," 96–97
2010 midterm gains, 36, 97–98
2018 resignations and retirements,
239
Republican Study Committee, 98,
188
Rice, Kathleen, 36, 141, 356, 359–60,
363, 365–66, 369, 371
Rice, Susan, 48
Richmond, Cedric, 92, 101, 139, 142
Risch, Jim, 145
RNC (Republican National
Committee), 291
Roberti, Vin, 348
Roberts, John, 303
Roberts, Pat, 52, 66, 145
Roby, Martha, 267
Rodgers, Cathy McMorris, 46–47,
164, 165, 221, 229
Rogers, Hal, 128
Rogers, John, 296, 297, 311
Romney, Mitt, 73, 221, 236, 319
Rose, Max, 351
Rosenstein, Rod, 319
Roskam, Peter, xi, 99, 341–42, 353
Ross, Dennis, 263–64
Ross, Wilbur, 130
Rubiner, Laurie, 304

Russia investigations, 181–84, 206,
294–95, 300
Ryan, Janna, 216–17, 283
Ryan, Paul, 2, 11–31, 45, 53, 97, 148,
181, 182, 192, 261, 379. *See also*
Ryan, Paul — retirement decision
after the 2018 midterms, 356–57,
358, 359
at the Camp David retreat, 175,
177, 180
as fund-raiser, 60, 67, 219–21, 227,
234–36, 239, 283, 311–12
and immigration/border policy,
190–91, 255, 256, 260–69, 375
and the January 2018 funding bill,
202, 203–4, 206, 209, 212
and Obamacare repeal, 75, 78, 79,
83, 84–85, 86, 87, 91, 220
and Scalise's shooting, 93, 106,
108–9
Speakership challengers and
speculation, 13–19, 28, 29, 94,
219, 222–23, 343
and tax reform, 154, 155–56, 158,
162–67, 169, 170, 172
and Trump as president, xi,
46, 123, 215–16, 217, 221–22,
345–46, 406
and Trump's candidacy, 12–13,
14–16, 20–25, 27, 29–31
and Trump's election, 26–27, 29–31
Trump's opinions of, xi, 13, 27, 31
and the 2017 debt limit extension/
hurricane aid bill, 118, 121, 122
and the 2018–2019 shutdown
crisis, 380, 381–87
and the 2018 midterms, 310, 327,
345–46, 349
Ryan, Paul — retirement decision, xi,
16, 214–33, 260
announcements of, 214–15, 217–18,
221–22, 226, 227, 229, 230
decision-making process, 215,
218–21
discussions about who should
serve as next Speaker, 223–32
reactions to, 217, 221–22, 223,
227–28
and Republican fund-raising, 219,
221, 223, 227, 239, 311–12

Ryan, Paul — retirement decision (*continued*)
and retention of the speakership, 219, 222–23, 227
Ryan, Tim, 40–42, 43, 356, 360–63, 365–66, 367

Salazar, Julia, 247
Salman bin Abdulaziz Al-Saud, 317–18
sanctuary cities, 201, 318
Sanders, Bernie, 51, 52–53, 242, 247–48, 252, 270–72, 276, 277–79, 282
Sanford, Mark, 98, 265
Sasse, Ben, 52
Saudi Arabia, Trump in, 317–18
Scalia, Antonin, 71
Scalise, Jennifer, 29, 94, 96, 105–6, 107–8
Scalise, Steve, 2, 92–101
at the Camp David retreat, 175, 176, 179, 180
and immigration/border policy, 212, 258, 259
and the January 2018 funding bill, 207, 208, 210
leadership aspirations, 99, 222–23, 226–31, 330, 342–44
and McCarthy, 93–99, 108, 109, 222, 223, 227–32, 330–31, 342–44, 406
and Obamacare repeal, 83, 84
and Pelosi, 96, 106
and Ryan's retirement, 221, 222–23, 226–32
shooting and recovery, 92–93, 105–9, 151, 207, 340–41
and tax reform, 155, 156, 165, 172
and Trump, 19, 20, 54–55, 106, 151, 330
and the Trump impeachment investigation, 408
and the 2016 election, 20, 24, 27–29
and the 2018 midterms, 310–12, 329–31, 341–42, 349
Scanlon, Mary Gay, 335
Scaramucci, Anthony, 8
Schatz, Brian, 145, 388

Schiff, Adam, 182, 184, 407–9
Schuler, Heath, 41
Schultz, Debbie Wasserman, 244
Schumer, Chuck, 11, 17, 26, 51, 58, 76, 272–77, 281
and the anti-Pelosi rebels, 363, 364–65
Clinton-era border security votes, 373, 374
and the December 2017–January 2018 shutdown threat, 195, 209–10, 211–12
and the Democrats' leftward shift, 272, 279–82
and Franken, 135–36, 137, 147, 148
and the Kavanaugh nomination, 304–5
and Trump, xii, 53, 72, 122–23, 132, 279–80
and the 2017 debt limit extension/hurricane aid bill, 110–11, 114–17, 119–20, 121–23, 125–26
and the 2017 prescription drug bill, 278
and the 2017 tentative immigration deal, 129–32
and the 2018–2019 shutdown crisis, 376–79, 390, 391, 396–98
Schwarzenegger, Arnold, 191
Scott, Austin, 204
Scott, Rick, 398
Scott, Tim, 52, 172
Seifert, Kevin, 16, 25–27, 66–67, 218, 221
Sena, Dan, 56–58, 60–63, 143–44, 237, 327–29, 336, 348, 351–52
Senate, 50–53, 76–77, 91, 99. *See also* judicial appointments; *specific senators and legislative topics*
filibuster rule, 82, 211, 267
sexual misconduct and, 135–38, 144–49
Trump impeachment trial in, 403, 410–11
Sessions, Jeff, 45, 162, 250
Sessions, Pete, 310
sexual misconduct, 133–49
background, 133–35
Conyers allegations, 138–43, 146–47

Franken allegations, 135–38, 143, 144–49

Kavanaugh allegations, 307–10, 313–16, 318–21

other allegations and resignations, 141–42, 148–49

the Trump *Access Hollywood* video, 21–23, 30–31, 135, 148

Shaheen, Jeanne, 145, 210

Shelby, Richard, 52, 390

Shelleby, Ed, 136

Sherrill, Mikie, 362

Short, Marc, 28, 50, 114–15, 121, 129, 160, 171–72, 207

Silberman, Laurence, 71

Silver, Nate, 178

Sloan, Melanie, 139, 142

Slotkin, Elissa, 246, 370

Smith, Jason, 220

social media, 61. *See also* Twitter

Social Security reform. *See* entitlement reform

Soderstrom, Sharon, 380

Sommers, Mike, 5

Soros, George, 333, 345

Souders, Pat, 114

Spanberger, Abigail, 351, 355

Sparks, Matt, 102, 103

special counsel. *See* Mueller investigation

special elections, 178, 237, 240, 271, 286

Balderson-O'Connor, 286–93, 295, 297

Sessions Senate seat, 137, 148, 162, 272

Speth, Andy, 16, 218

Spicer, Sean, 45, 50, 156

Stabenow, Debbie, 210

Starr, Kenneth, 302

State of the Union address, 54, 394, 397

Stern, Todd, 305

Stevens, Haley, 362

Stewart, Dave, 151, 156, 163, 170

Steyer, Tom, 333

Stivers, Steve, 65–66, 67, 219, 227, 237–42, 295, 299, 311–12, 325–26. *See also* National Republican Congressional Committee

on and after election day 2018, 348–49, 357, 358–59

and the Balderson-O'Connor special election, 288, 290, 291, 295, 297

Strange, Luther, 162

Sullivan, Dan, 172

super PACs, 66. *See also* American Action Network; Congressional Leadership Fund

Supreme Court appointments, 70, 71–74. *See also specific nominees*

Swetnick, Julie, 313, 320

Swett, Walt, 245

Tapper, Jake, 20, 79, 106

tariffs, 238–39. *See also* China; trade

Tarkanian, Danny, 241–42

TARP bailout, 98

tax reform, 9, 50, 117, 150–72, 175

background, 150, 153–54

border-adjustment tax proposal, 45, 155–56, 158

budget resolutions for, 157, 163–66

final negotiations and passage, 169–72

Freedom Caucus and, 45, 158–63, 172

House process, 150–52, 156–57, 163–66, 167

Obamacare individual mandate repeal, 167–69

political impact, 235, 237, 285, 327, 411–12

Ryan's interest in, 154, 155–56, 158, 162, 164, 170

Senate process, 157–58, 163, 167–69

and the Trump White House, 150–53, 155–66, 169, 171–72

and the 2017 debt limit extension/ hurricane aid bill, 116–17

Tea Party revolution, 97, 98, 113–14. *See also* elections of 2010; *specific candidates*

Tester, Jon, 4

Thapar, Amul, 301

Thomas, Clarence, 312

Thompson, James, 271

Thompson, Tommy, 221

Thune, John, 172, 276

Tiberi, Pat, 286–87

Tierney, John, 356

Tlaib, Rashida, 247, 392, 407

Todd, Chuck, 140–41, 231–32

Toomey, Pat, 168, 172

trade, 238–39. *See also* China

border-adjustment tax proposal, 45, 155–56, 158

House passage of the USMCA, 402–3

Traficant, James, 40

Trott, Dave, 256–57

Trump, Donald J. — candidacy and campaign (2015–16), 19–24. *See also* 2016 election

the *Access Hollywood* video, 21–23, 30–31, 135, 148

Election Day and immediate aftermath, 25–31

judicial candidate lists, 21, 72–73

Nunes and, 181

Ryan and, 12–16, 20–25, 27, 29–31

Trump, Donald J. — impeachment, 400–411. *See also* Trump, Donald J. — Ukraine affair

abuse of power charge, 402, 410

House investigations and hearings, 407–9

House Republicans and, 408, 409–10

House vote on impeachment articles, 400–401, 402, 409–10

obstruction of Congress charge, 402, 408–9, 410

Pelosi's hold on delivering impeachment articles, 410–11

Pelosi's initial resistance and growth of House support, 401–7

public opinion about, 403–4

Senate trial, 403, 410–11

Trump's comments about/ responses to, 408–9

Trump, Donald J. — Trump administration. *See also specific policy areas and specific individuals for their relationships with Trump*

administration's early days, 45–50

approval ratings and other public opinion about, 46, 236, 265, 285, 298–99, 326, 332, 379

Cabinet appointments, 47

the Camp David retreat, 175–80, 240

the Charlottesville incident, 117–18

conflicts among advisers and staff, 49–50

dealings with Democrats, 111, 123–25, 127, 128–32, 187, 194, 197, 209–12, 377

and Democratic strategy for the 2018 midterms, 64

ideological flexibility, 9, 10

impeachment talk/potential, 174, 226, 286, 297, 339, 369, 392

inauguration, 49, 57

Jordan on Trump's accomplishments, 409–10

and judicial appointments, 9, 21, 45, 70, 72–74, 301–3, 308, 316, 320–23

legislative agenda, 50

and the March 2018 omnibus spending bill, 216

and the media, 47, 49, 264

public opinion after the 2018 elections, 412

relations with Republican leadership and legislators, 45–49, 54–55, 86

and Republican concerns about the 2018 midterms, 174–78, 236, 326–27, 332, 341–42

and Russian election interference, 183

transition, 181

Trump on his presidency, xii

Trump's admiration for Democrats, 399

Trump's Twitter use, 45–46, 49, 176, 265, 266, 268–69, 346

and the 2017 debt cap/hurricane aid deal, 110–11, 120–25

and the 2018–2019 shutdown crisis, 372–73, 375–76, 378–79, 381, 383–99

2018 endorsements and campaign appearances, 240–42, 288–89, 291, 316–18

2018 midterm reactions, ix–xii, 352, 393

2019–2020 legislative victories, 402–3

and Washington norms, 7–8, 9–10, 44–50

Trump, Donald J. — Ukraine affair, 402, 407. *See also* Trump, Donald J. — impeachment public opinion about, 403

Trump, Donald, Jr., 318

Trump, Fred, 122

Trump Hotel (Washington, D.C.), 8

Trump, Ivanka, 121, 173–75, 176, 224, 265

Trump, Melania, 30, 31, 106, 317, 318

Tweeden, Leeann, 136–37

Twitter, 45–46, 49, 52, 89, 176, 265, 266, 268–69, 346

Ukraine affair. *See* Trump, Donald J. — Ukraine affair

Upton, Fred, 87, 239, 328

U.S. Congress. *See* Congress; House *entries;* Senate *entries; specific members of Congress*

USMCA (United States-Mexico-Canada Agreement), 402–3

Valadao, David, 255, 264, 353

Van Drew, Jeff, 370, 402

Van Hollen, Chris, 119, 120

voting rights legislation, 369

Wagner, Ann, 23, 386

Walberg, Tim, 127

Walden, Greg, 23, 382

Walker, Scott, 22, 24

wall funding. *See* border wall

Wall Street regulation, 280–81

Walorski, Jackie, 310

Walz, Tim, 360

Warner, Mark, 184

Warren, Elizabeth, 52, 53, 253, 276, 278, 280–81

Washington Crossing the Delaware, 334

Washington Post, 80, 105, 201, 307

Waters, Maxine, 318, 327

Weaver, John, 290–91

Webster, Daniel, 104

Weiner, Anthony, 4, 133–34

Weinstein, Harvey, 135

Weiss, Danny, 361

Welder, Brent, 271

Wenstrup, Brad, 93

Wexton, Jennifer, 349

whistleblower complaint (against Trump), 402, 407. *See also* Trump, Donald J. — impeachment; Trump, Donald J. — Ukraine affair

Whitehouse, Sheldon, 147, 398

White, Lamar, Jr., 100

white supremacy, 100–101, 117–18

Wicker, Roger, 210

Williams, Roger, 383

Winfrey, Oprah, 393

Wolff, Michael, 175–76, 180

Womack, Steve, 383

Women's March (2017), 62

Woodall, Rob, 310

Woodruff, Judy, 34, 35, 348

Xi Jinping, 151–52

Yoder, Kevin, 271, 328

Yoho, Ted, 358

Young, Don, 172

Young Guns (McCarthy, Ryan, and Cantor), 97

Young, Max, 304

Zeldin, Lee, 128, 409

Zelensky, Volodymyr, 402. *See also* Trump, Donald J. — Ukraine affair

Zinke, Ryan, 47

Zirkin, Nancy, 348

JAKE SHERMAN and ANNA PALMER are senior writers for *Politico* and the co-authors of *Politico Playbook*. Sherman is a graduate of George Washington University and Columbia University. A graduate of St. Olaf College, Palmer was previously a reporter for *Roll Call* and *Legal Times*.